Alix ... elo Pepper

The LONDON SCHOOL of Eco... ... ... es
2 Po.

Jem

ORGANIZATIONS IN TIME

Organizations in Time

History, Theory, Methods

EDITED BY
MARCELO BUCHELI AND R. DANIEL WADHWANI

OXFORD
UNIVERSITY PRESS

OXFORD
UNIVERSITY PRESS

Great Clarendon Street, Oxford, OX2 6DP,
United Kingdom

Oxford University Press is a department of the University of Oxford.
It furthers the University's objective of excellence in research, scholarship,
and education by publishing worldwide. Oxford is a registered trade mark of
Oxford University Press in the UK and in certain other countries

Published in the United States of America by Oxford University Press
198 Madison Avenue, New York, NY 10016, United States of America

British Library Cataloguing in Publication Data

Data available

Library of Congress Control Number: 2013943250

ISBN 978-0-19-964689-0

Printed and bound in Great Britain by
CPI Group (UK) Ltd, Croydon, CR0 4YY

Acknowledgements

This collection is the result of several years of work and discussions with an interdisciplinary group of scholars in several places around the world. The enthusiasm and thoughtful comments provided by participants in seminars, symposia, and panels were crucial for the successful completion of this project. We particularly benefited from discussions at the European Group of Organization Studies meetings in Gothenburg (2011) and Helsinki (2012), the Academy of Management meetings at Chicago (2010) and Austin (2011), and the Business History Conference (Philadelphia, 2012). Some of the early meetings that gave birth to this project resulted from the initiative of scholars like Hüseyin Leblebici, Michael Rowlinson, Roy Suddaby, and Matthias Kipping, and built on the previous efforts to integrate business history and organization studies by Margaret Graham, Mary O'Sullivan, and others. We are thankful for the feedback and discussions with Ludovic Caiullet, Carlos Davila, Stephanie Decker, Lars Engwall, Eric Godelier, Per Hansen, Sanjay Jain, Richard John, Mukti Khaire, Christopher McKenna, Andrew Popp, Christopher Kobrak, and Natalya Vinokurova. Of course, this volume would not have become a reality without the early support of David Musson, our editor at Oxford University Press. We also thank Emma Booth at OUP. Research assistants Anna Acettola, Danielle Jones, and Ishva Minefee provided us with crucial help at different moments. Our home institutions, the University of Illinois at Urbana-Champaign and the University of the Pacific, provided us with the resources we needed for the completion of this project. We finally would like to express our gratitude to Ericka Beckman and Emel Gökyigit Wadhwani for their support throughout the process.

Contents

III. Sources and Methods

List of Contributors

Howard E. Aldrich is Kenan Professor of Sociology, Chair of the Sociology Department, Adjunct Professor of Business at the University of North Carolina, Chapel Hill, Faculty Research Associate at the Department of Strategy & Entrepreneurship, Fuqua School of Business, Duke University, and Fellow, Sidney Sussex College, Cambridge University. His main research interests are entrepreneurship, entrepreneurial team formation, gender and entrepreneurship, and evolutionary theory. His latest book is *An Evolutionary Approach to Entrepreneurship: Selected Essays* (Elgar, 2012).

Marcelo Bucheli is Associate Professor of Business and History at the University of Illinois at Urbana-Champaign. He was the 2004–2005 Newcomen Fellow at Harvard Business School and a visiting scholar at the École Polytechnique (Paris) in 2013. His publications (including several award-winning articles and the book *Bananas and Business* (NYU Press, 2005)) focus on the relationship between multinational corporations and governments in a historical perspective. He earned his Ph.D. in history at Stanford University.

Jeffrey Fear is Professor of International Business History at the University of Glasgow. He previously taught at the University of Redlands, University of Pennsylvania, and Harvard Business School. His research interests include business history, international cartels, corporate governance, immigrant entrepreneurship, organizational learning, and the internationalization of small business. He is the author of *Organizing Control: August Thyssen and the Construction of German Corporate Management* (Harvard University Press, 2005), as well as numerous articles and chapters. He earned his Ph.D. in history at Stanford University.

William M. Foster is an Associate Professor of Management at the Augustana Campus of the University of Alberta. His research interests include social memory, strategic management, and rhetorical history. His current research focus is on corporate archivists/historians in Fortune 500 companies and how they use history to create a competitive advantage. He has published in a number of top management journals including *Journal of Business Ethics*, *Management and Organizational History*, and *Advances in Strategic Management*.

John Hassard is Professor of Organizational Analysis at Manchester Business School. Previously he taught at London Business School and the Universities of Cardiff and Keele. For many years he was Visiting Fellow in Management at Cambridge University. His research interests lie in business history, change management, and organization theory. He has published sixteen books and articles in journals such as *Academy of Management Review, Human Relations, Journal of Management Studies, Industrial Relations,* and *Organization Studies.*

Geoffrey Jones is the Isidor Straus Professor of Business History at the Harvard Business School. He taught previously at the London School of Economics, and Cambridge and Reading Universities in the UK. He is co-editor of the journal *Business History Review,* and the author or editor of over thirty books, primarily on the history of global business. He is currently completing a global history of green business.

Jin Uk Kim is a doctoral student in International Business at the University of Illinois at Urbana-Champaign. His research interests lie at the intersection between international business, economic sociology, and organization studies. He is particularly interested in how institutional environments influence the behavior of multinational enterprises. He has published on the Asian financial crisis and the relationship between globalization and localization.

Matthias Kipping is Professor of Policy and Chair in Business History at the Schulich School of Business, York University in Toronto, Canada. His research has focused on the international transfer of management knowledge, in particular the development and role of management consulting and business education. In general, he has been aiming to link historical research with organization theory and has published extensively in both business history and management journals.

David Kirsch is Associate Professor of Strategy and Entrepreneurship at the Robert H. Smith School of Business at the University of Maryland. His research focuses on innovation and entrepreneurship, technological and business failure, and industry emergence and evolution. With the Library of Congress, Kirsch established the Digital Archive of the Birth of the Dot Com Era, an archive that documents the commercialization of the internet. Kirsch received a Ph.D. in History of Technology from Stanford University.

Hüseyin Leblebici is Merle H. and Virginia Downs Boren Professor of Business Administration at the University of Illinois at Urbana-Champaign. His research focuses on three interrelated macro organizational domains: the co-evolutionary processes in the professions and organizational fields; the sociology of professional careers; and the evolution of business models and their impact on firms' competitive advantage. His work has appeared in journals such as *Administrative Science Quarterly, Social Forces, Organization Studies, Strategic Organization,* and *Strategic Management Journal.*

Kenneth Lipartito is Professor of History at Florida International University and former editor of *Enterprise & Society*. His areas of specialization are economic and business history and the history of technology. He has published books and articles on the history of the telecommunications industry, finance, law, and corporate governance. His most recent book is *Corporate Responsibility: The American Experience* (Cambridge, 2012).

Stephen Lippmann is Associate Professor of Sociology at Miami University in Oxford, Ohio. His research interests include the institutional and organizational dynamics of cultural industries, and employment flexibility and the employment relationship. His research has been published in *Journal of Broadcasting and Electronic Media, Social Science Research, and Social Forces*. Lippmann earned his Ph.D. in sociology at the University of North Carolina, Chapel Hill.

Albert J. Mills is Director of the Sobey Ph.D. at Saint Mary's University, Nova Scotia. His thirty-five books and edited collections include *The Routledge Companion to Management & Organizational History* (Routledge, 2014); *ANTi-History: Theorizing the Past, History, and Historiography in Management and Organizational Studies* (IAP, 2012); *Business Research Methods* (Oxford University Press, 2011); and *Sex, Strategy and the Stratosphere: The Gendering of Airline Cultures* (Palgrave/MacMillan, 2006).

Mahka Moeen is an Assistant Professor of Management at the Moore School of Business, University of South Carolina. She received her Ph.D. in Strategy and Entrepreneurship from the Robert H. Smith School of Business, University of Maryland. Her research focuses on firms' reconfiguration strategies and their implications for strategic renewal and evolution of nascent industries.

Michael Rowlinson is Professor of Organization Studies in the School of Business and Management, Queen Mary University of London. His interests are in organization theory, critical management studies, and management and organizational history. His research explores how companies use historical knowledge of the past in the present. He is a co-editor, along with John Hassard, for a Special Topic Forum of the *Academy of Management Review* on History and Organization Studies: Toward a Creative Synthesis.

Roy Suddaby is the Eldon Foote Professor of Law and Society at the Alberta School of Business, University of Alberta. His research focuses on processes of organizational change with a specific focus on the changing role of the corporation in society. He has published in leading management journals and has won best paper awards from the *Administrative Sciences Quarterly* and the *Academy of Management Review*. He is the editor of the *Academy of Management Review*.

Behlül Üsdiken is Professor of Management and Organization at the School of Management, Sabanci University in Istanbul, Turkey. He has contributed to journals such as *Organization Studies, Management Learning, Journal of Management Inquiry, Strategic Management Journal, British Journal of Management, Scandinavian Journal of Management*, and *Business History* as well as various edited collections. His research interests are in organization theory, history of management thought, and the history of business education.

R. Daniel Wadhwani is Fletcher Jones Associate Professor of Entrepreneurship and Management at University of the Pacific. His research, which has appeared in leading journals in both business history and management, has employed historical and comparative methods to examine the emergence of new industries, the evolution of organizational forms, and the establishment of novel market categories and valuation systems. He was the Newcomen Fellow at Harvard Business School in 2003, and earned his Ph.D. in history from the University of Pennsylvania.

JoAnne Yates is Sloan Distinguished Professor of Management at the MIT Sloan School of Management. She researches communication and information as they shape and are shaped by technology over time. She uses qualitative methods to study contemporary use of technologies such as electronic mail and BlackBerrys. Her historical books include *Control through Communication* and *Structuring the Information Age*. She is currently studying the history of voluntary consensus standards setting from 1900 to the present.

Introduction

1

The Future of the Past in Management and Organization Studies

R. Daniel Wadhwani and Marcelo Bucheli[1]

The purpose of this book is to examine why and how historical research and reasoning should be used in the study of management, organizations, and industries. It builds on recent efforts to incorporate historical perspective into management and organization studies. Our goal is to provide an intellectual foundation for both management scholars interested in the use of historical methods and historians interested in the promise of cross-disciplinary dialogue on the nature of organizations and markets.

The last two decades have witnessed a growing chorus of calls for the integration of history into organization studies (Zald, 1993; Kieser, 1994; Clark and Rowlinson, 2004), along with echoes in the related disciplines of strategy (Kahl et al., 2012), entrepreneurship (Wadhwani and Jones, 2007; Forbes and Kirsch, 2010), and international business (Jones and Khanna, 2006). Both management scholars and historians have argued for the expanding use of historical methods and explanations in organizational research, and historical assumptions and arguments have crept into scholarship in several schools of organizational thought, including neo-institutionalism (Suddaby and Greenwood, 2009), evolutionary theory (Aldrich and Ruef, 2006), and actor-network theory (Durepos and Mills, 2012). The turn toward history in business and organizational research reflects a broader interest across the social sciences (McDonald, 1996; Szreter, 2002; Pierson, 2004; Kaiser, 2009) and in mainstream intellectual discourse (Brooks, 2010; Schuessler, 2013) in the development of historically contextualized approaches to studying economic and social behavior. Surveying these developments, one could fairly conclude, as

[1] The authors wish to thank Natalya Vinokurova, Per Hansen, Jeff Fear, Jin-Uk Kim, and Mick Rowlinson for insightful comments on this chapter.

Clark and Rowlinson (2004) did, that we are in the midst of a "historic turn" in the study of management, organizations, and markets.

Yet, this apparent consensus masks as much as it reveals when it comes to understanding what a "historic turn" entails and how it might be valuable to the study of organizations. With some notable exceptions (Zald, 1993; Kieser, 1994; Üsdiken and Kieser, 2004; Leblebici and Shah, 2004; Booth and Rowlinson, 2006; Hansen, 2012; Ingram et al., 2013), there has until recently been little sustained effort within either organization studies or business history to examine the nature of historical reasoning and why it might be important to our understanding of organizations. While business history has become more open to new topics and approaches (Jones and Hertner, 1986; Jones and Zeitlin, 2008; Amatori and Jones, 2003; Scranton and Fridenson, 2013), this re-evaluation of the field has rarely (Zeitlin, 2008; Hansen, 2012; Raff, 2013) included deeper consideration of the nature of historical reasoning, why it is important to the study of organizations, or how historical methods actually work. Likewise, mainstream organizational studies have seen growing attention to longitudinal research and historical settings (Ventresca and Mohr, 2002; Leblebici, this volume), but largely due to the extension of existing social scientific reasoning and techniques to longer timeframes rather than through any deliberate reflection on the theoretical and methodological challenges and opportunities involved in an engagement with the past. Ironically, then, the growing insistence that "history matters" in management and organizational studies has been accompanied with little reflection or dialogue about what is meant by "history" and exactly why and how it matters for understanding managers, organizations, and markets.

This book seeks to fill that need. Separately and together, the chapters emphasize the importance and value of recognizing that historical reasoning emerged out of a distinct epistemic and research tradition that cannot and should not be reduced to a longitudinal version of the functional social sciences. Unlike the general theory building and hypothesis testing methods valued by most economic, sociological, and psychological approaches to organizational studies, historical reasoning emphasizes temporally contextualized explanations of organizations and markets and the methodological challenges of assigning significance and meaning to incomplete and temporally distant evidence from the past. The future of history in management and organization studies, we argue, rests on the extent to which historical research and reasoning can be understood and utilized because of these *differences*. The real promise of a historic turn in organization studies, in this regard, lies not in a longitudinal perspective on what economists, sociologists, and psychologists already know or in the application of this theoretical knowledge to temporally remote settings. Rather, it lies in the promise of new perspectives on the nature of organizations and their behavior, perspectives that challenge settled assumptions about the way most organization scholars *and* business historians currently think about organizational choice and action, the methodological challenges posed by evidence, and the nature of understanding and explanation for the subject under consideration. This book examines these differences in historical epistemology, theory, and methods in order to provide a foundation for a meaningful dialogue about the incorporation of history into the study of organizations.

This introduction contextualizes the chapters that follow within these broader epistemic, theoretical, and methodological considerations. As we show, the growing interest in the incorporation of the past into organization studies has created an opportunity for a "historic turn" following a period when history was largely marginalized by the experimental-science inspired aspirations of organization studies. However, we point out that the barriers to such a historic turn remain significant and include the limited dialogue between organization scholars and historians over the nature of historical reasoning and its relevance to organizations, the opacity of historical methods, and the separation of organization scholars and business historians into distinct intellectual communities.

The first section traces the development of interest in historical approaches to management and organization studies, and explains why we think this is an opportune moment for a deeper dialogue between management scholars and business historians about the nature and value of historical methods. The second section examines the challenges posed by the epistemological differences between "historical reasoning" and "management science," and considers how organizational research can still effectively incorporate history given these differences. The third section demonstrates *how* historical reasoning offers unique insights into the choices and behavior of entrepreneurs, managers, organizations, and markets which the more functional social sciences often miss. The fourth section discusses issues of methodology, and proposes solutions to problems of evidence, analysis, and interpretation that arise concurrently with the insights of historical approaches. The conclusion examines a number of practical considerations and challenges involved in more fully incorporating history into management and organization studies.

ORIGINS OF THE "HISTORIC TURN"

Like the organizations we study, the "historic turn" has had its own history. That history provides a useful perspective on the prospects and challenges of incorporating historical reasoning into organizational research.

In their examination of the role of historical reasoning in organization studies over the course of the 20th century, Üsdiken and Kipping (this volume) show that recent efforts to integrate historical research into organization studies are not entirely new. Indeed, history was an integral element of what eventually became foundational works on organizations and institutions, including Weber (1978 [1922]; 2003 [1905]), Bendix (1956), Selznick (1949, 1957), Smelser (1959), Stinchcombe (1965), and Chandler (1962, 1977). Moreover, throughout the early and mid-20th century, history was part of the streams of research and teaching that would later come to be identified as organizational studies, especially in the United States. Üsdiken and Kipping show that it was not until the 1950s and 1960s, when organization studies embraced the identity of a *particular form* of inquiry inspired by the laboratory sciences, that history became increasingly marginal. As happened in other social science fields, organization studies gradually gravitated towards a form of science that emphasized general theory, propositional claims, and the separation and testing of independent and dependent variables as ends in themselves. History, in this context, seemed less and less relevant to knowledge formation.

Paradoxically, the foundations for the eventual re-emergence of history at the turn of the century were laid during the height of organization studies' scientific aspirations. In particular, organizational theories that sought to provide longitudinal perspectives on organizational phenomena raised questions about time and process that led scholars back into an engagement with the past. Organization ecology (Hannan and Freeman, 1977) and institutional theory (DiMaggio and Powell, 1983), for instance, integrated temporal dynamics into research that relied on historical data to test assertions in remote time periods (Haveman and Rao, 1997). Likewise, evolutionary theory (Nelson and Winter, 1982; Malerba et al., 1999; Aldrich and Ruef, 2006), process research (Pettigrew, 1992; Langley 1999) and, to a degree, transaction cost economics (Williamson, 1993) seemed open to questions of temporality. Over time, these theories have led many organization scholars into deeper encounters with longitudinal data, historical settings, and archival sources (Ventresca and Mohr, 2002).

Even so, it was the limited manner in which historical reasoning was incorporated in such longitudinal studies that eventually prompted calls for a more self-conscious "historic turn" in organization studies. As Clark and Rowlinson (2004) argued, most longitudinal theories hinged on ahistorical assumptions about the universalism of human and organizational behavior and a timeless present. Leblebici and Shah (2004) called for organization research that neither subsumed history into existing longitudinal theory nor relied only on historical particularity, but rather developed "intrinsically historical theories" (p. 355). These critiques and calls for a more reflective integration of history into organization studies were built on a series of landmark articles by Zald (1990, 1993, 1995) and Kieser (1994) that challenged organization scholars to move beyond the confines of the economic, sociological, and psychological disciplinary orientations in their research and to consider the deeper epistemic, theoretical, and methodological issues that a turn to history raised.

The re-emergence of history in organization studies has occurred in parallel with business historians' ongoing reconsideration of the scope and aims of their own field. Like organization studies, historical studies of business moved in a scientistic direction beginning in the 1960s. This was particularly true in economic history, but was also reflected in business history during the height of Alfred Chandler's influence. Chandlerian business history slowly evolved from the contextualized narrative approach reflected in his 1962 classic *Strategy and Structure* to the more systematic, stylized, and universalist aspirations espoused by his 1990 study, *Scale and Scope*. Although Chandler's works won recognition for business history as a relevant discipline in business schools and among practitioners, many historians found the narrow focus on the organizational structure of big business to be out of step with the broad scope and contextualized knowledge that characterized most other forms of history (John, 1997; Lipartito, 1995).

By the 1990s, critiques by historians and historical sociologists of Chandler's emphasis on the efficiency of big business, along with research showing the vitality of other organizational forms, had opened business history to new topics and approaches (Scranton, 1997; Sabel and Zeitlin, 1997; Fligstein 1993). In recent years, the re-examination of the boundaries of the discipline has resulted in an expansion of the subjects business historians engage (Friedman and Jones, 2011; Lipartito and Sicilia, 2004; Scranton and Fridenson, 2013). The field now encompasses a broad array of topics, including organizational culture, politics, aesthetics, class, race, gender, the environment, and other issues. This expansion has led to a re-engagement with mainstream history, which is itself increasingly returning to topics related to organizations and markets under the banner of the "history of capitalism" (Mihm, 2009; Ott, 2011; Hyman, 2011). The re-examination has also (more slowly) led a few business historians to question the assumptions underlying how we understand and interpret the past (Zeitlin, 2008; Sabel and Zeitlin, 1997; Hansen, 2012) and how we treat sources (Decker, 2013; Schwarzkopf, 2012).

Developments in both business history and organization studies thus suggest that we should be at a conjuncture of flourishing cross-disciplinary thought and engagement. Yet, to date, meaningful dialogue over what are indeed common concerns in these two disciplines has not been forthcoming. Skepticism and misunderstanding across disciplinary boundaries along with the self-critique that good cross-disciplinary dialogue entails remain real obstacles. On the one hand, many historians bridle at explaining to non-historians how an interpretation was produced, embracing what historian John Lewis Gaddis (2002) has called a "Don't ask, we won't tell" policy. On the other hand, while few organization scholars would argue against the claim that "history matters," many still see history in relatively narrow terms, namely as a chronicle, as the past, as a longitudinal perspective, or as background information secondary to the kind of "real" analysis and rigor the social sciences provide. Moreover, while most leading organization and management journals seem to have embraced longitudinal studies and the use of archival data as legitimate, very few articles employ an explicitly historical approach, in part because of uncertainty about what historical reasoning and methods actually entail (Leblebici, this volume).

The challenges involved in integrating historical reasoning and methods into mainstream management and organization studies should not be underestimated. As Leblebici (this volume) argues, these challenges lie in epistemic differences between history and the other social sciences and how each understands common subjects of study. It is only by more fully understanding such challenges that the promise of cross-disciplinary dialogue between historians and organization scholars can be realized. Failing to do so would simply lead to a reenactment of the old and all-too-common problem of cross-disciplinary engagements that historian Ferdinand Braudel referred to as the "dialogue of the deaf"—the notion that historians and other social scientists tend to talk past one another even as they discuss the same phenomena. In the next section we consider briefly some of the underlying reasons for this tendency and explain the prospects, examined in a number of the chapters of this book, for dealing with the problem.

TRANSCENDING THE DIALOGUE OF THE DEAF

Efforts to incorporate historical research and reasoning into organization studies confront difficult epistemological challenges (Bernardi and Greenwood, forthcoming). Social scientists, for instance, assert that historical research often lacks broad theoretical claims and fails to specify independent and dependent variables, making it seem unrecognizable as research. Historians bridle that such a priori requirements are ahistorical and illegitimate as a means to explain organizational behavior and thought in the past. The prospects for a historic turn in management and organization studies necessarily rest on understanding these epistemic differences, the reasons for their existence, and their implications for *how* to incorporate historical research and reasoning into organization studies. The chapters in Part I: History and Theory, propose alternative ways to overcome these seemingly irreconcilable differences.

Previous efforts to clarify the differences between history's epistemic assumptions and those of the mainstream social sciences have often utilized comparisons to the sciences or to the humanities. Zald (1993) and Clark and Rowlinson (2004), for instance, point to history's humanistic assumptions in order to contrast it with the scientific aspirations of mainstream organizational science. Gaddis (2002), in contrast, suggests that historical reasoning is similar to the approaches used by "historical sciences" (e.g., paleontology, geology, and evolutionary biology), while mainstream social sciences (including organization studies) follow an "experimentalist" approach. Although we recognize the usefulness of these comparisons, we believe they also hide as much as they reveal about the sources of the epistemic differences between history and organization studies. They also tend to predispose readers to value or discount history based on their orientations as researchers pursuing humanistic or scientific aims.

We, instead, highlight disciplinary differences in *temporal perspective* (Hassard, 1990) in order to account for the points of tension between the epistemic assumptions of historical and functional social scientific research. As Sewell (2005) has pointed out, historical perspectives on time in social and economic research differ from the predominant social scientific understanding of it. This is true not only of cross-sectional social scientific accounts of actions—which separate behavior from time altogether—but also of most "longitudinal" social scientific studies, which imagine time as a clock variable and hence arrange events and action into a chronology, as if observed by the researcher in an unfolding present. In contrast, historical reasoning hinges on the perspective of a researcher looking back on an action, and assessing its relationship in time to developments before and after it occurred. As the philosopher of history Arthur Danto (1965) points out, histories are not mere chronicles of events in the past, but rather employ a retrospective point of view to establish the significance of an event or action in light of antecedent and subsequent developments. This interpreted "significance" may take various forms, including establishing an action's causes, consequences, meanings, and possible implications for alternative paths of development. The use of historical perspective raises a host of theoretical and methodological issues (to which we will return later), but it also helps us understand the basis for several of the more common tensions between historical and functional social scientific accounts of organizations and markets.

First, it highlights why historical research views *actors and actions as temporally situated*. In historical perspective, the significance of an action can only be understood by its relationship to what came before it *and* after it—to its place in time. As Sewell (2005: 6) notes, historical explanations treat time as "fateful" in the sense that "action, once taken, or an event, once experienced, cannot be obliterated." This assumption about time is based on how one experiences action and events in daily life (Carr, 1986); after all, one cannot undo actions once they have taken place and subsequent actions are hence always subject to previous ones. One important implication of this assumption is the relevance of sequence and context. The use of time in historical research differs from the use of time in ahistorical versions of social science, in that in the latter actions are potentially universal and hence may be analyzed as a product of atemporal "determinants" separately from the time in which they occurred (Braudel, 1982).

Moreover, historical reasoning usually involves a complex understanding of time in which confluences of *multiple temporal processes operate together to explain an action at a particular moment* (Braudel,1982; Sewell, 2005). The temporal embeddedness of action in history does not simply mean taking into consideration a set of events on a timeline. Hence, a particular organizational action may be best explained by how a momentary event, a process that had been emerging over several years, and a decades- or centuries-long set of ideas come together in the moment of the action being explained. Braudel (1982: 27) called this the "multiplicity of time" in historical understanding.

Second, historical reasoning emphasizes that explanations of human action require an "*understanding of the subjective motives and contextualized world-views of the actors being studied*" (or *Verstehen*, as discussed in detail in the chapters by Leblebici and Fear in this volume). Unlike those social scientific approaches based on a model of natural science, most branches of modern historical thought are premised on the assertion that, in order to understand human action in the past, one needs to take into account the perspective of the subjects of study (Dilthey, 2002 [1910]), which in turn requires insight into their world (Herder, 1968 [1791]). These subjective motives and concerns need not be the only or even primary factors historical explanations take into account; historical reasoning is also open to the effects of natural environments and behavioral considerations. However, in studying such innately human subjects as organizations, historical approaches often emphasize the importance of reconstructing subjective perspectives and mentalities (Collingwood, 1994 [1946]) rather than giving a priori authority to economically or socially functional forces.

Third, the temporal specificity of historical reasoning points to why historical explanations are based on *embedded generalizations and theoretical claims* rather than universal ones. For historians, social actions and relationships cannot be universal if they are temporally situated and dependent on the actors' perspectives. This does not mean, however, that historians have not tried to discover covering or universal laws in history. Indeed, the debate over whether universal laws could be found in history remained hotly contested through the middle of the 20th century (Hempel, 1942), but was eventually abandoned in the face of significant criticism. Universal and predictive laws and grand, objective syntheses do not easily emerge from historical research given the temporal contingency of the subject and the diversity of perspectives of its actors (Appleby et al., 1994).

Yet, this insistence on temporal specificity and the subjectivity of actors does not mean that historical reasoning is antithetical to theorizing or generalization. Indeed, histories could not be written without generalizations and theorizations about the studied actors and actions. But, as with all else, historical reasoning embeds theoretical generalizations in time—that is, to what came before and what might arise afterwards. As Gaddis (2002: 62) has put it, historians "embed our generalizations within our narratives" while social scientists often "embed narratives within generalizations." In more prosaic terms, historical knowledge posits that generalizations are context bound and subject to "scope conditions" based on time, place, and the perspective of actors; understanding the scope conditions is at least as important as the generalization or theory itself.

And, fourth, taking into consideration the foregoing points, historical understanding is based on identifying the *interdependency of variables over time* rather than the identification of independent and dependent variables at any one moment in time (Gaddis, 2002). Historical perspective allows that the causal direction between independent and dependent variables can change over time and recognizes that feedback loops, learning, and innovation can change both the fundamental identity of variables and the relationships between them. This perspective requires understanding relationships between actions as contingent and evolving over time. We need to emphasize that this perspective does not preclude the use of quantitative methods to explain causes and effects during particular times (which is something historians often do), but it does indicate the ways in which historical understanding values complex explanations over time that eschew an a priori stance on parsimony and endogeneity.

The epistemic differences between historical and ahistorical social scientific knowledge lead to challenging questions about how to incorporate historical research and reasoning into management and organizational studies. First, given the epistemic differences involved, *why* turn to history at all? And, second, if history is to be engaged, *how* is this to be done given the existing epistemic tensions? The chapters in Part I of this volume address these questions.

In his chapter, Leblebici is skeptical of interdisciplinary approaches that seek to tightly integrate history into management and organization research. Given the significant differences in epistemic culture, such an interdisciplinary approach would likely require compromises on the part of one discipline or the other. He argues that such interdisciplinary efforts—in areas such as "economic history" and "historical sociology"—have not been particularly impactful because of inherent tensions with the core disciplines. Leblebici also points out that, although trends in management dissertations and articles in top organization studies' journals indicate that researchers are increasingly engaging with historical evidence and longitudinal designs, this research rarely describes its approach as historical—a pattern that may suggest underlying tensions about research assumptions and expectations. He posits that instead of pursuing interdisciplinary scholarship researchers interested in the incorporation of history into organization studies should consider a "transdisciplinary" approach in which scholars accept the differences between the disciplines as distinct ways of studying the same phenomena. The transdisciplinary research he advocates would focus on "critical managerial problems and effective solutions rather than traditional theory based research so that both [historians and organization scholars] could work together without being questioned about the adequacy of their cultures of inquiry."

Focusing on institutional theory, the chapter by Suddaby, Foster, and Mills offers an alternative. The authors see history's epistemic assumptions as not only compatible with institutional theory, but also crucial to a better understanding of certain aspects of institutionalization. "[I]nstitutions or processes of institutionalization contain within them an assumptive historical dynamic that goes beyond mere temporality and which, largely, remains unarticulated in institutional theory," they argue. They suggest that important aspects of institutionalization are lost in the functionalist assumptions that predominate in neo-institutional research and point to Selznick's (1949) classical study of the Tennessee Valley Authority (TVA) as an example of the potential value of historical approaches to the study of institutionalization. In particular, they indicate a number of ways in which a (re)turn to "historical institutionalism" could better account for processes of isomorphic diffusion, bring actors back into institutional theory, and provide a more nuanced way to understand entrepreneurship and embedded agency.

Taking a third approach, Lippmann and Aldrich's chapter suggests that evolutionary theory may prove especially useful for integrating historical reasoning into mainstream organization theory. Like the other authors, they acknowledge the epistemic differences between contextualized narrative approaches to organizational research, like history, and the "deductive/ structural, data driven approaches to theory testing" that predominated in management and organizational science in the mid-20th century. They worry, however, that historical research risks becoming isolated from mainstream scholarship on organizations if its findings and approaches cannot be related to traditional deductive scholarship. "Too frequently, debates about the merits of what we would call 'deductive/structural' versus 'narrative/interpretive' historical approaches have been framed in all or nothing terms, and a true integration of the approaches has seemed impossible," they write. Evolutionary theory offers a meta-theoretical framework for the task through its heuristic processes of variation, selection, and retention, which, they suggest, accommodates interpretive, contextualized findings within a general frame that allows deductive and structural claims as well.

Lastly, Rowlinson and Hassard's chapter argues that neither the universal claims offered by traditional organization studies nor the conventional narratives of traditional business history can adequately capture the promise of a historic turn in organizational studies. Drawing on critical and cultural theory, they assert that epistemic challenges presented by a historic turn require "deconstructionist history" that analyzes the narrative accounts presented in organizational settings but does so in a way that is itself reflex-ive. A deconstructionist approach would have strong implications for the way both organization scholars and business historians have read and should read their primary sources. In this way, the authors advocate a type of histori-cal research in which the researcher's position before the sources is critically analyzed.

In sum, the authors in Part I show that although there are important and intrinsic epistemic differences between mainstream organization studies and history, there is still a range of possible paths for the incorporation of his-torical research and reasoning into the study of management, organizations, and markets. The premises of historical reasoning certainly do suggest that there are ways in which it should *not* be used—including for the develop-ment of atemporal or predictive theory—but there are still a rich array of options for historical reasoning to flourish within the scholarship on man-agement and organizations. A glance at the intellectual landscape beyond the boundaries of organization studies and business history suggests that historical reasoning does in fact thrive in endeavors as diverse as many of the sciences (Wilson, 1999) and humanities (Greenblatt, 1991), in addition to the social sciences.

Indeed, we suggest that scholars should be receptive and attentive to the multiple ways in which historical research and reasoning may be effec-tively used in management and organization studies. History, it seems to us, can be simultaneously used to address the subject-based research questions that Leblebici has in mind, to contribute to the development of theories that are sensitive to time and change as Suddaby, Foster, and Mills and Lippmann and Aldrich point out, and to provide a critical perspective on established understandings, including its own narrative composition, as Rowlinson and Hassard recommend. Confining historical research to only one of these paths would be unfortunate because each approach pro-vides unique insights into organizational research and engages in different types of cross-disciplinary dialogue. Lippman and Aldrich's integration-ist approach, for instance, would use history to contribute to mainstream research on the mechanisms shaping organizations and organizational fields over time, while Rowlinson and Hassard's call for deconstruction of historical narratives would provide a critical stance on these same expla-nations. Researchers should simply be explicit and reflective about exactly why and how they are turning toward historical reasoning in a particular study or stream of research.

This array of options still leaves unanswered the question of exactly *how* historical reasoning works to produce unique insights into the phenomena of interest, temporal processes, and critical analyses discussed by the authors in Part I. It is to this question that we turn next.

THE LOGICS OF HISTORY: CONSTRUCTIVE,
COGNITIVE, CRITICAL

What exactly is it that historical reasoning does and how is it different from other social sciences in the ways it explains organizational action? What unique perspectives can it provide on topics of interest to management and organization scholars? Regardless of whether researchers turn to history to deepen their understanding of a particular phenomenon, to elaborate on theories that deal with change over time, or to gain a critical perspective on seemingly settled issues and theories, they ought to understand *how* historical reasoning will help achieve their scholarly ends.

To understand how historical reasoning works, one must return to the topic of temporal perspective. As we have already emphasized, historical reasoning rests on a retrospective viewpoint, looking back on an action and assessing its relationship in time to developments before and after it occurred.[2] Such a perspective allows the researcher to zoom in and out (Gaddis, 2002) on an action, using different temporal lenses in order to understand its significance, including its causes, consequences, meanings, and possible implications for alternative paths of development.

Hargadon and Douglas's study (2001) of how Thomas Alva Edison's design decisions for electric light overcame institutional constraints provides a useful example. The authors explain that they turn to history because it offers "opportunities to examine social processes in ways that both cross-sectional and even current longitudinal research cannot" (p. 480). Indeed, it is by using different temporal lenses to zoom in and out on Edison's decisions that they are able to arrive at their claim that "robust design" of electric light facilitated change "by exploiting the established institutions while simultaneously retaining the flexibility to displace them" (p. 476). For instance, they begin by taking a long view to show that electric light technologies had been available since the early 19th century and that the development of incandescent light was under way "forty years before Edison's work" (p. 482), hence excluding technology as the primary reason for Edison's success. They also show how the "gas industry had become a highly institutionalized field in the half century since it overturned oil lamps and candles" (p. 484). At other points, they focus on Edison's specific thought process, to show that his design decisions were intended to present "to the public a lighting system already familiar to them" (p. 487). Further, the authors zoom out again to look back on the decision not only from the point of view of the successful adoption of electric light by 1892, but also from the perspective of "over a century later": by doing so, they

---

[2] Historians will sometimes try to actively put aside this perspective in order to better interpret sources in context from the past "forward." But the very effort to do this hinges on the initial insight that one is viewing sources in retrospect.

can explain why the industry's evolution reflected Edison's design for a system of light based on centralized power generation, and not J. P. Morgan's alternative vision of an industry "composed of scores of manufacturers, each providing its own line of electricity production and distribution equipment." By viewing Edison's decision from different temporal perspectives, the authors establish the causes, consequences, and meanings of the action they study, as well as the alternative paths of development that the action foreclosed.

Historical narratives, like the one presented by Hargadon and Douglas, commonly use multiple temporal lenses to explain an event or action, but rarely explicitly acknowledge this approach. (Braudel's classical study of the Mediterranean, in this sense, is arguably the most famous exception.) For the purposes of exposition, however, it is useful to tease out the different ways historical reasoning operates and the analytical and interpretive purposes it thereby serves. The terms "historical logics" (Sewell, 2005), historical lenses, and temporalities (Braudel, 2000 [1958]) can be used to denote the variety of ways historical perspective is used to interpret the significance of organizational actions by relating them in time to antecedent, contemporaneous, and subsequent developments. For heuristic purposes, we group these historical logics into three varieties, but neither the specific logics nor the categorization are meant to be definitive and comprehensive. Whereas Braudel (1982) highlighted the use of different temporal spans of time in historical perspective, our classification is used to illustrate the types of research questions historical perspective can be used to address. In each case, we point to existing examples of the use of such logics in management and organizational studies. We also introduce how these logics are used by the contributors to Part II: Actors and Markets, to explain the value of history in studying organizations, entrepreneurs, industries, and the state.

One set of historical logics deals with the question of how time and temporality *constructs* behavior by *shaping and constraining* the actions of organizational actors. It addresses how behavior, action, or events at one point in time relate to behavior or action at another time due to the temporal relationship between them. Historical perspective, in this sense, offers insights into the complex relationship of organizational actions across time—sometimes over long spans of time—that are best or only understood from a retrospective point of view (Goodman et al., 2001).

This approach to historical reasoning, based on how temporality constructs actions, is probably the most widely accepted and used in management and organizational studies. Examples of such temporal mechanisms in organizations include path dependence (Schreyögg and Sydow, 2011; Schreyögg et al., 2011), organizational imprinting (Marquis, 2003; Johnson, 2007, 2008), routines (Cohen et al. 1996), formative events (Lampel and Meyer, 2008) and institutionalization processes (Suddaby et al., this volume). Lawrence et al. (2001) and Leblebici et al. (1991), for instance, analyze a process of institutionalization as one taking place at varying rates, followed by a period of stabilization that also varies between organizations. In their analysis of how technological oversights and foresights occur, Garud et al. (1997) and Langlois (1997) argue that technological choices are constrained by the past and this constraint in turn determines technological innovation.

As several chapters in Part II of this volume point out, other related lines of reasoning on the temporal construction of organizations and markets remain either unexplored or only partially explored and offer management and organizational researchers opportunities for further development. For instance, in his chapter Jeffrey Fear points to the use of *periodization* in history as a tool for organizing and contextualizing organizational behavior over time and argues that periodization is one way in which historical approaches can further contribute to organizational research. Such "period effects" have also been identified by Aldrich and Ruef (2006) as theoretically relevant to evolutionary theory, but remain relatively unexplored in empirical research and Fear suggests that embracing periodization can even be a useful tool in contextualizing organization theory itself. Similarly, in their chapter on entrepreneurship, Wadhwani and Jones point out that periodization of entrepreneurial behavior based on institutional environments reveals how entrepreneurial risks and resource allocation processes have been variably organized over time. They point to Baumol's (1990) use of periodization to develop the theoretical distinction between productive, unproductive, and destructive entrepreneurship as a promising example of the relevance of such an approach to other kinds of entrepreneurial phenomena.

Other chapters point to the value of examining *antecedents* that shape the behavior of actors and markets. Bucheli and Kim highlight the role of a nation state's antecedents in determining how it acts to confer legitimacy on organizations within its boundaries. As they point out, while the political legitimacy of organizations has received attention in management research, little consideration has been given to the antecedent dynamics shaping the legitimacy of the state. Understanding the antecedents of state legitimacy in different national contexts, they argue, could shed light on the ways in which states in turn legitimize organizations. Similarly, the chapter on industry emergence by Kirsch et al. posits that antecedents of industries have been ignored. The standard "industry life-cycle model" focuses on the point of a new technology's commercialization as the moment of industry origin. However, as the authors point out, antecedent developments also shape industry characteristics. Studying the antecedent developments provides an opportunity to consider the conditions under which a new technology *fails* to be commercialized.

A second variety of historical logic uses a *cognitive* lens to consider how the identity of actors and their motivations for actions are themselves constructed by these same actors' perception of their place in historical time (Sabel and Zeitlin, 1997; Hansen, 2007; Popp and Holt, 2013). The cognitive perspective emerges from the historical tradition that warns against imposing presentist conceptions on actors in the past (Herder, 1968 [1791]; Dilthey, 2002 [1910]; Collingwood, 1994 [1946]). It thus emphasizes the value of understanding actors on their own terms as historical agents rather than as primarily responsive to economic, social, and political conditions. Actors, in this sense, understand themselves, their choices, and their own actions as historically situated (Carr, 1986). This approach to historical temporality may emphasize either constraining, taken-for-granted characteristics of actors' historical rationality or its reflective and agentic possibilities—which, in effect, can be considered two sides of the same coin, both taking the actors' historical consciousness seriously.

In the context of management and organizational studies, work in this tradition is relatively new but is rapidly growing. From this perspective, organizational actors' rationale for behavior is based in large part on their own understanding and "uses of history" (Hansen, 2012). In some studies, the historical identities of actors are subject to change in part because external conditions create a "shock" to their taken-for-granted historical understandings. But perhaps even more interesting and promising is research that takes organizational actors as historically reflective and hence capable of agency, rather than as reactive to the prevailing social, political, and economic factors or by the received and taken-for-granted histories of their time. New approaches, such as "rhetorical history" (Suddaby et al., 2010), examine the creative and strategic possibilities that emerge from taking the reflective historical capabilities of organizational actors seriously.

Several of the chapters in Part II explore these possibilities. In their chapter, Kirsch et al., for instance, posit that such an approach would allow us to re-think our understanding of industry emergence. Industries, they point out, frame stories of their development based on participants' historical understanding of their own creation as they "emerge," and these stories are often passed down unquestioned to scholars, too often becoming a basis of the "stylized" facts that form theory. Instead, Kirsch et al. argue for a more critical view of industry historical narratives in understanding the formation of an industry's own identity. Likewise, Wadhwani and Jones argue that this approach can help researchers better understand the creativity of entrepreneurs and entrepreneurship, and shed light on the nature of entrepreneurial "opportunities." And Fear emphasizes the value of such an approach in the formation of organizational knowledge and identity. Even more than the first approach, the treatment of organizational actors as historically conscious and reflective subjects strikes us as particularly promising in organizational research.

A third approach uses historical perspective to gain a *critical* angle on the taken-for-granted categories, explanations, and theories that predominate in management and organizational studies. From this perspective, a deeper lens on time, a wider lens on place, or the broadening of perspectives to include

include overlooked organizational actors facilitates a critical view of the assumptions that cross-sectional or longitudinal perspectives take for granted.

The wave of organizational scholarship that has re-examined the conventional history of the Hawthorne Studies provides an example of the use of history to gain a critical stance on organizational issues. In the conventional account, the Hawthorne Studies—which were conducted at Western Electric's Hawthorne Works in the late 1920s and early 1930s—are seen as a scientific breakthrough in knowledge of organizational behavior that played a pivotal role in shifting managerial thought from a focus on "scientific management" to one based on "human relations." Deeper historical research, however, has shown that not only were the effects of the studies well understood within Western Electric before the experiments (Gillespie, 1991), but also that the motivations of the researchers in establishing the Studies' "findings" were shaped by political and career motivations (O'Connor, 1999) and connections to powerful interests (Bruce and Nyland, 2011). The contextualization of the studies within the history of Western Electric, as Hassard (2012) has shown, reveal that the company practiced the basic elements of human relations policies *before* the experiments, both for strategic reasons and because of the particular history it had with its labor force. Deeper examination of the received history is thus used to question assumptions held in the present about the relationship between scientific research on organizations and its motivations and effects (Hassard, 2012).

The chapters in Part II introduce several potential uses for this approach to historical reasoning. Bucheli and Kim, for instance, use historical perspective to critique the depiction of "the state" as it has come to be understood in management theory, primarily from the point of view of institutional theory, as a source of authority capable of conferring legitimacy on organizations. They argue that this assumption is based largely on the ways in which states themselves achieved legitimacy through struggles between competing interests, but that the pattern often seen in Western states cannot be assumed to apply to other regions of the world over time. They suggest that understanding the legitimacy of organizations and organizational fields may mean different things in different national contexts and that this requires a historicization of the state. Wadhwani and Jones, likewise, critique entrepreneurship theory as it has developed in the last three decades, and advocate that the theory should be contextualized in a particular moment of time when large industrial firms experienced a period of stagnation (Wadhwani, 2010). A historical perspective on the concept of entrepreneurship, they argue, helps us better understand the phenomenon and shows us the contextual limits of most definitions of entrepreneurship used today.

For the purposes of exposition, we have separated out distinct temporal lenses or logics in order to show how different ways of using historical perspective may provide insights into different kinds of action in the past. Many management and organization researchers may find value in focusing on one type of logic in order to examine a subject of interest—a step toward the incorporation of history into management studies that we would welcome. In many cases, however, good historical explanations hinge on weaving together multiple logics or temporalities into complex historical narratives or representations (White, 1975; Ankersmit, 2001). Historians, indeed, may protest such a dissection of historical reasoning into distinct parts and processes which artificially separates out logics that in fact intersect and interact in historical explanations. We agree that historical narratives and representations that employ "multiplicities of time" (Braudel, 1982) should have a central place in organizational research, but also suggest that there is room for both more focused and discrete efforts to examine particular logics more deeply, as well as opportunities to pursue full narrative accounts of subjects in the past. Indeed, we see no reason why a clearer understanding of *how* one is using historical reasoning would not contribute to deeper understanding of both studies that focus on one type of historical reasoning and complex narratives that bring together multiple temporal lenses into a whole representation of the past.

The "logics of history" and historical narratives hence offer extensive opportunities for new and unique insights into the behavior of actors, organizations, industries, and states. But the use of historical perspective also raises methodological questions about how historical research actually goes about using evidence to come to valid explanations and interpretations about the past. If historical reasoning involves interpretations that assign significance to events in systematic ways, how do we understand how and on what grounds historians make such designations? And, how can such methods be used to distinguish good from bad history? It is to this question that we turn in the final part of the book.

THE HISTORIAN'S CRAFT REVISITED

"Either all minds capable of better employment must be dissuaded from the practice of history, or history must prove its legitimacy as a form of knowledge," wrote the historian Marc Bloch in the classical *The Historian's Craft* (2004 [1946]). Bloch's reflections are all the more poignant because he wondered aloud "whether he has spent his life wisely" (p. 3) as he sat in Nazi captivity awaiting his eventual execution. Indeed, Bloch's bold challenge to the legitimacy of historical knowledge strikes at the heart of the value of historical perspective in management and organizational research. History's legitimacy as a way of understanding management and organizations rests not only on recognizing how history offers unique insights into its subjects of examination, but also in reflecting on how exactly historical knowledge of organizations and markets is produced. While work on the former issue is expanding, work on the equally important latter question is just beginning.

Unfortunately, business history has not been particularly transparent or reflective about its methods, and business historians are often reticent about explaining their research process (Schwarzkopf, 2012; Decker, 2013). Mainstream history, particularly in the United States, has not been much more open. As we pointed out earlier, historians often take what Gaddis (2002: 92) has called a "Don't ask, we won't tell" stance on methodology. To some extent, this stance is understandable, for many historians see themselves as producing historical narratives for "informed general readers" and perceive the social scientific norm of explaining methods as a kind of ugly and burdensome post hoc justification that detracts from the integrity of the narrative. Indeed, the reticence to discuss methods seems to arise at least partly from the sense that exposing the inner gears and springs of historical clockwork is bad craftsmanship.

This position is hardly conducive to dialogue across disciplines, where the reasonable question of "how did you do that" is necessary in establishing understanding. This attitude has left even sympathetic management and organization scholars with the impression that history simply means reporting "one damn fact after another," in which there is not much interest in engaging with theory (Taylor et al., 2009). Or, perhaps worse yet, that historical methods basically conform to Leopold von Ranke's (1973 [1881]) dictum that historians just try to tell it "as it actually happened."

Not surprisingly, then, most of the growing body of research on the past in mainstream management and organizational journals has avoided the explicit characterization of the work as "historical." Rather, organization and management scholars have opted for approaches that extend their accepted methods of analysis to historical data. For instance, Ventresca and Mohr (2002: 810) distinguish a "new archivalism" in management research that uses primary sources in rigorous ways "steeped in the ethos and methods of formal social science" and hence distinct from the "historiographical tradition" (which is characterized as "essentially ethnographic studies of organizations conducted through the medium of archival materials"). In other cases, history has had to be snuck into management publications using methodological Trojan horses, such as "discourse analysis," (Khaire and Wadhwani, 2010) and "case study methodology" (Tripsas and Gavetti, 2000; Kaplan and Murray, 2010; Bucheli and Kim, 2012). As a result, even scholars interested in historically informed research on organizations and markets are not engaging historical traditions themselves when defining their methodological approach.

The neglect of historical methodology is unfortunate because history's use of the retrospective viewpoint raises unique and important questions about the nature of historical evidence and interpretation. Unlike experimental data, historical evidence is not created in circumstances under the control or even under the observation of the researcher. It is usually comprised of incomplete and fragmented traces of the past that raise methodological questions of why and how the evidence being used was preserved. Moreover, even when sufficient data exists for quasi-experimental analysis, questions arise about its interpretation in context. How does one assess evidence in a way that takes into account the time and place of its creation? In short, the use of historical perspective raises unique methodological questions that the extension of traditional social scientific techniques to the past cannot, by themselves, address.

Despite the historical practice of avoiding extensive methodological discussions within narrative accounts, history actually has a considerable but often overlooked tradition of engaging the methodological issues referred to previously. Somewhat akin to common law systems, historical standards and rules have been embedded in historical practice and explained in separate treatises rather than codified in procedures. These practices and treatises are a good starting point for considering the nature of historical methods and how they differ from other methodologies in management and organization research. The chapters of Part III in this volume introduce some of these traditions, methods, and practices and consider them in the context of the questions, needs, and interests of management and organizational research.

Yates' chapter begins by orienting readers to historical methods within the scope of methods currently familiar to organization scholars. She draws on the central distinction between quantitative methods—which tend to be deductive and hypothesis-testing in orientation—and qualitative methods—which tend to be interpretive and oriented toward theory building. Yates notes that historical methods are certainly closer to qualitative research in this basic classification system, but she cautions that there are important distinctions related to the temporal character of historical research. In particular, historical research's temporal perspective is different from most other approaches in organizational studies both in its consideration of evidence and in its approach to analysis and interpretation. The last two chapters of the book, by Lipartito and by Kipping et al., address these issues of evidence and analysis in greater depth.

While questions of what constitutes evidence and how to identify it are at the heart of both history and organization science, the two disciplines in fact tend to view evidence in different ways. As Lipartito points out, there are important implications embedded in the distinction between the social scientific approach to evidence as "data" to be tested and the historical approach to evidence as "sources." The distinction is important because "sources" imply that the evidence has not been directly observed and that the passage of time between its production and its analysis has created important methodological challenges to its interpretation. Moreover, Lipartito points out that sources are in fact just traces of the past that, in order to be interpreted, must be engaged in relation to one another and in relation to the questions being posed. Historical research processes hence integrate source identification with theorization and analysis in iterative processes of abduction, deduction, and induction rather than considering data collection as a discrete phase of research. Lipartito additionally points to the historical tradition of source and archival criticism, including the examination of the political and institutional processes involved in source preservation, as a crucial part of historical methods.

Finally, Kipping et al. propose a set of basic methods for the analysis and interpretation of sources in management and organizational research. While traditional historical publications rarely explain their methods, researchers interested in the use of history in management and organizational studies will certainly need to be more explicit about the processes they use in moving from sources used to the analyses and interpretations they present. The authors draw on traditions and debates extending to the origins of history as a professional discipline in the 19th century to illuminate the analytical and interpretive processes used in historical research. Specifically, they argue that the interpretive process includes drawing on the traditions of source criticism, the triangulation of sources, and the hermeneutic foundations of interpretation. Such an approach, they argue, allows researchers to take into account the temporal and fragmented nature of sources as well as to reconstruct the perspective of historical actors themselves, while recognizing the limits on such reconstructive engagement that time and the researcher's own perspective create.

In sum, the chapters in Part III begin a dialogue on the nature of historical methods and their inclusion within organization studies. The discussion of methods highlights the need to deepen and critique more clearly and openly how historical research arrives at interpretations of the past, just as the contextualized generalizations discussed in Part II suggest possibilities for how the past may be theorized in management and organizational studies. But just as important to the success of such efforts are the more practical and prosaic concerns of how and by whom such questions will be engaged. It is with this question that we conclude.

(RE)INVENTING TRADITIONS, (RE)IMAGINING COMMUNITIES

In this introduction, we have shown how the chapters of this book lay out new directions for thinking about the incorporation of historical reasoning and research into the study of management, organizations, and markets. While differences in disciplinary epistemic assumptions pose challenges, this volume shows how thoughtful efforts to incorporate history can deepen understanding of particular subjects, lead to new insights into processes involving time and change, and allow critical perspectives onto settled ideas and categories, and that such efforts hold much promise in management and organizational studies. Historical perspectives and reasoning provide unique insights by allowing researchers to "look back" on organizational behavior and thought in order to identify relationships and processes over time, to consider the historical consciousness of organizational actors, and to take new temporal, spatial, and social angles onto organizational issues. Such a perspective raises unique methodological challenges and opportunities pertaining to the identification, interpretation, and analysis of sources that hold the promise of contributing to new ways of studying organizations.

Still, the historic turn faces challenges because it requires new ways of *acting* and not just new ways of *thinking*. The institutionalization of disciplinary boundaries and professional practices creates obstacles for the incorporation of history into management and organizational studies. For instance, differences in preferred publication genres between history and organization studies lead to divergent understandings of what is considered valid or legitimate scholarship. Articles published in a few top academic journals drive perceptions of scholarly value in management and organizations research, while historians prize books published by respected academic presses. Extended and explicit discussions of methodology are required in peer-reviewed management journals, while they are often considered inappropriate in business history. Accrediting bodies or those determining business school rankings do not give much weight to research monographs or articles in historically oriented journals, something that discourages rising schools from supporting such research by their faculty. Business historians and management scholars also belong to different scholarly associations and develop networks and communities that rarely overlap. Add to these differences in tenure expectations, typical career trajectories, and departmental pressures, and one gets a clearer sense of how institutionalized practices pose serious practical challenges for those who see the intellectual promise of the incorporation of history into management and organization studies.

Addressing these issues will require a different type of historic turn, one in which management scholars and business historians are willing to use historical perspective to reflect on their own institutionalized practices. Historical reasoning, as we have shown, suggests that institutions are often not as rigid or deterministic as functionalist perspectives sometimes make them out to be; taken-for-granted routines and practices are not timeless codes or templates. Rather, such myths are often the product of what Hobsbawm and Ranger (1983) called "invented traditions," collective understandings of the past that on closer inspection show themselves to be of surprisingly recent origin and subject to change through historical reflection and critique.

Many of the institutionalized practices that seem so intractable and work against a historic turn are in fact recently invented traditions—the result not of deep and timeless disciplinary differences but of collective memories that have been contrived to make them seem so. The distinction between scholarly books and articles in business schools, for instance, is of relatively recent vintage; indeed, many of the most impactful organizational research was, until the last couple of decades, published in books. Likewise, business historians' reluctance to discuss methods and engage in theory development belies a deeper history that suggests that explicit interdisciplinary engagement with theory and methods was central to the origins of the discipline itself.

Changing institutional structures and the settled habits of entire fields may at first seem like a Herculean task, requiring the intervention of powerful institutional entrepreneurs. However the first decade of the 21st century has been marked by a series of promising developments that suggest that a more subtle shift is needed, and is in fact underway. There are clear signs that management and organization scholars not only see the promise of a historic turn, but have also begun to act in ways that look beyond the limits imposed by institutionalized practices. Prominent business historians and management scholars have begun to actively reflect on the nature of historical knowledge and its value in understanding organizations and markets (Hansen, 2012; Ingram et al., 2012). Scholars studying non-OECD countries have challenged accepted ideas of how organizations work through business historical studies (Decker, 2010; Dávila, 2004). New journals have appeared to promote the historic turn (Booth and Rowlinson, 2006), established ones have become more open to cross-disciplinary work (Friedman and Jones, 2011), and major management journals have published special issues on historical research (Graham and O'Sullivan, 2010; Godfrey et al., 2013). The number of co-authored articles and collaborations between historians and organization scholars also seem to be increasing. And cross-disciplinary groups of scholars at conferences such as the European Group for Organization Studies (EGOS) and the Academy of Management (AoM) are engaging in ongoing research pertaining to the historical analysis of management, organizations, and markets. Such developments raise the chances of re-examination and re-invention of those traditions that artificially limit the use of historical reasoning in organizational research, and suggest that the future of history in organization studies depends in large part on how thoughtfully we understand our own past.

REFERENCES

Aldrich, H., and Ruef, M. (2006). *Organizations Evolving*. London: Sage.

Amatori, F., and Jones, G. (eds.) (2003). *Business History Around the World*. Cambridge: Cambridge University Press.

Ankersmit, F. (2001). *Historical Representation*. Palo Alto: Stanford University Press.

Appleby, J., Hunt, J., and Jacob, M. (1994). *Telling the Truth About History*. New York: Norton.

Baumol, W. (1990). "Entrepreneurship: Productive, Unproductive, and Destructive," *Journal of Political Economy*, 98(5): 893–921.

Bendix, R. (1956). *Work and Authority in Industry: Managerial Ideologies in the Course of Industrialization*. New York: John Wiley.

Bernardi, A., and Greenwood, A. (Forthcoming). "Understanding the Rift, the (Still) Uneasy Bedfellows of History and Organization Studies," *Organization*.

Bloch, M. (2004 [1946]). *The Historian's Craft*. Manchester: Manchester University Press.

Booth, C., and Rowlinson, M. (2006). "Management and Organizational History: Prospects," *Management & Organizational History*, 1: 5–30.

Braudel, F. (1982). *On History*. Chicago: University of Chicago Press.

Braudel, F. (2000 [1958]). *The Mediterranean and the Mediterranean World in the Age of Philip II*. London: Folio Society.

Brooks, D. (2010). "History for Dollars," *The New York Times*, June 28, p. A27.

Bruce, K., and Nyland, C. (2011) Elton Mayo and the Deification of Human Relations, *Organization Studies*, 32: 383–405.

Bucheli, M., and Kim, M.-Y. (2012). "Political Institutional Change, Obsolescing Legitimacy, and Multinational Corporations: The Case of the Central American Banana Industry," *Management International Review*, 52(6): 847–877.

Carr, D. (1986). *Time, Narrative, and History*. Bloomington: Indiana University Press.

Chandler, A. D. (1962). *Strategy and Structure: Chapters in the History of the American Industrial Enterprise*. Cambridge, MA: MIT Press.

Chandler, A. D. (1977). *The Visible Hand: The Managerial Revolution in American Business*. Cambridge, MA: Harvard University Press.

Chandler, A. D. (1990). *Scale and Scope: The Dynamics of Industrial Capitalism*. Cambridge, MA: Harvard University Press.

Clark, P., and Rowlinson, M. (2004). "The Treatment of History in Organization Studies: Towards a 'Historic Turn'?" *Business History*, 46(3): 331–52.

Cohen, M., Burkhart, R., Diosi, G., Egidi, M., Marengo, L., Warglien, M., and Winter, S. (1996). "Routines and Other Recurring Action Patterns of Organizations: Contemporary Research Issues," *Industrial and Corporate Change*, 5(3): 653–98.

Collingwood, R. G. (1994 [1946]). *The Idea of History*. Oxford: Oxford University Press.

Danto, A. C. (1965). *Analytical Philosophy of History*. Cambridge: Cambridge University Press.

Dávila, C. (2004). "Historia de la empresa y teoría de la organización. Un diálogo necesario. A propósito de la historiografía empresarial colombiana de la última década." In Grupo de Historia Empresarial (ed.), *Las regiones y la historia empresarial*. Medellín: Universidad Eafit: 26–72.

Decker, S. (2010). "Postcolonial Transitions in Africa: Decolonization in West Africa and Present-day South Africa," *Journal of Management Studies*, 47(5): 791–813.

Decker, S. (2013). "The Silence of the Archives: Business History, Post-Colonialism, and Archival Ethnography," *Management and Organizational History*, 8(2): 155-73.

Dilthey, W. (2002 [1910]). *The Formation of the Historical Work in Human Sciences*. Princeton: Princeton University Press.

DiMaggio, P., and Powell, W. W. (1983). "The Iron Cage Revisited: Institutional Isomorphism and Collective Rationality in Organizational Fields," *American Sociological Review*, 48(2): 147–60.

Durepos, G., and Mills, A. (2012). *ANTi-History: Theorizing the Past, History, and Historiography in Management and Organization Studies.* Charlotte, NC: Information Age Publishing.

Fligstein, N. (1993). *The Transformation of Corporate Control.* Cambridge, MA: Harvard University Press.

Forbes, D., and Kirsch, D. (2010). "The Study of Emerging Industries: Recognizing and Responding to Some Central Problems," *Journal of Business Venturing,* 26(5): 589–602.

Friedman, W., and Jones, G. (2011). "Business History: Time for Debate," *Business History Review*, 85(1): 1–8.

Gaddis, J. L. (2002). *The Landscape of History: How Historians Map the Past.* Oxford: Oxford University Press.

Garud, R., Nayyar, P., and Shapira, Z. (1997). "Technological Innovation: Oversights and Foresights." In R. Garud, P. Nayyar, and Z. Shapira (eds.), *Technological Innovation: Oversights and Foresights.* Cambridge: Cambridge University Press: 3–12.

Gillespie, R. (1991) *Manufacturing Knowledge: A History of the Hawthorne Experiments.* Cambridge: Cambridge University Press.

Godfrey, P., Hassard, J., O'Connor, E., Rowlinson, M., and Ruef, M. (2013). "History and Organization Studies: Toward a Creative Synthesis," *Academy of Management Website* (<http://www.aom.org/STF-2014> accessed February 28, 2013).

Goodman, P., Lawrence, B., Ancona, D. G., and Tushman, G. (2001). "Introduction," *Academy of Management Review*, 26(4): 507–11.

Graham, M., and O'Sullivan, M. (2010). "Moving Forward by Looking Backward: Business History and Management Studies," *Journal of Management Studies*, 47(5): 775–90.

Greenblatt, S. (1991). *Marvelous Possessions: The Wonder of the New World.* Oxford: Oxford University Press.

Hannan, M., and Freeman, J. (1977). "The Population Ecology of Organizations," *American Journal of Sociology*, 82(5): 929–64.

Hansen, P. (2012). "Business History: A Cultural and Narrative Approach," *Business History Review*, 86(4): 693–717.

Hansen, P. H. (2007). "Organizational Culture and Organizational Change: The Transformation of Savings Banks in Denmark, 1965–1990," *Enterprise and Society*, 8(4): 920–53.

Hargadon, A. B., and Douglas, Y. (2001). "When Innovations Meet Institutions: Edison and the Design of the Electric Light," *Administrative Science Quarterly*, 46(3): 476–501.

Hassard, J. (1990). *The Sociology of Time.* London: Macmillan.

Hassard, J. (2012). "Rethinking the Hawthrone Studies: The Western Electric Research in its Social, Political, and Historical Context," *Human Relations*, 65: 1431–61.

Haveman, H., and Rao, H. (1997). "Structuring a Theory of Moral Sentiments: Institutional and Organizational Coevolution in the Early Thrift Industry," *American Journal of Sociology*, 102(6): 1606–51.

Hempel, C. (1942). "The Function of General Laws in History," *Journal of Philosophy*, 39: 35–48.

Herder, J. G. (1968 [1791]). "Reflections on the Philosophy of the History of Mankind." In F. E. Manuel (ed.), *Classic European Historians*. Chicago: University of Chicago Press: 79–118.

Hernes, T. (2014). *A Process Theory of Organization*. Oxford: Oxford University Press.

Hobsbawm, E., and Ranger, T. (1983). *The Invention of Tradition*. Cambridge: Cambridge University Press.

Hyman, L. (2011). *Debtor Nation: The History of America in Red Ink*. Princeton: Princeton University Press.

Ingram, P., Rao, H., and Silverman, B. S. (2012). "History in Strategy Research: What, Why, and How," *Advances in Strategic Management*, 29: 241–73.

John, R. (1997). "Elaborations, Revisions, Dissents: Alfred D. Chandler's *The Visible Hand* After Twenty Years," *Business History Review*, 71: 151–200.

Johnson, V. (2007). "What Is Organizational Imprinting? Cultural Entrepreneurship in the Founding of the Paris Opera," *American Journal of Sociology*, 113(1): 97–127.

Johnson, V. (2008). *Backstage at the Revolution: How the Royal Paris Opera Survived the End of the Old Regime*. Chicago: University of Chicago Press.

Jones, G., and Hertner, P. (1986). *Multinationals: Theory and History*. Aldershot: Gower.

Jones, G., and Khanna, T. (2006). "Bringing History (Back) into International Business," *Journal of International Business Studies*, 37(4): 453–68.

Jones, G., and Zeitlin, J. (2008). "Introduction." In G. Jones and J. Zeitlin (eds.), *The Oxford Handbook of Business History*. Oxford: Oxford University Press: 1–6.

Kahl, S., Silverman, B., and Cusumano, M. A. (2012). *History and Strategy*. Bingley: Emerald.

Kaiser, W. (2009). "Bringing History Back into the Study of Transnational Networks in European Integration," *Journal of Public Policy*, 29(2): 223–39.

Kaplan, S., and Murray, F. (2010). Entrepreneurship and the Construction of Value in Biotechnology. *Research in the Sociology of Organizations*, 29, 107–47.

Khaire, M., and Wadhwani, R. D. (2010). "Changing Landscapes: The Construction of Meaning and Value in a New Market Category Modern Indian Art," *Academy of Management Journal*, 53(6): 1281–304.

Kieser, A. (1994). "Why Organization Theory Needs Historical Analyses—And How This Should Be Performed," *Organization Science*, 5(4): 608–20.

Lampel, J., and Meyer, A. D. (2008). "Field-configuring Events as Structuring Mechanisms: How Conferences, Ceremonies, and Trade Shows Constitute New Technologies, Industries, and Markets," *Journal of Management Studies*, 45(6): 1025–35.

Langley, A. (1999). "Strategies for Theorizing from Process Data," *Academy of Management Review*, 24(4): 691–710.

Langlois, R. (1997). "Cognition and Capabilities: Opportunities Seized and Missed in the History of the Computer Industry." In R. Garud, P. Nayyar, and Z. Shapira (eds.), *Technological Innovation: Oversights and Foresights*. Cambridge: Cambridge University Press: 71–94.

Lawrence, T., Winn, M., and Jennings, P. D. (2001). "The Temporal Dynamics of Institutionalization," *Academy of Management Review*, 26(4): 507–11.

Leblebici, H., and Shah, N. (2004). "The Birth, Transformation and Regeneration of Business Incubators as New Organisational Forms: Understanding the Interplay between Organisational History and Organisational Theory," *Business History*, 46(3): 353–80.

Leblebici, H., Salancik, G. R., Copay, A., and King, T. (1991). "Institutional Change and the Transformation of Interorganizational Fields: An Organizational History of the US Radio Broadcasting Industry," *Administrative Science Quarterly*, 36(3): 333–63.

Lipartito, K. (1995). "Culture and the Practice of Business History," *Business and Economic History*, 24, 1–42.

Lipartito, K., and Sicilia, D. (2004). *Constructing Corporate America: History, Politics, Culture.* Oxford: Oxford University Press.

Malerba, F., Nelson, R., Orsenigo, L., and Winter, S. (1999). "History Friendly Models of Industry Evolution: The Case of the Computer Industry," *Industrial and Corporate Change*, 8(1): 3–40.

Marquis, C. (2003). "The Pressure of the Past: Network Imprinting in Intercorporate Communities," *Administrative Science Quarterly*, 48: 655–89.

McDonald, T. J. (ed.) (1996). *The Historical Turn in the Human Sciences.* Ann Arbor: University of Michigan Press.

Mihm, S. (2009). *A Nation of Counterfeiters: Capitalists, con men, and the making of the United States.* Cambridge, MA: Harvard University Press.

Nelson, R., and Winter, S. (1982). *An Evolutionary Theory of Economic Change.* Cambridge, MA: Harvard University Press.

O'Connor, E. (1999) "The Politics of Management Thought: A Case Study of the Harvard Business School and the Human Relations School," *Academy of Management Review*, 24: 117–31.

Ott, J. (2011). *When Wall Street Met Main Street: The Quest for an Investors' Democracy.* Cambridge, MA: Harvard University Press.

Pettigrew, A. M. (1992). "The Character and Significance of Strategy Process Research," *Strategic Management Journal*, 13(S2): 5–16.

Pierson, P. (2004). *Politics in Time: History, Institutions, and Social Analysis.* Princeton: Princeton University Press.

Popp, A., and Holt, R. (2013). "The Presence of Entrepreneurial Opportunity," *Business History*, 55(1): 9–28.

Raff, D. (2013). "How to Do Things with Time," *Enterprise and Society*, 14(3): 435–66.

Ranke, L. (1973 [1881]). *The Theory and Practice of History.* Bobbs-Merrill: Indianapolis.

Sabel, C. F., and Zeitlin, J. (eds.) (1997). *World of Possibilities: Flexibility and Mass Production in Western Industrialization.* Cambridge: Cambridge University Press.

Schreyögg, G., and Sydow, J. (2011). "Organizational Path Dependence: A Process View," *Organization Studies*, 32(3): 321–35.

Schreyögg, G., Sydow, J., and Holtmann, P. (2011). "How History Matters in Organizations: The Case for Path Dependence," *Management and Organizational History*, 6(1): 81–100.

Schuessler, J. (2013). "In History Departments, It's Up with Capitalism," *New York Times*, April 6, p. A1.

Schultz, M. and Hernes, T. (2013). "A Temporal Perspective on Organizational Identity," *Organization Science*, 24(1): 1–21.

Schwartzkopf, S. (2012). "What Is an Archive—And Where Is It? Why Business Historians Need Constructive Theory of the Archive," *Business Archives*, 105: 1–9.

Scranton, P. (1997). *Endless Novelty: Specialty Production and American Industrialization.* Princeton: Princeton University Press.

Scranton, P., and Fridenson, P. (2013). *Reimagining Business History.* Baltimore: Johns Hopkins University Press.

Selznick, P. (1949). *TVA and the Grassroots.* Berkeley: University of California Press.

Selznick, P. (1957). *Leadership in Administration: A Sociological Interpretation.* Berkeley: University of California Press.

Sewell, W. (2005). *The Logics of History: Social Theory and Social Transformation.* Chicago: University of Chicago Press.

Smelser, N. (1959). *Social Change in the Industrial Revolution: An Application of Theory to the British Cotton Industry.* Chicago: University of Chicago Press.

Stinchcombe, A. L. (1965). "Social Structure and Organizations." In J. G. March (ed.), *Handbook of Organizations.* Chicago: Rand McNally: 142–93.

Suddaby, R., and Greenwood, R. (2009). "Methodological Issues in Researching Institutional Change." *The Sage Handbook of Organizational Research Methods.* Los Angeles: Sage: 177–95.

Suddaby, R., Foster, W. M., and Trank, C. Q. (2010). "Rhetorical History as a Source of Competitive Advantage," *Advances in Strategic Management*, 27, 147–73.

Szreter, S. (2002). "The State of Social Capital: Bringing Back in Power, Politics, and History," *Theory and Society*, 31(2): 573–621.

Taylor, S., Bel, E., and Cook, B. (2009). "Business History and the Historiographical Operation," *Management and Organizational History*, 4: 151–66.

Tripsas, M., and Gavetti, G. (2000). "Capabilities, Cognition, and Inertia: Evidence from Digital Imaging," *Strategic Management Journal*, 21(10–11): 1147–61.

Üsdiken, B., and Kieser, A. (2004). "Introduction: History in Organization Studies," *Business History*, 46(3): 321–30.

Ventresca, M., and Mohr, J. (2002). "Archival Research Methods." In J. Baum (ed.), *The Blackwell Companion to Organizations.* New York: Blackwell: 818–19.

Wadhwani, R. D. (2010). "Historical Reasoning and the Development of Entrepreneurship Theory." In H. Landstrom and F. Lohrke (eds.), *Historical Foundations of Entrepreneurship Research.* Cheltenham: Edward Elgar: 343–62.

Wadhwani, R. D., and Jones, G. (2007). "Schumpeter's Plea: Historical Approaches to the Study of Entrepreneurship," *Frontiers of Entrepreneurship Research*, 27(16): 5.

Weber, M. (1978 [1922]). *Economy and Society.* Berkeley: University of California Press.

Weber, M. (2003 [1905]). *The Protestant Ethic and the Spirit of Capitalism.* Mineola, New York: Dover.

White, H. (1975). *Metahistory: The Historical Imagination in Nineteenth-Century Europe.* Baltimore: Johns Hopkins University Press.

Williamson, O. (1993). "Transaction Cost Economics and Organization Theory," *Industrial and Corporate Change*, 2(2): 107–56.

Wilson, D. C. (1999). *A Guide to Good Reasoning.* New York: McGraw-Hill.

Zald, M. (1990). "History, Sociology, and Theories of Organization." In J. E. Jackson (ed.), *American Political and Economic Institutions.* Ann Arbor: University of Michigan Press: 81–108.

Zald, M. (1993). "Organization Studies as Scientific and Humanistic Enterprise: Toward a Reconceptualization of the Foundations of the Field," *Organization Science*, 4(4): 513–28.

Zald, M. (1995). "Progress and Cumulation in the Human Sciences After the Fall," *Sociological Forum*, 10(3): 455–79.

Zeitlin, J. (2008). "A Historical Alternatives Approach." In G. Jones and J. Zeitlin (eds.), *The Oxford Handbook of Business History*. Oxford: Oxford University Press: 120–40.

Part I

History and Theory

2

History and Organization Studies: A Long-Term View

Behlül Üsdiken and Matthias Kipping

INTRODUCTION

This chapter examines how the relationship between history and what is now known as "organization studies" has unfolded over the past 100 years, beginning well before the latter gained a distinct disciplinary identity. The chapter considers both the factors that have led to distancing as well as the recent attempts towards reviving a closer relationship. By taking such a long-term view, it aims to help understand better the prospects and challenges of engaging with history when studying organizations and organizational fields.

The central argument of the chapter is that the significance of history has been shaped largely by the evolution of the broader field of business education and research—with some geographic variation. Thus, during the first half of the 20th century there was a fairly strong link between history and what was at the time called "business administration"—albeit confined almost exclusively to business schools in the United States (US), where business history emerged as a discipline in the mid-1920s and often obtained a place in the curricula of undergraduate and the few available graduate programs. However, this link weakened significantly after the 1950s due to the post-war shift in the US towards making the study of business administration more "scientific," together with concomitant alterations in curricula and the rise of the graduate Master of Business Administration (MBA) degree. Distancing became even more pronounced with ensuing specialization and fragmentation into sub-fields, which not only led to organization studies gaining a separate disciplinary identity, but also served to isolate "business history" as well as "management history" within business education and research. While there have been intermittent attempts to rebuild the relationship, calls for a deeper engagement with history surfaced only over the past two decades. Interestingly, it was the theoretical and epistemological pluralism, which emerged within the field of organization studies—in particular in Europe—that paved the way for an increased interest in recovering the links with history.

The chapter traces these developments in five main chronologically organized sections. The first examines the strong ties that came to be established in the first half of the 20th century within US business schools. The following section considers the two decades after World War II when there were promising signs of an emerging research relationship, but also the beginnings of a movement towards making business administration a "science," within the context of broader currents in US social sciences at the time. The third section then traces the definitive "scientistic" (or neo-positivist) turn in the 1960s and the 1970s within the US business school environment, together with the consolidation of sub-fields in business and then management. The following section considers the developments from the 1980s onwards, specifically within the field of organization studies. The final section then shows how sporadic voices calling for greater attention to history, initially in the US and then more so in Europe, have led to a variety of statements promulgating a rediscovery of history in studying organizations. The conclusion summarizes our main argument and points to the promises of such a revival of interest in "taking history seriously" in view of the multitude of approaches that it has engendered.

CLOSE ORIGINS: HISTORY IN THE EDUCATION FOR BUSINESS ADMINISTRATION, 1920s TO THE 1950s

The late 19th century saw the creation of business or commercial schools in both the US and various European countries. There were differences however, as in the US they were housed within existing universities, whereas in Europe they were established outside the university sector, often by the chambers of commerce (Engwall, Kipping, and Üsdiken, 2010). The orientations of these schools were also different. The US version, as exemplified by its pioneer, the Wharton School, espoused a strong liberalizing mission for educating future businessmen, which meant including liberal arts courses in the first two years of the curriculum. Among its European counterparts, the French had only a two-year program which was distinctly vocational in character, including some teaching of commercial history (Meuleau, 1981). It was the German variants that had the strongest aspirations for creating an economics- and accounting-based "science of business," which eventually led to their inclusion within the universities as faculties of *Betriebswirtschaftslehre* (business economics), distinct from economics and with no room for history (Locke, 1984).

By contrast, history did have a place in US business schools since their early days, initially through the teaching of economic history. This had to do with the significant influence that the German historical school had on the formation of American economic thought in the late 19th century, not least because of those who were trained in Germany (Dorfman, 1955). Thus, two separate studies carried out in the mid and late 1920s showed, respectively, that 39 percent and 50 percent of the AACSB (American Assembly of Collegiate Schools of Business) member schools required a course in economic history before graduation (Wren and Van Fleet, 1983: 30–31).

It was within this context that the Harvard Graduate School of Business Administration (HBS) served as the birthplace of "business history" through the founding of the Business History Society in 1925, the first publication of its *Bulletin* in 1926 [to become the *Business History Review* (BHR) in 1954], and the endowment of the first professorship in 1927 (Supple, 1959). This came with a mandate for research that would involve writing "from the study of specific situations as they came to businessmen and their communities in the past" (cited by Redlich et al., 1962: 61). Though not without its critics, business history was able to carve a space for itself, as it narrowed down in the 1930s and the 1940s towards company history not least due to the post-depression reduction in resources for research (Redlich et al., 1962). It distanced itself from economic history with claims of a focus on business administration and, unique as it may have been to the US, an identity derived from the strong links with business schools. An added justification came from the use, particularly at HBS, of the case method, which was practically oriented and involved no claims to being theoretical and therefore fit well with history (Supple, 1959; Goodman and Kruger, 1988).

MIXED LINKS AND THE SEEDS OF RUPTURE: HISTORY IN THE IMMEDIATE POST-WORLD WAR II PERIOD

Together with initiatives in the late 1940s, again at HBS, for moving towards studying entrepreneurs, business history appeared to be consolidating its presence in US business schools in the aftermath of World War II. According to an "informal survey" in 1949, fifteen such schools offered courses in business history (Wren and Van Fleet, 1983: 31). Although it is difficult to judge how much of a spread this indicates, there appeared to be an air of optimism as one author at least proclaimed that there was a "relatively recent boom in business history as a valid field of study for students in schools of business administration" (Steigerwalt, 1959: 212). A 1962 survey carried out by the editors of the *Business History Review* (covering mostly US institutions but also some in Canada, Australia, and Japan) showed that "business history courses are offered almost exclusively in schools of business administration and economics departments separately or within a school of business" and that there was a "notable rate of increase between 1949 and 1957," when a slowdown had begun to set in. In all, some two-thirds of the respondents reported that a business history or related course was taught in their schools ([Editors], 1962: 362).

However, some soul-searching with regard to the past and possible futures of the discipline and its links with business schools had also begun. Claims to a distinct identity and separation from economic history generated controversy. This was coupled with concerns about the predominance of company history and whether business history could produce "useful knowledge," which was thought to be a major yardstick for maintaining its position in schools of business administration (Redlich et al., 1962; Supple, 1959). More importantly, there was the recognition that business administration had begun to turn towards the social sciences, which were moving in a scientistic direction. This was coupled with calls to "raise more general questions" (Redlich et al., 1962: 85) and for "a joining of hands in joint ventures, between the historians, including business historians, and other students of business administration," which would involve learning each other's methods and studying organizations not only of "today" but also of the past as a way of making up for the inability to experiment, among others, in "organizational behavior" (Redlich et al., 1962: 73).

These hopes seemed to have come true with the publication of Chandler's (1962) *Strategy and Structure*, which has since been hailed as a prime example of how business history could feed into the study of business administration (Hendry, 1992; Jeremy, 2002; Kipping and Üsdiken, 2008; Madansky, 2008; Zald, 1990). Through a survey of the largest industrial corporations in the United States and a detailed historical study of four cases, Chandler (1962) examined the development and dissemination of the decentralized multidivisional form and deduced his general thesis that "structure follows strategy." Not only did this spur additional research in other countries, both at the time and today (e.g., Whittington and Mayer, 2000; Colli et al., 2011), it also lasted as a major theme in what was later to become a separate strategy field. Chandler's thesis was also incorporated into "structural contingency theory" (e.g., Thompson, 1967), which turned out to be, as will be shown later in the chapter, highly instrumental in organization studies gaining a distinct identity.

It was not all good news however, as there were also signs of parting. There was, for one, a push for reverting business history to its roots by re-establishing a closer link with economics and economic theory (Redlich et al., 1962). By this time, business history had traveled to the United Kingdom (UK) and a number of other countries, though it did not necessarily find a home in business schools ([Editors], 1962). In the UK, a new journal, *Business History* (BH) was established in 1958 and the first university position was created in 1959 (Warren and Tweedale, 2002: 212). However, unlike the early stages of development in the US, business history came to be associated with history, economic history, or, occasionally, economics departments and not with the schools of business, as the latter did not actually exist in the UK at the time (Bourn, 1975; Holmes and Ruff, 1975; Kipping and Üsdiken, 2008; Tiratsoo, 2004).

Equally, or with hindsight perhaps more notably, the quest for turning business administration into a "professional science" had also begun. As a part of this new orientation an academic literature distinct from the earlier work of practitioner authors and with a specific focus on organizations started to develop in the US, based on longitudinal case studies by sociologists who were influenced by Weber's writings on bureaucracy. These studies were laying the foundations for treating organizations as a distinct unit of analysis, which was to be followed by claims for an "administrative science" as a field within business (as well as public) administration at par with specialties such as marketing, finance, or operations research (March and Simon, 1958; Thompson, 1956). Although there were proponents of building on the prior practitioner literature (e.g., Koontz, 1961), the aspirations for developing an "administrative science" rested on the sociological orientation, though with an accent on moving away from the unique to a search for general patterns. This was very much in line with the strong currents in the US at the time for making sociology and social sciences more scientific (Zald, 1991).

Although the more frontal attack of those calling for an "administrative science" was against the "principles" and the "lore" of the earlier practitioner authors, the scientistic turn also called for an engagement with the present—rather than the past—through large-scale comparative studies (e.g., Thompson, 1956). Simon (1952: 1135), for example, in one of the earliest attempts to justify organizations as a distinct level of analysis, argued that the "historical data appealed to by the Weberians need supplementation by analysis of contemporary societies, advanced and primitive." Likewise, Delany (1960: 449) in his invitation for a systematic approach to study organizations was advising that "an emphasis upon current and immediately observable organizations in the interests of full and rigorous data" was needed and that "historical research, while not ruled out, is given second-level priority and rigorous comparative studies substituted at the first-priority level." That these calls for a reorientation were bearing their almost immediate fruits was shown by Boulding's (1958) examination of the articles published in the first two years of the *Administrative Science Quarterly* (ASQ), which epitomized the scientistic turn in the US. There was a marked shift, even from one year to the next, from "theory and philosophy," "methodology," and "history and description" to "research" papers.

The drive to be scientific was being accompanied by initiatives to reform business education in the US. The central premise was that in the first half of the century business education had been oriented towards vocationalism (Simon, 1991). Although the two landmark "foundation reports" (Gordon and Howell, 1959; Pierson, 1959; for their impact see Engwall et al., 2010) did take a liberal arts perspective—with Gordon and Howell (1959: 170), for example, pointing to "the importance to the businessman of historical perspective"—what attracted much more attention was their emphasis on making business education science-based. Together with financial support, within the Cold War context, from US philanthropic foundations, the science project was put firmly in place, accompanied by the shift towards the MBA as the archetypal professional degree in business (Khurana, 2007). Becoming a science promised not only greater prestige in academia, but also enhanced legitimacy in management circles (Zald, 1993). As a result, neither of the two footings for studying business, namely, scientism and managerialism (Üsdiken and Leblebici, 2001), had a place for history since it was perceived as being too limited, on the one hand, in providing generalizations and, on the other, in offering recipes for managerial action (Goldman, 1994; Kieser, 1994; Mathias, 1975).

HISTORY MARGINALIZED: DEVELOPMENT AND FULLY FLEDGED SCIENTIZATION OF ORGANIZATION STUDIES, 1960s TO THE 1980s

The scientization project encouraged the flow of faculty trained in social science disciplines into US business schools (Zald, 1993). With a longer research tradition and the precedent of the human relations literature in its background, the psychological stream led the way with empirical research on individual, group, and leadership behavior. The interest of earlier practitioner authors in organizing as well as the sociologists' encounter with Weber's description of bureaucracy soon prompted empirical research on internal structures of organizations, with contributions from both the US and the UK (Üsdiken and Leblebici, 2001). These soon culminated in structural contingency theory (e.g., Thompson, 1967), which spurred throughout the 1970s a large number of cross-sectional studies on the effects of variables like size, technology, environment, and strategy on organizational structures. Explicitly ahistorical in character, structural-contingency theory thus became the prevalent perspective on internal organization, its attractiveness arising from both its science-based character and the recipes it offered to managers as to proper means of organizing for enhancing effectiveness. It also paved the way for the separation between "organizational behavior," which focused on individual and group phenomena, and "organization theory" with more macro concerns centering on internal structures and organization-environment relationships.

This emergent division between the "micro" and the "macro" in studying organizations was an indication of broader tendencies of specialization within what was now being referred to as "management," an umbrella term increasingly replacing its precursor, "administrative science," not least because of its affinity to private business rather than the public sector. This also had to do with the expansion of the US Academy of Management (AoM), which was founded in 1936 but began to be more active in the late 1940s. The drift towards specialization within management became perhaps most manifest when the AoM set up seven "interest groups" in 1969 and then 10 "professional divisions" in 1971 based largely on the former (Lounsbury and Ventresca, 2002: 12). Two elements in this process are particularly noteworthy: The first is the creation of separate divisions for "organizational behavior" and "organization and management theory," thus providing explicit acknowledgement of the latter becoming a sub-field of its own, at least in the US academic setting of the time. The second is the inclusion of "management history" even in the very first list of seven interest groups and then as one of the initial set of professional divisions.

That management history was accorded a status within the AoM at par with the likes of business policy, personnel and industrial relations, organizational behavior, and organization theory may be attributed to the extent of development of management as an academic field and the limited degree of specialization that had emerged until then. It may also be associated with a view that, as an establishing profession, management needed to have a history of its own (Duncan, 1971). Indeed, it was in early 1960s that William Scott (1961: 8) proposed a stages model of "theories of organization" encapsulated for the first time under what he called "classical," "neo-classical," and "modern" forms, which he argued had "influenced management thought and practice." This particular formulation was to have a lasting effect on prominent examples of evolutionary histories of "management" and "management thought" that soon followed, such as those by George (1968) and Wren (1972). The same was to be the case with histories that found a place in introductory chapters of textbooks on management, organizational behavior, organization theory, and personnel management.

This surge of books and a number of doctoral dissertations led Bedeian (1976: 96), for example, to conclude optimistically that "[t]he number of publications dealing with the history of management thought has multiplied over the last decade." A 1975 study on AACSB member schools also showed that a history of management thought course was offered in more than a third of the undergraduate programs, and in about 60 percent of the graduate schools (Mahmoud and Frampton, 1975: 409). There also appeared to be a non-negligible interest in management history as a research area. In a 1967 survey among the AoM membership, close to 20 percent of the respondents indicated history of management thought as an area of research interest. This was as much as a half of those who mentioned organization theory, which topped the list, and put history of management at a rank well above the middle of the subject list (Young et al., 1967: 206).

There also seemed to be some opportunities in the 1970s and early 1980s to turn this interest into publications, though increasingly by moving out of leading journals. Articles could initially be found in the *Academy of Management Journal* (AMJ), such as the pieces by Wrege and Perroni (1974) on scientific management pioneer Frederick W. Taylor and by Giglioni and Bedeian (1974) on control. As publishing in the AMJ started to become more difficult, some of this work, and more so those that turned to reporting on the history of particular management concepts, migrated to the AoM's new journal, the *Academy of Management Review* (AMR), as exemplified by Van Fleet and Bedeian (1977) on the span of control, Wrege and Stotka (1978) as well as Locke (1982) on Taylor, Bracker (1980) on strategy, and Greenwood (1981) on management by objectives. Once obtaining space in AoM journals became practically impossible (Mowday 1997: 1404; Van Fleet et al., 2006: 484), the next new journal in line was the *Journal of Management*, where Greenwood, Bolton, and Greenwood (1983) on the Hawthorne Studies and Keller (1984) on the development of organization theory provided some of the increasingly rare examples of articles on management history. So, after what looked like a promising start, management history was driven to the margins of management research within about a decade. Moreover, concerns began to be expressed that history did not obtain the share that it deserved within the undergraduate and graduate curricula of US business schools (Wren and Van Fleet, 1983). Similar complaints had already been voiced in the UK, as a rapprochement was sought between business history and management education in the early 1970s (e.g., Bourn, 1975; Holmes and Ruff, 1975; Mathias, 1975).

The establishment of the management history division consummated a split with business history. This separation reflected an institutional and ideational division. As Wren and Hay (1977) have shown, members of the management history division were management professors with an interest in history, not historians. Most members of the Business History Conference (BHC; established in 1954), by contrast, came from history or economics departments, where economic history also continued to be taught and researched. Only a few, if any, business historians were likely to be affiliated with business schools, Chandler being the notable exception when he moved to HBS in 1970. Also as an institution HBS remained an exception with few other North American business schools creating chairs in business history—until more recently.

Business history thus evolved separately from management history, developing what Galambos (1970: 280) called an "organizational synthesis," which looked at the development of "large-scale, national, formal organizations . . . characterized by a bureaucratic structure of authority." As suggested by this characteristic, the organizational synthesis claimed a Weberian heritage in addition to relying on "traditional tools of historical thought" (Galambos, 1970: 279). These formal organizations were not only seen to have emerged in business, as studied by Chandler, but also, for instance, in professions and labor unions. Explicitly rejecting statistical analyses and hypothesis testing, this approach ran afoul of the scientization, which moved management, and later on organization studies, in a different direction. This left business history largely isolated not only in terms of its institutional home (which was occupied by "management history"), but also in terms of its key underlying assumptions and methodologies. Not surprisingly therefore, following the original appeal of *Strategy and Structure*, Chandler's subsequent books found less of a resonance among management scholars and practitioners (John, 1997).

All of this was happening within a context where sub-fields in management were solidly settling on a scientist route with empirical research increasingly characterized by quantification, as shown for the case of ASQ by Daft (1980) and later for the AMJ by Goodrick (2002). This was clearly the case for organization studies together with the advent and dominance of structural contingency theory, a predicament shared, as acknowledged more lately, by neighboring sub-fields such as strategy (Hendry, 1992; Jeremy, 2002) and international business (Jones and Khanna, 2006). Neither did the newer resource dependence perspective bring in a historical view, although it did serve to expand the domain of organization theory beyond the narrow concerns with internal structure. There was no significant place for history either in economistic approaches such as transaction cost and agency theory, which also arose at about the same time and later infiltrated organizational research. Perhaps the only major exception was organization theorists taking a Marxist approach, Benson (1977: 6–7) probably being first in pointing to the ahistorical character of organizational analysis at the time. The other singular exception was Stinchcombe (1965) with his far ranging essay in the very first *Handbook of Organization*, where he explicitly recognized the need for locating organizational analysis in an historical context due the lasting effects that social structure could have on organizations founded at a particular point in time. Greater awareness of Stinchcombe's (1965) theses in organizational research, however, had to wait for more than a decade (Lounsbury and Ventresca, 2002: 10).

HISTORY BY OTHERS: ORGANIZATION STUDIES TURNS LONGITUDINAL, 1980s ONWARDS

The 1980s saw the beginnings of major changes in organization studies. Most notably perhaps, organization studies entered a stage of theoretical pluralism (Üsdiken and Leblebici, 2001). This had to do with the new theoretical currents that originated in the US, including two other approaches in addition to those already mentioned (i.e., the resource dependence view and organizational economics), namely, organizational ecology and neo-institutionalism. Although the ecological and neo-institutionalist research programs differed in their central concerns, the key concepts they employed, and their levels of analyses, both brought a longitudinal orientation to organization theory. Together they signified a turn away from cross-sectional research that had come to characterize structural contingency theory and the newer resource dependence as well as organizational economics perspectives.

Of the two, organizational ecology took the lead in carrying out longitudinal empirical studies on the dynamics of populations of organizations. Some of this work employed data that spanned very long periods of time, for example, the full 19th century for Argentine and the 19th and 20th centuries for Irish newspapers (Carroll and Delacroix, 1982) or a period of 200 years for Finnish newspapers (Miner, Amburgey, and Stearns, 1990). Such data were collected from a variety of archival resources and typically involved counts of organizational founding and mortality as well as population densities. They also included measures of context, though in a very coarse manner. This was because the main aim of the ecologists was to develop universal theories of organizational diversity, founding, survival, and change. Recourse to historical data had to do with the need for testing and refining the theories of population dynamics that were developed. History also featured in the structural inertia theory of the ecologists but again as one of the factors that constrained adaptive capabilities of organizations (Hannan and Freeman, 1984). Very rare was the ecological study that would dwell upon a single historical case, Langton's (1984) work on Wedgewood pottery probably being the only example.

Institutional theory started out with a broad range of ideas and a looser set of arguments and concepts. One strand of institutional thinking was preoccupied with explaining conformity of organizations to regulative and socio-cultural pressures within fields in which they were located (DiMaggio and Powell, 1983). In this particular formulation, unlike the "old" version of institutionalism, an organization's history had little role to play in view of the current demands from the institutional environment. Nevertheless, there were views from the outset, which granted greater significance to influences from the past, especially in the development of organizational fields (Scott, 1983). Methodologies in early empirical work also varied. They included, for example, cross-sectional investigations based on secondary (e.g., Tolbert, 1985) as well as interview and secondary data (Boeker, 1989). There have also been longitudinal quantitative studies (e.g., Baron, Dobbin, and Jennings, 1986) or a combination of historical and quantitative (e.g., Rowan, 1982) as well as purely qualitative historical analyses (e.g., DiMaggio, 1991).

Indeed, as neo-institutionalist research ventured into field-level investigations and studies of institutionalization, institutional change, institutional entrepreneurship, and institutional logics there has been a greater recognition of historical effects and incorporation of historical research. Notable examples included Leblebici et al.'s (1991) historical analysis of the US radio broadcasting field, which showed that institutional change was prompted by the actions of marginal players, Holm's (1995) study of the transformation in institutional forms of Norwegian fisheries over the period 1930–1994, and Farjoun's (2002) detailed historical analysis of changes in pricing conventions in the online database industry in the 1971–1994 period. Likewise, Hargadon and Douglas (2001) examined, through a historical study, Edison's introduction of electric lighting as a case of institutional entrepreneurship.

Researchers taking an institutional logics approach have also studied how changes in logics have affected various organizational phenomena. They have often used archival data albeit in ways where qualitatively documented historical changes served as a basis for formulating hypotheses, which were then tested quantitatively through methods such as event-history analysis. Lounsbury (2002), for example, has shown how a shift from a regulatory to a market logic in the financial services field in the US over the 1945–1993 period affected, together with the growth of expert knowledge, the founding of professional associations and the professionalization of finance. Thornton (2002) also used historical analysis, together with interviews, to identify the shift in the US textbook publishing industry from an editorial to a market logic in the 1958–1990 period, to then demonstrate how structural alterations took place in line with the new predominant logic.

The move towards longitudinal analysis also had some effects on research in the resource dependence tradition. Mizruchi and Stearns (1988), for example, drawing in part upon resource dependence arguments on cooptation, examined the addition of directors from financial institutions to boards of major US corporations over the 1956–1983 period and showed that general economic conditions had significant effects on such appointments. Indeed, there have also been proposals to include history within, for example, transaction cost theory to enable the consideration of constraints posed by past governance choices (Argyres and Liebskind, 1999).

Accompanying this broad reorientation in theorizing on organizations and organizational fields towards longitudinal approaches was an early recognition by some strategy researchers of the value of taking a long-term perspective in studying the formation of strategies (Mintzberg, 1978) and strategic change (Pettigrew, 1985). This strand of work extended its domain to studying change more broadly at the organizational level of analysis (e.g., Pettigrew, Woodman, and Cameron, 2001) and to the development of "process" theories of organizational dynamics (Langley, 1999). Unlike much of the longitudinal studies within organization theory, which empirically tested and refined preset theories through quantitative methods, theory development in this new strand of research was based on in-depth, qualitative study of processes (Langley, 1999). Moreover, process theorists explicitly acknowledged that history matters as one of the elements enabling or inhibiting change (Pettigrew et al., 2001). History also features in process theorizing as a source of data, collected through primary documents or retrospective interviews, though almost invariably together with current data. This is not only because of the central premise that history shapes or exists within the present, but also due to a primary concern with developing theory. Nevertheless, process research has been one of the ways through which studies of organizational phenomena and history have more recently come to be connected.

NEW BEGINNINGS OR DEAD ENDS? RE-ENGAGING WITH HISTORY IN VARIED WAYS

As mainly US-based organizational research was moving towards longitudinal approaches, other ways of engaging with history were also surfacing, together with explicit calls, especially in the past two decades, for incorporating history into organizational research.

The sub-field of management history was continuing very much in the form that it had taken by the 1980s, with no links to organization studies. Concerns with limited teaching of history persisted in much the same way (e.g., Bedeian, 1998; Wren, 1987), surveys repeatedly showing that there were no signs of growth in the share of history in the curricula of US business schools (Gibson, Hodgetts, and Blackwell, 1999; Van Fleet and Wren, 2005). The literature base of management history also appeared to be increasingly confined to a single text making repeated editions (Wren, 1972; now Wren and Bedeian, 2009 in the sixth edition). Appearance in major journals became an extremely rare event, publications being confined to AoM's proceedings or having to migrate to the specialist *Journal of Management History* (JMH) established in 1995, which quickly became incorporated in 2000 as a section into *Management Decision* (a journal founded in 1963) but then re-emerged as a separate journal in 2006 (Madansky, 2008: 556). There was even some progress within the AoM's Management History division, not only due to the birth and re-birth of a specialist journal but also because some management historians took the opportunity to voice their concerns and pleas (and engage in debates) in the pages of the AoM's new journal, *Academy of Management Learning & Education* (e.g., Bedeian, 2004; Madansky, 2008; Smith, 2007; Wright, 2010).

Perhaps more notably, however, a literature began to appear in major US journals by authors from outside management history circles, who took a critical position and questioned the received historiography of management. Miller and O'Leary (1989), for example, sought to demonstrate how hierarchy was reconciled with American political culture and rendered functional in early management writings. Barley and Kunda's (1992) study showed that management thought did not follow a linear path of progress as it has typically been told in the management history literature but rather oscillated between "rational" and "normative" forms of control, the emergence of each wave being conditioned, respectively, by economic expansion and contraction. Shenhav (1995) argued that viewing organizations as systems was in place in the US already by the early 1930s, shaped as it was by the professionalization concerns of mechanical engineers, the political context, and labor unrest. In a similar manner, O'Connor (1999a) showed the political agendas involved in the human relations movement and the way the ideas and techniques that were propagated served to justify managerial authority and control.

This critical line then began to move towards non-US journals as exemplified by O'Connor's (1999b) companion article on human relations and Cooke's (1999) attempt to show that ideas in the organizational change and development literature were appropriated from the political left, which was then "written out" of its own historiography. More recent examples in this stream have been Frenkel and Shenhav's (2006) postcolonial take on the history of management and organization studies and the actor-network theory perspective that Bruce and Nyland (2011) have brought to understanding how human relations got to be established as a humanistic initiative, while scientific management was demonized (see Booth and Rowlinson, 2006 for further literature of this kind).

The latter examples are especially notable as the alternative models for studying organizational phenomena that gained currency from the 1980s onwards in Europe, in particular the UK, turned out to be inattentive, if not antithetical, to history. These currents developed in the form of interpretive, critical, and postmodern approaches. With respect to these alternative orientations, Rowlinson and Procter (1999), for example, argued that interpretivist views do not really allow for historical research because of the inherent subjectivism, the reliance on unraveling meanings through in-depth interviewing, which confines research to the recent past, and the common tendency of not revealing organizational identities. Cooke (1999) pointed to a lack of historical awareness in some of the work considered as critical. Postmodernist orientations in organization studies have had an uneasy relationship with history too, much of the work in this tradition not having an historical element and, those that did, following Foucault and his critique of the more conventional ways of doing historical research (Rowlinson and Carter, 2002). Nevertheless, the idea of developing a closer relationship between history and organization studies was to be picked up more readily in Europe, after a few early calls from US authors.

Perhaps in the very first of these calls, Lawrence's (1984: 307–8) emphasis was on taking a historical perspective, which she defined as a methodological tool and distinguished from historical research. The purpose of the former was to enable a better understanding of the present, whereas the latter was for learning about the past. More concerned with individual level analyses, for her, the value of the historical perspective rested on being able to separate what was truly universal from that which was not and, more importantly perhaps, to identify the boundaries of theories and empirical results. Goodman and Krueger (1988), on the other hand, turned to historiography as a research technique, attempting to counter typical criticisms and pointing to what it could offer to management research, which they listed as variable selection, theory construction, and hypothesis generation.

Then came the more influential series of papers by Zald (1990, 1991, 1993), this time with specific reference to organization studies. In these, Zald looked first into the relationships between history, sociology, and organization theory, and then to the issues that arose as sociology and organization studies had come to be framed as a science. Zald (1991) expressly pointed to the overall ahistorical character and timeless claims of organization theory. His broader agenda involved forging closer links with the humanities, including literary theory, history, and philosophy. The main problem for Zald (1993: 516; emphasis in original) was how to "*combine* a positivistic programme of theoretical and empirical cumulation with the enriching possibilities of the humanities." With respect to history, to go beyond a "history-for-itself approach" and to "combine" history and organization theory, the avenues that were open included (a) working through cases so that they could be related to more abstract and general issues, (b) using history to test general propositions, (c) developing "historical theories of organizations" in which "time dependent events or processes are (made) critical in explaining later states and events of organizations" (e.g., Stinchcombe, 1965), and (d) using comparative historical data from different societal contexts to specify and understand the core components of organizational forms and major transformations in them (Zald, 1990: 101–3).

Along similar lines, Kieser (1994: 609–11) turned to Weber to suggest that in its roots the study of organizations had a close connection to history. He argued that by re-establishing this relationship organization studies could benefit in a number of ways, such as explaining organizational differences across national settings or examining theories about change over long periods of time. Kieser (1994: 617–18) also proposed that there could be three ways in which organization theory might be employed in historical analysis, namely, by (a) using general conceptions as frameworks for explanation, (b) applying "ideal-typical" formulations to historical cases, and (c) employing alternative hypotheses or deriving hypotheses inductively from historical data.

These earlier calls have either ascribed a "supplementary" role to history (as a research tool or a source of variable selection, theory construction, or hypothesis generation) or sought ways of (partial) "integration" with organization theory (Üsdiken and Kieser, 2004). They have then been joined by those who have gone beyond this and looked into possibilities of forging links specifically with business and company history (Rowlinson and Procter 1999) or have, more broadly, "claimed organization for history," implicating that organization studies should move away from its scientist orientations and its concomitant search for general models towards the narrative in history (Carter, McKinlay, and Rowlinson, 2002). These calls for a "historical turn" in organization studies (Clark and Rowlinson, 2004) were made possible not only by the alternative currents that had gained currency in organization studies but also by changes in the orientation of history as a discipline, which had also trickled down into business history.

Within history, there was, as Fridenson (2008: 21) has noted, a "spectacular boom of cultural history since the 1980s" (see also Lipartito, 2008) and increasing attention was paid to issues such as gender or ethnicity. Cultural history, which included postmodern approaches, first affected technology history (where the main journal is now called *Technology and Culture*) and then also "exerted a growing influence on business history" (Fridenson, 2008: 21). This trend was strengthened (and institutionalized) through the establishment of the journal *Enterprise & Society* (E&S) by the Business History Conference in 2000, which also—but far from exclusively—publishes this kind of research.

These developments, together with the aforementioned calls for a humanistic or historical turn in organization studies, opened up new opportunities for bringing history into organizational analyses. A new journal called *Management & Organizational History* (MOH) was founded in 2006 with the explicit aim "to publish high quality, original, historical research that would 'inform organization and management theory.'" There are other encouraging signs too. Over the last decade or so, more business schools have created courses and positions in business history—partly as a reaction to critiques highlighting their narrow economistic focus, which has also led to a new emphasis on business ethics and corporate social responsibility. Somewhat surprisingly, some of these positions have been difficult to fill, which might show a lack of interest by historians to work in business schools, but is probably most likely due to the differences in the criteria for recruitment and promotion (i.e., A-journal articles vs. books). Many historians actually do work "undercover" in business schools or management departments, teaching a broad variety of courses, while pursuing their own research as well as trying to publish in the journals listed by the different ranking systems. Networking events at the annual meetings of the BHC regularly attract between thirty and fifty participants. There are also new points of contact at some of the major management conferences, with several specific professional development workshops at the AoM meetings and, since 2011, a standing working group on "Historical Perspectives in Organization Studies" at the annual colloquium of the European Group for Organizational Studies (EGOS). It is probably too early to judge the as yet meager results of all these efforts, but there is perhaps some room for hope.

CONCLUDING REMARKS

This chapter has traced the development of the relationship between history and organization studies over the past century. While close at the beginning of the period (in the form of "business history" and "business administration"), these two fields became increasingly distant as time went by and almost completely isolated from each other since the mid-1960s—a development followed by some calls for renewed engagement since the 1990s, which have as yet to show significant tangible results. The chapter has described this evolution in some detail and has tried to link it to the broader evolution of not only organization studies but "business administration" and then "management" as a whole, which was marked by two processes: one of "scientization" within a largely neo-positivist paradigm, where historical methodology had only limited, if any, legitimacy; and a second of an increasing specialization and, consequently, fragmentation of the different academic disciplines over time. Thus, what is now referred to as "organization theory," or more broadly "organization studies," originated as part of business administration, then turning into administrative science, then management, before becoming a separate (sub-)field, distinct also from organizational behaviour, which focuses more on the micro-level. These processes marginalized management history and at the same time separated it from business history, which in turn became increasingly differentiated from economic and general history.

It was again broader developments since the late 1980s that opened possible avenues for closer contact and cooperation: (a) a dissatisfaction and sometimes vociferous critique, more so in Europe than the US, of the scientistic/neo-positivist paradigm in organization studies, the "engineering model" as Zald (1993) has called it; (b) an interest in postmodern, narrative and, particularly, critical approaches to the study of organizations, especially in Europe, as a tangible alternative to the dominant neo-positivism; and (c) developments within history itself, with a strong growth of interest in cultural history, which for institutional and ideational reasons trickled down to business history. All of these developments opened opportunities for bridging the gaps that had arisen earlier and prompted the aforementioned calls.

With these developments in the background, two broad orientations seem likely in furthering the relationship between history and organization studies. One of these would be geared towards "integrating" history and historical research into organization studies while maintaining its social scientistic and theory building aspirations. As discussed earlier, this orientation can be seen most readily in process theorizing and institutionalist approaches. Process studies, in particular, offer an opportunity to benefit from detailed, micro-level historical research, as there is a concern with explaining present day phenomena by recourse to what happened in the past. With regard to institutionalist approaches this is not to suggest that all of institutional research will or needs to become historical but that there might be an increasing awareness of the value of incorporating history for a better understanding of institutional processes and outcomes (see, e.g., Greenwood et al., 2010). This is one of the avenues in which the "integrationist" project could come into its own, which, as Schneiberg and Clemens (2006: 205) have observed, is exemplified by some of the field-level studies that "combine the attention to historical processes and complexity demanded by historians with the systematic analysis and rigour demanded by organizational researchers."

The second orientation for collaboration seems to be with respect to the narrative turn in both organization studies and history. This involves, as Booth and Rowlinson (2006: 9) have put it, "historically informed writing in organization theory and historical research informed by organization theory." Not only is this route likely to entail new ways of a rapprochement with business history but also to cultivate stronger ties with critical management studies. It could also serve to generate and develop the debate around historical writing, and theory and philosophy of history as they pertain to organization studies (Rowlinson, Jacques, and Booth, 2009).

Whatever direction is taken, rebuilding the relationship between history and organization studies calls for openness from both sides and requires points of contact, which is probably where most progress has been made over the last decade or so. There are now more forums and more journals where historical work on organizations can be presented and published. What probably would be most important is to have more "historical" research published in leading organization journals, which despite the repeated calls by their editors for diverse approaches to the study of organizations has yet to materialize (with most of the exceptions noted in this chapter).

As historians (should) know, the future is always uncertain, but recent developments have at least opened a variety of avenues to gradually (re)build a closer relationship between history and organization studies. It is up to the actors in both fields to pursue them.

REFERENCES

Argyres, N. S., and Liebeskind, J. P. (1999). "Contractual Commitments, Bargaining Power, and Governance Inseparability: Incorporating History into Transaction Cost Theory," *Academy of Management Review*, 24(1): 49–63.

Barley, S. R., and Kunda, G. (1992). "Design and Devotion: Normative Ideologies of Control in Managerial Discourse," *Administrative Science Quarterly*, 37(3): 363–99.

Baron, J. N., Dobbin, F. R., and Jennings, P. D. (1986). "War and Peace: The Evolution of Modern Personnel Administration in US Industry," *American Journal of Sociology*, 92(2): 350–83.

Bedeian, A. G. (1976). "Management History Thought," *Academy of Management Review*, 1(1): 96–7.

Bedeian, A. G. (1998). "Exploring the Past," *Journal of Management History*, 4(1): 4–15.

Bedeian, A. G. (2004). "The Gift of Professional Maturity," *Academy of Management Learning & Education*, 3(1): 92–8.

Benson, J. K. (1977). "Organizations: A Dialectical View," *Administrative Science Quarterly*, 22(1): 1–21.

Boeker, W. (1989). "Strategic Change: The Effects of Founding and History," *Academy of Management Journal*, 32(3): 489–515.

Booth, C., and Rowlinson, M. (2006). "Management and Organizational History: Prospects," *Management & Organizational History*, 1(1): 5–30.

Boulding, K. E. (1958). "Evidences for an Administrative Science: A Review of the Administrative Science Quarterly, Volumes 1 and 2," *Administrative Science Quarterly*, 3(1): 1–22.

Bourn, A. M. (1975). "Business History and Management Education," *Business History*, 17(1): 17–25.

Bracker, J. (1980). "The Historical Development of the Strategic Concept," *Academy of Management Review*, 5(2): 219–24.

Bruce, K., and Nyland, C. (2011). "Elton Mayo and the Deification of Human Relations," *Organization Studies*, 32(3): 383–405.

Carroll, G. R., and Delacroix, J. (1982). "Organizational Mortality in the Newspaper Industries of Argentina and Ireland: An Ecological Approach," *Administrative Science Quarterly*, 27(2): 169–98.

Carter, C., McKinlay, A., and Rowlinson, M. (2002). "Introduction: Foucault, Management and History," *Organization*, 9(4): 515–26.

Chandler, A. D. (1962). *Strategy and Structure: Chapters in the History of the Industrial Enterprise*. Cambridge, MA: MIT Press.

Clark, P., and Rowlinson, M. (2004). "The Treatment of History in Organisation Studies: Towards an 'Historic Turn'?" *Business History*, 46(3): 331–52.

Colli, A., Iversen, M. J., and Abe de Jong, A. (2011). "Mapping Strategy, Structure, Ownership and Performance in European Corporations: Introduction," *Business History*, 53(1): 1–13.

Cooke, B. (1999). "Writing the Left out of Management Theory: The Historiography of the Management of Change," *Organization*, 6(1): 81–105.

Daft, R. L. (1980). "The Evolution of Organization Analysis in ASQ, 1959–1979," *Administrative Science Quarterly*, 25(4): 623–36.

Delany, W. (1960). "Some Field Notes on the Problem of Access in Organizational Research," *Administrative Science Quarterly*, 5(3): 448–57.

DiMaggio, P. J. (1991). "Constructing an Organizational Field as a Professional Project: U.S. Art Museums, 1920–1940." In W. W. Powell and P. J. DiMaggio (eds.), *The New Institutionalism in Organizational Analysis*. Chicago: The University of Chicago Press: 267–92.

DiMaggio, P. J., and Powell, W. W. (1983). "The Iron Cage Revisited: Institutional Isomorphism and Collective Rationality in Organizational Fields," *American Sociological Review*, 48(2): 147–60.

Dorfman, J. (1955). "The Role of the German Historical School in American Economic Thought," *American Economic Review*, 45(2): 17–28.

Duncan, W. J. (1971). "Professionalism in Management and the History of Administrative Thought: Comment," *Academy of Management Journal*, 14(4): 515–18.

[Editors]. (1962). "Survey of the Teaching of Business History in Colleges and Universities in the United States, Canada, Australia, and Japan," *Business History Review*, 36(3): 359–71.

Engwall, L., Kipping, M., and Üsdiken, B. (2010). "Public Science Systems, Higher Education, and the Trajectory of Academic Disciplines: Business Studies in the United States and Europe." In R. Whitley, J. Gläser, and L. Engwall (eds.), *Reconfiguring Knowledge Production: Changing Authority Relationships in the Sciences and Their Consequences for Intellectual Innovation*. Oxford: Oxford University Press: 325–53.

Farjoun, M. (2002). "The Dialectics of Institutional Development in Emerging and Turbulent Fields: The History of Pricing Conventions in the On-Line Database Industry," *Academy of Management Journal*, 45(5): 848–74.

Frenkel, M., and Shenhav, Y. (2006). "From Binarism Back to Hybridity: A Postcolonial Reading of Management and Organization Studies," *Organization Studies*, 27(6): 855–76.

Fridenson, P. (2008). "Business History and History." In G. Jones and J. Zeitlin (eds.), *The Oxford Handbook of Business History*. Oxford: Oxford University Press: 9–36.

Galambos, L. (1970). "The Emerging Organizational Synthesis in Modern American History," *Business History Review*, 44(3): 279–90.

George, C. S. (1968). *The History of Management Thought*. Englewood Cliffs, NJ: Prentice-Hall.

Gibson, J. W., Hodgetts, R. M., and Blackwell, C. W. (1999). "The Role of Management History in the Management Curriculum: 1997," *Journal of Management History*, 5(5): 277–85.

Giglioni, G. B., and Bedeian, A. G. (1974). "A Conspectus of Management Control Theory, 1900–1972," *Academy of Management Journal*, 17(2): 292–305.

Goldman, P. (1994). "Searching for History in Organizational Theory: Comment on Kieser," *Organization Science*, 5(4): 621–23.

Goodman, R. S., and Kruger, E. J. (1988). "Data Dredging or Legitimate Research Method: Historiography and its Potential for Management Research," *Academy of Management Review*, 13(2): 315–25.

Goodrick, E. (2002). "From Management as a Vocation to Management as a Scientific Activity: An Institutional Account of a Paradigm Shift," *Journal of Management*, 28(5): 649–68.

Gordon, R. A., and Howell, J. E. (1959). *Higher Education for Business*. New York: Columbia University Press.

Greenwood, R. (1981). "Management by Objectives: As Developed by Peter Drucker, Assisted by Harold Smiddy," *Academy of Management Review*, 6(2): 225–30.

Greenwood, R. G., Bolton, A. A., and Greenwood, R. A. (1983). "Hawthorne a Half Century Later: Relay Assembly Participants Remember," *Journal of Management*, 9(2): 217–31.

Greenwood, R., Díaz, A. M., Li, S. X., and Lorente, J. C. (2010). "The Multiplicity of Institutional Logics and the Heterogeneity of Organizational Responses," *Organization Science*, 21(2): 521–39.

Hannan, M. T., and Freeman, J. (1984). Structural Inertia and Organizational Change. *American Sociological Review*, 49(2): 149–64.

Hargadon, A. B., and Douglas, Y. (2001). "When Innovations Meet Institutions: Edison and the Design of the Electric Light," *Administrative Science Quarterly*, 46(3): 476–501.

Organizations in Time

Hendry, J. (1992). "Business Strategy and Business History: A Framework for Development," *Advances in Strategic Management*, 8: 207–25.

Holm, P. (1995). "The Dynamics of Institutionalization: Transformation Processes in Norwegian Fisheries," *Administrative Science Quarterly*, 40(3): 398–422.

Holmes, G., and Ruff, H. (1975). "The Perils of Entrepreneurial History," *Business History*, 17(1): 26–43.

Jeremy, D. J. (2002). "Business History and Strategy." In A. Pettigrew, H. Thomas, and R. Whittington (eds.), *Handbook of Strategy and Management*. London: Sage: 436–60.

John, R. R. (1997). "Elaborations, Revisions, Dissents: Alfred D. Chandler, Jr.'s, 'The Visible Hand' After Twenty Years," *Business History Review*, 71(2): 151–200.

Jones, G., and Khanna, T. (2006). "Bringing History (Back) into International Business," *Journal of International Business Studies*, 37(4): 453–68.

Keller, R. T. (1984). "The Harvard 'Pareto Circle' and the Historical Development of Organization Theory," *Journal of Management*, 10(2): 193–203.

Khurana, R. (2007). *From Higher Aims to Hired Hands: The Social Transformation of American Business Schools and the Unfulfilled Promise of Management as a Profession*. Princeton: Princeton University Press.

Kieser, A. (1994). "Why Organization Theory Needs Historical Analysis—And How This Should Be Performed," *Organization Science*, 5(4): 608–20.

Kipping, M., and Üsdiken, B. (2008). "Business History and Management Studies." In G. Jones and J. Zeitlin (eds.), *The Oxford Handbook of Business History*. Oxford: Oxford University Press: 96–119.

Koontz, H. (1961). "The Management Theory Jungle," *Academy of Management Journal*, 4(3): 174–88.

Langley, A. (1999). "Strategies for Theorizing From Process Data," *Academy of Management Review*, 24(4): 691–710.

Langton, J. (1984). "The Ecological Theory of Bureaucracy: The Case of Josiah Wedgewood and the British Pottery Industry," *Administrative Science Quarterly*, 29(3): 330–54.

Lawrence, B. S. (1984). "Historical Perspective: Using the Past to Study the Present," *Academy of Management Review*, 9(2): 307–12.

Leblebici, H., Salancik, G. R., Copay, A., and King, T. (1991). "Institutional Change and the Transformation of Interorganizational Fields: An Organizational History of the U.S. Radio Broadcasting Industry," *Administrative Science Quarterly*, 36(3): 333–63.

Lipartito, K. (2008). "Business Culture." In G. Jones and J. Zeitlin (eds.), *The Oxford Handbook of Business History*. Oxford: Oxford University Press: 603–28.

Locke, E. A. (1982). "The Ideas of Frederick W. Taylor: An Evaluation," *Academy of Management Review*, 7(1): 14–24.

Locke, R. R. (1984). *The End of the Practical Man: Entrepreneurship and Higher Education in Germany, France and Great Britain*. Greenwich, CT: JAI Press.

Lounsbury, M. (2002). "Institutional Transformation and Status Mobility: The Professionalization of the Field of Finance," *Academy of Management Journal*, 45(1): 255–66.

Lounsbury, M., and Ventresca, M. J. (2002). "Social Structure and Organizations Revisited," *Research in the Sociology of Organizations*, 19: 1–36.

Madansky, A. (2008). "Teaching History in Business Schools: An Outsider's View," *Academy of Management Learning & Education*, 7(4): 553–62.

Mahmoud, S., and Frampton, C. (1975). "An Evaluation of Management Curricula in the American Association of Collegiate Schools of Business," *Academy of Management Journal*, 18(2): 407–11.

March, J. G., and Simon, H. A. (1958). *Organizations*. New York: John Wiley and Sons.

Mathias, P. (1975). "Business History and Management Education," *Business History*, 17(1): 3–16.

Meuleau, M. (1981). *Histoire d'une Grande École: HEC, 1881–1981*. Jouy-en-Josas: Ecole des Hautes Etudes Commerciales.

Miller, P., and O'Leary, T. (1989). "Hierarchies and American Ideals, 1900–1940," *Academy of Management Review*, 14(2): 250–65.

Miner, A. S., Amburgey, T., and Stearns, T. M. (1990). "Interorganizational Linkages and Population Dynamics: Buffering and Transformational Shields," *Administrative Science Quarterly*, 35(4): 689–713.

Mintzberg, H. (1978). "Patterns in Strategy Formation," *Management Science*, 24(9): 934–48.

Mizruchi, M. S., and Stearns, L. B. (1988). "A Longitudinal Study of the Formation of Interlocking Directorates," *Administrative Science Quarterly*, 33(2): 194–210.

Mowday, R. T. (1997). "Celebrating 40 Years of the Academy of Management Journal," *Academy of Management Journal*, 40(6): 1400–13.

O'Connor, E. (1999a). "The Politics of Management Thought: A Case Study of the Harvard Business School and the Human Relations School," *Academy of Management Review*, 24(1): 117–31.

O'Connor, E. (1999b). "Minding the Workers: The Meaning of 'Human' and 'Human Relations' in Elton Mayo," *Organization*, 6(2): 223–46.

Pettigrew, A. M. (1985). *The Awakening Giant: Continuity and Change in ICI*. Oxford: Blackwell.

Pettigrew, A. M., Woodman, R. W., and Cameron, K. S. (2001). "Studying Organizational Change and Development: Challenges for Future Research," *Academy of Management Journal*, 44(4): 697–713.

Pierson, F. C. (1959). *The Education of American Business Men*. New York: John Wiley & Sons.

Redlich, F., Glover, J. D, Johnson, A. M., Taylor, G. R., and Overton, R. C. (1962). "Approaches to Business History/Comment," *Business History Review*, 36 (1): 61–86.

Rowan, B. (1982). "Organizational Structure and the Institutional Environment: The Case of Public Schools," *Administrative Science Quarterly*, 27(2): 259–79.

Rowlinson, M., and Carter, C. (2002). "Foucault and History in Organization Studies," *Organization*, 9(4): 527–47.

Rowlinson, M., and Procter, S. (1999). "Organization Culture and Business History," *Organization Studies*, 20(3): 369–96.

Rowlinson, M., Jacques, R. S., and Booth, C. (2009). "Critical Management and Organizational History." In M. Alvesson, T. Bridgman, and H. Willmott (eds.), *The Oxford Handbook of Critical Management Studies*. Oxford: Oxford University Press: 286–303.

Schneiberg, M., and Clemens, E. S. (2006). "The Typical Tools for the Job: Research Strategies in Institutional Analysis," *Sociological Theory*, 24(3): 195–227.

Scott, W. G. (1961). "Organization Theory: An Overview and an Appraisal," *Journal of Academy of Management*, 4(1): 7–26.

Scott, W. R. (1983). "The Organization of Environments: Network, Cultural, and Historical Elements." In J. W. Meyer and W. R. Scott (eds.), *Organizational Environments: Ritual and Rationality*. London: Sage: 155–75.

Shenhav, Y. (1995). "From Chaos to Systems: The Engineering Foundations of Organization Theory," *Administrative Science Quarterly*, 40(4): 557–85.

Simon, H. A. (1952). "Comments on the Theory of Organizations," *American Political Science Review*, 46(4): 1130–9.

Simon, H. A. (1991). *Models of My Life*. New York: Basic Books.

Smith, G. E. (2007). "Management History and Historical Context: Potential Benefits of its Inclusion in the Management Curriculum," *Academy of Management Learning & Education*, 6(4): 522–33.

Steigerwalt, A. K. (1959). "Business History in Schools of Business Administration," *Business History Review*, 33(1): 212–13.

Stinchcombe, A. L. (1965). "Social Structure and Organizations." In J. G. March (ed.), *Handbook of Organizations*. Chicago: Rand McNally & Company: 142–93.

Supple, B. E. (1959). "American Business History—A Survey," *Business History*, 1(2): 63–76.

Thompson, J. D. (1956). "On Building an Administrative Science," *Administrative Science Quarterly*, 1(1): 102–11.

Thompson, J. D. (1967). *Organizations in Action*. New York: McGraw-Hill.

Thornton, P. H. (2002). "The Rise of the Corporation in a Craft Industry: Conflict and Conformity in Institutional Logics," *Academy of Management Journal*, 45(1): 81–101.

Tiratsoo, N. (2004). "The 'Americanization' of Management Education in Britain," *Journal of Management Inquiry*, 13(2): 118–26.

Tolbert, P. S. (1985). "Institutional Environments and Resource Dependence: Sources of Administrative Structure in Institutions of Higher Education," *Administrative Science Quarterly*, 30(1): 1–13.

Üsdiken, B., and Kieser, A. (2004). "Introduction: History in Organisation Studies," *Business History*, 46(3): 321–30.

Üsdiken, B., and Leblebici, H. (2001). "Organization Theory." In N. Anderson, D. S. Ones, H. K. Sinangil, and C. Viswesvaran (eds.), *Handbook of Industrial, Work and Organizational Psychology*. London: Sage, Vol. 2: 377–97.

Van Fleet, D. D., and Bedeian, A. G. (1977). "A History of the Span of Management," *Academy of Management Review*, 2(3): 356–72.

Van Fleet, D. D., and Wren, D. A. (2005). "Teaching History in Business Schools, 1982–2003," *Academy of Management Learning & Education*, 4(1): 44–56.

Van Fleet, D. D., Bedeian, A. G., Downey, H., Griffin, R., Dalton, V., Vecchio, R., Kacmar, K, and Feldman, D. (2006). "The Journal of Management's First 30 Years," *Journal of Management*, 32(4): 477–506.

Warren, R., and Tweedale, G. (2002). "Business Ethics and Business History: Neglected Dimensions in Management Education," *British Journal of Management*, 13(3): 209–19.

Whittington, R., and Mayer, M. (2000). *The European Corporation: Strategy, Structure, and Social Science*. Oxford: Oxford University Press.

Wrege, C. D., and Perroni, A. G. (1974). "Taylor's Pig-Tale: A Historical Analysis of Frederick W. Taylor's Pig-Iron Experiments," *Academy of Management Journal*, 17(1): 6–27.

Wrege, C. D., and Stotka, A. M. (1978). "Cooke Creates a Classic: The Story Behind F. W. Taylor's Principles of Scientific Management," *Academy of Management Review*, 3(4): 736–49.

Wren, D. A. (1972). *The Evolution of Management Thought*. New York: Ronald Press.

Wren, D. A. (1987). "Management History: Issues and Ideas for Teaching and Research," *Journal of Management*, 13(2): 339–50.

Wren, D. A., and Hay, R. D. (1977). "Management Historians and Business Historians: Differing Perceptions of Pioneer Contributors," *Academy of Management Journal*, 20(3): 470–5.

Wren, D. A., and Van Fleet, D. D. (1983). "History in Schools of Business," *Business and Economic History*, 12: 29–35.

Wright, R. E. (2010). "Teaching History in Business Schools: An Insider's View," *Academy of Management Learning & Education*, 9(4): 697–700.

Young, S., George, C. S., Johnson, R. A., Pederson, C. A., Reed, K. A., and Shull, F. A. (1967). "Research Activities and Interests of the Academy Membership—A Summary," *Academy of Management Journal*, 10(2): 205–7.

Zald, M. N. (1990). "History, Sociology, and Theories of Organization." In J. E. Jackson (ed.), *Institutions in American Society: Essays in Market, Political and Social Organizations*. Ann Arbor, MI: University of Michigan: 81–108.

Zald, M. N. (1991). "Sociology as a Discipline: Quasi-Science and Quasi-Humanities," *The American Sociologist*, 22(3): 165–87.

Zald, M. N. (1993). "Organization Studies as a Scientific and Humanistic Enterprise: Toward a Reconceptualization of the Foundations of the Field," *Organization Science*, 4(4): 513–28.

3

History and Organization Theory: Potential for a Transdisciplinary Convergence

Hüseyin Leblebici

Since the beginning of the 21st century, there have been high expectations of an imminent coalition between organization theory and business history scholars to build what is called the "historic turn" (Clark and Rowlinson, 2004). As Weatherbee and his colleagues amply point out in a new special issue on organization studies and history (Weatherbee et al., 2012), efforts to promote the interaction between these two fields have been increasing exponentially since the turn of the century. In theory, the close interaction between historical and organizational research, at least at the macro level, has had the potential to turn the ongoing discussions about the role of history in organizational studies beyond simple ideological debates into a more substantive agreement over the proper theoretical role and methodological contributions of history in socio-logical studies of management and organizations. As Booth and Rowlinson put it in their discussion of the prospects of the new journal, *Management and Organizational History*, "In parallel with the historic turn in management and organization theory, business history has become more open to an engage-ment with theory from sociology and cultural studies, even if many business historians remain in thrall to economics" (Booth and Rowlinson, 2006: 21). But if that kind of clarifying, substantive integration is in fact to material-ize, organization theory and business history scholars need to be a lot more explicit, and a lot more honest, about what their fundamental epistemological as well as ontological assumptions are and how their unique perspectives lead not only to substantive debates but also an eventual integration.

The purpose of this chapter is to explore whether such integration is feasible or even desirable and what its domain should be. That may sound a bit strange, since so many of the recent papers about the relationship between organization theory and history claim that such integration is necessary in order to advance both fields. New macro theories about organizational fields, industries, and organizational change all emphasize how important it is for organization theory to be history friendly (Malerba et al., 1999); business historians are equally serious about such joint ventures and insist that unlike traditional historians within history departments, historians in business schools are serious and actually willing to talk in detail about theory development that is meaningful to their organization theory counterparts. Yet, as I will try to demonstrate in this chapter, the reality might be very different and the eventual integration much more complex. What organization theory scholars may consider as history friendly research might simply look like highly flimsy historical research to historians. Similarly, while historians may use the term "theory" in their papers, they may mean something substantively and rhetorically different in its usage. Indeed, it is possible to argue that the old cultural debates between history and sociology of the last century are alive and well within the domain of organizational research.

Thus, my approach in this paper is to explore some of the most fundamental similarities and differences between organization theory and business history scholars and show how these variations shape the ongoing debates. In the first section, I will provide some empirical data to explore the interactions between organization theory and business history. The data I use are based on the dissertations completed in the first ten years of this century and the academic articles published in major management journals (*Academy of Management, Administrative Science Quarterly, Organization Science*, and *Organization Studies*). Later in this section I also look at ongoing attempts at interdisciplinary research between historians and economists as well as sociologists. The basic objective of these explorations is to understand both the ongoing trends and the ultimate consequences of these interactions for these different cultures of inquiry (Hall, 1999) in terms of research questions and actual patterns of interdisciplinary work. In the second section, I explore possible explanations of why the observed patterns of interactions exist and how scholars within sociology, economics, organization theory, and history justify or repudiate the nature of their interactions. In the final section, I offer some alternative strategies on how a more productive interaction between organization theory and history could be developed and examine the kind of best practices that could be transferred from other academic fields.

ORGANIZATION THEORY, SOCIOLOGY, ECONOMICS, AND HISTORY: NATURE OF INTERACTIONS AND SOME STYLIZED FACTS

It is a received fact today that history as a scholarly activity should be an integral part of the organizational scholar's research toolbox. Since the early 1990s organization theorists have been arguing consistently that history as a discipline should be incorporated into their scholarship (Booth and Rowlinson, 2006; Jacques, 2006; Kieser, 1994; Soulsby and Clark, 2007). Various business and management journals have been specifically set up to generate interdisciplinary research such as *Accounting History, Business History, Business History Review, Business and Economic History, Journal of Management History*, and *Management and Organizational History*. Similarly, recent edited books by various scholars in the management disciplines have been exploring how history could be integrated into their disciplines (Ingram, Rao, and Silverman, 2012).

These trends and arguments reflect themselves in various ways in the research produced by organizational scholars. Two specific indicators are uniquely instructive in accounting for how researchers incorporate the historical understanding of the phenomena they study. One indicator is the trend in doctoral dissertations produced within business schools and their use of historical data or perspectives. As shown in Figure 3.1, there has been a steady increase in the number of such dissertations completed in the first decade of this century.

Two additional trends could also be observed from this figure. One is that organization theory and strategy researchers were in the forefront of using historical observations. The second is the fact that most of the research conducted relies on secondary sources and does not encompass historical methods or historiography as understood by historians. Moreover, these investigations rely on single historical case studies rather than comparative investigations.

A close examination of these dissertations reveals that most of these "historical" studies are more like panel data analyses or time series data that are

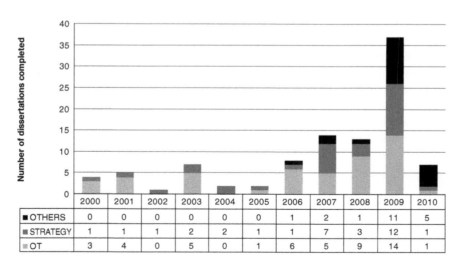

Figure 3.1 Number of management and organization theory dissertations using historical data or analyses 2000–2010

commonly used by institutional or ecological researchers. It is clear that neither institutional theorists nor organizational ecologists incorporate historical methods or rely on source material. Out of the hundred dissertations completed within business schools and analyzed for this paper that could be considered historical, only a few are based on organizational or industry history that could acceptable to business historians. (Please refer to Appendix 3.1 for a list of the dissertations used for this analysis.)

Most of the historical dissertations written in organization or management departments in the first decade of the 21st century follow a well-established traditional pattern. They usually start with a core theoretical claim based on the prevailing organizational theories. Then the dissertation focuses on the histories of a particular industry, institutional field, or managerial practice. These historical accounts are usually based on original documents, archival data sources, and sometimes oral histories based on interviews with the industry insiders. The collected data are then analyzed either in the form of statistical analyses to test some specific hypothesis or in the form of a historical narrative to see the relationship between the theoretical claims and the historical observations. For instance, Christopher Marquis in his dissertation on the historical transformation of the banking sector in the US focuses on how changes in the institutional, technical, legal, and economic environments produced changes in banking organizations and how these changes ultimately influenced the institutional and economic environments these banks are part of (Marquis, 2005). His objective is to demonstrate that the relationship between organizations and their environments is historically contingent and the founding environments of organizations have a path-dependent impact on the subsequent evolution of individual banks as well as the banking field. In other words, the mutual interdependency between organizations and their environments evolves in a historically contingent manner.

A similar dissertation looks at the evolution of the electric utility industry in the US (Sine, 2001). Wesley Sine, in his investigation of the structural changes in this industry between 1935 and 1978, shows how the taken-for-granted practices of a well-established industry could erode because of the crisis it faced and produce alternative institutional practices and the founding of new organizational forms. As in Marquis' dissertation, Sine focuses on original sources such as popular press articles, congressional hearings, and interdisciplinary academic articles on the electric utility industry.

Both of these dissertations are clear examples of what organizational scholars consider as doing valid historical research. The core questions of the inquiries are solidly based on theoretical questions in the field of organization theory and the selections of the historical settings are mostly determined by the accessibility of historical records and data. The convenience of data availability dominates all the dissertations included in Appendix 3.1.

A second indicator of the trend is the number of historically based articles published in major academic journals within organizational studies. Similar observations could be made about the increasing trend in the number of articles published that are historical in nature. As Figure 3.2 shows, a steady increase in the number of articles, particularly in two journals (*Administrative Science Quarterly* and *Organization Studies*), points to the changing nature of the research questions being asked by organizational scholars. (Please refer to Appendix 3.2 for a list of the articles and journals used for this analysis.) As the field of organization studies has moved into questions dealing with evolutionary processes, networks, social institutions, and the emergence (and the decline) of industries, traditional research techniques ranging from surveys to participant observations have become less and less useful for researchers in the field. Even in the case of traditional event history studies conducted by organizational ecologists or strategy scholars, it has become necessary to incorporate industry history into the traditional narrative. One peculiar observation that is not revealed in the data presented in Figure 3.2 (and Appendix 3.2) is the constant avoidance of the term "history" in the abstracts of these articles or in the main body of the texts. Most authors, it seems, prefer terms such as longitudinal investigation or "historical case study" in describing their research (e.g., Guler, Guillén, and Macpherson, 2002; Hargadon and Douglas, 2001; Suddaby and Greenwood, 2005).

For instance, Hiatt and his colleagues, in their study on the role of social movements in disrupting existing organizational fields and industries focus on the development of the Woman's Christian Temperance Union (WCTU), the

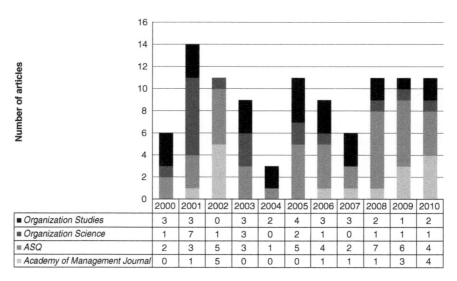

	2000	2001	2002	2003	2004	2005	2006	2007	2008	2009	2010
■ Organization Studies	3	3	0	3	2	4	3	3	2	1	2
■ Organization Science	1	7	1	3	0	2	1	0	1	1	1
■ ASQ	2	3	5	3	1	5	4	2	7	6	4
▨ Academy of Management Journal	0	1	5	0	0	0	1	1	1	3	4

Figure 3.2 Number of published historical articles in major organization theory and management journals

leading organizational representative of the American temperance movement, and its impact on breweries and soft drink producers (Hiatt, Sine, and Tolbert, 2009). It is interesting to observe that even though most of the critical research on the subject of social movements cited in the paper are historical, the narrative form of this and similar papers follows the traditional social science discourse with specific theoretical focus and testing of hypotheses. Similar papers on social movements, such as ones that examine the effects of Progressive-era movement organizations on the emergence of new types of thrift organizations (Haveman, Rao, and Paruchuri, 2007) and the effects of the organic food movement on the rise of alternative forms of food production (Lee, 2009), maintain a theory testing narrative. The opening lines of these papers and their abstracts focus on a conceptual rather than a historical question. This is one of the reasons why traditional database searches (e.g., ISI) fail to detect all the papers that have historical dimensions.

Another example of a traditional historical research topic within management literature is institutional diffusion of managerial practices or industry evolution, such as the research done on the formation of business incubators as new organizational forms (Leblebici and Shah, 2004) or the antecedents and consequences of establishing new national stock exchanges in developing countries (Weber, Davis, and Lounsbury, 2009). The basic theoretical question is to understand the diffusion process behind these core organizational arrangements whether it is the idea of business incubators or of financial globalization. Even though all the data are historical, the basic narratives of the papers are based on theoretical narrative or hypotheses testing as expected in management research.

These trends partly explain why there has been an increasing call for a historical emphasis in organizational studies. The introduction of time relevant arguments as well as key measurements has necessitated at least a renewed way of paying attention to what historians could provide for organization theory researchers. It is unclear, however, how such an interaction between these two cultures of inquiry could be beneficial to both parties. Neither institutional theory nor organizational ecology specifically relies on source material as historians understand it. And because the empirical research is always coupled with a particular theoretical approach, the search for supporting evidence is not built around the description of a particular phenomenon in historical time and space.

In order to ascertain how these generally tenuous but welcome interactions would evolve during the next decade of the 21st century, it would be instructive to look at some other social science fields where such interactions started much earlier. I have specifically selected two such interactions between the fields of economics and sociology with history. Both of these fields are an integral part of macro-organizational research. Moreover, economic history and historical sociology have a long intellectual relationship with the discipline of history that goes back more than half a century. Learning from their experiences could be very instructive in developing our expectations and avoiding their mistakes.

History, Economics and the Field of Cliometrics

It was more than sixty years ago that economists started to apply economic theory to historical settings. The basic idea was to combine the rigor of economic thinking and historical evidence to understand and to a degree test the power of economic models. The Cliometrics tradition (the term combines the Muse of History, Clio, one of the nine daughters of Zeus in the Greek mythology, and metrics for measurement) has been one of the major attempts to integrate history with a well-established social science discipline. Since then various journals, such as *Journal of Economic History*, *Economic History Review*, and *Cliometrica* among others, have evolved to provide an interdisciplinary forum to discuss the nature and role of markets, labor institutions, organizational and related business innovations, and the role of political and social institutions in economic development (Whaples, 1991). The early attempts mainly focused on the application of traditional neoclassical economics to past historical data. Early research, however, failed to incorporate the role of governments, history of property rights, transaction costs, or political institutions as endogenous forces that shaped economic history (Greif, 1997). In the late 1980s, however, the influence of the traditional neoclassical economics declined and the introduction of new ideas such as evolutionary game theory and historical and comparative institutional analysis (Greif, 1998) narrowed the conceptual gap between economic theory and economic history.

The long history of interdisciplinary work in economics, however, has been limited in its impact. Recent debates among economic historians show that the divide between economic historians and traditional economists has not really closed but might actually have been widened by making economic history a marginal player within both disciplines. As Whaples has argued recently:

> In these turbulent times, it became obvious to almost everyone that understanding economic history is useful, indeed essential, and economic historians are indispensable. And yet many economic historians have the sense that their discipline is a neglected field, a field on the margins, caught in a no man's land between two disciplines: ignored and underappreciated by economists and misunderstood, feared, and perhaps even despised by historians. Most economic historians sense that the discipline has almost always been on the margins and that this marginalization has increased appreciably since the end of a brief golden age that glimmered during the 1960s and into the 1970s. (Whaples, 2010: 17)

Most of today's economic historians use history as a part of their empirical laboratory for economics. Because of their strong economics training, they are mostly oblivious to the concerns of the historians. Moreover, because most of these researchers are housed in traditional economics departments and most of the interdisciplinary journals select editors from the economics departments, their concerns are more aligned with testing economic theories. Similarly, historians are equally unsympathetic to the needs of the economists. They are not only untrained in economic logic but subscribe to different assumptions, approaches, and ideological perspectives (Ryden, 2011).

The following tables show the degree of relatedness among journals in the fields of economics and economic history. The degree of relatedness among journals listed in the following tables is based on the reports prepared by ISI Web-of-Knowledge Journal Citation Reports. As described on the Journal Citation Reports, the relatedness values are generated by taking into account the number of citations between two journals (<http//admin-apps.webof-knowledge.com/JCR/help/h_relatedjrnl.htm#relatedjournals>) based on the algorithm adopted by the Web of Knowledge (Pudovkin and Garfield, 2002). The first column shows the citations from focal journal to related journals (j) and the second column shows the citations from related journals (j) to the focal journal. As indicated by Web of Knowledge, related journals data are available only for journals that have been cited more than 100 times. The journals at the top of each table are more likely to have a stronger subject connection to the journal selected for analysis than the journals at the bottom of the table. In preparing these tables I eliminated journal pairs if each journal cited the other less than twenty-five times if the number of related journals specified by the Web of Knowledge was more than fifteen to keep the number of journals at a reasonable number. The objective of these tables is ultimately to see if interdisciplinary history journals receive any attention from their core disciplinary journals.

The evidence clearly indicates that the degree of interaction among mainstream economists and economic historians is not only low but when there is an interaction it is unidirectional where the major disciplinary journals are cited by the interdisciplinary journals but not the other way around. Moreover, the journals at the top of each table represent interdisciplinary journals. For instance, *American Economic Review* is at the bottom of the journal lists for *Journal of Economic History* and *Economic History Review* (Tables 3.1a and 3.1b) and is not included at all in *Cliometrica* (Table 3.1c).

Some economic historians have argued that the lack of participation among historians in economic history could be explained by their rejection of the idea that universal models of economic behavior could be used to explain historical events (Ryden, 2011). Another possible explanation is that for many mainstream and intellectual historians economic history and particularly Cliometrics simply produce unreliable historical data and trivial results (Wickberg, 2009).

Table 3.1a The degree of interactions among economic history and other mainstream economics and history journals: *Journal of Economic History*

Related journal (j)	Relatedness (R)	
	J ECON HIST to j	j to J ECON HIST
European Review of Economic History	268.39	1521.02
Journal of Economic History	1242.99	1242.99
Explorations in Economic History	372.12	954.94
Economic History Review	311.63	874.88
Cliometrica	78.45	821.17
Revista de Historia Económica	95.61	635.81
Business History	20.81	473.33
Journal of Political Economy	373.96	71.08
Journal of Law and Economics	191.23	239.65
Business History Review	76.49	231.03
Journal of Interdisciplinary History	95.61	227.27
Journal of Economic Literature	203.98	214.73
Quarterly Journal of Economics	199.54	85.03
Continuity and Change	101.99	184.37
Journal of Institutional and Theoretical Economics	41.35	169.68
Agrarian History	107.36	161.08
Journal of Monetary Economics	106.73	142.88
Economica	56.66	120.94
American Economic Review	118.34	75.79
Journal of Economic Perspectives	106.73	50.06
Econometrica	106.24	105.27

Table 3.1b The degree of interactions among economic history and other mainstream economics and history journals: *Economic History Review*

Related journal (j)	Relatedness (R)	
	ECON HIST REV to j	j to ECON HIST REV
Journal of Economic History	874.88	311.63
European Review of Economic History	387.76	311.37
Explorations in Economic History	351.78	336.25
Business History	175.41	231.71
Rural History	221.02	40.88
Continuity and Change	196.46	127.46
Business History Review	135.07	191.67
Journal of Interdisciplinary History	168.84	185.19
Revista de Historia Económica	76.74	150.71
Journal of Economic Literature	147.35	16.97
Past and Present	141.89	74.09
Journal of British Studies	118.56	41.35
Journal of Law and Economics	92.09	56.81
Journal of Economic Growth	40.93	62.56
Enterprise and Society	58.47	19.81
Australian Economic History Review	56.67	55.45
Journal of Contemporary History	53.1	11.53
Journal of Global History	23.39	44.73
Journal of Historical Geography	44.08	36.18
American Historical Review	39.61	11.77
American Economic Review	34.2	5.61

Table 3.1c The degree of interactions among economic history and other mainstream economics and history journals: *Cliometrica*

Related journal (j)	Relatedness (R)	
	CLIOMETRICA to j	j to CLIOMETRICA
Journal of Economic History	821.17	78.45
Explorations in Economic History	552.38	68.13

History and Sociology

Philip Corrigan and Derek Sayer in their editorial remarks for the inaugural issue of the *Journal of Historical Sociology* quoted Philip Abrams' book *Historical Sociology* (Abrams, 1982) in the following way:

> In my understanding of history and sociology there can be no relationship between them because, in terms of their fundamental preoccupations, history and sociology are and always have been the same thing. Both seek to understand the puzzle of human agency and both seek to do so in terms of the process of social structuring. ... [I]t is the task that commands the attention, and not the disciplines. (Corrigan and Sayer, 1988: 1)

The editors justified the establishment of the journal by stating that good sociology or anthropology must be historical and good history must also rely on social sciences. The objective was not really to eliminate the disciplinary boundaries but rather to build substantive and insightful understanding of human agency by leveraging their disciplinary differences. *Journal of Historical Sociology* is but only one example of such efforts. Journals such as *Social Science History* and *Past & Present* have been pursuing similar agendas for the last half century. Unfortunately, the results of such attempts have not necessarily been any more successful than those of the economic historians. Tables 3.2a

Table 3.2a The degree of interactions among *Historical Sociology* and other mainstream sociology and history journals: *Journal of Historical Sociology*

Related journal (j)	Relatedness (R)	
	J HIST SOCIOL to j	j to J HIST SOCIOL
History Workshop Journal	59.15	72.94
American Historical Review	55.33	24.45
Past and Present	38.12	38.47
Economic History Review	31.76	28.34

Table 3.2b The degree of interactions among *Historical Sociology* and other mainstream sociology and history journals: *Social Science History*

Related journal (j)	Relatedness (R)	
	SOC SCI HIST to j	j to SOC SCI HIST
American Journal of Sociology	465.95	48.1
Journal of Interdisciplinary History	138.99	427.81
Annual Review of Sociology	178.93	78.96
History of the Family	65.41	103.02
Journal of Historical Geography	76.03	91.95
Journal of Urban History	86.48	30.26
Demography	67.39	30.75
Urban Geography	38.34	49.24
International Journal of Urban and Regional Research	44.26	44.69
Annals of the Association of American Geographers	28.88	19.13

and 3.2b provide the relatedness among the historical sociology journals and other sociological or historical publications.

In some sense the results are much more discouraging. *Journal of Historical Sociology* interacts only with four other journals, two of which are economic history journals. No major sociology journal regularly cites their papers. The situation is not any better for the journal *Social Science History*. Even though there is a closer relationship between this journal and the *American Journal of Sociology*, it is again basically unidirectional, that is, *American Journal of Sociology* is cited by *Social Science History* but not vice versa.

Management and History

I have conducted a similar analysis for business history to see if the interdisciplinary relationship between management research and history is any different. As Tables 3.3a, 3.3b, and 3.3c show, the situation is not any different in the case of interdisciplinary journals in the business history field. Other than *Organization Studies*, no other major organization theory journals (e.g., *Administrative Science Quarterly* or the *Academy of Management Journal*) are included in these tables. The following tables collectively give the impression that interdisciplinary specialized journals are relatively isolated in the field even though there are a variety of major outlets where historical research is published. As I pointed out earlier (Figure 3.2), major journals in the areas

Table 3.3a The degree of interactions among business history and other mainstream business and history journals: *Business History Review*

Related journal (j)	Relatedness (R)	
	BUS HIST REV to j	j to BUS HIST REV
Business History	181.05	411.59
Enterprise and Society	398.98	240.64
Journal of Economic History	231.03	76.49
Economic History Review	191.67	135.07
Industrial and Corporate Change	17.92	69.41
Journal of International Business Studies	57.5	65.55
Research Policy	8.57	31.63
Past and Present	21.91	25.01
Organization Science	24.64	17.5
Organization Studies	23.1	17.81
Journal of Management Studies	13.32	15.23

Table 3.3b The degree of interactions among business history and other mainstream business and history journals: *Enterprise and Society*

Related journal (j)	Relatedness (R)	
	ENTERP SOC to j	j to ENTERP SOC
Business History Review	240.64	398.98
Business History	65.48	219.52
Journal of Economic History	100.27	72.85
Economic History Review	19.81	58.47

of management and organizational studies have been continuously increasing their intake of articles with a strong historical bent.

Thus, based on the data and the analyses, it is possible to provide a set of stylized facts about the state of affairs between history and organization theory as well as other social sciences such as economics and sociology. I use the term "stylized facts" here in order to emphasize that the findings reported here are open to debate and my own empirical observations are simply guideposts to speculate the future trajectory of cooperation between these two fields. The

Table 3.3c The degree of interactions among business history and other mainstream business and history journals: *Business History*

	Relatedness (R)	
Related journal (j)	BUS HIST to j	j to BUS HIST
Journal of Economic History	473.33	20.81
Business History Review	411.59	181.05
Economic History Review	231.71	175.41
Enterprise and Society	219.52	65.48
Revista de Historia Industrial	109.76	158.55
Journal of Macromarketing	63.32	19.9
Explorations in Economic History	44.5	45.19
Service Industries Journal	6.59	7.07

empirical observations provided are simply a stylized view of the informal model of the trends in this interdisciplinary domain of history.

1. Even though there has been a substantial increase in historically based research in organization theory, especially in the domain of institutional theory and organizational ecology, the term "history" is not commonly used to describe this research.

2. Because most historians, including organizational historians, are uncomfortable with the notion that there are universal, general, or covering theories explaining social behavior, their narratives never makes their theoretical arguments explicit.

3. Historically friendly research conducted by organization theorists gives the impression that they consider history as an empirical laboratory to test their specific theories.

4. The degree of interaction and interdisciplinary conversation is not strongly encouraged by either the historians or the other social science disciplines. Given the degree of epistemological and methodological differences between these two cultures of inquiry, the interdisciplinary journals have had limited impact on the development of an interdisciplinary culture of inquiry.

In order to build a more durable bridge between history and organization theory, we need to explore the critical conceptual and methodological fault lines that separate these two academic communities.

CONCEPTUAL FOUNDATIONS OF LIMITED
INTEGRATION: TYPES OF UNDERSTANDING
AND HISTORICAL ORGANIZATION THEORY
RESEARCH

What these historical analyses show is that the conventional proposals to improve the relationship between history and other social science disciplines including organization theory have not been as productive as expected. The question then is what could explain such a disconnect between the enthusiasm of the participants, on the one hand, and the collective inability to produce an interdisciplinary dialogue, on the other hand. One way to search for potential answers is to provide a meta-theoretical toolset that could address some of the debates between historians and other social scientists.

The main meta-theoretical issues behind these debates are two distinct but related philosophical controversies. The first is the classic question of the *methodenstreit,* or whether or not social sciences are unique in terms of their own methodological requirements. And the second is the Weberian question of *verstehen,* whether or not an adequate understanding of human action requires an understanding of the subjective motives and objectives of the actual participants (Calhoun, 1998). In other words, as social scientists and historians do we have the right methodological tools to accurately report historical events; to understand the motivations and justifications of the historical agents in action; to explain theoretically both the agents' behavior as well as the events they are involved in; and, finally to provide an evaluation of these actions based on the moral or political sensibilities that the researchers render in understanding the rationalization used by actors in question? These elements are the unavoidable byproducts of reflexivity in social/historical research.

One solution for this quandary is offered by Runciman, who argues that in terms of explanation alone, social sciences are no different from any other scientific activity. According to Runciman, what does make the social sciences different is that additional types of understanding are required to make sense of human action. "The first of these is the need to understand in the primary sense what the action is [an accurate reporting or what he calls *reportage*]; to understand in the secondary sense why it comes about or what caused it or *explanation*; and to understand in the tertiary sense what it was like for the agent to do it, *description*" (Runciman, 1983: 15). At a meta-theoretical level, social sciences could not be simply satisfied with the "explanation" in the secondary sense but they also need an understanding in a tertiary sense, the *description* which provides for the reader a sense of what the historical actors' experiences were like for "them" and; finally, *evaluation*, the explicit discussion of the judgments made by the social scientist as to whether the actions of the historical agents, the path-dependencies created by the historical process, could be assessed as "good" or "bad" in a moral, esthetical, or political sense. Evaluation as another type of understanding is necessary in order to explore the political or societal biases that are present in the researchers involved in historical analysis.

Even if we agree that historical science should be based on the systematic and critical investigation of primary source documents with the aim of showing the past as it "actually was," it is still important to distinguish between reportage, evaluation, and description. Reportage refers to the data and information that are available and collectively understood in the same way. An initial public offering, for instance, should mean the same thing and should be different from the company annual report in terms of its legal significance and production. When an historian talks about people in an organization and describes them as employees, the term employees is clear in the minds of other researchers. In other words, its validity is accepted by the organizational researcher as well as the historian.

If the proper function and the objective of history is to recover the past in as close an approximation of how it actually was, it is expected that historians must keep their prejudices, beliefs, and presupposition away (Spiegel, 2009). In other words, if we acknowledge that history is the product of "contemporary mental representations of the absent past that bear with them strong ideological or political imprints" (Spiegel, 2009: 4), the question of reportage is not as straightforward as imagined in historical or in organization theory. Moreover, both business historians and organizational researchers select their topic of study, the historical setting, or the industry in part by the interests that shape their inquiry. The object of historical inquiry could not be directly tied to the historical events themselves but the choices made by the researchers. As Hall argues, historical as well as organizational analyses emerge from the questions being posed, the value commitments the researchers have, and the accumulated knowledge available to the researchers (Hall, 1992). Thus, accurate reportage and evaluation are common problems for both cultures of inquiry but they manifest themselves in different ways.

Description, on the other hand, requires a different type of understanding. When Whyte in his book *The Organization Man* (1956) described employees as persons who not only worked for the organization, but also belonged to it, his focus was on how these individuals understood their organizational life. In Whyte's understanding, organization men believed in their firms as "the source of creativity and in belongingness as the ultimate need of the individual" (Randall, 1987: 460). His description provided an understanding of the motives and incentives of the agents in organizations. Such an understanding of an employee more than fifty years ago has been reevaluated, challenged, and reinterpreted in successive periods and by successive researchers. Since Whyte, the topic of commitment has been explored extensively. Early explorations of the subject have simply assumed that high levels of commitment are good and organizations should motivate their employees by increasing their commitments. Later research, however, has shown that the original organization man was neither the norm nor morally acceptable in today's managerial environment (Bennett, 1990; Randall, 1987).

Similarly, Betty Friedan's research on women's role in society during the 1960s described how well-educated women at the time understood their lives (Friedan, 1963). She was able to articulate the unexpressed feelings of house-wives (description) and not only explained why they are in their situation (explanation) but also how this must change (evaluation), in turn contributing to the feminist movement in the US. Alternative methodologies within sociology, such as frame analysis (Goffman, 1974), describing not only how individuals come to understand and experience "what is going on here and now" in a situation but also how it is that they seem to so easily arrive at consensus about the nature of this social reality (Goffman, 1974: 9). The use of frame analysis as well as other similar tools to understand how subjective meaning is assigned to social events is necessary not only for sociologists but also for historians (see the discussion of hermeneutic interpretation in the chapter by Kipping et al.) to address the problem of description (Diehl and McFarland, 2010).

Reportage, description, explanation, and evaluation are the elements of a toolkit that are critical for understanding the social realities of the past. How each field of inquiry implicitly or explicitly employs the elements of this meta-theoretic toolkit may help explain why we continue to have the debates among organization theorists and organizational historians. This is especially true in the case of explanation. Historical scholarship is not simply an inductive exercise based on "facts" or reportage where the historian arbitrarily collects archival data. The ultimate objective is to test a set of historical claims and further extend some of these claims to new historical events. In that sense, historians have their own explanatory theories even though these theories are expressed implicitly. The narrative form of the organizational historians is in a sense a form of theoretical explanation. Even when the organizational historians make their theories more explicit, they do so in order to challenge its historical presuppositions. By relying on narrative, they search for contingencies and sequentiality of events; and thus they believe in the theoretical value of the narrative.

Organization theorists, on the other hand, demand an explanatory theory as a starting point of doing research. As in the case of sociology and economics, they argue that a theory is essential in order to select relevant facts, to search for generalizable causal mechanisms, to accumulate evidence within different historical settings, and to ultimately test theories and generate better theories (Kiser and Hechter, 1998). General theories as explanations must specify both relations between causal factors and the mechanisms by which casual process is completed. Such explanations are assumed to be independent of the experiences of the actors as they perceived them. This does not mean that descriptions are not important but organizational, sociological, or economic explanations rely more on general theories such as rational choice, resource dependency, or institutional diffusion and less on the power of the narrative itself.

Historians as well as organizational researchers are implicitly concerned about their own historical setting both in terms of the wider cultural context in which they interpret the past but also in terms of the personal experiences and commitments they may have towards a particular ideology, social class, or political view (Bernardi and Greenwood, 2012). Both disciplines understand the need for a certain degree of detachment in their research practices. One way to address these possible prejudices is to take the task of evaluation seriously and explicitly question how our views may shape our understanding.

A similar common ground exists between these two disciplines in terms of explanations as well. Like social scientists, historians look at the broader structural and social factors that produce events. Especially in certain branches of historical research, such as the Annales School, which broke radically with traditional historiography by insisting on the importance of taking all levels of society into consideration, a theoretical narrative becomes an integral part of historical narrative discourse. Structural explanations that are part of a theoretically specified account of historical phenomena have been one of the major criticisms of the Annales School because it has minimized the individual importance of human agency in history making (Bernardi and Greenwood, 2012).

Table 3.4 provides a summary of the basic differences between historical organization theory, which is firmly based on the organizational studies discipline, and organizational history, which subscribes to the tenets of business history. These two disciplines produce two unique cultures of inquiry in terms of alternative frames in the types of understanding presented earlier in the chapter (Runciman, 1983). Column 2 provides a sharp comparison of the two cultures of inquiry which are based on the way each defines history. The next four columns on the right provide comparisons of the two disciplines within each type of understanding by emphasizing what is made explicit by organization theory and business history.

Historical organization theory, based on universal history, subscribes to an understanding of history that implicitly claims the existence of a temporally dynamic but holistic social system moving through objective time (Hall, 1992: 182). Such an understanding is necessary to develop a theoretical account of historical processes. In some sense, a universal history assumes the feasibility of applying a social theory to specific historical cases. Organizational history, on the other hand, is based on specific history where the focus is on relatively self-contained sets of events, sequences, patterns, or outcomes rendered coherent by the historian's claim about their collective meaningfulness. The task of the historian is to evaluate alternative plots in relation to historical evidence but within a particular value system. Because the values of historians are situational and located in the present, terms such

Table 3.4 Business history and organization theory approaches to historical research

Disciplines	Cultures of inquiry	Types of understanding			
		Reportage	Description	Explanation	Evaluation
Organization Theory	Historical Organization Theory based on universal history	"What actually happened" could be described through objective history	Observer's interpretation of meaning in objective context	The use of narrative to explain specific cases as an application of a specific theory	Implicit within the basic assumptions of the theory in use
Business History	Organizational History based on specific history	Uniqueness of individual events and the historical actors requiring subjective interpretation	Observer's interpretation of subjective meaning in historical context	The use of narrative to identify unique causes of events or historical processes	Explicit within a self-contained historical period and made coherent by the historical actors as meaningful

as the Industrial Revolution, globalization, or the Great Depression change their meanings and require alternative reinterpretations within different regimes of evaluation. Such a perspective changes not only the methodologies of inquiry but the degree of emphasis put on the types of understanding by each discipline.

Hall (1992) points out: "For every theory that falls short of accounting completely for phenomena, for every narrative that transcends the simple chronicling of events, the question 'why?' inevitably raises the possibility of explanation as a distinctive form of discourse" (p. 172). In other words, explanation is a required component of historical as well as theoretical understanding. For explanations, neither theory nor the historical narrative may be sufficient, however. Most organizational theories are limited in their power of explaining why certain organizational events take place within a particular historical context. The accounts of why specific events, such as the replacement of a CEO, the introduction of a new production technology, or the diffusion of managerial practices take place may not even require explanations that employ a theory. In other words, explanations are thus open to particularistic or idiosyncratic sequences of factors and could only be meaningful within the narrative historical account. This is why the ongoing disagreements between the two disciplines focus on the differences highlighted in the column dealing with "explanation."

The debate between organizational historians and organization theory scholars on the merits of "general theory" and "the narrative as theory" is partly a function of what each party understands by the term theory. For organization theorists a theory provides an omni-temporal explanation that would produce similar results under different contextual settings. A transaction cost argument should lead to similar outcomes whether the events described occur in the 19th-century textile factory or the 21st-century software development firm. It is supposed to provide the explanatory guidelines necessary to attack substantive problems in the field of organizations. For organization scholars, such theories are parts of economic, sociological, or behavioral paradigms that can lead to research programs. They consist of explicit assumptions about causal relations, mechanisms, abstract models, and conditions delimiting the scope of such assumptions. Together these elements can be used to generate testable causal propositions. The assumptions, mechanisms, and models are essential parts of explanatory theory. This is similar to the definition of "explanation" offered within Runciman's model.

The response of the historians, whether they are business, economic, or sociological historians, is usually in the form of not rejecting the idea of a theory, but rather pleading for a different type of theory—a narrative history that can help to build theory. For the organizational historian, whatever their ideological persuasions, the contemporary organizational world is a specific configuration produced by historical struggles. In other words, the social and economic world of organizations as it presents itself at one time or another is a unique and singular conjuncture, and is understood by the participants at the time in a unique way as well. To say, for example, that a particular society was predominantly capitalist was not only to indicate what theory would fit best with many replicable empirical data within it, but it was also to characterize the whole and to locate it in history. In a sense, this is a theoretical claim based on a specific understanding of causality in history (Calhoun, 1998; Froeyman, 2009).

The conceptualizations of theory only in terms of causal explanations could result in the exclusion of many important efforts to achieve relatively general understandings of organizational events (Schreyögg and Sydow, 2011). What makes theoretical explanations unique, however, is the introduction of abstract categories that are an integral part of developing explanatory models. For instance, the term "inflation" is an economic concept that may explain social unrest, state policies, or managerial turnover independent of the participants' understanding of its relation to money. Even if the understanding of the actors and their interpretations of the events do not refer to "inflation," the monetary theory could explain the relationship between "the value of money" and other social or economic events.

The traditional arguments on the distinction between historians and organization theorists have rested on the nature of explanation and the methods used by both sides. A historian may pursue "explanations" through the presentation of evidence and counter-evidence in an attempt to let the historical facts speak for themselves without any preconceived explicit hypotheses from the beginning. The use of narrative becomes the major methodological device to provide explanation. An organization theorist, on the other hand, could rely on a general theory to generate the hypotheses to be tested within a historical context. The early attempts at interdisciplinary work were based on the assumption that its value rests chiefly upon the exchange of methods. For historians this meant that they could acquire new methods with which to tackle old problems ranging from content analysis to comparative methods, or even more sophisticated sampling procedures (Hofstadter, 1958). Similarly, organization theorists could learn to be sensitive to the nature of narrative in developing explanations in historical context. But neither would be able to go beyond multidisciplinary research where each discipline works in its self-contained world with little cross-fertilization or synergy in the outcomes of research.

Thus, the basic difference between an organizational historian and an organization theorist could not be reduced simply to the differences in the methodological tools each uses to drive conclusions from their observations. As I tried to summarize in Table 3.4, explanation is only one kind of understanding and reportage, description, and evaluation are equally important in order to make sense of history. Historical approaches to events and agents must take into account these forms of understanding whether they are conducted by organizational researchers or business historians. Thus, a good starting point is to acknowledge the potential implications of making other types of understanding more explicit in our historical research.

The continuing discussions between historians and organizational scholars could be more productive if the debate shifts to these other forms of understanding involving reportage, description, and evaluation where the historians have much to contribute. Unfortunately, the ongoing discourse has been biased towards explanation and its role in social science research. I strongly believe that a broader perspective on the classical question of "*verstehen*" with its four distinct forms could bring history and organization theory closer without forcing one to be like the other, allowing us to appreciate the richness each side contributes to scholarly research.

CHALLENGES AND FUTURE DIRECTIONS

The empirical observations based on dissertations, as well as the management articles published during the first ten years of the 21st century, demonstrate that there is a consistent interest among organization theorists in producing research based on history. The slope of this trend is actually positive in the case of organization theory research that deals with institutions, networks, diffusion of managerial practices, path dependencies, and evolutionary perspectives. This trend is not only a byproduct of the empirical requirements of these types of research, but also of their theoretical foundations. The fundamental questions asked by organization theory researchers today are part of the sociological and economic traditions in which history has been taken seriously.

Such history friendly research, however, has had limited success in producing a strong interdisciplinary research agenda that links historians with organization theorists or in creating a cohesive intellectual community with common academic outlets. The relatedness data presented earlier provide a picture about the state of affairs for interdisciplinary journals that reflect this reality. The question it raises is how to maintain the ongoing engagement between the two fields by rethinking the types of questions they could ask collectively and by relying on the unique strengths of each discipline. As I tried to explore in the previous section, one potential approach is to reimagine what we mean by socio-historical "understanding."

In this concluding section my objective is to provide a summary of the various approaches to cross-disciplinary engagement developed in the literature and to assess their potential feasibility and impact in developing better interaction between organization theory and history, more specifically business history. These approaches could be categorized into three main camps. The first group mainly argues that a forced interdisciplinary strategy would simply produce research appreciated neither by historians nor by organization theorists; thus, they argue that history should simply be methodological in terms of its contribution to organization theory. The second group argues that the lack of better integration between history and organization theory requires strong interdisciplinary research. The third group proposes a transdisciplinary research agenda where both history and organization theory retain their disciplinary boundaries and their research contributions should be assessed by the criteria of their own disciplines.

Within organizational studies, the first group is sometimes called the factual approach (Rowlinson, 2004) or *Supplementarist* (Üsdiken and Kieser, 2004). In this approach, history is assigned the role of discovering facts. Most traditional organizational research, ranging from population ecology to industry studies, could be included in this category. As demonstrated within this research tradition, the past could be contained within a series of historical facts interpreted through the lens of a specific organizational theory. Such a clear demarcation between the two disciplines could be beneficial to each in its own trajectory of development and does not imply a lack of interaction between them. Cross-border interactions between the fields could still focus on the nature of causality, the importance of theory, or the use of narrative, without challenging the other side for its lack of rigor or relevance.

Most of the recent calls for a stronger interaction between history and organizational studies could be categorized within the second group. Üsdiken and Kieser call this approach *Integrationist* (Üsdiken and Kieser, 2004). The goal of this approach is to enrich organization theory by developing links with fields in the humanities without abandoning its social science orientation (Booth and Rowlinson, 2006). Such an approach ultimately requires developing a strong partnership between these two cultures of inquiry (Hall, 1999) supported by appropriate training in theoretical thinking and research methodologies. Such an approach would eventually yield mutually beneficial research without compromising the fundamental premises of either party. Such an approach would help produce research that is conventionally deep with respect to the analysis of primary sources, but at the same time address the theoretical interests of the organizational scholars (Harvey and Wilson, 2007). Recent research shows that this is do-able when the research objective is to engage with and refine theory based on evidence provided by historical analysis (Bucheli, Mahoney, and Vaaler, 2010; Lamberg and Pajunen, 2010).

A related camp within the second group, which is called *reorientationist* by Üsdiken and Kieser (2004), argues that the agenda for interdisciplinary research between history and organization theory should focus on critical reexamination of existing theories of organizations for their ahistorical premises. Others argue that the focus should be on the discursive process between the past and the present and how events are read by the historians and presented in historical narrative (Weatherbee et al., 2012). Such an approach not only points out the problems in organizational research but also the problematic character of historiography (Booth and Rowlinson, 2006; Jacques, 2006).

I maintain that none of these approaches resolves the basic dilemma that interdisciplinary solutions face in most fields of inquiry—one discipline becomes the driver of the research agenda making the other discipline a secondary contributor. I argue that a better alternative is to develop a transdisciplinary approach. The basic argument behind a transdisciplinary approach is to identify a basic disjuncture between the two orientations: the sociological study of history and the historian's use of sociology. The distinction focuses on the sociologists' emphasis on a theory that could be applicable to multiple cases; and the historians' emphasis on comprehensive analysis of a single phenomenon (Hall, 1992). Even though both cultures of inquiry solve the problems of reportage, description, explanation, and evaluation (what Hall (1999) calls values, social theory, narrative, and explanation), each discipline provides its own comparative advantages which they may lose under a strong interdisciplinary agenda. What is important to maintain is the richness each perspective provides for the questions being generated collectively. If we look at some of the most successful examples of business history, such as Chandler's work on US corporations (Chandler, 1962, 1992) or Christensen's work on technology (Christensen, 1993), it is clear that what made this research successful was not that it fit the mold of traditional organizational theory but because they are historians. Alternative theoretical interpretations of what these studies signify could then be investigated and reinterpreted by management scholars that would enrich both fields (Bucheli et al., 2010).

Compared to an interdisciplinary approach, transdisciplinary research is needed when knowledge about managerially relevant problems is constantly changing and thus requires new concepts, models, or theories. When the concrete nature of the managerial problems is disputed and when the society (or the business world) demands unique prescriptions to address these problems, transdisciplinary research provides transformational knowledge (Hadorn et al., 2008). Neither entrepreneurship nor innovation as conceptual categories has been part of early management theory or managerial history. But today there are constant debates not only about their importance for the economic or social well-being of societies but historical explorations involving these phenomena. As reflexive organizational researchers, it is imperative that we explore why the writers of the earlier periods failed to include them in their vocabulary. Such questions require descriptive explanations. This is where organizational historians, who focus on the original source material, could generate potential insights and open doors for future research questions. Transdisciplinary research could deal with such subjects where the abstract concepts in organization theory could be linked to case-specific historical knowledge without undermining the value of one or the other. Other disciplines ranging from natural to medical sciences have been proposing such an approach for a long time with some degree of success (Klein, 2008)

A transdisciplinary research perspective provides support for both organization theorists and historians without sacrificing their unique contributions to their fields. A historical organization theorist subscribes to a meta-theory of history; applies organization theory to explain specific historical cases; tests hypotheses through comparative analysis of multiple cases; and, uses historical explanation to identify unique effects on the process. An organizational historian, on the other hand, is situational; concentrates on explaining a particular phenomenon; uses social theory to frame the research; and concentrates on identifying unique causes of events (Hall, 1992: 175–88). These strategies could make both the organization theorists and organizational historians not only feel at home but also help us organize the practice of research.

A transdisciplinary approach also refocuses researchers' attention to managerial and organizational issues that demand contemporary solutions but are informed by historical analyses. Topics such as corporate governance, business cycles, and globalization demand new solutions and historians could provide new insights and alternative interpretations based on historical attempts to solve these urgent problems. Recent reinterpretations of influential past business history research involving business cycles (McCraw, 2006) or the strategy-structure relationship (O'Sullivan and Graham, 2010) show how a new partnership could be established between these disciplines. Contemporary research on corporate governance by historians (Fellman, Kuustera, and Vaara, 2008), or firm capabilities by strategy scholars (Helfat, 2003) shows how we could forge new types of interaction between the two fields.

In summary, in order to be successful in transdisciplinary research, three important conditions must be met. The first is a genuine willingness on both sides of the cultural divide to accept the potential contributions of the other. As I tried to point out earlier, such an acceptance requires a broader interpretation of what "understanding" is in social sciences. Second is an ongoing dialogue where the debate is not on methods but on research questions that are mutually interesting and relevant. Creation of unique interaction opportunities in the form of centers or institutes, where historians and organizational scholars could collectively focus on organizational problems using a broad set of tools and lenses, could accelerate such discourse. Third is the establishment of new publication outlets that are problem oriented rather than discipline oriented. For instance, *Journal of Industrial Corporate Change* publishes work on industrial change that is historical as well as empirical and theory driven. Other outlets in corporate governance, entrepreneurship, or technological change could also provide such opportunities for teams of research from different disciplines with a focused set of research questions.

As Stinchcombe (2005: 5) amply points out, historical methods "study sequences of conditions, actions, and effects that have happened in natural settings, in sufficient detail to get signs of sequences that are causally connected." What differentiates a historian from a social scientist is the fact that a historian conceptualizes temporality "as fateful, contingent, complex, eventful, and heterogeneous" (Sewell, 2005: 11). A social scientist, on the other hand, attempts to find patterns and the causal mechanism that could provide explanations in a conceptual fashion (Clemens, 2007). A strong *integrationist* perspective mostly favors the organization theorists over the historians. The *reorientationist* perspective, on the other hand, gives the upper hand to the historians. The transdisciplinary approach allows each side to retain their culture of inquiry and produce complementary research to address critical managerial problems that demand answers that could guide managerial action.

The traditional debates have been based on putting the burdens of argument either on the historians or the organizational researchers in terms of epistemology or methodology. The limitation of such arguments is that organization theorists have little business doing historical research and business historians are not traditional social scientists. Historians claim that if organization theorists do historical research well, they should simply be historians. More importantly, organizational scholars argue that historical research is poorly suited to generating the observations needed to advance organizational research. In spite of these debates and disagreements, the first decade of the 21st century has witnessed a steady stream of productive research and publications in major scholarly outlets. As Figures 3.1 and 3.2 clearly demonstrate the interest in historically informed organizational research has been growing. As I tried to argue in this chapter one way to accelerate this trend is to reimagine the nature of socio-historical research and rethink the nature of the ongoing debate. A better way to reimagine socio-historical research is to make room for reportage, description, and evaluation as well as explanation. A better way to frame the traditional debate is to argue that most management problems are the products of complex historical processes, path dependencies, and contemporary contingencies (Goldstone, 1998). In other words, if we wish to develop better theories to address managerial issues, we have to accept the fact that our theories must themselves be intrinsically historical. The history of most influential social theories, including Marx's *Capital*, Durkheim's *Division of Labor*, and Weber's *Protestant Ethic*, demonstrate that addressing contemporary concerns and solutions require both a historical turn and an appreciation of a theoretical lens.

APPENDICES

Appendix 3.1: List of doctoral dissertations completed in business schools that are based on historical data or analyses 2000–2010

Appendix 3.1

Author	Title	Granting institution	Year
de Andrade Junior, Flavio	Essays in government guaranteed credit and asset pricing	Northwestern University	2010
Hiebert, Thomas E	How is the value of real estate affected by the Department of Defense Base Realignment and Closure process?	The University of North Carolina at Charlotte	2009
Li, Yuan	Rhetoric in elite-led radical change: China's capitalist transformation from 1978–2008	University of Southern California	2009
Tian, Jie	CEO selection performance: Does board experience matter?	University of Southern California	2008
Posey, Raymond L., Jr.,	Analysis of the terms of bank lending and risk measurement: Three essays on small business loans	Cleveland State University	2010

Appendix 3.1 (Continued)

Author	Title	Granting institution	Year
Popescu, Denisa,	Determinants of effective information transfer in international regulatory standards adoption	The George Washington University	2010
Xiouros, Costas	Asset prices and trading in complete market economies with heterogeneous agents	University of Southern California	2009
Promboon, Wipawin	Capital flows, institutions, and financial fragility	The University of North Carolina at Chapel Hill	2009
Anderson, Kyle J.,	Essays on online price comparison site competition	Indiana University	2009
Sierra- Jimenez, Jesus Antolin,	Essays on interest rate determination in open economies	University of Southern California	2009
So, Jongil,	Essays on political connections and firm value	The University of North Carolina at Chapel Hill	2009
Geyer, Richard A.,	Fallen ivory towers: Avoiding collapse through analysis of the antecedents leading to university decline	Nova Southeastern University	2009
Major, David Lanier	How firm resources and behavior impact firm performance: An examination of firm resources, competitive actions and performance	University of Maryland, College Park	2009
Bliss, Gary	Moral hazard and Certified Development Companies participating in SBA 504 loans	Nova Southeastern University	2009
Al Amin, Mona,	Organizational ecology and the proliferation of specialty hospitals	Temple University	2009
Kothari, Tanvi H.,	The ball is in their court: Changing role of multinational companies from emerging nations	Temple University	2009
Horne, John Richard	The effect on corporate performance of firms that won the Malcolm Baldrige National Quality Award	Nova Southeastern University	2009
Giorgi, Simona	Culture in action: Cultural competence and agency in institutional	Northwestern University	2010
Bermiss, Yerodin Sekou	The emergence and evolution of professional service industries	Northwestern University	2009

Appendix 3.1 (Continued)

Author	Title	Granting institution	Year
Major, David Lanier,	How firm resources and behavior impact firm performance: An examination of firm resources, competitive actions and performance	University of Maryland, College Park	2009
Pfarrer, Michael Donald	Information in the marketplace: Two essays on firm strategies and stakeholder perceptions	University of Maryland, College Park	2007
Niro, Michyael M.,	Asset allocation with the inclusion of the owner-occupied home	Cleveland State University	2010
Pavone, Carla,	Opportunity re-evaluation: How risk dimensions influence post-investment venture capital decisions	University of Minnesota	2010
Hart, Timothy	An examination of the drivers of exploratory and exploitative search	The University of Oklahoma,	2009
Chai, Lin	Community structure as collective identity construction and resource search	University of Southern California	2009
Lawlor, Kenneth Blaine	Relationship of CEO and TMT pre-merger power characteristics of acquiring and target firm with post-merger effectiveness	Oklahoma State University	2009
Gotsopoulos, Aleksios,	Resource space dynamics in the evolution of industries: formation, expansion, and contraction of the resource space, and its effects on the survival of organizations	The University of Chicago	2009
Bewaji, Tolulope	Resources: The effect of top management team characteristics and outside influences on the knowledge management of small entrepreneurial firms	Temple University	2009
Kiyatkin, Lori	Employee health: A value creating organizational resource	University of Maryland, College Park	2009
Nandialath, Anup	Essays on the role of unobservables in corporate strategy	The Ohio State University	2009

Appendix 3.1 (Continued)

Author	Title	Granting institution	Year
Zhang, Dongli	Quality exploitation versus quality exploration: Measurement, antecedents, and performance implications	University of Minnesota	2009
Tan, David	Status ambiguity and conflict in the market	Emory University	2009
Wu, Zheying	Three essays on distance: Examining the role of institutional distance on foreign firm entry, local isomorphism strategy and subsidiary performance	University of Southern California	2009
Lee, Mina	Spin-offs and innovation	Purdue University	2009
Pozner, Jo Ellen	An exploration of the social mechanisms driving the consequences of earnings restatements for organizational elites	Northwestern University	2007
Lehman, David W.,	"Going for it" on fourth down: Organizational risk-taking in the National Football League	Purdue University	2007
Kazanjian, Robert K.	Old mindsets and new opportunities: How the composition of founding teams affects the survival of new ventures	Emory University	2009
Block, Emily Sarah	The emergence of self-regulatory organizations as institutional change	University of Illinois at Urbana-Champaign	2009
Gao, Jijun	The evolution of business sustainability: Historical trajectory and structural relationships	The University of Western Ontario (Canada)	2009
Chng, Han Ming Daniel,	The effects of interests and institutional influences on organizational adoptions over time and across practices	The University of Texas at Austin	2006
Rider, Christopher	Network positions and processes: Evidence from U.S. private equity	University of California, Berkeley	2008
Desai, Vinit Madhukar	Constraints on organizational learning from poor performance in the modern American railroad industry, 1978–2003	University of California, Berkeley	2007
Rawley, Evan,	Organization and firm performance: Evidence from microdata	University of California, Berkeley	2007

Appendix 3.1 (Continued)

Author	Title	Granting institution	Year
Madsen, Peter Micah	The co-diffusion of organizational and policy innovations: The spread of a new organizational form and its supporting legislation in the United States insurance industry	University of California, Berkeley	2006
Bigelow, Lyda S.	The evolution of the boundaries of the firm: Transaction cost alignment and organizational survival in the early American automobile industry	University of California, Berkeley	2001
Roy, Aradhana	Mobilization and performance effects of firms' participation in social movements: Firms in the open source movement	University of Michigan	2008
Neuman, Eric J.	Public policy and entrepreneurship: The development of the competitive local telephone service industry	University of Michigan	2008
Fleischer, Anne Bowers	The creation and performance of classification schemes: Rating systems in United States broker–dealers, 1993–2000	University of Michigan	2008
Toh, Puay Khoon	Structure–scope matching: A study of the interrelationship between organization structure and innovation in the United States communications industry	University of Michigan	2007
Wooten, Melissa	The evolution of the black higher education field, 1854–1996	University of Michigan	2006
Gruber, Daniel A.	Dollars and sensemaking: The mindful pipeline between firms and the financial media	University of Michigan	2009
Kacperczyk, Aleksandra J.	Inside or outside: The social mechanisms of entrepreneurship choices. Evidence from the mutual fund industry	University of Michigan	2009
Marquis, Christopher	Historical environments and the transformation of twentieth-century United States banking	University of Michigan	2005

Appendix 3.1 (Continued)

Author	Title	Granting institution	Year
Weber, Klaus	Does globalization lead to convergence? The evolution of organizations' cultural repertoires in the biomedical industry	University of Michigan	2003
Kovacs, Balazs	Essays on the similarity of organizations	Stanford University	2009
Pontikes, Elizabeth George	Fitting in or starting new? An analysis of invention, constraint, and the emergence of new categories in the software industry	Stanford University	2008
Luo, Xiaoqu	How mergers and acquisitions affect organizational growth rates	Stanford University	2008
Switanek, Nicholas J.	Ideological competition and the rise of business collaboration among U.S. environmental nonprofits	Stanford University	2008
Wang, Chunlei	Social networks, competition, and institutionalization: An integrated perspective on social influence in innovation diffusion	Stanford University	2008
Spiro, Jarrett	The impact of network position and network mobility on collaborative strategies, novelty, and innovation: The case of the artists network in the U.S. film industry, 1909–2005	Stanford University	2008
Rhee, Mooweon,	The liability of good reputation	Stanford University	2003
Lee, Brandon H.	Cultivating the niche: A study of the origins and consequences of standards-based certification organizations in the United States organic food industry	Cornell University	2007
Shukla, Prem Chandra	An ecological model of institutional change in normative organizational fields	Cornell University	
David, Robert James	The emergence and evolution of an "expert" field: The origins, growth, and competitive dynamics of the management consulting industry	Cornell University	2001
Szafara, Kristina Louise	In, out, up, or sideways: The effect of executive group structure on executive job mobility	Cornell University	2003

Appendix 3.1 (Continued)

Author	Title	Granting institution	Year
Perretta, Heather Geraci	Better dead than coed?' The survival and decline of single-sex colleges in the United States	Cornell University	2007
Sine, Wesley David	Paradise lost: A study of the decline of institutions and the restructuring of organizational fields in the United States power industry	Cornell University	2001
Lee, Chang Kil	The institutionalization of growth and decline in government employment: Economics, politics, and imitation	Cornell University	2001
Drozdova, Ekaterina (Katya)	Organizations, technology, and network risks: How and why organizations use technology to counter or cloak their human network vulnerabilities	NYU	2008
Conley, Caryn Alison	Design for quality: The case of open source software development	NYU	2008
Phelps, Corey C.	Technological exploration: A longitudinal study of the role of recombinatory search and social capital in alliance networks	NYU	2003
Zietsma, Charlene Ellen	Determinants and processes of institutional change in the British Columbia coastal forest industry	The University of British Columbia (Canada)	2003
Milanov, Hana	"One is known by the company one keeps": The imprinting effects of a firm's network entry on its status	Indiana University	2007
Bradley, Steven W.	Resources and resourcefulness: The role of slack and the environment on entrepreneurial outcomes	Indiana University	2007
Green, Kimberly	Learning and knowledge management in corporate entrepreneurship	Indiana University	2007
Upham, Samuel Phineas	Communities of innovation: Three essays on new knowledge development	University of Pennsylvania	2006
Corredoira, Rafael A.	Embedded exploration: The role of inter-firm networks in channeling organizational search	University of Pennsylvania	2009

Appendix 3.1 (Continued)

Author	Title	Granting institution	Year
Cohen, Linda M.	Physical organization and strategic firm geography: Within- and between-firm physical structures as a source of heterogeneity and competitive advantage	University of Pennsylvania	2008
Schneper, William D.,	When goals collide: Essays on corporate governance, stakeholders, and the concept of the firm	University of Pennsylvania	2006
Rye, Colleen Beecken	The role of institutional incentives in the resource allocation processes of pharmaceutical and biotechnology companies	University of Pennsylvania	2009
Wu, Xun (**Brian**) ,	Capacity-constrained capabilities, market maturity, and corporate diversification: Theory and evidence from the cardiovascular medical device industry, 1976–2004	University of Pennsylvania	2007
Guler, Isin	A study of decision making, capabilities and performance in the venture capital industry	University of Pennsylvania	2003
Kim, Hann Ohl	Technological evolution at the producer consumer interface	University of Pennsylvania	2000
Gupta, Anuja	Value creation and destruction: A study of the US medical devices industry	University of Pennsylvania	2010
Kaul, Aseem	Innovation, resources and corporate transactions: The dynamics of technology and corporate scope	University of Pennsylvania	2009
Lavie, Dovev	The interconnected firm: Evolution, strategy, and performance	University of Pennsylvania	2004
Puranam, Phanish	Grafting innovation: The acquisition of entrepreneurial firms by established firms	University of Pennsylvania	2001
Martens, Martin L.	Mapping risk, strategy, and performance in IPO organizational knowledge structures	The University of British Columbia (Canada	2002
Okhmatovskiy, Ilya	Content, structure, and performance implications of board interlocks: The role of institutional contingencies	University of Southern California	
El Haddad, Christine M.	Exploring the role of learning in contract design: Empirical evidence using buyer–supplier IT services contracts	University of Southern California	2007

Appendix 3.1 (Continued)

Author	Title	Granting institution	Year
Baack, Sally Ann,	Board involvement in monitoring and strategy making: Antecedents and consequences	University of Southern California	2000
Fong, Eric Alan,	Chief Executive Officer (CEO) responses to CEO compensation equity	University of Florida	2004
Kim, June Young	Organizational experience and institutional innovation: The effects of task and industry experience on power marketer registration in the United States electric power industry, 1994–1998	The University of Wisconsin - Madison	2006
Kim, Ji Yub	Crash test without dummies: A longitudinal study of interorganizational learning from failure experience in the United States commercial banking industry, 1984–1998	The University of Wisconsin - Madison	2000
Schwab, Andreas	Management practices in short-term network organizations: The performance impact of the shadow of the future and psychological contracts in the United States movie industry, 1931–1940	The University of Wisconsin - Madison	2000
Gok, Kubilay	Dynamics in the diffusion and institutionalization of site-based management reform in the United States of America	The University of Wisconsin - Madison	2009
Fischer, Harald M.	Dynamics of internal selection: The effects of intra-firm managerial migration and network structure on business unit divestiture	The University of Wisconsin - Madison	2005
Rivard, Peter E.	Change agency and a culture of patient safety at Veterans Administration hospitals	Boston College	2006
Ferguson, John Paul	Contest, social valuation and change in American labor-union organizing, 1961 to 2004	Massachusetts Institute of Technology	2009
Struben, Jeroen J. R.	Essays on transition challenges for alternative propulsion vehicles and transportation systems	Massachusetts Institute of Technology	2006

APPENDIX

Appendix 3.2: List of articles published in major management journals between 2000 and 2010 that are based on historical data, analyses, or narrative

Abrahamson, E., and Eisenman, M. (2008). "Employee-management Techniques: Transient Fads or Trending Fashions?" *Administrative Science Quarterly*, 53(4): 719–44.

Ahmadjian, C. L., and Lincoln, J. R. (2001). "Keiretsu, Governance, and Learning: Case Studies in Change from the Japanese Automotive Industry," *Organization Science*, 12(6): 683–701.

Alvarez, V. S., and Merino, T. G. (2003). "The History of Organizational Renewal: Evolutionary Models of Spanish Savings and Loans Institutions," *Organization Studies*, 24(9): 1437–61.

Arndt, M., and Bigelow, B. (2005). "Professionalizing and Masculinizing a Female Occupation: The Reconceptualization of Hospital Administration in the Early 1900s," *Administrative Science Quarterly*, 50(2): 233–61.

Arthaud-Day, M. L., Certo, S. T., Dalton, C. M. D., and Dalton, D. R. (2006). "A Changing of the Guard: Executive and Director Turnover Following Corporate Financial Restatements," *Academy of Management Journal*, 49(6): 1119–36.

Augier, M., and Teece, D. J. (2008). "Strategy as Evolution with Design: The Foundations of Dynamic Capabilities and the Role of Managers in the Economic System," *Organization Studies*, 29(8–9): 1187–208.

Barley, S. R. (2010). "Building an Institutional Field to Corral a Government: A Case to Set an Agenda for Organization Studies," *Organization Studies*, 31(6): 777–805.

Barley, S. R., and Kunda, G. (2001). "Bringing Work Back In," *Organization Science*, 12(1): 76–95.

Bartunek, J. M. (2007). "Academic-Practitioner Collaboration Need not Require Joint or Relevant Research: Toward a Relational Scholarship of Integration," *Academy of Management Journal*, 50(6): 1323–33.

Baum, J. A. C., Rowley, T. J., Shipilov, A. V., and Chuang, Y.-T. (2005). "Dancing with Strangers: Aspiration Performance and the Search for Underwriting Syndicate Partners," *Administrative Science Quarterly*, 50(4): 536–75.

Benner, M. J., and Tushman, M. (2002). "Process Management and Technological Innovation: A Longitudinal Study of the Photography and Paint Industries," *Administrative Science Quarterly*, 47(4): 676–706.

Boone, C., Brdcheler, V., and Carroll, G. R. (2000). "Custom Service: Application and Tests of Resource-Partitioning Theory among Dutch Auditing Firms from 1896 to 1992," *Organization Studies*, 21(2): 355–81.

Boone, C., De Brabander, B., and Hellemans, J. (2000). "Research Note: CEO Locus of Control and Small Firm Performance," *Organization Studies*, 21(3): 641–46.

Carlsen, A. (2006). "Organizational Becoming as Dialogic Imagination of Practice: The Case of the Indomitable Gauls," *Organization Science*, 17(1): 132–49.

Cattani, G., Ferriani, S., Negro, G., and Perretti, F. (2008). "The Structure of Consensus: Network Ties, Legitimation, and Exit Rates of U.S. Feature Film Producer Organizations," *Administrative Science Quarterly*, 53(1): 145–82.

Chuang, Y.-T., and Baum, J. A. C. (2003). "It's All in the Name: Failure-Induced Learning by Multiunit Chains," *Administrative Science Quarterly*, 48(1): 33–59.

D'Aunno, T., Succi, M., and Alexander, J. A. (2000). "The Role of Institutional and Market Forces in Divergent Organizational Change," *Administrative Science Quarterly*, 45(4): 679–703.

Dobrev, S. D., and Tai-Young, K. (2006). "Positioning among Organizations in a Population: Moves between Market Segments and the Evolution of Industry Structure," *Administrative Science Quarterly*, 51(2): 230–61.

Dobrev, S. D., Tai-Young, K., and Carroll, G. R. (2002). "The Evolution of Organizational Niches: U.S. Automobile Manufacturers, 1885–1981," *Administrative Science Quarterly*, 47(2): 233–64.

Dunn, M. B., and Jones, C. (2010). "Institutional Logics and Institutional Pluralism: The Contestation of Care and Science Logics in Medical Education, 1967–2005," *Administrative Science Quarterly*, 55(1): 114–49.

Emrich, C. G., Brower, H. H., Feldman, J. M., and Garland, H. (2001). "Images in Words: Presidential Rhetoric, Charisma, and Greatness," *Administrative Science Quarterly*, 46(3): 527–57.

Faerman, S. R., McCaffrey, D. P., and Van Slyke, D. M. (2001). "Understanding Interorganizational Cooperation: Public-Private Collaboration in Regulating Financial Market Innovation," *Organization Science*, 12(3): 372–88.

Farjoun, M., and University, T. A. (2002). "The Dialectics of Institutional Development in Emerging and Turbulent Fields: The History of Pricing Conventions in the On-line Database Industry," *Academy of Management Journal*, 45(5): 848–74.

Fiss, P. C., and Zajac, E. J. (2004). "The Diffusion of Ideas over Contested Terrain: The (Non)adoption of a Shareholder Value Orientation among German Firms," *Administrative Science Quarterly*, 49(4): 501–34.

Fleischer, A. (2009). "Ambiguity and the Equity of Rating Systems: United States Brokerage Firms, 1995–2000," *Administrative Science Quarterly*, 54(4): 555–74.

Frenkel, M., and Shenhav, Y. (2006). "From Binarism Back to Hybridity: A Postcolonial Reading of Management and Organization Studies," *Organization Studies*, 27(6): 855–76.

Galaskiewicz, J., Bielefeld, W., and Dowell, M. (2006). "Networks and Organizational Growth: A Study of Community Based Nonprofits," *Administrative Science Quarterly*, 51(3): 337–80.

Glynn, M. A., and Abzug, R. (2002). "Institutionalizing Identity: Symbolic Isomorphism and Organizational Names," *Academy of Management Journal*, 45(1): 267–80.

Greenwood, R., Díaz, A. M., Li, S. X., and Lorente, J. C. (2010). "The Multiplicity of Institutional Logics and the Heterogeneity of Organizational Responses," *Organization Science*, 21(2): 521–39.

Greve, H. R. (2002). "Sticky Aspirations: Organizational Time Perspective and Competitiveness," *Organization Science*, 13(1): 1–17.

Guler, I., Guillén, M. F., and Macpherson, J. M. (2002). "Global Competition, Institutions, and the Diffusion of Organizational Practices: The International Spread of ISO 9000 Quality Certificates," *Administrative Science Quarterly*, 47(2): 207–32.

Hargadon, A. B., and Douglas, Y. (2001). "When Innovations Meet Institutions: Edison and the Design of the Electric Light," *Administrative Science Quarterly*, 46(3): 476–501.

Haveman, H. A., Russo, M. V., and Meyer, A. D. (2001). "Organizational Environments in Flux: The Impact of Regulatory Punctuations on Organizational Domains, CEO Succession, and Performance," *Organization Science*, 12(3): 253–73.

Hiatt, S. R., Sine, W. D., and Tolbert, P. S. (2009). "From Pabst to Pepsi: The Deinstitutionalization of Social Practices and the Creation of Entrepreneurial Opportunities," *Administrative Science Quarterly*, 54(4): 635–67.

Higgins, M. C., and Gulati, R. (2003). "Getting Off to a Good Start: The Effects of Upper Echelon Affiliations on Underwriter Prestige," *Organization Science*, 14(3): 244–63.

Hinings, C. R., and Greenwood, R. (2002). "Disconnects and Consequences in Organization Theory?" *Administrative Science Quarterly*, 47(3): 411–21.

Huygens, M., Van Den Bosch, F. A. J., Volberda, H. W., and Baden-Fuller, C. (2001). "Co-Evolution of Firm Capabilities and Industry Competition: Investigating the Music Industry, 1877–1997," *Organization Studies*, 22(6): 971–1011.

Ingram, P., and Simons, T. (2000). "State Formation, Ideological Competition, and the Ecology of Israeli Workers' Cooperatives, 1920–1992," *Administrative Science Quarterly*, 45(1): 25–53.

Ingram, P., and Torfason, M. T. (2010). "Organizing the In-between: The Population Dynamics of Network-weaving Organizations in the Global Interstate Network," *Administrative Science Quarterly*, 55(4): 577–605.

Iyer, D. N., and Miller, K. D. (2008). "Performance Feedback, Slack, and the Timing of Acquisitions," *Academy of Management Journal*, 51(4): 808–22.

Jennings, P. D., Schulz, M., Patient, D., Gravel, C., and Yuan, K. (2005). "Weber and Legal Rule Evolution: The Closing of the Iron Cage?" *Organization Studies*, 26(4): 621–53.

Jensen, M. (2003). "The Role of Network Resources in Market Entry: Commercial Banks' Entry into Investment Banking, 1991–1997," *Administrative Science Quarterly*, 48(3): 466–97.

Jensen, M. (2006). "Should We Stay or Should We Go? Accountability, Status Anxiety, and Client Defections," *Administrative Science Quarterly*, 51(1): 97–128.

Johnston, S., and Selsky, J. W. (2006). "Duality and Paradox: Trust and Duplicity in Japanese Business Practice," *Organization Studies*, 27(2): 183–205.

Jones, C. (2001). "Co-Evolution of Entrepreneurial Careers, Institutional Rules and Competitive Dynamics in American Film, 1895–1920," *Organization Studies*, 22(6): 911–44.

Kalev, A., Shenhav, Y., and De Vries, D. (2008). "The State, the Labor Process, and the Diffusion of Managerial Models," *Administrative Science Quarterly*, 53(1): 1–28.

Khaire, M., and Wadhwani, R. D. (2010). "Changing Landscapes: The Construction of Meaning and Value in a New Market Category—Modern Indian Art," *Academy of Management Journal*, 53(6): 1281–304.

Kijkuit, B., and van den Ende, J. (2010). "With a Little Help from Our Colleagues: A Longitudinal Study of Social Networks for Innovation," *Organization Studies*, 31(4): 451–79.

King, B. G. (2008). "A Political Mediation Model of Corporate Response to Social Movement Activism," *Administrative Science Quarterly*, 53(3): 395–421.

King, B. G., and Soule, S. A. (2007). "Social Movements as Extra-institutional Entrepreneurs: The Effect of Protests on Stock Price Returns," *Administrative Science Quarterly*, 52(3): 413–42.

King, M. D., and Haveman, H. A. (2008). "Antislavery in America: The Press, the Pulpit, and the Rise of Antislavery Societies," *Administrative Science Quarterly*, 53(3): 492–528.

Kochan, T. A., and Rubinstein, S. A. (2000). "Toward a Stakeholder Theory of the Firm: The Saturn Partnership," *Organization Science*, 11(4): 367–86.

Kraatz, M. S., and Zajac, E. J. (2001). "How Organizational Resources Affect Strategic Change and Performance in Turbulent Environments: Theory and Evidence," *Organization Science*, 12(5): 632–57.

Kuilman, J. G., and Li, J. (2009). "Grades of membership and legitimacy spillovers: Foreign Banks in Shanghai, 1847–1935," *Academy of Management Journal*, 52(2): 229–45.

Lamberg, J.-A., and Laurila, J. (2005). "Materializing the Societal Effect: Organizational Forms and Changing Patterns of Dominance in the Paper Industry," *Organization Studies*, 26(12): 1809–30.

Lammers, C. J. (2003). "Occupation Regimes Alike and Unlike: British, Dutch and French Patterns of Inter-Organizational Control of Foreign Territories," *Organization Studies*, 24(9): 1379–403.

Lange, D., Boivie, S. and Henderson, A. D. (2009). "The Parenting Paradox: How Multibusiness Diversifiers Endorse Disruptive Technologies while their Corporate Children Struggle," *Academy of Management Journal*, 52(1): 179–98.

Lounsbury, M. (2002). "Institutional Transformation and Status Mobility: The Professionalization of the Field of Finance," *Academy of Management Journal*, 45(1): 255–66.

Lubatkin, M. H., Lane, P. J., Collin, S.-O., and Very, P. (2005). "Origins of Corporate Governance in the USA, Sweden and France," *Organization Studies*, 26(6): 867–88.

Marquis, C., and Huang, Z. H. I. (2010). "Acquisitions as Exaptation: The Legacy of Founding Institutions in the U.S. Commercial Banking Industry," *Academy of Management Journal*, 53(6): 1441–73.

McKendrick, D. G., and Carroll, G. R. (2001). "On the Genesis of Organizational Forms: Evidence from the Market for Disk Arrays," *Organization Science*, 12(6): 661–82.

McKinley, W. (2007). "The March of History: Juxtaposing Histories," *Organization Studies*, 28(1): 31–6.

Meyer, A. D., Gaba, V., and Colwell, K. A. (2005). "Organizing Far from Equilibrium: Nonlinear Change in Organizational Fields," *Organization Science*, 16(5): 456–73.

Mezias, S. J., and Boyle, E. (2005). "Blind Trust: Market Control, Legal Environments, and the Dynamics of Competitive Intensity in the Early American Film Industry, 1893–1920," *Administrative Science Quarterly*, 50(1): 1–34.

Mutch, A. (2007). "Reflexivity and the Institutional Entrepreneur: A Historical Exploration," *Organization Studies*, 28(7): 1123–40.

Navis, C., and Glynn, M. A. (2010). "How New Market Categories Emerge: Temporal Dynamics of Legitimacy, Identity, and Entrepreneurship in Satellite Radio, 1990–2005," *Administrative Science Quarterly*, 55(3): 439–71.

Newton, T. (2004). "From Freemasons to the Employee: Organization, History and Subjectivity," *Organization Studies*, 25(8): 1363–87.

Oliver, A. L. (2001). "Strategic Alliances and the Learning Life-Cycle of Biotechnology Firms," *Organization Studies*, 22(3): 467–89.

Osterman, P. (2006). "Overcoming Oligarchy: Culture and Agency in Social Movement Organizations," *Administrative Science Quarterly*, 51(4): 622–49.

Pettigrew, A. M., Woodman, R. W. and Cameron, K. S. (2001). "Studying Organizational Change and Development: Challenges for Future Research," *Academy of Management Journal*, 44(4): 697–713.

Phillips, D. J. (2002). "A Genealogical Approach to Organizational Life Chances: The Parent-Progeny Transfer among Silicon Valley Law Firms, 1946–1996," *Administrative Science Quarterly*, 47(3): 474–506.

Phillips, D. J. (2005). "Organizational Genealogies and the Persistence of Gender Inequality: The Case of Silicon Valley Law Firms," *Administrative Science Quarterly*, 50(3): 440–72.

Poppo, L., Zhou, K. Z., and Sungmin, R. (2008). "Alternative Origins to Interorganizational Trust: An Interdependence Perspective on the Shadow of the Past and the Shadow of the Future," *Organization Science*, 19(1): 39–55.

Roberts, P. W., and Amit, R. (2003). "The Dynamics of Innovative Activity and Competitive Advantage: The Case of Australian Retail Banking, 1981 to 1995," *Organization Science*, 14(2): 107–22.

Rodrigues, S. B. (2006). "The Political Dynamics of Organizational Culture in an Institutionalized Environment," *Organization Studies*, 27(4): 537–57.

Rojas, F. (2010). "Power through Institutional Work: Acquiring Academic Authority in the 1968 Third World Strike," *Academy of Management Journal*, 53(6): 1263–80.

Romanelli, E., and Khessina, O. M. (2005). "Regional Industrial Identity: Cluster Configurations and Economic Development," *Organization Science*, 16(4): 344–58.

Ruef, M., and Harness, A. (2009). "Agrarian Origins of Management Ideology: The Roman and Antebellum Cases," *Organization Studies*, 30(6): 589–607.

Ruef, M., and Patterson, K. (2009). "Credit and Classification: The Impact of Industry Boundaries in Nineteenth-century America," *Administrative Science Quarterly*, 54(3): 486–520.

Russo, M. V. (2001). "Institutions, Exchange Relations, and the Emergence of New Fields: Regulatory Policies and Independent Power Production in America, 1978–1992," *Administrative Science Quarterly*, 46(1): 57–86.

Sarasvathy, S. D., Dew, N., Read, S., and Wiltbank, R. (2008). "Designing Organizations that Design Environments: Lessons from Entrepreneurial Expertise," *Organization Studies*, 29(3): 331–50.

Sherer, P. D., and Lee, K. (2002). "Institutional Change in Large Law Firms: A Resource Dependency and Institutional Perspective," *Academy of Management Journal*, 45(1): 102–19.

Short, J. L., and Toffel, M. W. (2010). "Making Self-Regulation More Than Merely Symbolic: The Critical Role of the Legal Environment," *Administrative Science Quarterly*, 55(3): 361–96.

Simons, T., and Ingram, P. (2003). "Enemies of the State: The Interdependence of Institutional Forms and the Ecology of the Kibbutz, 1910–1997," *Administrative Science Quarterly*, 48(4): 592–621.

Sine, W. D., and Lee, B. H. (2009). "Tilting at Windmills? The Environmental Movement and the Emergence of the U.S. Wind Energy Sector," *Administrative Science Quarterly*, 54(1): 123–55.

Sorenson, O., and Stuart, T. E. (2008). "Bringing the Context Back In: Settings and the Search for Syndicate Partners in Venture Capital Investment Networks," *Administrative Science Quarterly*, 53(2): 266–94.

Sorge, A., and Brussig, M. (2003). "Organizational Process, Strategic Content and Socio-Economic Resources: Small Enterprises in East Germany, 1990–94," *Organization Studies*, 24(8): 1261–81.

Suddaby, R., and Greenwood, R. (2005). "Rhetorical Strategies of Legitimacy," *Administrative Science Quarterly*, 50(1): 35–67.

Tai-Young, K., Dongyoub, S., Hongseok, O., and Young-Chul, J. (2007). "Inside the Iron Cage: Organizational Political Dynamics and Institutional Changes in Presidential Selection Systems in Korean Universities, 1985–2002," *Administrative Science Quarterly*, 52(2): 286–323.

Thornton, P. H. (2001). "Personal Versus Market Logics of Control: A Historically Contingent Theory of the Risk of Acquisition," *Organization Science*, 12(3): 294–311.

Thornton, P. H. (2002). "The Rise of the Corporation in a Craft Industry: Conflict and Conformity in Institutional Logics," *Academy of Management Journal*, 45(1): 81–101.

Toms, S., and Filatotchev, I. (2004). "Corporate Governance, Business Strategy, and the Dynamics of Networks: A Theoretical Model and Application to the British Cotton Industry, 1830–1980," *Organization Studies*, 25(4): 629–51.

Tripsas, M. (2009). "Technology, Identity, and Inertia Through the Lens of 'The Digital Photography Company,'" *Organization Science*, 20(2): 441–60.

Tsui-Auch, L. S. (2005). "Unpacking Regional Ethnicity and the Strength of Ties in Shaping Ethnic Entrepreneurship," *Organization Studies*, 26(8): 189–1216.

Unger, B. (2000). "Innovation Systems and Innovative Performance: Voice Systems," *Organization Studies*, 21(5): 941–69.

Wasserman, N. (2003). "Founder-CEO Succession and the Paradox of Entrepreneurial Success," *Organization Science*, 14(2): 149–72.

Weber, K., Davis, G. F. and Lounsbury, M. (2009). "Policy as Myth and Ceremony? The Global Spread of Stock Exchanges, 1980–2005," *Academy of Management Journal*, 52(6): 1319–47.

Weber, K., Heinze, K. L., and DeSoucey, M. (2008). "Forage for Thought: Mobilizing Codes in the Movement for Grass-fed Meat and Dairy Products," *Administrative Science Quarterly*, 53(3): 529–67.

Zaheer, A., and Soda, G. (2009). "Network Evolution: The Origins of Structural Holes," *Administrative Science Quarterly*, 54(1): 1–31.

Zelner, B. A., Henisz, W. J., and F., Holburn, G. L. (2009). "Contentious Implementation and Retrenchment in Neoliberal Policy Reform: The Global Electric Power Industry, 1989–2001," *Administrative Science Quarterly*, 54(3): 379–412.

Zhu, Z. (2007). "Reform without a Theory: Why Does it Work in China?" *Organization Studies*, 28(10): 1503–22.

REFERENCES

Abrams, P. (1982). *Historical Sociology*. Ithaca, NY: Cornell University Press.
Bennett, A. (1990). *The Death of the Organization Man*. New York: William Morrow & Company.
Bernardi, A., and Greenwood, A. (2012). "Understanding the Rift, the (Still) Uneasy Bedfellows of History and Organization Studies," *European Group of Organization Studies (EGOS) Annual Colloquium*. Helsinki, Finland.
Booth, C., and Rowlinson, M. (2006). "Management and Organizational History: Prospects," *Management & Organizational History*, 1(1): 5–30.
Bucheli, M., Mahoney, J. T., and Vaaler, P. M. (2010). "Chandler's Living History: The Visible Hand of Vertical Integration in Nineteenth Century America Viewed Under a Twenty-First Century Transaction Costs Economics Lens," *Journal of Management Studies*, 47(5): 859–83.
Calhoun, C. (1998). "Explanation in Historical Sociology: Narrative, General Theory, and Historically Specific Theory," *American Journal of Sociology*, 104(3): 846–71.
Chandler, A. D. (1962). *Strategy and Structure: Chapters in the History of the Industrial Enterprise*. Cambridge, MA: MIT Press.
Chandler, A. D. (1992). "Organizational Capabilities and the Economic History of the Industrial Enterprise," *The Journal of Economic Perspectives*, 6(3): 79–100.
Christensen, C. M. (1993). "The Rigid Disk Drive Industry: A History of Commercial and Technological Turbulence," *The Business History Review*, 67(4): 531–88.
Clark, P., and Rowlinson, M. (2004). "The Treatment of History in Organisation Studies: Towards an 'Historic Turn'?" *Business History*, 46(3): 331–52.
Clemens, E. S. (2007). "Toward a Historicized Sociology: Theorizing Events, Processes, and Emergence," *Annual Review of Sociology*, 33: 527–49.
Corrigan, P., and Sayer, D. (1988). "Editorial," *Journal of Historical Sociology*, 1(1): 1–5.
Diehl, D., and McFarland, D. (2010). "Toward a Historical Sociology of Social Situations," *American Journal of Sociology*, 115(6): 1713–52.
Fellman, S., Kuustera, A., and Vaara, E. (eds.). (2008). *Historical Perspectives on Corporate Governance*. Helsinki: Finnish Academy of Science and Letters.
Friedan, B. (1963). *The Feminine Mystique*. New York: W. W. Norton.
Froeyman, A. (2009). "Concepts of Causation in Historiography," *Historical Methods*, 42(3): 116–28.
Goffman, E. (1974). *Frame Analysis: An Essay on the Organization of Experience*. New York: Harper & Row.
Goldstone, J. A. (1998). "Initial Conditions, General Laws, Path Dependence, and Explanation in Historical Sociology," *American Journal of Sociology*, 104(3): 829–45.
Greif, A. (1997). "Cliometrics After 40 Years," *The American Economic Review*, 87(2): 400–3.
Greif, A. (1998). "Historical and Comparative Institutional Analysis," *The American Economic Review*, 88(2): 80–4.

Guler, I., Guillén, M. F., and Macpherson, J. M. (2002). "Global Competition, Institutions, and the Diffusion of Organizational Practices: The International Spread of ISO 9000 Quality Certificates," *Administrative Science Quarterly*, 47(2): 207–32.

Hadorn, G. H., Hoffmann-Riem, H., Biber-Klemm, S., Grossenbacher-Mansuy, W., Joye, D., Pohl, C., Wiesmann, U., and Zemp, E. (eds.). (2008). *Handbook of Transdisciplinary Research*. Berlin: Springer.

Hall, J. R. (1992). "Where History and Sociology Meet: Forms of Discourse and Sociohistorical Inquiry," *Sociological Theory*, 10: 164–93.

Hall, J. R. (1999). *Cultures of Inquiry: From Epistemology to Discourse in Sociohistorical Research*. Cambridge: Cambridge University Press.

Hargadon, A. B., and Douglas, Y. (2001). "When Innovations Meet Institutions: Edison and the Design of the Electric Light," *Administrative Science Quarterly*, 46(3): 476–501.

Harvey, C., and Wilson, J. (2007). "Redefining Business History: An Editorial Statement," *Business History*, 49(1): 1–7.

Haveman, H. A., Rao, H., and Paruchuri, S. (2007). "The Winds of Change: The Progressive Movement and the Bureaucratization of Thrift," *American Sociological Review*, 72(1): 117–42.

Helfat, C. E. (ed.). (2003). *The SMS Blackwell Handbook of Organizational Capabilities: Emergence, Development, and Change*: Strategic Management Society Book Series. Malden, MA, Oxford, and Carlton, Australia: Blackwell.

Hiatt, S. R., Sine, W. D., and Tolbert, P. S. (2009). "From Pabst to Pepsi: The Deinstitutionalization of Social Practices and the Creation of Entrepreneurial Opportunities," *Administrative Science Quarterly*, 54(4): 635–67.

Hofstadter, R. (1958). "History and the Social Sciences." In F. Stern (ed.), *The Varieties of History: From Voltaire to the Present*. New York: Meridian Books, Inc.: 359–70.

Ingram, P., Rao, H., and Silverman, B. S. (2012). "History in Strategy Research: What, Why, and How?" In S. J. Kahl, B. S. Silverman, and M. A. Cusumano (eds.), *History and Strategy (Advances in Strategic Management)* Vol. 29. New York: Emerald Group Publishing: 241–73.

Jacques, R. S. (2006). "History, Historiography and Organization Studies: The Challenge and the Potential," *Management & Organizational History*, 1(1): 31–49.

Kieser, A. (1994). "Why Organization Theory Needs Historical Analyses—And How This Should Be Performed," *Organization Science*, 5(4): 608–20.

Kiser, E., and Hechter, M. (1998). "The Debate on Historical Sociology: Rational Choice Theory and Its Critics," *American Journal of Sociology*, 104(3): 785–816.

Klein, J. T. (2008). "Evaluation of Interdisciplinary and Transdisciplinary Research: A Literature Review," *American Journal of Preventive Medicine*, 35(2, Supplement): S116–S123.

Lamberg, J. A., and Pajunen, K. (2010). "Agency, Institutional Change, and Continuity: The Case of the Finnish Civil War," *Journal of Management Studies*, 47(5): 814–36.

Leblebici, H., and Shah, N. (2004). "The Birth, Transformation, and Regeneration of Business Incubators as New Organizational Forms: Understanding the Interplay Between Organizational History and Organizational Theory," *Business History*, 46(3): 353–80.

Lee, B. H. (2009). "The Infrastructure of Collective Action and Policy Content Diffusion in the Organic Food Industry," *Academy of Management Journal*, 52(6): 1247–69.

Malerba, F., Nelson, R., Orsenigo, L., and Winter, S. (1999). "History Friendly Models of Industry Evolution," *Industrial and Corporate Change*, 8(1): 3–40.

Marquis, C. (2005). *Historical Environments and the Transformation of Twientieth-Century United States Banking.* Unpublished dissertation, University of Michigan.

McCraw, T. K. (2006). "Schumpeter's Business Cycles as Business History," *Business History Review*, 80(2): 231–61.

O'Sullivan, M., and Graham, M. B. W. (2010). "Guest Editors' Introduction," *Journal of Management Studies*, 47(5): 775–90.

Pudovkin, A. I., and Garfield, E. (2002). "Algorithmic Procedure for Finding Semantically Related Journals," *Journal of the American Society for Information Science & Technology*, 53(13): 1113–19.

Randall, D. M. (1987). "Commitment and the Organization: The Organization Man Revisited," *Academy of Management Review*, 12(3): 460–71.

Rowlinson, M. (2004). "Historical Perspectives in Organization Studies: Factual, Narrative, and Archeo- Genealogical." In D. E. Hodgson and C. Carter (eds.), *Management Knowledge and the New Employee*. Burlington, VT: Ashgate Publishing: 8–20.

Runciman, W. G. (1983). *A Treatise on Social Theory: The Methodology of Social Theory.* Cambridge: Cambridge University Press.

Ryden, D. B. (2011). "Perhaps We Can Talk," *Social Science History*, 35(2): 209–12.

Schreyögg, G., and Sydow, J. (2011). "Organizational Path Dependence: A Process View," *Organization Studies*, 32(3): 321–35.

Sewell, W. (2005). *Logics of History: Social Theory and Social Transformation.* Chicago: University of Chicago Press.

Sine, W. D. (2001). *Paradise Lost: A Study of the Decline of Institutions and the Restructuring of Organizational Fields in the United States Power Industry.* Unpublished dissertation, Cornell University.

Soulsby, A., and Clark, E. (2007). "Organization Theory and the Post-Socialist Transformation: Contributions to Organizational Knowledge," *Human Relations*, 60(10): 1419–42.

Spiegel, G. M. (2009). "The Task of the Historian," *American Historical Review*, 114(1): 1–15.

Stinchcombe, A. L. (2005). *The Logic of Social Research.* Chicago: University of Chicago Press.

Suddaby, R., and Greenwood, R. (2005). "Rhetorical Strategies of Legitimacy," *Administrative Science Quarterly*, 50(1): 35–67.

Üsdiken, B., and Kieser, A. (2004). "Introduction: History in Organisation Studies," *Business History*, 46(3): 321–30.

Weatherbee, T. G., Durepos, G., Mills, A., and Mills, J. H. (2012). "Theorizing the Past: Critical Engagements," *Management & Organizational History*, 7(3): 193–202.

Weber, K., Davis, G. F., and Lounsbury, M. (2009). "Policy as Myth and Ceremony? The Global Spread of Stock Exchanges, 1980–2005," *Academy of Management Journal*, 52(6): 1319–47.

Whaples, R. (1991). "A Quantitative History of the Journal of Economic History and the Cliometric Revolution," *The Journal of Economic History*, 51(2): 289–301.

Whaples, R. (2010). "Is Economic History a Neglected Field of Study?" *Historically Speaking*, 11(2): 17–20.

Whyte, W. H. (1956). *The Organization Man*. New York: Simon and Schuster.

Wickberg, D. (2009). "Is Intellectual History a Neglected Field of Study?" *Historically Speaking*, 10(4): 14–17.

4

Historical Institutionalism

Roy Suddaby, William M. Foster, and
Albert J. Mills

INTRODUCTION

Institutional theory has become a dominant and influential perspective to study management and organizations. The popularity of institutional theory is driven, in part, by its effectiveness in offering explanations of social phenomena in counterpoint to prevailing economic analyses. A core insight of institutional theory is that business organizations sometimes attend to social pressures and influences that are distinct from material or technical factors. As a result, organizations often act in ways that are not necessarily rational, in an economic sense, but are consistent with "rules, norms and ideologies of the wider society" (Meyer and Rowan, 1977: 84).

The rising prominence of institutional analysis, however, has raised questions about its theoretical integrity. That is, as the institutional lens becomes applied to broader ranges of organizational and managerial phenomena, there is a concern that the theory now lacks "scope conditions" or an assessment of the external contingencies under which the theory will or will not apply (Suddaby, 2010). Others indicate that there is a need to address core questions that underpin the theoretical foundation of neo-institutionalism but which remain unanswered (see Barley and Tolbert, 1997; Hallett, 2010; Lawrence and Suddaby, 2006; Hallett and Ventresca, 2006)—what is an institution? How are they formed? How do they change? What role do individual actions play in institutional processes?

There is an implicit historical theme to these questions. That is, the questions are each derived from an assumption that institutions or processes of institutionalization contain within them an assumptive historical dynamic that goes beyond mere temporality and which, largely, remains unarticulated in institutional theory. This is perhaps most apparent in examining the various definitions of institutions in the literature—"*settled* habits of thought" (Veblen, 1919: 239, emphasis added), "*durable* social structures that are relatively resistant to change" (Scott, 2008: 48, emphasis added), "*enduring* features of social life" (Giddens, 1984: 24, emphasis added)—each of which contain a core element of historicity.

Similarly, the central processes that underpin institutional theory contain a fundamental but unarticulated reliance on history (i.e., the role of past events on current practices). Diffusion, for example, is a critical component of institutionalization (DiMaggio and Powell, 1983; Strang and Meyer, 1993) that contains within it a series of central, and as yet unresolved, questions about the role of history. Are the motivations of early adopters of diffused practices different from late adopters (Tolbert and Zucker, 1983)? Do diffused practices change as they move through time and space (Sahlin and Wedlin, 2008)? Is there a sedimentation effect in which the adoption of earlier practices influences the expression of later practices (Cooper, Hinings, Greenwood, and Brown, 1996)? What exactly is the role of history in processes of diffusion (Djelic, 2007)? The key observation of this paper is that institutional theory contains within it a central but unarticulated assumption of historical methods and theory.

This chapter seeks to address this gap in our understanding of the role of history in institutions and institutional processes. Our central argument is that neo-institutional theory is predicated on a critical but unarticulated set of assumptions about the role of history and historical methods. We further argue that because history has only been weakly theorized by neo-institutionalism, institutional research has been limited by an overly narrow and often positivist understanding and application of historical methods. Following the tradition of critical social theorists (i.e., Foucault, 1972) and philosophers of history (Carr, 1986; 2008) we argue for a more nuanced and socially constructivist use of history in institutional analysis.

Our chapter proceeds as follows. First, we sketch out the assumptive historical basis of institutional theory and demonstrate why neo-institutionalism needs more explicit and dedicated historical methods. Second, we offer a review of the, relatively limited, common historical methods and constructs used by neo-institutional researchers. We then offer an epistemological critique of this narrow view of history in neo-institutionalism and demonstrate how institutional research might benefit from adopting a more explicit view of history and historical methods. Specifically, we argue for the adoption of historical method as narrative and the use of narrative analytic techniques to study institutions and processes of institutionalization. Finally, we offer some suggestions as to what a historically informed view of institutionalism might look like.

THE HISTORICAL PREMISE OF
INSTITUTIONAL THEORY

History is an implicit, but often invisible, element of institutional theory. This is, perhaps, most evident in the early discussions of processes of institutionalization offered by Berger and Luckman (1967) who explicity draw from 19th- and 20th-century historical thought as antecedents to their arguments about the social construction of reality. Berger and Luckman (1967) observed that institutions arise and persist as a result of historical processes of participation in patterns of reciprocal categorizations. Reciprocal categorizations are social categories that become routinely reproduced through texts and social action. Gender, status, nationality, and class are all examples of reciprocal categorizations that have become institutionalized.

Once institutionalized, practices become cognitively embedded or so taken-for-granted they become invisible and entrenched because no one questions their history. As Krippendorf (2004) notes, "our lack of history fuels institutional controls." To be institutionalized means to become taken-for-granted because individuals have lost the capacity to question their origin or how they are maintained.

Early studies of institutions—that is, the so-called "old" institutionalism— adopted an explicitly historical perspective, often couched in the narrative style of a historical case study. Perhaps the best example of this is Selznick's (1949) now classic study of the Tennessee Valley Authority. Later, Selznick (1957: 16) explained the role of history in processes of institutionalization:

> Institutionalization is a *process*. It is something that happens to an organization over time, reflecting the organization's own distinctive history, the people who've been in it, the groups it embodies and the vested interests it has created, and the way it has adapted to its environment.

In Selznick's view, because institutionalization is an inherently historical process, it can only be understood through historical analysis. Selznick (1957: 16) concludes that "in the search for more general connections between policy and social structure, something may be gained from the study of organizational histories."

Old institutionalism, as a result, is replete with detailed analytic accounts of the "life histories" (or what, today, would be called "historical case studies") of organizations or industries. So, for example, in early sociological studies of organizations detailed historical accounts were written about the institutionalization of norms and practices in unions (Lipset et al., 1956) and in the textile industry (Bendix, 1956). In organizational sociology similar life histories were produced on a variety of organizations including a gypsum plant (Gouldner, 1956), a clerical agency (Crozier, 1964), political parties (Michels, 1949), and a medical school (Becker et al., 1961) among others.

A limited number of studies within "new" institutionalism have maintained the historical premise of institutional theory. Leblebici and colleagues (1991) for example offered an insightful historical account of institutional change in the radio broadcasting industry. Their core insight was that institutional changes emerged from the margins of the field or from actors not fully embedded in the norms and taken-for-granted assumptions within the field. Their methods however are historical in so far as they attempt to analyze the influence of past events on current practices and adopt a stage-based analytic technique that identifies three distinct periods of institutionalization in this industry.

Another powerful use of historical methods in organizational institutionalism is Hargadon and Douglas's (2001) analysis of the design techniques used by Edison to legitimate the innovation of electric light. Their core insight is to delineate elements of "robust design" or attributes within the innovated object that directly manipulate consumers' perceptions of the degree of historical novelty of the innovation. One such design technique is the adoption of *skeumorphs* or design characteristics that comfort the consumer by making semiotic reference to familiar objects from the past. In this case, early light bulbs were designed to look like candle flames.

This article is notable, however, in how the authors explicitly articulate the need to use historical methods to understand institutional innovation and change. Hargadon and Douglas (2001: 480) specifically reject rationalist methods and explain the need to embrace the emphasis on the particularistic empirical detail of time and place offered by historical techniques:

> Historical case studies...offer ways to examine social processes in ways that both cross-sectional and even current longitudinal research cannot...cognition, whether individual (e.g. DiMaggio, 1997) or organizational (e.g. Weick, 1979; Levitt & March, 1988) serves as the nexus between existing institutions and the actions they guide. Cultural elements shape both interpretation and action and any analysis of the relationship between them must account for the context in which they are embedded (Geertz, 1973)....Careful analysis of moments in history when innovations rapidly change the landscape of existing institutions offers the opportunity to observe these larger systems of meaning.

There are a limited number of other neo-institutional analyses within organization theory that adopt a historical or historical case study perspective: Hoffman's (1999) analysis of the chemical industry, Suddaby and Greenwood's (2005) analysis of multidisciplinary practices in the professions, Maguire and Hardy's research on DDT (2009), Arndt and Bigelow's (2005) study of the gendered history of hospital administration and, more recently, Rojas' (2010) study of the 1968 Third World Strike.

These studies, however, are the exceptions. Most current studies of institutions within organizational theory (i.e., neo-institutionalism) have replaced historical methods and epistemology with a rational-deductive (or what Thelen (1999) would term a "rational choice") perspective. Doing so has had serious and limiting consequences for our understanding of institutions. In the following section we elaborate the differences between the historical premise of old institutionalism and the rational-deductive premise of neo-institutionalism.

WHAT IS A HISTORICAL EPISTEMOLOGY AND HOW DOES IT DIFFER FROM RATIONAL DEDUCTION?

Although the early case studies of old institutionalism did not necessarily articulate an explicit historical perspective in their methodology (Selznick being a clear exception), the studies contain, and help to articulate, an implicit historical epistemology. This epistemology is characterized by four distinct emphases.

Truth Claims: First, historical studies of institutions tend to make *particularist* and localized, rather than *universal*, truth claims. In these studies it was assumed that institutions were the products of very specific elements of time and space. This is, perhaps, most evident in Selznick's classic study of the TVA where the reader is made acutely aware of the unique confluence of factors—the intent to create a federal institution closely connected to grassroots organizations, the territorial reaction of other federal agencies, the co-optation by agricultural interests, all against the backdrop of New Deal policy initiatives—that served as a crucible for institutional creation.

It is important to note that even though Selznick makes evident that the TVA was a product of highly localized factors, it did not diminish his ability to distil generalized principles. Co-optation, the unintended consequences of purposive action, and the process of infusion of value beyond mere technical requirements are three key theoretical insights produced from this study and which populate a wide range of subsequent studies of institutions. However, Selznick makes no overt attempt toward generalization, nor does he make universal truth claims from the study.

Causality: Second, historical studies of institutions focus on *complex*, rather than *unitary* causality. This is the important difference noted by Hargadon and Douglas (2001), where they observe that historical studies acknowledge the fact that institutions are founded in complex sedimentations of culture and meaning in ways that rational-deductive studies are not. Perhaps the best illustration of this emphasis arises from the observation made by Hoffman (1999) at the conclusion of his study of the origins of environmentalism in the US chemical industry about the ways in which neo-institutionalism has simplified the notion of "events." In commenting on the limitations of his study Hoffman (1999: 366) observes that

> a question remains as to how events drive institutional change. What distinguishes events that cause change from others that do not? Is there some way that events can be classified as to the characteristics that enable them to alter the institutional order? Do single events cause change or are only event chains responsible for social change? The answers to these questions appear to lie in the process by which events are socially constructed within a field...it is important to consider how events are socially constructed through a contest over meaning among the players within an organizational field (Hannigan, 1995). Similar events occurring at different points in history can be constructed in different ways so that their impacts vary.

Here Hoffman is commenting on the limitations of applying hypo-deductive constructs and methods that flow from a rational choice epistemology to questions that require a historical perspective. Historians understand that events acquire different meanings over time and, as a result, it becomes difficult to construct a coherent narrative around a single cause (Carr, 2008; Sewell, 2005).

Motivations: Third, the motivations for historical studies of institutions tend to be driven by *empirical phenomena* or puzzles rather than *gaps in theory*. For Phillip Selznick (1996) this was one of the defining differences between the "old" and "new" institutionalisms. He begins his essay on the differences between old and new institutionalism with a quote from the American pragmatist John Dewey (1938) that argues for a greater focus motivated by observations in nature, rather than problems generated by theories. "Any problem of social inquiry," Dewey (1938: 499) wrote, "that does not grow out of actual (or 'practical') social conditions is factitious; it is arbitrarily set by the inquirer instead of being objectively produced and controlled." Selznick (1996: 270) thus criticizes neo-institutionalism for its navel-gazing focus on theory, noting that social science "should be guided by problems of life and practice rather than intellectually self-generated conceptions and techniques."

Institutional explanations: Fourth, historical analyses of institutions tend to focus on *endogenous* rather than *exogenous* explanations for institutions. The reason for this, according to Selznick (1996), is that old institutionalism does not reify social structures, like organizations or institutions, in the same way that new institutionalism does. That is, old institutionalism is not afraid of methodological individualism, but rather accepts the notion that broader social structures are composed of human beings. Selznick (1957: 4) explains that "no social process can be understood save as it is located in the behavior of individuals, and especially in their perceptions of themselves and each other. The problem is to link the larger view with the more limited one, to see how institutional change is produced by, and in turn shapes, the interaction of individuals in day to day situations."

A historically informed view of institutions, thus, offers a place for the individual within institutional theory. This is an oft criticized element of neo-institutionalism (Hallett and Ventresca, 2006; Barley and Tolbert, 1997; Suddaby, 2010) which, as Hallett (2010) notes, was originally built on a premise of micro-sociology but has gradually evolved to exclude individuals entirely. Meyer and Jepperson (2000) observe that institutions were once thought to be socially constructed by humans, but increasingly neo-institutionalism has reversed this assumption by arguing, erroneously, that individuals are the products of institutions.

Historical analyses of institutions may help to correct this logical fallacy by exploring the relationship between sedimented human interactions and institutional practices and through revealing how understandings of institutions change over time. The historical case studies of old institutionalism adopt a specific narrative analytical style in which the theoretical findings of the study are embedded in descriptive accounts of specific individuals and their interactions. This might have been a narrow timeframe restricted by a specific event, such as a wildcat strike (Gouldner, 1956) or a much longer period of time with analytic emphasis on the life history of an organization, like the TVA (Selznick, 1949). Hallett and Ventresca (2006) demonstrate the utility of this technique by adopting a symbolic interactionist re-reading of Gouldner's (1956) classic historical case study. They observe an essential role for individuals and their interpretive interactions in shaping the institution in which they work, a process the authors term "inhabited institutionalism."

In sum, the differences between the historical assumptions and methods of old institutionalism and the more scientistic or rational-deductive assumptions and methods of new institutionalism become embedded in the preferred level of analysis adopted by each camp. One example is that old institutionalism tends to study intra-organizational aspects of institutionalization and new institutionalism tends toward field level studies. An unfortunate outcome, however, is that as neo-institutionalism has grown in prominence, its sensitivity to historical methods, assumptions, and epistemology has waned. This has created serious problems for neo-institutionalism, which we elaborate in the following section.

WHAT PROBLEMS ARE CREATED WHEN NEO-INSTITUTIONALISM NEGLECTS HISTORY

An unfortunate outcome from the shift from old to new institutionalism in organization studies, thus, is that *the new institutionalism has become ahistorical*. That is, in their search for scientific legitimacy—that is, the ability to make broad theoretical generalizations and claims of universal knowledge—contemporary organizational institutionalists have minimized or obscured the role of history. That is, they have taken the subjective and interpretive elements of historical methods and replaced them with the more objective and measurable assumptions of "events" measured over "time" (Suddaby, Foster, and Quinn-Trank, 2010).

When institutional researchers treat history as an objective, measurable phenomenon, two distinct problems arise. First, research tends to become *essentialist*. That is, the analysis becomes fixed and objective and the nuances of time and place, which are essential in a truly historical epistemology, become supplanted by methods that purport to be attentive to history, but which transform the richness of history to the somewhat sterile variable of time. History, in such a rational-deductive logic, is something to be measured and controlled, as in the use of "event-history analysis" in which all events are coded as relatively discrete and equivalent experiences (Alison, 1984). Thus, complex and contextualized historical processes are reduced to a series of events—"adoption" or "diffusion"—that are analyzed in relative isolation from each other.

What is lost in the act of transforming history into an essentialist and objective series of events is the ability to understand the social and cultural embeddedness of institutions and the role of complex processes—that is, the critical or crucible events in the emergence, development, and alteration of institutions. Khurana (2007: 14–15) notes that neo-institutional research has lost this appreciation of history in explaining institutional change:

> [It] is essential to examine an institution's birth—its emergence out of an interaction with the larger society and culture, the evolution of its internal dynamic and the interface between the two . . . The key here is to show organizations responding to particular problems posed by history.

Contemporary neo-institutionalism tends to see history as a set of underlying conditions that are relatively constant and which express themselves relatively consistently over time and space. Moreover, time itself is treated as a relatively discrete—that is, ordered and measured—phenomena.

Such an essentialist view, however, overlooks the critical role of narrative and interpretation in history. History isn't so much the measurement of events over time as the ability to unearth and document the shift of collective interpretations over time (Lowenthal, 1985). This is an inherently subjective process that requires considerable discretion and interpretive skill on the part of the historian (Carr, 2008). Historians emphasize some facts and deemphasize others. They reinterpret and synthesize various competing perspectives on similar events and, ultimately, they impose a narrative order, coherence, and structure on the relatively undifferentiated stream of "facts" that constitute the past (White, 1973).

Another consequence of treating history in a rational-deductive manner is the tendency toward *functionalism*. Ahistorical approaches to understanding institutions tend to view issues from the past through the eyes of the present. As a result, they tend to privilege the present by assuming that surviving present day institutions represent higher standards of legitimacy, adoptability, or superior logics (Kieser, 1994). The success of present day institutions is used to impose a unifying causal logic on the sequence of historical events. That is, rather than acknowledging the complex causality that is typically associated with historical events, particularly when studied as an unfolding process, rational-deductive approaches tend to impose a unifying causality *post-hoc* on a sequence of events (Booth and Rowlinson, 2006).

This is perhaps best illustrated by the popularity of path-dependence as an explanatory narrative in neo-institutional research both in economic and organization theory which, as critics have observed, tend to generate simplified and functionalist explanations of socially embedded and historical complex processes. In economics, path dependence refers to the observation that incremental early choices (in product design, industrial standards, etc.) can often produce inefficient long-term consequences. So, for example, the adoption of standard gauge railway tracks (Puffert, 2000; 2002), QWERTY keyboards (Arthur, 1990; 1994), and video formats (Cusumano, Mylonadis, and Rosenbloom, 1992) have each been described as economically inferior choices imposed on society by the burden of history. This view of path dependence, thus, interprets history narrowly as a set of constraining contingencies.

An alternative view of path dependence, however, derived from political science, sociology, and historians, sees history not as a constraint but as generating a series of specific moments of choice, each of which creates multiple paths of different historical trajectories or outcomes (Dobbin, 1994; Leibowitz and Margolis, 1990; 1995). An analysis that is determinately historical in methods and assumptions, however, does not necessarily assume that surviving institutional forms and practices are successful because of objective laws or principles of, for example, legitimacy, but rather because they survive as the result of a series of specific decisions and past choice opportunities, whether intentional or implicit (Kieser, 1994).

A good example of the use of historical epistemology to avoid functionalism is offered by Leblebici et al.'s (1991) historical analysis of transformations in the US radio broadcasting industry. The purpose of the study is to identify the primary mechanisms for change in an organizational field. Instead of using the more typical longitudinal cross-sectional research design, the authors employed an analysis of "historically grounded descriptive material" (Leblebici et al., 1991: 333) that combined both quantitative and qualitative archival material. Adopting a historically sensitive methodology combined with the use of rich textual data sources generated a study of institutional change that avoided the inherent tendency to focus on a simple and single causal explanation. Rather than analyzing the diffusion of a single innovation in the field, the authors identify a series of "consecutive transformations of [the radio industry's] institutionalized mechanism of exchange" (Leblebici et al., 1991: 357)—analogies, private agreements, and conventions. More significantly, their core insight identified an explanation of institutional change as an *endogenous process*—that is, they conclude that the more legitimate a new practice becomes, the more it erodes the power of incumbent actors and the institutional resources that support them.

In contrast to functionalism, a more determinately historical analysis of institutions draws researchers' attention away from using historical data to explain the "success" of existing arrangements in terms of the functions they provide to contemporary society and, instead, focuses attention on understanding that present day standards of efficiency and success are, themselves, historical products (Kieser, 1994). As a result, in order to understand where existing institutional arrangements came from requires a degree of suspension of present-day assumptions about standards of efficiency and success.

Functionalist views of history, however, tend to limit our understanding of institutions by imposing present day assumptions, standards, and questions on historical data. As a result, functionalist researchers are much less interested in explaining origins than they are in explaining the present. That is, they care less about understanding where institutions originate than they do in explaining how existing institutions survived.

In sum, the shift from old to new institutionalism has come at a cost. Adopting a rational-deductive perspective limits our understanding of institutions as the outcome of historical processes. It forces us to treat institutions as things, rather than as processes and encourages the reduction of complex causality into simple variables. The impoverished view of history in neo-institutional theory is a critical source of this limited view of institutions. By ignoring the richness of an interpretive view of history, neo-institutionalism has adopted a flat, mechanical, and barren view of temporal processes that are central to institutional theory. Neo-institutionalism ignores the role of individuals or groups in processes of institutional creation, maintenance, and change. It also tends to privilege explanations derived from the present and impose them on the past. Unfortunately, old institutionalism never fully articulated a historical methodology for the study of institutions. In the following section we offer a preliminary sketch of what an institutional historiography might look like.

HISTORICAL INSTITUTIONALISM

Our earlier review of the use of history in neo-institutionalism revealed a small sample of studies that explicitly adopted historical methods or a historical perspective in analyzing institutions. Three observations follow from our review of these studies. First, with one exception (Hargadon and Douglas,

2001), none of the accounts we examined explicitly make reference to the use of history as a method of analysis. Instead, references are made to history as something that a person or organization *has*; suggesting that history is there to be uncovered and represented in some kind of historic account that does not draw upon a formal method. Thus, while historians have an explicit method or "craft" (Bloch, 1953), institutional theorists who use historical methods appear to be unwilling or unable to articulate what that method is.

Second, in constructing histories, the notion of the past is often conflated with history (Durepos, Mills, and Weatherbee, 2012). That is, there is a tendency to treat history as little more than a sequence of events or an analysis with a temporal or a longitudinal component. There is little conscious reflection on the myriad of choices that must be made when one analyses the past—that is, which facts are selected and which are ignored, how periods are imposed on events, and which events are identified as "crucibles" or "critical junctures" and which are not. Indeed, the construct of "events" is, itself, under-theorized.

Third, while the various authors go to some lengths to explain some of the limitations of their chosen methods *for the subject at hand* they rarely, if at all, reflect on how those methods contribute to embedded notions of the past and history. Nor do they reflect on the role of such things as historical narrative (Carr, 1986; 2008) or rhetorical history (Suddaby, Foster, and Trank, 2010) in developing supposed traces of the past.

Path dependence[1] for example, in utilizing the metaphor of a narrow and linear trail, overlays on the past a template for viewing how events are selected for consideration and what effect they have on present outcomes, thus providing a sequential inevitability or teleology to present decision making. It does not take into account such things as the way that events become prioritized and change in meaning through historical-discursive processes (Foucault, 1965, 1970). Nor does the notion of path dependence adequately deal with disjunctures, ruptures, and serendipity, each of which serve to change the logics and taken-for-granted assumptions of groups of people, communities, or societies (Burguiere, 2009).

In a similar vein, constructs like "tracking" (Mintzberg et al., 1986), "evolution" (Baum and Singh, 1994), or "imprinting" (Stinchcombe, 1965) each carry embedded ways of reducing the rich complexity of historical analyses to the fairly narrow, deterministic, and often antiseptic notion of the past (Bryman et al., 2011). The result is the construction of institutional histories that mask their largely socially constructed and often highly fictionalized nature.

---

[1] Note that here we use the term "path dependence" in the narrow view of economics in which history is viewed as a burden that delimits choice, rather than the broader view of sociology in which the term is used to indicate junctures of time that generate a proliferation of different choice trajectories, as discussed earlier in the chapter.

HOW HISTORICAL INSTITUTIONALISM
CAN ENRICH OUR UNDERSTANDING OF
INSTITUTIONS

The core of our argument is that by adopting a greater epistemological and methodological sensitivity to the past and the study of history, neo-institutional researchers can enrich our understanding of institutions. More specifically, we suggest that adopting a historical approach to studying institutions will enhance our understanding of institutions as a historical process rather than as abstract, reified structures. Moreover, we believe that a renewed historical understanding of institutions will help to address key limitations of institutional theory by enriching our understanding of three core constructs that underpin the theory. These constructs are diffusion, actors, and embedded agency. In the balance of this section we elaborate the critiques of each of these constructs followed by a short description of how a historically aware approach might address the limitations of each construct. Before doing so, however, we describe briefly what we mean by a historically sensitive approach to institutions.

Historical Institutionalism: Institutional theory is based on a core foundation of phenomenology, that is, over time individuals create social structures out of shared assumptions about the nature of social reality. Berger and Luckman (1967: 54–5) argued that social structures, or institutions, form as a result of human interactions becoming habituated or reproduced over time and that this process is inherently a historical one:

> Reciprocal typifications of action are built up in the course of a shared history. They cannot be created instantaneously. Institutions always have a history, of which they are the products. It is impossible to understand an institution adequately without an understanding of the historical process in which it is produced.

We can draw three key insights from this statement. First, institutions are clearly to be understood as a historical process, that is, the outcomes of past events and interpretations of those events. Second, this process is underpinned by the interactions of *individuals*. Third, over time, the collective interpretations of these actions, and the social significance attached to them, change.

These key insights form the basis of our understanding of historical institutionalism. We define historical institutionalism to mean *the socio-historical process by which habituated actions and meanings become reified as objective social structures*. Each of these key insights has been lost or forgotten in contemporary neo-institutional theory. This is perhaps, most obvious, in the core construct of diffusion, which we elaborate next.

Diffusion: Isomorphic diffusion is a central concept in institutional theory (Greenwood et al., 2008). The core idea is that over time organizations in a common field adopt characteristics that make them appear similar to each other (DiMaggio and Powell, 1983). Critically, organizations are motivated to adopt these characteristics for social reasons, such as legitimacy, rather than for reasons of technical efficiency, such as improving performance. A more nuanced elaboration of isomorphic diffusion is the "two-stage" adoption model in which organizations first adopt an innovation for technical reasons, but later adoptions do so only because they want to appear similar to other organizations in the field (Tolbert and Zucker, 1983). Further elaborations of the diffusion construct observe that, under conditions of ambiguity, organizations will adopt the characteristics of exemplars or leading organizations in the field (Haveman, 1993a and b). Considerable research has been devoted to amassing empirical evidence to support the argument of isomorphic adoption (i.e., Davis, 1991; Burns and Wholey, 1993; Greve, 1995; Kraatz and Zajac, 1996; Lee and Pennings, 2002).

Although the notion of isomorphic diffusion seems well settled, empirically, the theoretical foundation of the construct has attracted considerable criticism. First, critics note that we often do not actually understand the motives for adopting organizations, thus making it difficult to know if adoption occurred because of blind mimicry, thus supporting the institutional premise, or because it actually improves performance (Donaldson, 1995). Second, much of the empirical support for diffusion assumes that an organizational practice or characteristic diffuses intact across all organizations in a field without any variation, distortion, or adaptation to local conditions (Sahlin-Andersson, 1996; Boxenbaum and Jonsson, 2008). Finally, prior research has failed to demonstrate how a practice or characteristic becomes elaborated *inside* the organization post-adoption (Suddaby, 2010).

Each of these shortcomings of the construct of mimetic diffusion is the result of the absence of a historical perspective and the lack of historical methods. Acts of adoption and the movement of templates through time and space are studied as scientific abstractions using cross-sectional methods that are inattentive to the complex and often subjective interpretive processes that occur temporally in each act of adoption as an organizational characteristic or practice diffuses across an organizational field. Quantitative research, unfortunately, tends to treat adoption as a discrete (i.e., "yes" or "no") event without acknowledging the possibility that adoption may, in some cases, be a continuous event, with degrees of partial adoption combined with ongoing processes of adaption or "translation" (Czarniawski and Sevon, 1996; Sahlin-Andersson, 1996; Boxenbaum and Jonsson, 2008).

A historical approach to diffusion would address most, if not all, of these issues. Foremost, historical research is more sensitive to issues of process in organizations (Tsoukas and Chia, 2002). More significantly, historical research views organizations and institutions as the outcome of complex causal processes with multiple and often conflicting motivations for action (Eisenstadt, 1964; Selznick, 1949). As a result, historical approaches to understanding institutions see the process of mimetic adoption as a messy and often chaotic process (Bennett and Elman, 2006). Perhaps the best example of this is Holm's (1995) historical analysis of the Norwegian fishing industry in which he attributes macro-structural change to multiple institutional pressures operating within multiple organizational fields (political, organizational, economic, and cultural).

Schneiberg (2007), similarly, used historical methods to understand the emergence and institutionalization of US cooperatives as a new organizational form in the first half of the 20th century. He concludes that the new organizational form was not the result of simple mimetic adoption and diffusion of a newly legitimate form, as would be predicted by neo-institutional theory. Rather, he shows the emergence of the cooperative as an adaption of the cast-off elements of previously dominant forms of organizing, an outcome of what he describes as the "institutional detritus" of a process of experimentation with different models of capitalism. Historical research, thus, is sensitive to adoption as a complex process rather than a discrete outcome.

Historical approaches to institutions, specifically narrative historiography, are also more likely to be attentive to the powerful role of interpretation of meaning over time and space. Dobbin (1994) studied differences in the adoption of railway standards and systems in Britain, France, and the US. Again, in contrast to both neo-institutional and path-dependence theorists, Dobbin explains the differences in the structural organization of national rail systems (i.e., the adoption of standards, public versus private ownership, etc.) as the outcome of cultural differences in core assumptions about the appropriate way of creating social order.

Finally, using historical methods to study institutions is also sensitive to the powerful effects of prior institutions on present decisions to adopt or reject a new organizational characteristic or practice. In a study of the adoption of corporate managerial practices in a professional services firm, Cooper et al. (1996) adopt a genealogical perspective (Foucault, 1972) on institutional change and find that the adoption of new templates of organization is highly influenced by the residue or sedimentation of prior templates. They conclude that the institution of professional partnerships does not change by discrete choices of adoption or non-adoption, but rather is the outcome of long processes of learning and incremental change in which old models of management are adapted in the context of complex layers of prior models upon which the new models become sedimented.

Individuals, Actors and Actorhood: As already noted, early expressions on institutional theory reserved a powerful role for individuals in the production, maintenance, and alteration of institutions. Berger and Luckman (1967) describe institutionalization as an inherently human process in which the subjective interpretations and interactions of individuals in social groups become manifest in enduring patterns of behavior that, ultimately, become reified as institutions. An important consequence of this is that the process of institutionalization, although it is an inherently human activity produced by individuals, tends to objectify individuals into socially constructed categories—that is, roles, occupations, genders, classes—or different constellations of "actorhood" (Meyer and Jepperson, 2000; Hwang and Colyvas, 2011).

Contemporary neo-institutional theory, however, has focused exclusively on the reified outcomes of institutionalization, that is, roles and occupational categories, with little or no attention to the role of individuals in producing, maintaining, and modifying those outcomes. So, for example, considerable research has been devoted to understanding the emergence and diffusion of occupational categories (Dobbin, 2009; Baron, Dobbin, and Jennings, 1986), gendered organizational roles (Arndt and Bigelow, 2005), or professional work (Greenwood, Suddaby, and Hinings, 2002). The role of individuals in producing these categories, however, is largely absent in these theoretical accounts. As noted previously, neo-institutional theory has empirically attended to the objectified outcomes of individual interactions but has failed to "inhabit" these outcomes with an understanding of the individuals who produce them (Hallett, 2010; Hallett and Ventresca, 2006). The individual has, largely, become invisible in contemporary institutional theory and research (Suddaby, 2010; Lawrence, Suddaby, and Leca, 2009).

Adopting a more historically informed approach to institutional research can help correct this deficiency. An emerging new stream of historical research has identified a distinction between "human" history and "natural" history. The latter is more clearly understood as traditional history with a focus on generating a scientifically accurate description of the past. This view of history, thus, is largely empirical, driven to identify rational accounts by which actions and events are linked temporally and causally. Human history, by contrast, is much more interpretive in orientation in that what ultimately will constitute history are not necessarily the empirical events, but the collective interpretation of those events over time. Indeed it is this collective reinterpretation of historical events that eventually becomes objectified as institutions. Noted historian R. G. Collingwood (1999: 46) elaborated the connection between human history and institutions:

> [A] great many things which deeply concern human beings are not, and never have been, traditionally included in the subject-matter of history. People are born, eat and breathe and sleep, and beget children and become ill and recover again, and die; and these things interest them, most of them at any rate, far more than art and science, industry and politics and war. Yet none of these things have been traditionally regarded as possessing historical interest. Most of them have given rise to institutions like dining and marrying and the various rituals that surround birth and death, sickness and recovery; and of these rituals and institutions people write histories; but the history of dining is not the history of eating, and the history of death-rituals is not the history of death.

Here Collingwood is offering a characterization of historical research that we share about neo-institutionalism—both have become obsessed with the outcomes of historical and institutional processes at the expense of studying the processes themselves.

The construct of "institutional work" has arisen to address the lack of attention to process in neo-institutional research. Institutional work refers to the "purposive action of individuals and organizations aimed at creating, maintaining, and disrupting institutions" (Lawrence and Suddaby, 2006: 215). Like Berger and Luckman's (1967) concept of institutionalization, institutional work contains an inherent element of historical process within it. This is perhaps most evident in the growing number of empirical applications of institutional work that involve historical methods.

Rojas (2010) adopted a historical case study method to examine the institutional work employed by university administrators such as S. I. Hayakawa in their effort to expand administrative authority at San Francisco State College during the Third World Strike in 1968–69. In justifying the use of archival data and historical methods in the study Rojas (2010) indicates that much of institutional work involves the use of embedded power which is difficult, if not impossible, to capture in contemporary contexts because of the totalizing effects of institutions on human cognition. That is, when power has been properly institutionalized, those subject to it are most likely unaware of its existence. When examined from the distance of time, however, institutionalized power becomes more apparent, particularly when examining periods of historical disruption:

> Barley (1986) observed that institutions can be "totalizing." Actors in organizations take rules for granted and may not be aware of how those rules were created, developed and challenged... Therefore power and institutional work may be poorly documented and difficult to observe. However there are institutional disruptions, moments where practices are disrupted and become publicly questioned. These moments allow researchers to examine the otherwise opaque work of organizations. (Rojas, 2010: 1267)

There are a number of other empirical applications of institutional work that employ historical methods. Hirsch and Bermiss (2009), for example, describe the institutional work involved in decoupling externally imposed financial reforms from day-to-day economic life in the Czech Republic after the collapse of the Soviet Union in 1989. Dacin, Munir, and Tracey (2010) describe how everyday rituals of dining draw from history to maintain institutional norms at Cambridge University. Collectively, these studies demonstrate a powerful new approach for using historically informed methods to focus research attention on the deeper historical and individual processes by which institutions are produced, rather than analyzing the somewhat superficial outcomes of institutions.

A related study that addresses the historical processes by which actors and actorhood are socially constructed is offered by Arndt and Bigelow's historically grounded analysis of hospital administrators. The researchers were interested in understanding the gender specificity of contemporary hospital administrators. Through a historical analysis of the leading journal of hospital administration, these researchers discovered that extant portrayals of "men rather than women as the appropriate practitioners" (Arndt and Bigelow, 2005: 233) mask the fact that hospital administration had originated and developed as a female-dominated occupation. The current gendered structure was not the outcome of objective assessments of the relative merits of male and female administrators but rather was rooted in historical-social changes at the turn of the 20th century. Arndt and Bigelow (2005: 233) conclude that the "rhetorical use of gender created a male image of the generic practitioner and the occupation, while an internal boundary segregated women within the occupation."

Entrepreneurship and Embedded Agency: A recent trend in neo-institutional theory is to examine instances of institutional change, often in counterpoint to early statements of neo-institutionalism which had been framed around trying to understand why organizations were so similar (DiMaggio and Powell, 1983). The point of departure for this research has been DiMaggio's (1988) articulation of the "institutional entrepreneur," an actor with sufficient resources and motivation to generate profound socio-economic change at the level of the organizational field. A mass of subsequent research has been devoted to studying institutional change (see the Special Issue of *Academy of Management Journal* edited by Dacin, Goodstein, and Scott, 2002) much of it focusing on the role of institutional entrepreneurs (see Hardy and Maguire, 2008 for a summary review).

Institutional entrepreneurship has, however, created a logical problem for neo-institutional theory. The problem is often termed the "paradox of embedded agency" and refers to the epistemological contradiction inherent in the question: "If institutions are cognitively totalizing social structures, how can actors ever identify the possibility of change?" Answers to this question invariably derive from outside the core assumptions of institutional theory. Thus, researchers have explained institutional entrepreneurship by suggesting that such entrepreneurs come from the periphery of an organizational field (Leblebici et al., 1991) or because of their size they span multiple fields (Greenwood and Suddaby, 2006) and, in both cases, are therefore not subject to the cognitive influence of institutions.

Critics however decry these explanations as relying on a "hypermuscular" view of institutional entrepreneurs (Powell and Colyvas, 2008; Suddaby, 2010). These explanations rely on a mythical actor that exists outside the sphere of institutional power. Where, they ask, are the *endogenous* explanations of institutional change? How can individuals or groups of individuals ever amass the awareness and power to instigate institutional change?

Again, the application of historically informed methods and theory can help address the problem of embedded agency where it focuses on the interpretations that people bring to situations and how those interpretations become embedded in institutional practices. At its core the paradox of embedded agency asks how it is that some individuals can acquire sufficient reflexivity to understand the institutional environment within which they exist and, as a result of that reflexivity, engage in actions designed to change them.

Historical materialists will recognize the paradox of embeddedness to be similar, if not identical to the issue of false consciousness in Marxist theory. The working class is subject to powerful ideological control by social elites in a capitalist society that obscures their own motives and their capacity for social mobility. Individuals escape false consciousness through education that allows workers to understand that commodities are their own products, rather than that of the elites. False consciousness and embedded agency, thus, are both overcome by actors acquiring a degree of insight or reflexivity into the institutional structures which they participate in reproducing.

Institutional theorists, thus, could gain greater theoretical and empirical traction by employing the techniques and methods of historical sociology in analyzing the agency of elites in social fields. Historians use a variety of methods here including prosopography or "the investigation of the common background characteristics of a group of actors in history by means of a collective study of their lives" (Stone, 1971: 46). The purpose of a prosopography is to identify common patterns in the personal biographies of social groups to help explain ideological or cultural change (Stone, 1971). Broadly speaking, prosopography offers a unique means of analyzing biographical data in an effort to understand how some individuals or groups attain greater institutional reflexivity than others.

CONCLUSION

The purpose of this chapter has been to articulate the need for an enhanced sensitivity to the inherent historical nature of institutions. The very term "institution" connotes a social structure infused with the capacity to endure. Early attempts to theorize institutions were highly sensitive to the important role of history and historical processes. Recent scholarship on institutions, however, has lost this sensitivity to history. Neo-institutionalism, we argue, employs cross-sectional methods that focus on the outcomes of institutional processes and the reified or more objective elements of institutional structures. What is lost in this approach to understanding institutions is an awareness that these outcomes and objective elements of institutions would not exist without the active participation of individuals and groups in practices that reproduce and maintain their objectivity over time (viz. historically).

We propose the term "historical institutionalism" to reinforce our understanding of institutions as the outcome of enduring historical processes. We argue that by adopting a heightened sensitivity to the historical foundation of institutions and the importance of history in maintaining and reproducing institutions, scholars can address a series of epistemological and methodological challenges encountered by contemporary institutional researchers. We illustrate this with a series of empirical studies that are attempting to use historical methods to better understand institutions as historical processes of human interpretation and re-interpretation through which our social world is ordered.

REFERENCES

Alison, P. D. (1984). *Event History Analysis: Regression for Longitudinal Event Data*. Thousand Oaks, CA: Sage.

Arndt, M., and Bigelow, B. (2005). "Professionalizing and Masculinizing a Female Occupation: The Reconceptualization of Hospital Administration," *Administrative Science Quarterly*, 50(2): 233–61.

Arthur, W. B. (1990). "Positive Feedbacks in the Economy," *Scientific American* 262(2): 92–9.

Arthur, W. B. (1994). *Increasing Returns and Path Dependence in the Economy*. Ann Arbor: University of Michigan Press.

Barley, S. R. (1986). "Technology as an Occasion for Structuring: Evidence From Observations of CT Scanners and the Social Order of Radiology Departments," *Administrative Science Quarterly*, 31(1): 78–108.

Barley, S. R., and Tolbert, P. (1997). "Institutionalization and Structuration: Studying the Links Between Institutions and Action," *Organization Studies*, 18(1): 93–117.

Baron, J., Dobbin, F., and Jennings, P. D. (1986). "War and Peace: The Evolution of Modern Personnel Administration in U.S. Industry," *American Journal of Sociology*, 92(2): 350–83.

Baum, J. A. C., and Singh, J. (1994). *Evolutionary Dynamics of Organizations*. New York: Oxford University Press.

Becker, H. S., Geer, B., Hughes, E. C., and Strauss, A. (1961). *Boys in White: Student Culture in Medical School*. Chicago: University of Chicago Press.

Bendix, R. (1956). *Work and Authority in Industry*. Berkeley, CA: University of California Press.

Bennett, A., and Elman, C. (2006). "Qualitative Research: Recent Developments in Case Study Methods," *Annual Review of Political Science*, 9: 455–76.

Berger, P., and Luckman, T. (1967). *The Social Construction of Reality*. New York: Anchor.

Bloch, M. (1953). *The Historian's Craft*. Toronto: Random House.

Booth, C., and Rowlinson, M. (2006). "Management and Organizational History: Prospects," *Management & Organizational History*, 1(1): 5–30.

Boxenbaum, E., and Jonsson, S. (2008). "Isomorphism, Diffusion and Decoupling." In R. Greenwood, R. Suddaby, C. Oliver, and K. Sahlin-Anderson (eds.), *Handbook of Organizational Institutionalism*: 78–98. New York: Sage.

Bryman, A., Bell, E., Mills, A. J., and Yue, A. R. (2011). *Business Research Methods. First Canadian Edition.* Toronto: Oxford University Press.

Burguiere, A. (2009). *The Annales School: An Intellectual History.* Translated by A. M. Todd. Ithaca, NY: Cornell University Press.

Burns, L. R., and Wholey, D. R. (1993). "Adoption and Abandonment of Matrix Management Programs: Effects of Organizational Characteristics and Interorganizational Networks," *Academy of Management Journal,* 36(1): 106–38.

Carr, D. (1986). "Narrative and the Real World: An Argument for Continuity," *History and Theory,* 25(2): 117–31.

Carr, D. (2008). "Narrative Explanation and its Malcontents," *History and Theory,* 47(1): 19–30.

Collingwood, R. G. (1999). *The Principles of History: And Other Writings on the Philosophy of History.* Oxford: Oxford University Press.

Cooper, D. J., Hinings, C. R., Greenwood, R., and Brown, J. (1996). "Sedimentation and Transformation in Organizational Change: The Case of a Canadian Law Firm," *Organization Studies,* 17(4): 623–47.

Crozier, M. (1964). *The Bureaucratic Phenomenon.* Chicago: University of Chicago Press.

Cusumano, M. A., Mylonadis, Y., and Rosenbloom, R. S. (1992). "Strategic Maneuvering and Mass-Market Dynamics: The Triumph of VHS over Beta," *Business History Review,* 66(1): 51–94.

Czarniawska, B., and Sevón, G. (1996). *Translating Organizational Change.* Berlin: Walter de Gruyter.

Dacin, M. T., Goodstein, J., and Scott, W. R. (2002). "Institutional Theory and Institutional Change," *Academy of Management Journal,* 45(1): 45–57.

Dacin, M. T., Munir, K. and Tracey, P. (2010). "Formal Dining at Cambridge Colleges: Linking Ritual Performance and Institutional Maintenance," *Academy of Management Journal,* 53(6): 1393–418.

Davis, G. F. (1991). "Agents Without Principles? The Spread of the Poison Pill Through the Intercorporate Network," *Administrative Science Quarterly,* 36(4): 583–613.

Dewey, J. (1938). *Logic: The Theory of Inquiry.* New York: Holt.

DiMaggio, P. J. (1988). "Interest and Agency in Institutional Theory." In L. Zucker (ed.), *Institutional Patterns and Culture,* Cambridge: Ballinger Publishing: 3–22.

DiMaggio, P. J. (1997). "Culture and Cognition," *Annual Review of Sociology,* 23: 263–87.

DiMaggio, P. J., and Powell, W. W. (1983). "The Iron Cage Revisited: Institutional Isomorphism and Collective Rationality in Organizational Fields," *American Sociological Review,* 48(2): 147–60.

Djelic, M. L. (2007). "Sociological Studies of Diffusion: Is History Relevant?" Uppsala Lectures in Business 2007—Lecture II, presented at Uppsala University, Thursday, September 27, 2007.

Dobbin, F. (1994). *Forging Industrial Policy: The United States, Britain, and France in the Railway Age.* New York: Cambridge University Press.

Dobbin, F. (2009). *Inventing Equal Opportunity.* Princeton: Princeton University Press.

Donaldson, L. (1995). *American Anti-Management Theories of Organization: A Critique of Paradigm Proliferation.* Cambridge: Cambridge University Press.

Durepos, G., Mills, A. J., and Weatherbee, T. G. (2012). "Theorizing the Past: Realism, Relativism, Relationalism & the Reassembly of Weber," *Management & Organizational History*, 7(3): 267–81.

Eisenstadt, S. N. (1964). "Social Change, Differentiation and Evolution," *American Sociological Review*, 29(3): 375–86.

Foucault, M. (1965). *Madness and Civilization: A History of Insanity in the Age of Reason*. New York: Pantheon.

Foucault, M. (1970). *The Order of Things*. New York: Pantheon.

Foucault, M. (1972). *Archaeology of Knowledge*. New York: Pantheon.

Geertz, C. (1973). *The Interpretation of Cultures: Selected Essays*. New York: Basic.

Giddens, Anthony (1984). *The Constitution of Society: Outline of the Theory of Structuration*. Cambridge: Cambridge University Press.

Gouldner, A. W. (1956). *Patterns of Industrial Bureaucracy*. New York: Free Press.

Greenwood, R., and Suddaby, R. (2006). "Institutional Entrepreneurship in Mature Fields: The Big Five Accounting Firms," *Academy of Management Journal*, 49(1): 27–48.

Greenwood, R., Oliver, C., Sahlin, K., and Suddaby, R. (2008). "Introduction." In R. Greenwood, C. Oliver, K. Sahlin, and R. Suddaby (eds.), *The Sage Handbook of Organizational Institutionalism*. London: Sage.

Greenwood, R., Suddaby, R., and Hinings, C. R. (2002). "Theorizing Change: The Role of Professional Associations in the Transformation of Institutionalized Fields," *Academy of Management Journal*, 45(1): 58–80.

Greve, H. R. (1995). "Jumping Ship: The Diffusion of Strategic Abandonment," *Administrative Science Quarterly*, 40(3): 444–73.

Hallett, T. (2010). "The Myth Incarnate," *American Sociology Review*, 75(1): 52–74.

Hallett, T., and Ventresca, M. (2006). "Inhabited Institutions: Social Interactions and Organizational Forms in Gouldner's Patterns of Industrial Democracy," *Theory and Society*, 35(2): 213–36.

Hannigan, J. (1995). *Environmental Sociology*. New York: Routledge.

Hardy, C., and Maguire, S. (2008). "Institutional Entrepreneurship." In R. Greenwood, C. Oliver, K. Sahlin, and R. Suddaby (eds.). *The Sage Handbook of Organizational Institutionalism*. London: Sage: 198–217.

Hargadon, A. B., and Douglas, Y. (2001). "When Innovations Meet Institutions: Edison and the Design of the Electric Light," *Administrative Science Quarterly*, 46(3): 476–501.

Haveman, H. (1993a). "Follow the Leader: Mimetic Isomorphism and Entry into New Markets," *Administrative Science Quarterly*, 38(4): 593–627.

Haveman, H. (1993b). "Organizational Size and Change: 'Diversification in the Savings and Loan Industry After Deregulation,'" *Administrative Science Quarterly*, 38(1): 20–50.

Hirsch, P., and Bermiss, S. (2009). "Institutional Dirty Work: Preserving Institutions Through Decoupling." In T. B. Lawrence, R. Suddaby, and B. Leca (eds.), *Institutional Work: Actors and Agency in Institutional Studies of Organization*, Cambridge: Cambridge University Press: 262–83.

Hoffman, A. (1999). "Institutional Evolution and Change: Environmentalism and the US Chemical Industry," *Academy of Management Journal*, 42(4): 351–71.

Holm, P. (1995). "The Dynamics of Institutionalization: Transformation Processes in Norwegian Fisheries," *Administrative Science Quarterly*, 40(3): 398–422.

Hwang, H., and Colyvas, J. A. (2011). "Problematizing Actors and Institutions in Institutional Work," *Journal of Management Inquiry*, 20(1): 62–6.

Khurana, R. (2007). *From Higher Aims to Hired Hands: The Social Transformation of American Business Schools and the Unfulfilled Promise of Management as a Profession.* Princeton: Princeton University Press.

Kieser, A. (1994). "Why Organization Theory Needs Historical Analyses—And How This Should Be Performed," *Organization Science*, 5(4): 608–20.

Kraatz, M. S., and Zajac, E. J. (1996). "Exploring the Limits of New Institutionalism: The Causes and Consequences of Illegitimate Organizational Change," *American Sociological Review*, 61(5): 812–36.

Krippendorf, K. (2004). *Content Analysis: An Introduction to its Methodology.* Thousand Oaks, CA: Sage.

Lawrence, T. B., and Suddaby, R. (2006). "Institutions and Institutional Work." In S. Clegg, C. Hardy, and T. B. Lawrence (eds.), *Sage Handbook of Organization Studies*, London: Sage.

Lawrence, T. B., Suddaby, R., and Leca, B. (eds.) (2009). "Institutional Work: Actors and Agency in Institutional Studies of Organizations." Cambridge: Cambridge University Press.

Leblebici, H., Salancik, G. R., Copay, A., and King, T. (1991). "Institutional Change and the Transformation of Interorganizational Fields: An Organizational History of the U.S. Radio Broadcasting Industry," *Administrative Science Quarterly*, 36(3): 333–63.

Lee, K., and Pennings, J. (2002). "Mimicry and the Market: Adoption of a New Organizational Form," *Academy of Management Journal*, 45(1): 144–62.

Levitt, J. G., and March, J. (1988). "Organizational Learning," *Annual Review of Sociology*, 14: 319–40.

Liebowitz, S. J., and Margolis, S. E. (1990). "The Fable of the Keys," *Journal of Law and Economics*, 33(1): 1–25.

Liebowitz, S. J., and Margolis, S. E. (1995). "Path Dependence, Lock-In, and History," *Journal of Law, Economics, and Organization*, 11(1): 204–26.

Lipset, S., Trow, M., and Coleman, J. (1956). *Union Democracy: The Internal Democracy of the International Typographical Union.* Glencoe: Free Press.

Lowenthal, D. (1985). *The Past Is a Foreign Country.* Cambridge: Cambridge University Press.

Maguire, S., and Hardy, C. (2009). "Discourse and Deinstitutionalization: The Decline of DDT," *Academy of Management Journal*, 52(1): 148–78.

Meyer, J. W., and Jepperson, R. L. (2000). "The 'Actors' of Modern Society: The Cultural Construction of Social Agency," *Sociological Theory*, 18(1): 100–20.

Meyer, J. W., and Rowan, B. (1977). Institutionalized Organizations: Formal Structure as Myth and Ceremony. *The American Journal of Sociology*, 83(2): 340–63.

Michels, R. (1949). *Political Parties: A Sociological Study of the Oligarchical Tendencies of Modern Democracy.* Illinois: The Free Press.

Mintzberg, H., Brunet, J. P., and Waters, J. A. (1986). "Does Planning Impede Strategic Thinking? Tracking the Strategies of Air Canada from 1937 to 1976," *Advances in Strategic Management*, 4: 3–41.

Powell, W. W., and Colyvas, J. A. (2008). "Microfoundations of Institutional Theory." In R. Greenwood, C. Oliver, K. Sahlin, and R. Suddaby (eds.), *The Sage Handbook of Organizational Institutionalism*. Thousand Oaks, CA: Sage: 276–98.

Puffert, D. J. (2000). "The Standardization of Track Gauge on North American Railways, 1830–1890," *Journal of Economic History*, 60(4): 933–60.

Puffert, D. J. (2002). "Path Dependence in Spatial Networks: The Standardization of Railway Track Gauge," *Explorations in Economic History*, 39(3): 282–314.

Rojas, F. (2010). "Power Through Institutional Work: Building Academic Authority in the 1968 Third World Strike," *Academy of Management Journal*, 53(6): 1263–80.

Sahlin, K., and Wedlin, L. (2008). "Circulating Ideas: Imitation, Translation and Editing." In R. Greenwood, C. Oliver, K. Sahlin-Andersson, and R. Suddaby (eds.), *The Handbook of Organizational Institutionalism*, Thousand Oaks, CA: Sage: 218–42.

Sahlin-Andersson, K. (1996). "Imitating by Editing Success. The Construction of Organizational Fields and Identities." In B. Czarniawska and G. Sevón (eds.), *Translating Organizational Change*. Berlin: De Gruyter: 69–92.

Schneiberg, M. (2007). "What's on the Path? Path Dependence, Organizational Diversity and the Problem of Institutional Change in the U.S. Economy, 1900–1950," *Socio-Economic Review*, 5(1): 47–80.

Scott, R. W. (2008). *Institutions and Organizations: Ideas and Interests*. Thousand Oaks, CA: Sage.

Selznick, P. (1949). *TVA and the Grassroots: A Study in the Sociology of Formal Organization*. Berkeley, CA: University of California Press.

Selznick, P. (1957). *Leadership in Administration: A Sociological Interpretation*. Evanston, IL: Harper & Row.

Selznick, P. (1996). "Institutionalism 'Old' and 'New.'" *Administrative Science Quarterly*, 41: 270–7.

Sewell, W. H. (2005). *Logics of History*. Chicago: University of Chicago Press.

Stinchcombe, Arthur L. (1965). "Social Structure and Organizations." In J. March (ed.) *Handbook of Organizations*. New York: Rand McNalley: 142–93.

Stone, L. (1971). "Prosopography," *Daedalus* 100(1): 46–79.

Strang, D., and Meyer, J. W. (1993). "Institutional Conditions for Diffusion," *Theory and Society*, 22(4): 487–511.

Suddaby, R. (2010). "Challenges for Institutional Theory," *Journal of Management Inquiry*, 19(1): 14–20.

Suddaby, R., and Greenwood, R. (2005). "Rhetorical Strategies of Legitimacy," *Administrative Science Quarterly*, 50(1): 35–67.

Suddaby, R., Foster, W. M., and Quinn-Trank, C. (2010). "Rhetorical History as a Source of Competitive Advantage." In J. Baum and J. Lampel (eds.), *Advances in Strategic Management: The Globalization of Strategy Research*, Vol. 27. Bingley, UK: Emerald Group Publishing Limited: 147–73.

Thelen, K. (1999). "Historical Institutionalism in Comparative Politics," *Annual Review of Political Science*, 2: 369–404.

Tolbert, P. S., and Zucker, L. G. (1983). "Institutional Sources of Change in the Formal Structure of Organizations: The Diffusion of Civil Service Reform, 1880–1935," *Administrative Science Quarterly*, 28(1): 22–39.

Tsoukas H., and Chia, R. (2002). "On Organizational Becoming: Rethinking Organizational Change," *Organization Science*, 13(5): 567–82.

Veblen, T. (1919). *The Place of Science in Modern Civilization and Other Essays.* New York: P. W. Hubsch.

Weick, K. E. (1979). *The Social Psychology of Organizing.* Reading, MA: Addison-Wesley.

White, H. (1973). *Metahistory: The Historical Imagination in Nineteenth-Century Europe*, Baltimore, MD: Johns Hopkins University Press.

5

History and Evolutionary Theory

Stephen Lippmann and Howard E. Aldrich

The historical turn in organization studies has brought with it increased attention to context, contingency, and the importance of time and place. For all scholars of organizations, this comes as welcome news. Organizations, as fundamentally social units, have a reciprocal relationship with their socio-historical environments. Just as organizations shape and give meaning to social life, they are themselves shaped by the worlds they inhabit. Given the complexity of organizations and their environments, it is likely that no two organizations have identical experiences, even in the same historical era or during the same event. A new wave of research focusing on the historical dynamics within and external to organizations highlights these nuances.

However, the growth of historical research on organizations seems somewhat disconnected from the trajectory of mainstream organizational scholarship. If anything, the new historical literature may well be developing on a path parallel and unconnected to more traditional, deductive research on organizations and organizational dynamics. Much of this divergence can be traced (as has been done skillfully in other chapters in this volume) to the continuing tension between narrative/interpretive historical approaches and the deductive/structural approaches that came to the fore not only in organization studies but also in the other social and management sciences in the mid-20th century. Indeed, over the past decade, several commentaries in the *Academy of Management Journal* have attempted to persuade a seemingly skeptical readership about the value of the narrative/interpretive qualitative analysis of "cases." The commentators tried to assuage fears that historical scholarship poses a threat to the mainstream, as they treated case studies of the sort conducted by historically minded organizational scholars as a preliminary step to "real" theory building and testing (Eisenhardt and Graebner, 2007; Siggelkow, 2007). Though they are not identical, historical research on organizations shares with qualitative research an attention to narrative and interpretive inquiry. In this regard, the new historical research, along with other narrative/interpretive approaches such as ethnography and grounded theory, risks becoming isolated from other research on organizations.

When placed in the context of the history of social sciences, the divergence between these approaches makes sense. Theories of the middle-range and the deductive/structural, data-driven approaches to theory testing that characterized mid-20th-century social science attempted to closely resemble the natural sciences and had little use for highly contextualized, case-based approaches that focused on process tracing and interpretive narratives. A similar trend away from context has more recently characterized mainstream management science (Aldrich, 2009). We fear that these parallel but separate trajectories are working against the best interests of organizational scholars and the research on organizational dynamics that they produce.

Although several other chapters in this volume privilege an interpretive/ narrative approach over what they label "modernist" or "constructivist" approaches, we believe that points of complementarity and commonality exist. More communication between proponents of the several approaches, coupled with more attention to alternative approaches in individual research agendas, could produce more perceptive and powerful findings. Unfortunately, given the current state of affairs, this intermingling seems problematic. Too frequently, debates about the merits of what we would call "deductive/structural" versus "narrative/interpretive" historical approaches have been framed in all or nothing terms, and a true integration of the approaches has seemed impossible (Hall, 1992; Burke, 2004).

In this chapter, we contend that a potential solution to this problem can be found in the framework provided by evolutionary theory. In particular, recent developments in evolutionary theory in the social sciences provide a robust set of mechanisms through which we can partially reconcile the divergent approaches of narrative/interpretive and deductive/structuralist scholars, while incorporating the conceptual and empirical strengths of both. A focus on *variation* within and among organizations and on mechanisms of *selection* and *retention*, which are the hallmarks of the evolutionary approach, forces scholars to consider both uniqueness (i.e., the nature of meaningful variations in a particular organizational population, given a specific research question) and context (i.e., selection mechanisms exogenous to organizations, including environmental shocks and historical events), while at the same time understanding the conditions under which these vital and, we believe, universal organizational processes occur.

The evolutionary approach encompasses many of the best features of historical research on organizations. Evolutionary theory in organizational analysis is a set of heuristic propositions about how entities develop through time (Aldrich, 1979; Langton, 1984). It uses and adapts Darwinian theories of natural selection, in combination with probability and complexity theories, resulting in a meta-theoretical framework that explains how organizational emergence, change, and reproduction occur through the interaction of blind and intentional variations with environmental selection forces (Aldrich and Martinez, forthcoming). Recent developments in evolutionary theory have emphasized two things. First, they have focused on the multi-level nature of evolutionary processes between groups within organizations, across organizations, and across populations and communities. Second, they have demonstrated the interdependence of selection and adaptation processes. When organizational actors adapt to their environments by actively choosing particular variations, they not only select them into their own organizations but also introduce new selection forces into organizational populations through a variety of learning and isomorphic processes (Argote and Miron-Spektor, 2011).

Although the approach has been around for some time (Haldane, 1932; Parsons, 1964), evolutionary perspectives on organizations have emerged with renewed vigor in recent decades (Nelson and Winter, 1982; Nelson, 1994; Aldrich and Ruef, 2006). Evolutionary theory is particularly useful for explaining how particular kinds of organizations come to exist in specific historical and environmental circumstances. At any given time, a tremendous amount of variation is reflected in the diverse organizations that comprise populations and communities. When we examine such diversity in dynamic terms—as it unfolds over time and in space—those meaningful variations among and within organizations provide the raw material for processes of selection.

The evolutionary approach is useful not only because it focuses attention on these variations, but also because of its focus on selection forces, which necessarily draws attention to environments, events, and contexts. Evolutionary theory examines the dynamic interaction of variations within and between organizations and selection mechanisms that retain or reject particular variations. As we argue later, such an approach combines the best aspects of historical studies—a focus on temporality, context, and the role of events in the structuring and development of social life, carried out with sensitivity to the *meaning* of events in their contexts—with a generalizable framework from which hypotheses can be generated and tested, a hallmark of more structurally oriented approaches.

We argue that evolutionary theory provides a conceptual framework to allow meaningful engagements between the generalization-oriented social scientific approach to history and the context-centered narrative humanistic approach. We explain why an integration of both approaches using the "bridge" of evolutionary theory will permit scholars on both sides to benefit from the achievements each approach has contributed to scholarship. We proceed by introducing four major differences in the "deductive/structural" versus "narrative/interpretive" approaches, including relative emphases on context, the generalizability of research results, the role of events in explanations, and the value of unique phenomena. After our discussion of each difference, we offer evolutionary concepts and examples that can bridge the gaps between the approaches.

POINTS OF STRENGTH AND POINTS OF DIVERGENCE

Methodological, practical, and even paradigmatic differences between the deductive/structural and narrative/interpretive approaches to studying organizations have made reconciliation difficult. Aldrich (2009) provided one perspective on the divide by describing the two approaches as the "all unique" approach that focuses on a particular context, as in narrative-based historical studies of organizations, versus the "all alike" approach driven by deduction, data, and generalization, and favored by structuralists. The "all unique" approach is one of "extreme contextualization," in which results are rarely generalized to other settings. While studies that adopt this approach appear infrequently in top organization studies journals, this approach might apply to narrative/interpretive and case studies at their most extreme. At the other end of the continuum are those studies that adopt the "all alike" approach, which Aldrich (2009: 23) referred to as one of "extreme decontextualization." These studies are close to the deductive/structural ideal, and at the extreme make (or perhaps simply imply) claims about the generalizability of their findings across infinite time and space. While few such truly general processes likely exist, these studies are more likely to appear in the top management and social science journals than their "all unique" counterparts.

These different approaches are apparent in a variety of disciplines and research methodologies, and the deductive/structural and narrative/interpretive approaches to organizations discussed in this volume are exemplars. According to many historians, despite advances in interdisciplinary collaborations across the humanities and social sciences in recent decades, we still lack an ongoing dialogue between historians and social scientists, who at root are interested in the same thing: the functioning and development of social life (Hall, 1992; Evans, 1997; Sewell, 2005). Despite this shared interest, however, deep differences remain. Historians begin with a topic of interest and produce a narrative about how a topic unfolds over time, based on extensive research using primary documents and archival sources. Although they often have an implicit theory of temporality, historians tend to construct their explanations as a particular sequencing of events, usually those that punctuate social life or change the course of history (Braudel, 1958; Sewell, 2005). The result, then, is an "all unique" approach that unearths the details of events and interprets the meanings of the processes through which they unfold.

Structuralists, in contrast, tend to gloss over such fine-grained temporal patterns and contextualized events, and instead focus on structure (in a variety of different guises). Such a focus on structure implies permanence, stability, and durability. They also implicitly rank their explanatory mechanisms in terms of their importance, often using tools of statistical inference to do so. While historians may rejoice in the discovery of a new or subtly nuanced explanation for a series of events, or an overlooked occurrence upon which something important depended, structuralists tend to downplay these sorts of things if they seem unique to a particular case. We are left with two approaches that, despite their once common language and common interests, advance their tasks from different perspectives, with different methods, and with different ends in mind (Hall, 1992).

At the most general levels, narrative/interpretive historians, at least implicitly, have theories of temporality and events at their disposal to explain the past, while social scientists focus on more abstract notions of process and structure that (they hope) transcend time and space. In an attempt to distance themselves from the humanities and to emulate the physical sciences, structuralists have largely ignored time, place, and the importance of events in favor of the "all alike" approach. Within this general difference, we identify four specific areas of divergence between the narrative/interpretive and deductive/structural approaches and offer an evolutionary perspective on how these differences, when acknowledged, add value to research and stretch the scope of explanations.

The first is the role that context plays in the research strategies of the two camps. While purely deductive/structural research strives to transcend particular contexts, narrative/interpretive research focuses explicitly on the variety of social, economic, political, and other contexts in which social processes unfold. We argue that evolutionary theory provides a useful middle ground between these two divergent approaches. Second, the findings produced by deductive/structural research should, in their ideal form, be generalizable across contexts. Narrative/interpretist approaches favored by many historical scholars, however, revel in the particular. Evolutionary theory acknowledges that while no two organizations or particular organizational processes are alike, general forces, given a particular set of case conditions, guide organizations and organizational populations over time, allowing us to identify the general mechanisms that operate in specific cases. Third, deductive/structural research, as our label for it suggests, favors a focus on durable structures, while the narrative/interpretive approach focuses on important and pivotal events. While the two are related, deductive/structural approaches tend to ignore events, at least as unique historical occurrences, in favor of more durable social forms. However, if we employ an evolutionary perspective and consider events as a class of selection forces, they can be more fully incorporated into our deductive theories of how organizations operate. Finally, deductive/structural

methodologies typically require and employ large-N approaches in which sufficient variation is necessary to test hypotheses, while narrative/interpretive
approaches assume that virtually all cases are unique, and while they may be
considered examples of certain "classes" of phenomena, their real scholarly
value is in their own unique details. As a meta-theory, the evolutionary perspective allows us to scan and collect a wealth of detailed studies on unique
cases and comb them for similarities and differences, as a more deductive/
structural approach would dictate. For the sake of exposition, we have framed
the issues that differentiate the approaches as dichotomies, but scholars are
arrayed across the spectrum represented by the two central tendencies.

Contextualization

A brief tour of theoretical and methodological treatises produced by deduc-
tive/structuralist and narrative/interpretive scholars highlights a fundamental
difference in their relative emphases on context in their explanatory schemes.
According to Sewell (2005: 10, emphasis in original), historians' deep focus
on temporality "implies that understanding or explaining social practices
requires *historical contextualization* ... Historians tend to explain things not by
subsuming them under a general or 'covering' law, but by relating them to their
context." Deductive/structural approaches to social life, in contrast, not only
avoid highly detailed portraits of contexts, but also see contextual factors as
limits to good theory. In Reynolds' (1971: 12) classic text on social theory construction, he argued that the most desirable feature of scientific knowledge is
its "abstractness (or) independence of time and space" (also see Stinchcombe,
1968, for a discussion of the value of abstraction in social theory).

Over time, however, it has become clear that context does matter for the
ways in which humans, groups, and organizations act and the ways in which
organizational processes unfold. Stinchcombe's (1965) path-breaking essay on
organizational imprinting argued that the contextual conditions at the time of
an organization's founding continue to exert an influence on organizational
structure and outcomes across its life, as shown in the persistence of core
structural features. Moreover, he argued that imprinting characterized entire
populations of organizations, with characteristics of specific industries persist-
ing over decades after coming into existence.

More recent work in economic sociology has also demonstrated the powerful effects historical contexts can have on the life-history of organizations, even
over centuries. Morgan and Prasad's (2009) compelling study of tax policy
development in the US and France, for example, revealed how two important
contextual features of turn-of-the-20th-century France and the US—industrial development and the consolidation of state power—shaped the divergent tax logics that developed in the two countries over the course of the 20th

century. In the US, growing industrialization threatened agrarian interests and raised the suspicions of labor and the public against the power of big business. These groups favored—and ultimately achieved—a more progressive income tax. In France, these interests felt a weaker threat and were thus less vocal in their support of a progressive tax. Also, a more centralized state structure in France made politicians careful not to appear to overstep their boundaries by installing a centralized tax structure. These important economic and political features of the two nations not only influenced the development of different tax policies in the 1910s and 1920s but also created the social and political contexts for the evolution of divergent welfare state policies over the rest of the 20th century. Clearly, in the case of macro-level outcomes, historical context matters greatly.

How can we more fully incorporate context into our theorizing and scholarship on organizations? The evolutionary approach offers powerful tools for accomplishing this task, without risking too narrow a focus on individual cases. Indeed, cases and the contexts in which they exist provide a more thorough understanding of how variation, selection, and retention processes occur. We argue that context should be interpreted broadly, along two key dimensions: time and space. These dimensions are important because the social and economic resources that all organizations need to start, survive, and grow exist in time and space. Attention to variations across time and space helps us to problematize the process of resource acquisition, by allowing us to see how entrepreneurs and organizations struggle with it in different contexts. In addition, time and space are also often proxies for other processes (Aldrich, 2009), including differing cultural norms and values, economic development, and demographic characteristics.

Time can include "clock time," measured in days, weeks, months, or years. Typically, we are limited in our applications of time in the "clock" sense due to constraints on the availability of data (i.e., census records may only be published once a year, or firms' quarterly reports every three months). Indeed, some organizational selection processes, including liabilities of newness and aging, are directly related to the passage of time (Ruef, 2002). However, narrative/interpretive scholars often reject clock time as theoretically meaningless in favor of time as socially constructed, with its conceptualization and interpretation dependent on particular cases or outcomes under investigation. At the most extreme, conceptions of time itself are social constructs, as Thompson (1967) has shown in his study of the necessity of time discipline during the transition to industrial capitalism. In the new system, employers demanded that workers observe "clock time" rather than coming and going as the mood, weather, and circumstances suited them. Subtler examples of the social construction of time in organizational processes also abound, as organizations construct time horizons based on available technology, stakeholder expectations, or the ways in which other "rules of the game" are established. Examples include dot-com firms, which have particular, usually longer-term, time horizons for going public that may change dramatically when venture capitalists get involved (Aldrich, 2001), or corporate time horizons, which may get considerably shorter in response to the demands of institutional investors and activist shareholders (Bushee and Cready, 2001). The evolutionary perspective, rather than emphasizing a rigid conception of time, instead focuses on how selection pressures are patterned by either socially constructed or "clock" time. Whichever conception we incorporate in our studies, it is important to be clear about how we use time in our studies and to justify our particular use of it.

However we define and operationalize time, though, there are methodological implications that must be taken into account in understanding organizational evolution. Most obviously, from a deductive/structural perspective, we need to follow groups, organizations, populations, and communities over time. For some, especially those with access to large-scale funding or those with few time constraints and an eye toward the future, this can be accomplished with survey data and a prospective panel design. The Panel Study of Entrepreneurial Dynamics (Gartner et al., 2004; Ruef, Aldrich, and Carter, 2003) is an example of one such undertaking.

For organizational researchers without the time, resources, or clairvoyance necessary to design a panel survey, historical research using a retrospective design offers an alternative approach. Looking back in time allows us to define time as befits our theoretical purposes (within the usual data and archival constraints) and to trace social units as they have passed through time. Although the past ultimately leads to a particular version of the present, investigating the past through an evolutionary lens allows us to capture the contingency of organizational outcomes in relation to historical-contextual factors. Given sufficient access to archival and secondary sources, narrative/interpretive research, with its focus on the totality and context of individual cases, allows scholars to more fully capture relevant contextual characteristics, and the ways in which organizations changed in response to those contexts, such as in Dobbin's (2011) study of the growth of equal opportunity practices in the US. Moreover, instead of mistakenly assuming that the present emerged smoothly out of the past or took the only "logical" path, a focus on variation and selection can help us to understand how and why, at important points in time, certain features of the social or organizational world made it to the next period, and why others did not.

A focus on time, and on the contingencies associated with it, requires that organizational scholars be attentive to feedback loops. We prefer the term "feedback loop" to the more common concept of "path dependence," which in our view implies too linear a concept of time and evolution, a false notion of the permanence of structures and processes associated with "lock-in," as well as deviation from an "optimal" path that was not pursued (also see

Steinmetz, 2005; Garud et al., 2010). Feedback loops, on the other hand, allow for unintended consequences, the contingencies of outcomes and processes associated with particular events, and uneven development of organizations and organizational populations. In addition, feedback loops can take a variety of functional forms, whereas path dependence is traditionally associated with formal codification in rules, regulations, or policies. The evolutionary perspective holds that selection and retention can occur on parallel tracks, and can be simultaneous and even messy processes. The variations that are selected into accepted practices during one era can become the institutionalized norms and practices against which future variations are judged, and then themselves become forces of selection. Recently in the financial services industry, for example, the institutionalization of innovative financial products (sub-prime mortgage securities offered by financial institutions) during a housing boom created new industry standards by which future risks were evaluated (Pozner et al., 2010)

In another example, in her study of the Paris Opera over a much longer period of time than in the financial services sector study, Johnson (2007: 99) demonstrated not only "how the original relationship between an organization and its founding (i.e., historical) context is produced," but how the embeddedness of this founding in a particular context continued to reassert itself across an organization's life, which in this case has lasted for centuries. To appeal to King Louis XIV, Opera founder Pierre Perrin proposed that the Paris Opera be established as a Royal Academy, an institution sponsored by the King and restricted to members only. However, after the King endorsed his proposal, he expanded the Opera's mission to include one of public enlightenment and uplift. Therefore, the Paris Opera represented a hybrid form, somewhere between the exclusive Royal Academy and a commercial entertainment organization. While Johnson's chief contribution was in demonstrating how important features of the historical context become imprinted into new organizations at the time of their founding, she also identified several mechanisms through which key aspects of an organization's initial structure may stay with the organization as it passes through changing contexts.

By incorporating time, both clock-based and socially constructed, into our research, we can better understand the important evolutionary processes through which ultimately flawed organizational forms (banks that created sub-prime mortgage securities) or unique organizational forms (the Paris Opera's hybrid form) come into being. From an evolutionary perspective, time matters critically for organizations because organizations and organizational populations are dynamic entities and are liable to change from one period to the next. As organizations pass through time, they change in response to selection forces that alter their activities, structures, and viability. Change may occur either because existing organizations do not survive, perhaps because they are replaced by organizations more suited to the new context, or because organizations adapt and are transformed to fit the new context. Our research must reflect these dynamic processes by following organizations and populations across time, with an eye towards environmental selection forces and issues of organizational adaptation and fitness that arise in response to them (for a discussion of methodological approaches beyond the scope of this chapter, see Woodside, 2010).

Space is another key context for understanding organizations and their evolution. Space is typically conceptualized as "differences due to location in particular geographic units, such as cities, regions, and nation states" (Aldrich, 2009: 24). It can also be conceptualized in an ecological manner, in terms of a collection of available resources upon which an organization may draw, or through identifying the potential collaborators or competitors in an organization's environment (Hannan, Carroll, and Pólos, 2003). However we measure space, it is important to keep it in the forefront of our analysis, because, as Abbott (1997: 1152) reminded us, "every social fact is situated, surrounded by other contextual facts and brought into being by a process relating it to past contexts." Too often, the push towards deductive, empirical approaches to organizations ignores this fundamental idea. We think the best way to capture the influence of space on organizational dynamics is to study organizations comparatively (Aldrich, 2009). Although there have been several shortcomings of comparative studies, which we discuss shortly, comparative research, particularly from an evolutionary perspective, allows us to see how space, and the variations in norms, laws, institutional structures, and other resources in a given geographical area affect organizational evolution.

Evolutionary theory challenges us to think clearly about space as the context within which organizational variations arise, selection processes operate, and some variations persist whereas others do not. For example, Hannan and Freeman (1986) argued that the balance between isolating and blending forces affects the extent to which new organizational populations arise and grow. Contexts that buffer variations from harsh selection forces give new kinds of social entities opportunities to proliferate and perhaps eventually diffuse. By contrast, more open and easily penetrated contexts may subject new social entities to such withering selection pressures that few survive. Thinking about space emphasizes the issue of the scale on which change occurs, as noted by Aldrich and Ruef (2006) in their nested analytic hierarchy of groups, organizations, communities, and societies.

A recent study of newspaper acquisitions accomplished this comparative task of highlighting the significance of context. Muehlfeld, Sahib, and Van Witteloostuijn (2012) conceptualized context in a variety of ways, but one of them is whether a newspaper acquisition took place within an acquirer's home country or outside of it. By doing so, they are able to examine how language and cultural contexts facilitate newspaper mergers. Those papers which targeted firms outside their home country, however, took a more deliberate approach to learning, which may lead to higher costs, but an expanded market for acquisitions. Local cultural and political contexts matter deeply in the newspaper industry, and comparing merger activity across these contexts demonstrates how space matters for organizational outcomes.

The evolutionary perspective provides the tools to theorize explicitly about how context matters for organizational development and change. Specifically, it focuses on two general elements of context—time and space—and focuses our attention toward the ways in which variations exist (or fail to exist) across meaningful spatial contexts, and how and why particular variations exist (or fail to exist) from one period to another. Rather than simply using these contextual features as proxies for understanding process, these contextual features may themselves be the reasons for the ways in which particular organizations and populations evolve. Thorough and meaningful definitions of contextual factors, typical in historical studies, ultimately identify what it is about them that is important for organizational evolution.

Generalizability

Another fundamental difference between the approaches concerns the degree to which research findings of individual studies can be generalized across contexts. Authors of deductive/structural studies tend to generalize from their results, whereas narrative/interpretive scholars tend not to generalize. As the social sciences moved towards the deductive/structural model in the mid-20th century, the presumed generalizability of findings became a hallmark of good social science research. Most historians, by contrast, clearly rejected this move towards generalizability, because in their eyes such cross-case applications ignored context, contingency, and case-specific details (Evans, 1997). However, any pragmatic research agenda searching for valid explanations must somehow consider both perspectives. Indeed, historical and other empirical details will always remain of immense importance and thus we cannot expect to obtain a single explanatory theory of everything. However, as the triumph of evolutionary theory in the life sciences demonstrates, it is possible to derive a powerful over-arching theoretical framework in which theorists can develop auxiliary, domain-specific explanations. Evolutionary theory has the power to draw on the contextual strengths of narrative/interpretive perspectives while providing a deductive/structural general framework for understanding even the most idiosyncratic events.

Several recent examples of narrative/interpretive organizational research demonstrate how evolutionary thinking provides a framework to make sense of case dynamics, and how the specific case-level contexts, events, and processes can help refine evolutionary theory. In their study of the Clyde River shipbuilding industry in Scotland, Ingram and Lifschitz (2006) demonstrated how before the rise of corporate governance, family and friendship ties between family-owned shipbuilding companies helped those firms survive. However, when the corporate form rose to prominence, the benefit of such ties was lost, and family firms eventually succumbed to their corporate competitors. Through the lens of evolutionary theory, we see how certain economic environments—in this case, one dominated by family-owned firms—favored highly embedded firms, while subsequent environments—a highly rational and rule-bound corporate economy—selected against those same firms. In addition, without a singular focus on this highly networked and highly localized industry as it unfolded over a long period of time (almost 300 years), the contextual dynamics that matter for evolution would have been lost. Although the specifics of this case study are difficult to generalize, the findings are useful because they point to a more general principle, which is the contingent nature of social ties between firm owners. A focus on general principles drawn from specific cases makes evolutionary theory a powerful meta-theory for organizing and making sense of the results of accumulated case studies common in narrative/interpretive historical studies.

Shifting the focus from an industry to a single firm, Joseph and Ocasio (2012) examined how changes in the organizational architecture of General Electric between 1951 and 2001 created different contexts for processes by which managers focused their attention. Although the authors did not explicitly use evolutionary language, it is clear that over time, different environments created selection mechanisms that favored different kinds of managerial attention processes. In short, they found that over a fifty-year period, as new CEOs introduced new organizational architectures that increasingly introduced mechanisms of cross-coordination, managerial attention at the division level became easier to adapt to corporate priorities. A focus on these evolutionary processes can help us extrapolate the lessons provided by General Electric, which is unique in many ways, to other organizational contexts.

In another example, Langton (1984) applied the evolutionary perspective to the case of the Wedgewood Pottery company to explain arguably one of the most central puzzles of organizational theory over the past 125 years—the emergence of bureaucracy. His evolutionary analysis made it clear how bureaucracy emerged in a firm not only through the rational calculations of top managers, but also through variations that emerged out of workmen drinking on the job and more generally, being indifferent to inefficiencies in their job performance. Josiah Wedgewood set out to enact a workplace structure that constrained workers to rationalized and more efficient behaviors. Demand for earthenware by tea and coffee drinkers (among other factors) then created a selection environment that favored Wedgewood's more efficient and productive processes while selecting out less productive traditional manufactures.

The evolutionary approach's focus on variation, selection, and retention requires a focus on case-specific details. As stand-alone concepts, these mechanisms lack specificity. Most simply, explanations that stop at these processes may tell us *how* something happens or changes, but not *why* social entities evolve in the ways that they do. Specifically, evolutionary theories of social dynamics often frame their explanations at a very high level of abstraction. The earliest evolutionary perspectives in social science, including Mandeville (1724) and Smith (1776), described the incremental processes that led to the development of technology and the division of labor, but they did not explain the micro-level social, political, and economic processes that led to those outcomes (Nelson, 2007). More recently, in an effort to fully incorporate the Darwinian processes of replication and retention into organizational evolution, Hodgson and Knudson (2004) have applied the variation/selection/retention view to the evolution of organizational practices. In their view, organizational practices are behavioral dispositions that are subject to the selection forces of managerial decision making. In these evolutionary formulations, as in other approaches that take a highly deductive/structural point of view, contextual details appear to matter little (for a critique see Buenstorf, 2007).

However, as a general scheme for organizing our explanations of organizational development through time, evolutionary processes of variation, selection, and retention become powerful tools for understanding the dynamics of organizational and social structures in more static models, as well as change in more dynamic ones. While "Darwin's principles of evolution do not themselves provide... a complete theory of everything... these principles are a kind of 'meta-theory' or an overarching theoretical framework wherein theorists place particular explanations" (Aldrich et al., 2008: 585). In the case of narrative/interpretive studies of organizations, these particular explanations are derived heavily from historical contexts and processes. Evolutionary theory's focus on selection, for example, offers a broad definition of this process, and narrative/interpretive case studies can help us to create meaningful categories of selection processes to further refine the concept as it applies to organizations (Hodgson and Knudson, 2006).

Eventfulness

One of the major mechanisms employed in narrative/interpretive explanations of change is the "event," seen not as a "data point" but as a historical conjuncture laden with meaning that must be deconstructed. For historians, significant happenings punctuate and define social life, and are the external stimuli to which actors must respond. In doing so, the course of history often changes. Some singular events, such as the commercialization of the internet, can give meaning to particular historical time, while others, like the end of the Civil War in the American South, can usher in new historical eras, with new social structures, new cultural landscapes, and new forms of economic organization (see Ruef, 2004). However, deductive/structural analysis discounts or glosses over singular events precisely because they are unique and often unpredictable, which is antithetical to the hypo-deductive models that have come to dominate the social sciences.

Much of the problem for both groups is that both approaches lack a coherent and robust theory of events. Sewell (2005) offered one theory of events that focused on the relationships between structures and events, rather than their opposition. Sewell argued that events only have meaning if we also understand structures. Events are meaningful precisely because they violate the stability provided by structures. Only with an understanding of structures and the ways in which they regulate and stabilize social life can we see how events occur and why they matter. In addition, retrospective explanations of structural transformations—a major task of both historians and historically minded social scientists—can reveal the important role that events play in this process.

While Sewell's approach is useful for understanding the role that events play in conceptual terms, we believe that an evolutionary perspective allows for a fuller incorporation of events, and a framework for theorizing about how events matter for organizations. In particular, evolutionary models that focus on age, period, and cohort effects of events on organizations and organizational populations can allow us to theorize about the interaction of organizations, on the one hand, and their complex, contingent, and often unique environments on the other (see Aldrich and Ruef, 2006: chapter 8). We pay primary attention to period effects—or the ways in which historical events affect all organizations in a given time—and cohort effects—the ways in which organizations of different ages experience historical events differently, for a variety of reasons. From an evolutionary perspective, events operate as a selection force on organizations that are affected by them.

According to Aldrich and Ruef (2006: 169), four classes of period effects have been examined in organizational scholarship: "(1) political events and change in regimes; (2) legal and regulatory policy changes; (3) shifts in societal norms and values; and (4) changes in resource availability not otherwise due to any of the previous three changes." The identification of periods provides a useful way to conceptualize events and understand how those events affected all organizations that shared common features (e.g., Leblebici et al., 1991; Li and Walder, 2001). Periods are not given a priori but rather are identified by knowledgeable analysts who use their skills to interpret where researchers should place boundaries to mark off periods, a clear example of the distinction between simple "clock time" and socially-constructed time we mentioned earlier.

Cohort effects, by contrast, depend on when an event occurs in the life of an organization. Some historical events affect all organizations equally, but closer analysis of many events reveals that organizations of different ages, or those founded under different conditions, experience historical events differently.

Note here that, in keeping with the narrative/interpretive approach, "events" are classified in terms of their meanings and significance for the organizations involved, rather than being given a priori. In general terms, for example, younger organizations, which lack institutionalized routines and procedures, may be able to adapt more quickly to disruptive environmental change (Ranger-Moore, 1997). For example, research on the effect of the economic downturn at the start of the 21st century on organizational failure rates indicates that independent organizations from earlier cohorts experienced relatively higher mortality rates, possibly owing to their inertia (Bradley et al., 2011). Cohorts also matter within organizations. Bercovitz and Feldman (2008) found that members of academic departments from older cohorts were less likely to embrace an orientation to technology transfer programs largely because of the influence of the equally reluctant peers who comprised their cohort. It is clear, then, that a focus on cohort effects turns our attention to the importance of events, but also to the features of organizations and their structures that are important for understanding how particular events affect certain kinds of organizations and organizational outcomes, and in what ways.

An evolutionary approach that focuses on how organizations in a given time period or from the same cohort experience particular events can help deductive/structural accounts of organizational processes take events seriously and understand their effects on organizational outcomes. Events that alter the social, economic, political, or cultural arrangements of a given setting can, from an evolutionary perspective, be viewed as selection forces and incorporated into theoretical frameworks as such. Although things like Prohibition, the French Revolution, or dot-com collapse only occurred once, these events can be instructive for our organizational theories if we focus on the ways in which they change environments, and the manner in which they act as selection forces for organizations, and the ways in which organizations adapt, or fail to adapt, to them.

Uniqueness

A major criticism of narrative/interpretive studies of social phenomena, from a deductive/structural point of view, is that they are interested in particular events, processes, or outcomes. Their findings, as historians readily admit, cannot be generalized easily to other times, places, cases, or contexts. Although this is the nature of the discipline, it is also due to the nature of narrative/interpretive methods. Deductive/structural researchers, by contrast, use a variety of sampling and data collection techniques that capture variations in social behaviors and outcomes, and utilize methods that allow them to test causal hypotheses about regular patterns that exist (they assume) in a variety of social contexts.

Recently, there have been attempts—in sociology, most notably—to bridge the gap between narrative/interpretive and deductive/structural studies. The rise of "comparative-historical" sociology sought to blend the historians' appreciation for process and events with social scientists' ability to capture variation and test hypotheses. Prominent sociologists, including Theda Skocpol and Charles Tilly, carried out major projects on social revolutions, and others have carried the comparative methodological torch in explicitly organizational applications (Perrow, 2002; Dobbin, 1994; King et al., 2009). When historical sociologists choose cases to compare, they do so in hopes of isolating the effects of one condition while others (typically those subsumed by historical time) are essentially held constant. For this reason, the comparative approach of many historical sociologists has been offered as proof of its "scientific" legitimacy, and its variable-based correlational approach begrudgingly accepted by the sociological mainstream (Steinmetz, 2007).

Despite this renewed attention to history, some have objected to the new approaches to history, such as represented in the field of cliometrics, and have accused deductive/structural scholars of trying to force historical processes into a quasi-experimental, deductive approach. An oft-repeated criticism is that historical sociologists, following the precepts of the deductive/structural approach, start from the present by choosing outcomes of interest and then work backwards to identify the relevant collection of social arrangements (read: variables) that explain why something happened when or where it did. Such "teleological temporality," according to Sewell (2005), leaves us with historical models that are fraught with selection bias and misspecifications. In addition to selecting cases on the dependent variable, these studies also assume that their cases represent different values of the same variable (i.e., social class cohesiveness or organizational centralization) when in fact two different cases are rarely different only in degree. By ignoring relevant historical contexts, and trying to isolate the effects of specific variables, ahistorical social science fails to grasp the ways in which context continues to matter throughout the history of a social form and the ways in which historical mechanisms operate over time (Sewell, 2005; Demetriou, 2012).

A second problem with the quasi-experimental approach prominent in historical social science is that "it cuts up the congealed block of historical time into artificially interchangeable units" (Sewell, 2005: 95). When comparative scholars start with particular outcomes, and work backward in search of explanations, they come across what are perceived as root causes. Such a method rests on an assumption of "experimental" temporality, in which causes precede outcomes. However, given the messy, contingent, and external temporalities characterizing history, such an assumption is untenable. When we start by asking about differences in organizations that exist in the current era, and look back in time for causal mechanisms, their histories look neat, tidy, and linear.

However, in reality, the process of organizational emergence is typically quite the opposite (Aldrich and Ruef, 2006; Ruef, 2010).

For example, consider the case of commercial radio broadcasting industry and how an evolutionary approach differs from one based on teleological temporality. Investigators who began with the highly centralized network form of commercial broadcasting that was in place following World War II and then looked backwards might draw conclusions about selection forces based on efficiency, performance, and optimal design (Coase, 1959). By contrast, investigators who began with the activities of pioneering amateurs prior to World War I would come to a different conclusion. Such an event-driven project would identify the people and groups who laid the framework for the commercial industry but were eventually relegated to marginal positions on the airwaves and in the industry, and would offer explanations for industry selection dynamics that focus on power, struggle, and cooptation (Lippmann, 2010).

How can an evolutionary approach to historical research on organizations help us avoid such pitfalls? Evolutionary explanations focus on processes and are event driven (Aldrich, 2001). First, our research should not be driven solely by outcomes of interest, but should also recognize the need to identify event sequences (as determined by historically knowledgeable scholars). Starting with events, and following them and their effects forward to outcomes, helps us avoid the problem of selection bias, and opens our minds to contingency and alternative explanations. In addition, forward-looking research allows us to not only examine what did happen, but what *didn't* happen. This is particularly important in organization studies, where the biggest and most successful exemplars tend to occupy our attention, and we often start with those success stories, and look for explanations of their success without focusing on what happened to those that don't remain (Aldrich, 2001; Kovacs, 2008). When we do so, we tend to ignore the selection forces at work in organizational evolution.

CONCLUSION

Evolutionary theory is a powerful tool for explaining organizational structures, processes, outcomes, and change. This power largely derives from its meta-theoretical approach for integrating findings and orientations from a wide variety of theoretical perspectives (Aldrich and Ruef, 2006). In this chapter, we have argued that an evolutionary framework is also a potentially fruitful way of combining narrative/interpretive and deductive/structural orientations toward organizations. For a variety of reasons, these perspectives lack integration, despite their common substantive interests. Historians employing narrative methods—a common approach, particularly after the cultural turn in the humanities—focus on events, context, and contingency. Their structuralist counterparts, meanwhile, are more interested in using data to test causal theories to uncover generalizable causal mechanisms. While each approach has its strengths, it is clear that they each lack what the other has to offer.

A focus on the evolutionary mechanisms of variation, retention, and selection provides a general framework for understanding organizational processes and outcomes, and when applied to particular organizations, populations, or cases, forces scholars to understand the context in which those processes unfold. Evolutionary theory is best described as a meta-theory, because it is an overarching framework that allows for the integration and comparison of other theories of organizational and managerial dynamics (Aldrich and Martinez, forthcoming). While it may be argued that the mechanisms of change proposed by evolutionary theory are not falsifiable, a more accurate characterization of the evolutionary perspective would be that it provides a general set of mechanisms that, when applied to particular empirical examples by more specific theoretical perspectives, can help us develop testable hypotheses about the conditions under which organizational processes occur, and how they affect different kinds of organizations.

Attention to the relevant organizational dimensions, in addition to the complexities and contingencies introduced by events and other selection forces, is a hallmark of evolutionary theory. In particular, a focus on variation and selection requires that scholars understand the relevant dimensions along which organizations vary, and the contextual and environmental conditions unique to particular times and places that act as selection forces. Variation and selection, while general processes, unfold in real time, in real places, and affect real organizations. In addition to this attention to context, however, the evolutionary perspective also provides a generalizable set of mechanisms for understanding a wide range of organizational dynamics across a variety of levels. Specific historical cases can add to our understanding of how and under what circumstances the evolutionary processes of variation, selection, and retention operate. As a meta-theory of organizational processes, change, and outcomes, the evolutionary perspective provides the best opportunity to organize, incorporate, and accumulate historical research more fully into our models of organizational dynamics. Although the particulars of historical research may be difficult to generalize to other contexts, when we view historical processes as empirical examples of variation, selection, and retention, we can begin to apply the mechanisms underlying historical processes to other organizational contexts.

It is important to note that evolutionary theory does not necessarily assume functionality or intentionality. Just because an organization or population evolved in a particular way does not mean that a given outcome was inevitable, or even the best of all possible outcomes. Rather, selection forces may represent the interests of powerful actors or the results of significant struggle between competing interest groups. In addition, evolutionary processes applied to organizations should not be assumed to imply efficient or optimal outcomes (March, 1994). Selection forces do not act immediately upon all organizations. In fact, there is often a significant time lag between the emergence of selection forces and evidence of their effects. Variations in those time lags lead to different, and sometimes messy, outcomes. The choices that actors in organizations make at a given time may be poor ones, but they can be "locked in" and lead to suboptimal outcomes. Applications of evolutionary mechanisms that focus on human agency, contingencies, and counterfactuals in our historical studies of organizational processes will draw attention to these inefficient outcomes.

All empirical research is, in one way or another, about the past. For some, the past is meaningful in its own right, and helpful for understanding how we arrived to the present. For others, it is simply the only time period from which data can be collected. However, virtually all of our research also strives to help us understand what is to come, whether in an explicit manner through the predictive power of hypothesis testing and generalizable results, or in a more subtle manner, though a detailed contextual understanding of how organizations and organizational actors have behaved in the past, how they were affected by their environments, and how they navigated complexity. Both of these tasks are useful, but too often, those steeped in the research traditions associated with each ignore the findings of the other. However, it is clear that each approach has much to offer the other.

We are encouraged by the growing interest in history by organizational scholars, but a chasm remains between the approaches we have described as "narrative/interpretive" and "deductive/structural." The predictive power of research findings based on hypothesis testing and replication can only be strengthened by more attention to context and temporality, as the common nod to "scope conditions" acknowledges. In addition, when researchers make more direct connections between their cases and other, similar cases, they strengthen the findings of business historians and others interested in historical organizational studies. Although a full integration has proven difficult thus far, we are confident that the framework provided by evolutionary theory provides an exciting point of departure.

REFERENCES

Abbott, A. (1997). "Of Time and Space: The Contemporary Relevance of the Chicago School," *Social Forces*, 75(4): 1149–82.

Aldrich, H. E. (1979). *Organizations and Environments*. Saddle River, NJ: Prentice Hall.

Aldrich, H. E. (2001). "Who Wants to Be an Evolutionary Theorist? Remarks on the Occasion of the Year 2000 OMT Distinguished Scholarly Career Award Presentation," *Journal of Management Inquiry*, 10(2): 115–27.

Aldrich, H. E. (2009). "Lost in Space, Out of Time: How and Why We Should Study Organizations Comparatively." In B. King, T. Felin, and D. Whetten, (eds.), *Studying Differences Between Organizations: Comparative Approaches to Organizational Research*, Vol. 26. In *Research in the Sociology of Organizations*. Series Editor: M. Lounsbury. Bingley, UK: Emerald Group: 21–44.

Aldrich, H. E., and Martinez, M. (forthcoming). "Evolutionary Theory." In J. McGee and T. Sammut-Bonnici (eds.), *Strategic Management Encyclopedia*. Malden, MA: John Wiley & Sons.

Aldrich, H. E., and Ruef, M. (2006). *Organizations Evolving*, 2nd edn. London: Sage.

Aldrich, H. E., Hodgson, G. M., Hull, D. L., Knudson, T., Mokyr, J., and Vanberg, V. J. (2008). "In Defence of Generalized Darwinism," *Journal of Evolutionary Economics*, 18(5): 577–56.

Argote, L., and Miron-Spektor, E. (2011). "Organizational Learning: From Experience to Knowledge," *Organization Science*, 22(5): 1123–37.

Bercovitz, J., and Feldman, M. (2008). "Academic Entrepreneurs: Organizational Change at the Individual Level" *Organization Science*, 19(1): 69–89.

Bradley, S. W., Aldrich, H. E., Shepherd, D. A., and Wiklund, J. (2011). "Resources, Environmental Change, and Survival: Asymmetric Paths of Young Independent and Subsidiary Organizations," *Strategic Management Journal*, 32(5): 486–509.

Braudel, F. (1958). "Histoire et Sciences Sociales: La Longue Durée," *Annales Histoire, Sciences Sociales*, 13(4): 725–53.

Buenstorf, G. (2007). "How Useful is Generalized Darwinism as a Framework to Study Competition and Industrial Evolution?" *Journal of Evolutionary Economics*, 16(5): 511–27.

Burke, P. (2004). *History and Social Theory*. Ithaca: Cornell University Press.

Bushee, B. J., and Cready, W. M. (2001). "Do Institutional Investors Prefer Near-Term Earnings Over Long-Run Value?" *Contemporary Accounting Research*, 18(2): 207–56.

Coase, R. H. (1959). "The Federal Communications Commission," *Journal of Law and Economics*, 2: 1–40.

Demetriou, C. (2012). "Processual Comparative Sociology: Building on the Approach of Charles Tilly," *Sociological Theory*, 30(1): 51–65.

Dobbin, F. (1994). *Forging Industrial Policy: The United States, Great Britain, and France in the Railway Age*. New York: Cambridge University Press.

Dobbin, F. (2011). *Inventing Equal Opportunity*. Princeton: Princeton University Press.

Eisenhardt, K. M., and Graebner, M. E. (2007). "Theory Building from Cases: Opportunities and Challenges," *Academy of Management Journal*, 50(2): 25–32.

Evans, R.J. (1997). *In Defence of History*. London: Granta Books.

Gartner, W. B., Shaver, K. G., Carter, N. M., and Reynolds, P. D. (eds.). (2004). *Handbook of Entrepreneurial Dynamics: The Process of Business Creation*. Thousand Oaks, CA: Sage.

Garud, R., Kumaraswamy, A., and Karnøe, P. (2010). "Path Dependence or Path Creation?" *Journal of Management Studies*, 47(4): 760–74.

Haldane, J. B. S. (1932). *The Causes of Evolution*. New York and London: Harper & Brothers.

Hall, J. (1992). "Where History and Sociology Meet: Forms of Discourse and Sociohistorical Inquiry," *Sociological Theory*, 10(2): 164–93.

Hannan, M. T., and Freeman, J. H. (1986). "Where Do Organizational Forms Come From?" *Sociological Forum*, 1(1): 50–72.

Hannan, M. T., Carroll, G. R., and Pólos, L. (2003). "The Organizational Niche," *Sociological Theory*, 21(4): 309–40.

Hodgson, G. M., and Knudson, T. (2004). "The Firm as an Interactor: Firms as Vehicles for Habits and Routines," *Journal of Evolutionary Economics*, 14(3): 281–307.

Hodgson, G. M., and Knudson, T. (2006). "Why We Need a Generalized Darwinism: And Why a Generalized Darwinism is Not Enough," *Journal of Economic Behavior & Organizations*, 61(1): 1–19.

Ingram, P., and Lifschitz, A. (2006). "Kinship in the Shadow of the Corporation: The Interbuilder Network in Clyde River Shipbuilding, 1711–1990," *American Sociological Review*, 71(2): 334–52.

Johnson, V. (2007). "What Is Organizational Imprinting? Cultural Entrepreneurship in the Founding of the Paris Opera," *American Journal of Sociology*, 113(1): 97–127.

Joseph, J., and Ocasio, W. (2012). "Architecture, Attention, and Adaptation in the Multibusiness Firm: General Electric from 1951–2001," *Strategic Management Journal*, 33(6): 633–60.

King, B., Felin, T., and Whetten, D. (eds.). (2009). *Studying Differences Between Organizations: Comparative Approaches to Organizational Research*, Vol. 26. In *Research in the Sociology of Organizations*, Series Editor: M. Lounsbury. Bingley, UK: Emerald Group.

Kovacs, J. D. B. (2008). "Selective Sampling of Empirical Settings in Organizational Studies," *Administrative Science Quarterly*, 53(1): 109–44.

Langton, J. (1984). "The Ecological Theory of Bureaucracy: The Case of Josiah Wedgewood and the British Pottery Industry," *Administrative Science Quarterly*, 29(3): 330–54.

Leblebici, H., Salancik, G., King, T., and Copay, A. (1991). "Institutional Change and the Transformation of Interorganizational Fields: An Organizational History of the U.S. Radio Broadcasting Industry," *Administrative Science Quarterly*, 36(3): 333–63.

Li, B., and Walder, A. G. (2001). "Career Advancement as Party Patronage: Sponsored Mobility into the Chinese Administrative Elite, 1949–1996," *American Journal of Sociology*, 106(5): 1371–408.

Lippmann, S. (2010). "Boys to Men: Age, Identity, and the Legitimation of Amateur Wireless in the U.S." *Journal of Broadcasting and Electronic Media*, 54(4): 657–74.

Mandeville, B. (1970 [1724]). *The Fable of the Bees*. Harmondsworth: Penguin.

March, J. G. (1994). "The Evolution of Evolution," In J. Baum and J. Singh (eds.), *Evolutionary Dynamics of Organizations*. New York: Oxford University Press: 39–49.

Morgan, K. J., and Prasad, M. (2009). "The Origins of Tax Systems: A French-American Comparison," *American Journal of Sociology*, 114(5): 1350–1394.

Muehlfeld, K., Sahib, P. R., and Van Witteloostuijn, A. (2012). "A Contextual Theory of Organizational Learning from Failures and Successes: A Study of Acquisition Completion in the Global Newspaper Industry, 1981–2008," *Strategic Management Journal*, 33(8): 938–964.

Nelson, R. R. (1994). "Evolutionary Theorizing about Economic Change." In N. Smelser and R. Swedberg (eds.), *The Handbook of Economic Sociology*. Princeton: Princeton University Press: 108–136.

Nelson, R. R. (2007). "Universal Darwinism and Evolutionary Social Science," *Biology and Philosophy*, 22(1): 73–94.

Nelson, R. R., and Winter, S. (1982). *An Evolutionary Theory of Economic Change*. Cambridge, MA: Belknap.

Parsons, T. (1964). "Evolutionary Universals in Society," *American Sociological Review*, 29(3): 339–557.

Perrow, C. (2002). *Organizing America: Wealth, Power, and the Origins of Corporate Capitalism*. Princeton: Princeton University Press.

Pozner, J. E., Stimmler, M. K., and Hirsch, P. M. (2010). "Terminal Isomorphism and the Self-Destructive Potential of Success: Lessons from Subprime Mortgage Origination and Securitization." In M. Lounsbury and P. M. Hirsch (eds.), *Markets on Trial: The Economic Sociology of the U.S. Financial Crisis: Part A, Research in the Sociology of Organizations*, Vol. 30A. Bingley, UK: Emerald: 183–215.

Ranger-Moore, J. (1997). "Bigger May Be Better But Is Older Wiser? Organizational Age and Size in the New York Life Insurance Industry," *American Sociological Review*, 62(6): 903–20.

Reynolds, P. D. (1971). *A Primer in Theory Construction*. Indianapolis: Bobbs-Merrill Company.

Ruef, M. (2002). "Unpacking the Liability of Aging: Toward A Socially Embedded Account of Organizational Disbanding," *Research in the Sociology of Organizations*, 19: 195–228.

Ruef, M. (2004). "The Demise of an Organizational Form: Emancipation and Plantation Agriculture in the American South, 1860–1880," *American Journal of Sociology*, 109(6): 1365–410.

Ruef, M. (2010). *The Entrepreneurial Group: Social Identities, Relations, and Collective Action*, Princeton: Princeton University Press.

Ruef, M., Aldrich, H. E., and Carter, N. M. (2003). "The Structure of Founding Teams: Homophily, Strong Ties, and Isolation among U.S. Entrepreneurs," *American Sociological Review*, 68(2): 195–222.

Sewell, Jr., W. H. (2005). *Logics of History: Social Theory and Social Transformation*. Chicago: University of Chicago Press.

Siggelkow, N. (2007). "Persuasion with Case Studies," *Academy of Management Review*, 50(1): 20–4.

Smith, A. (1970 [1776]). *The Wealth of Nations*. Harmonsworth: Penguin.

Steinmetz, G. (2005). "The Epistemological Unconscious of U.S. Sociology and the Transition to Post-Fordism: The Case of Historical Sociology." In J. Adams, E. Clemens, and A. S. Orloff (eds.), *Remaking Modernity: Politics, History, and Sociology*. Durham, NC: Duke University Press: 109–57.

Steinmetz, G. (2007). "The Relations Between Sociology and History in the United States: The Current State of Affairs," *Journal of Historical Sociology*, 20(1): 1–12.

Stinchcombe, A. L. (1965). "Social Structure and Organizations." In J. G. March (ed.) *Handbook of Organizations*. New York: Rand McNally: 142–93.

Stinchcombe, A. L. (1968). *A Primer in Theory Construction*. Chicago: University of Chicago Press.

Thompson, E. P. (1967). "Time, Work-Discipline, and Industrial Capitalism," *Past & Present*, 38: 56–97.

Woodside, A. G. (2010). "Bridging the Chasm between Survey and Case Study Research: Research Methods for Achieving Generalization, Accuracy, and Complexity," *Industrial Marketing Management*, 39(1): 64–75.

6

History and the Cultural Turn in Organization Studies

Michael Rowlinson and John Hassard

From a historical perspective the rise of organizational culture studies can be seen as part of a much wider "cultural turn" in society during the last quarter of the 20th century (Burke, 2008: 2). The popular reception for the concept of corporate culture can be understood in the historical context of a widespread readiness to accept cultural explanations for everything from poverty and drug use through to corporate success. In academia there was also a "cultural turn" across the humanities and social sciences, including history and organization studies, and the rise of a distinctive field of "cultural studies." But the cultural turn is inseparable from the "culture wars" that broke out across the social sciences and humanities, responding to changes in wider society and politics, with multiculturalism contested in schools and churches, as well as universities. For historians these various conflicts coalesced into a morass of "history-theory culture wars," with battles, sieges, and wars as the dominant metaphors (Clark, 2004: 26, 105). Within academia these bitter disputes mostly take place in books and journals, with very occasional seminar or conference confrontations and even rarer accusations of libel and demands for an apology (for an entertaining example of a clash across the political and cultural divides see Ferguson, 2011; responding to Mishra, 2011).

Although the metaphor of "culture wars" was used for a while in organization studies, this was largely a local disagreement over the definition of organizational culture (Martin, 2002: 55). For the most part these so-called "wars" in organization studies were insulated from wider cultural conflicts over gender, race, sexuality, and class. An indication of this insulation is that the battle was only ever joined by the "critical studies" side (Martin and Frost, 1999), with little or no response from the unitarist mainstream that were the target of attack. Subsequently the critical studies camp seems to have called it all off without much ado (Martin, Frost, and O'Neill, 2006).

The culture wars in organization studies were always constrained by their location in business schools, where even the advocates of critical management studies prefer to avoid references to Marxism and class in case they put off management practitioners (e.g., Martin, 2002; Voronov, 2008; Perrow, 2008; for a critique of critical management studies see Rowlinson and Hassard, 2011). Within business schools, business history continues to be dominated by a cozy culture of consensus rather than conflict (cf. Galambos, 2003), with a hegemonic civility that sees any serious critique of its leading figures as unseemly. The metaphors of siege or war from the wider discipline of history would be out of place in business history.

In this chapter we will consider the implications of the cultural turn for business history and organization studies, and the prospects for a rapprochement between these neighboring fields brokered by cultural theory. We focus on the problematic issues of narrative and identity and the implications for conducting historical research in organization studies. The chapter is divided into four sections. The first section gives an outline of the cultural, or culturalist, turn in history, and its implications for business history. The second section then considers the prospects for a culturally informed "historic turn" (Clark and Rowlinson, 2004) or historical reorientation in organization studies (Üsdiken and Kieser, 2004). The third section identifies examples of what could be called deconstructionist history in organization studies. The final section then considers the prospects for a self-conscious return to narrative history, informed by cultural and organization theory.

In our view historical researchers face a dilemma of how to position themselves between business history, which is largely indifferent to the epistemological issues raised by the cultural turn, and organization studies which remains skeptical towards the epistemic status of historical narratives. In this chapter we have identified examples of empirical archival research from business history and organization studies that overcome this dilemma to some extent and provide a set of templates for business historians considering an engagement with organization studies, especially from a critical or cultural perspective, or for organizational researchers considering a foray into the archives. We are well aware that historians are skeptical towards interventions from self-appointed theorists who have never ventured into an archive, so we would note that our reflections are informed by our own forays into historical research (e.g., Rowlinson, 1988; Rowlinson and Hassard, 1993; Hassard and Rowlinson, 2002).

THE "CULTURALIST TURN" IN HISTORY

The strongest advocates of cultural theory in history prefer to talk about a "culturalist turn," rather than a cultural turn, in order to emphasize that it is not just about studying "the history of culture." The culturalist turn is more "a matter of epistemology," and "a concern with narrative, symbol and representation as recognized in both the activities of people in the past and in 'doing history' in the present" (Munslow, 2003: 142). Cultural theory in history can be understood as a critique of "historical objectivity or Rankean empiricism—that is to say, of a particular model or construction of history." The aim of the culturalist critique is to generate "qualitatively different histories" (Gunn, 2006: 9), and in this chapter we identify some examples and extend our previous discussions of what qualitatively different histories might look like in business history and organization studies (Rowlinson and Delahaye, 2009).

Jenkins (1991) crystallized many of the concerns that have subsequently shaped debate in theory and philosophy of history, making the case that the culturalist critique of history is intended to engender methodological reflection on what it is "that makes history so epistemologically fragile." Unfortunately business historians (e.g., Toms and Wilson, 2010; Jeremy and Tweedale, 2005), in common with other "practicing" historians (Clark, 2004), tend to cut themselves off from epistemological considerations. Evans's (1997) celebrated riposte to postmodernism, *In Defense of History*, is often cited as if it is the last word and the challenges of cultural theory can be safely ignored (Finney, 2005: 149). It should be noted that Evans (2001) actually takes these challenges seriously, and in response to critics he specifically endorsed the view that historians need to be more self-conscious about theory and epistemology.

This means that the culturalist turn represents a challenge to the implicit division of labor in history, whereby cultural theory was reserved for examining cultural and intellectual phenomena (e.g., Collini, 1988), while business and economic history could defer to economics (e.g., Coleman, 1988; Lamoreaux, Raff, and Temin, 2008), or occasionally management and organization theory (Kipping and Üsdiken, 2008). However, a brief look at history journals and textbooks suggests that for the most part cultural and intellectual historians have not ventured into the realms of business and management. Weber's *Protestant Ethic and the Spirit of Capitalism* may be claimed as one of "the greatest contributions to cultural history" for its examination of the cultural roots of Western capitalism (Burke, 2008: 10), but that doesn't seem to entail any engagement with the historical debates engendered by Weber's thesis in management and organization theory (see, e.g., du Gay, 2000). History textbooks (e.g., Tosh, 2010) may give ample consideration to the "cultural turn" and the critique of historical practices. But this is completely separate from the discussion of business history, which is prosaically defined as the "systematic study of individual firms on the basis of their business records," and subsumed by debates over "the mechanisms of economic expansion" (Tosh, 2010: 75).

For their part business historians have been able to accommodate the idea that "business makes culture," with accounts of cultural industries, as well as the "culture of consumption," and the growth of marketing and advertising (Lipartito, 2008: 613). They have also come to appreciate that "cultural representations of business and business people," such as novels, can be valuable sources (Popp, 2006; Maltby and Rutterford, 2006: 221). The influence of business on cultural phenomena has also received greater attention (Harvey, Press, and Maclean, 2011), and here there is some convergence with the "material turn" in cultural history (Daly, 2007; Rappaport, 2008).

As a leading business historian, Jones's (2010) history of the global cosmetics industry, *Beauty Imagined*, illustrates how forays into the history of a cultural industry can run into difficult questions of identity politics and multiculturalism associated with the "culture wars" (Burke, 2008; Gunn, 2006). Jones (2010: 4) is mainly concerned with conventional issues of business history, namely the role of "the entrepreneurs who built the industry" and how they constructed the market for beauty. However, he also tackles questions of legitimacy, and the industry's "controversial role in shaping broader constructions of gender, age, and ethnicity" (Jones, 2010: 4, 7).

One of the most controversial issues dealt with by Jones is the promotion of skin-lightening creams, such as Fair & Lovely launched by Unilever's Indian subsidiary in 1978. This became one of its most successful beauty products, subsequently launched in nearly 40 countries. Jones argues that for many urban professional women in India the skin "whitening fashion...was not an unwelcome relic from the past but widely associated with modernity and upward mobility." Jones maintains that critics of Fair & Lovely fail to take into account different local interpretations, such as in India where "the use of fairness creams was seen as providing one means for women to escape socially imposed limitations" (2010: 313).

A measure of the Jones's success in securing the attention of cultural theorists is the long review of his book in the *London Review of Books*. But the reviewer criticizes Jones's account of Fair & Lovely and concludes that "for all his facts and figures," Jones "just doesn't understand his own subject" (Wilson, 2010), suggesting that Jones's representation of beauty as a natural phenomenon threatened by artifice is at odds with any cultural interpretation of beauty itself as artifice (on the negative implications of Fair & Lovely for public welfare see Karnani, 2007). In other words Jones takes a conventional business history approach to a cultural industry, which almost inevitably raises objections from cultural theory. As Lipartito argues, "studies incorporating gender, race, and ethnicity into business challenge notions of business as a universal, affective-neutral act quantified by some transparent measure of profitability" (2008: 609). Cultural theory goes further, by undermining the acceptance of class, gender, and "race" as fixed categories, and highlighting the socially constructed and historically constituted nature of cross-cutting identities (Gunn, 2006), and how historians have conceptualized these categories in their writings (Munslow, 2003). So-called "socially imposed limitations" cannot simply be taken as given in order to exonerate corporations that profit from perpetuating them.

As Lipartito and Sicilia (2004b: 3) explain in the introduction to their important edited collection, *Constructing Corporate America: History, Politics, Culture*, in post-structural terms the corporation can be said to have been "reified as an economic actor," rather than "a social, cultural, and political one." But as they make clear, the social, cultural, and political dimensions are not simply optional extras, because they compel us to reconsider rational economic explanations for the rise of the corporation. In this sense cultural theory "offers an alternative to economics for the study of business history" (Lipartito, 2008: 619), as well as a critique of the dominance of economics. Lipartito (2004), for example, reconsiders the Weberian question of the cultural values that facilitated the rise of capitalism and the corporation in 19th-century America. Walker's (2004) chapter on "White Corporate America" traces how black employees are held back by the continuation of "plantation-type" attitudes in contemporary corporations. She makes the ironic observation that "there were more black managers on plantations during the age of American slavery than there has been in the era of the New Economy." She also makes the point that "the fervent anti-government rhetoric of many white business people" opposed to affirmative action programs has not stopped them receiving government assistance, an argument that could be made with more resonance since the bailouts in 2008.

Although Lipartito and Sicilia (2004a) set a new agenda for business history, shifting away from an economistic search for the secret of business success, for the most part their contributors follow the practices of conventional historians and avoid an engagement with the epistemological concerns of the cultural turn. An exception is Guthey's (2004) insightful analysis of the rhetoric in the new economy, for example tracing Bill Gates's progress from entrepreneurial hero to monopolistic villain—although now there would have to be a reprieve for Gates as philanthropic savior. Galambos (2004: 161) also widens the agenda, explaining that broadly speaking, business history has contributed to a consensus that opposes state intervention in business, in order to preserve "a system that involved a skewed distribution of power, wealth, and income, because it generated unique economic opportunities and the continued growth Americans sought." Even so these are primarily essays derived from secondary sources rather than research in corporate archives.

While business historians such as Lipartito have recognized that the culturalist historical challenge is not limited to questions of gender, race, or class, they have yet to take up the challenge of exploring the language and taken-for-granted assumptions of business history by subjecting them to a detailed critique (Scranton 2008). Far from distracting historians into what might be considered cultural epiphenomena, a culturalist historical critique would entail unraveling the historical rhetoric of the consensus that prevails in business history, both in terms of its historiography as well as its implicit epistemological claims.

Mayhew's (2009) book, *Narrating the Rise of Big Business in the USA*, represents a rare example of culturalist critique of the rhetoric of business history itself. Mayhew argues that the accounts of big business from economic and business history need to be analyzed as "stories" or "narratives," and offers "an explicitly postmodern reading of received texts" (Mayhew, 2009: 3) such as Alfred Chandler's *Visible Hand* (1977). Business historians may disagree with Chandler, indeed it now seems almost obligatory that they should, but they remain committed to the search for an "alternative synthesis" informed by economic theory (Lamoreaux, Raff, and Temin, 2004; Toms and Wilson, 2003). Scranton (2008) questions whether "solid modernist business histories," such as Chandler's, are of any interest to other historians who are engaged in "conversations about language, meaning, and practice, past and present." But Mayhew's detailed deconstruction, a model of deconstructionist close reading, represents exactly the kind of threat to the boundaries of business history and challenge to its identity that was feared from cultural theory (Galambos, 2003: 29; Lipartito, 2008: 620). The threat is that it undermines the accumulation of narrative corporate histories that underpins business history and provides the sources for the overarching syntheses, such as Chandler's *Visible Hand* or *Scale and Scope* (Kobrak and Schneider, 2011).

THE "HISTORIC TURN" IN ORGANIZATION STUDIES

Zald (1991, 1993, and 1996) initiated a debate about the contribution of history in organization studies with a series of articles making the case for a broader rapprochement with the humanities and broader social sciences. Barrett and Srivasta (1991) also reviewed the prospects for a more interpretive approach to history in organization studies, while Kieser (1994) set out how and why historical case studies should be conducted. Nevertheless, it remains questionable whether the increased interest in history could be said to constitute a culturalist "historic turn" (Clark and Rowlinson, 2004) in the sense of reorienting organization studies towards historical analysis informed by cultural theory (Üsdiken and Kieser, 2004). The treatment of history in organization studies can be understood, and critiqued, using a framework from culturalist historians.

From a culturalist perspective (Munslow, 2003), three epistemological positions in history can be identified: first, reconstructionist or modernist history, which presents itself as an unmediated truthful account of the past derived from close scrutiny of sources; second, constructionist or "late-modernist" history, which self-consciously invokes social scientific concepts to reveal the underlying patterns in the past; and finally, deconstructionist history, which sees itself primarily as a form of literature that derives its meaning as much from its representation of the past as from the sources or concepts used to interrogate them. These positions can be mapped onto organization studies.

Reconstructionist history is more or less ruled out from organization studies, which has banished descriptive narrative case studies as part of its embarrassing unscientific anecdotal pedagogical origins. History in organization studies is therefore identified with constructionist history and the use of data from the past to test theories of organization. Kipping and Üsdiken (2008) note that longitudinal quantitative studies have become synonymous with history in organization studies. But as with other forms of qualitative research (e.g., Eisenhardt, 1989), qualitative historical methods in organization studies have been advocated with an argument that they can be made sufficiently scientific for theory testing, rather than an interpretive view that they cannot. This is predicated on a misreading of philosophy of history. For example, Popper has been cited to suggest that historiography can be equated with science, where "the goal of testing theory should be to refute hypotheses" (Goodman and Kruger, 1988: 318).

Popper's view was that "*testable hypotheses*" are rare in history, and "*historical interpretation*," which constitutes the form of history that interested him and which he aspired to write, "cannot be formulated as a testable hypothesis" (2002 [1957]: 139–40). Historians generally agree that, for Popper, "history is not, and did not aim to be, a science" (Clark, 2004: 31). Unfortunately for positivistic organization theorists, history is inadmissible unless it is, or aims to be, scientific. It is difficult to resist the temptation to suggest that by and large organization theorists are what Popper called, "historicists, who despise old-fashioned history and wish to reform it into a theoretical science" (2002 [1957]: 133).

Popper (2002 [1957]: 133) explicitly defended the view, "so often attacked as old-fashioned by historicists, that *history is characterized by its interest in actual, singular, or specific events, rather than in laws or generalizations.*" This doesn't rule out quantitative methods or the use of theory, but it calls on theory to contribute towards "the causal explanation of a *singular* event" (Popper, 2002: 133). There is nothing intrinsic in an event that makes it singular or universal. As Friedman (1953: 14, 25) put it, a choice has to be made between two familiar half-truths: "History never repeats itself" (singularity), and "There is nothing new under the sun" (universality). Social science, including organization theory, tends to follow the example of positive economics by moving towards universality, supplying nostrums that can be applied in all situations. In general this move towards universality replaces narrative and events with contingencies and trends. But within organization theory, under the influence of "narrative positivism" (Abbott, 1992), events themselves are treated as replicable, amenable to technicist event-history analysis.

In order to win acceptance for history in organization studies, therefore, a constructionist case has been made, but in such a way that deconstructionist epistemological doubts are not admitted. The door has to be opened to theory and methodology, but then closed quickly so as not to let in cultural reflexivity. Thus Popper might be mentioned on the misapprehension that he saw history as a form of science, but with no hint that for historians Popper's opposition to historicism can be seen as incipient poststructuralism (Clark, 2004: 31). The editors (O'Sullivan and Graham, 2010: 780) of a special issue on Business History in the *Journal of Management Studies* exemplify this tendency when they refer to a "historical turn," but then dismiss any preoccupation with "more abstract concerns, including the various possibilities for historical research" that are usually associated with a historical reorientation. In other words they want history, but without any cultural "turn" that might involve difficult epistemological questions. With the exception of Decker's (2010) article on postcolonial transitions in Africa, which we discuss in more detail later on, the rest of the papers in the special issue are firmly within the constructionist camp both in terms of content and methods. The point to be made here is that if consensual business history is allowed to stand in for history within management and organization studies then it reinforces the constructionist stance in both fields, hegemonically crowding out deconstructionist culturalist approaches to history, or dismissing them as unnecessarily "abstract."

DECONSTRUCTIONIST HISTORY IN ORGANIZATION STUDIES

Deconstruction has made sporadic appearances within organization studies, as with Kilduff's (1993) close critical reading of founding texts in the field. The rise of critical management studies is also associated with increased interest in history. This serves as a counter to the alleged indifference to history from mainstream organization studies (Burrell, 1997), as well as the constructionist approach to history in the forerunners for critical management studies, such as labor process theory (Rowlinson, Stager Jacques, and Booth, 2009). Even so there is little sense of what constitutes a self-consciously critical approach to empirical historical research in organization studies. In this section we have identified two studies that combine critical and cultural approaches to empirical archival research in order to identify some distinguishing characteristics of what could be called deconstructionist history in organization studies.

Mills' (2006) history of gender and organizational culture in the commercial airline industry represents a major attempt to use organizational concepts in a detailed empirical historical study. Mills' main sources are the in-house newsletters, or company magazines of the commercial airways. These provide a valuable insight into the construction of gender in the industry, and specifically how the role of stewardess came to be identified with women, not least through the visual representations of women and men in the industry. Mills focuses on one organization, British Airways, and provides comparisons with Pan American Airlines (Pan Am), which avoids over-generalization as well as allowing Mills to question reductionist explanations that would see all gender divisions as somehow functional for business in the context of prevailing attitudes. Although Mills entered into a relationship with the archivist at British Airways, one that resembled that of ethnographer entering the field, he is careful to differentiate his own research from what he calls "company history," which focuses on a "selected company in terms of its stated purposes" and sets out "to document how well it met its stated objectives over time" (Mills, 2006: 10).

Commercial airlines clearly do not set out to construct gender identity; it is not one of their stated purposes. But through formal and informal practices, such as the feminization of certain jobs and the prohibition on women doing other jobs, as well as the marriage bar which operated for women for a long period, and expectations of femininity, often manifested in visual representations in company magazines, these business organizations clearly contributed to the construction of gender, as well as racial identities. In other words, instead of treating airlines as economic actors who simply acted within given "socially imposed limitations," Mills takes them seriously as social and political actors who constructed those limitations. Mills' interest in gender and history, as well as his sensitivity to the potential use of sources, is clearly informed by his exposure to feminist research, as well as organizational culture studies, and unlike most business historians he sets out his theoretical influences clearly in his introduction, thus allowing the reader to make an informed assessment of his interpretations. Although Mills' account is broadly chronological, with the "gendering of airline culture over time" divided into eight distinct periods, he tends to avoid narrativization in terms of attributing causation, let alone intentionality, to changes between periods. In a sense his periodization represents a series of fairly discrete ethnographic studies. Mills only defers to published corporate histories for the names of characters involved in the industry and key dates.

Our second example of deconstructionist history in organization studies is Decker's (2010) account of postcolonial Africanization in Ghana and Nigeria during the 1950s and 1960s. This derives from her research in the corporate archives of five British companies, including Unilever, that were well established in West Africa during that period. The article is actually couched in constructionist terms, with the application of concepts such as "social capital" and the "embeddedness of organizations" (2010: 792), but it represents a move in a culturalist direction in two senses. First in terms of content, unlike run of the mill business history the focus is not on business success or failure, but the effectiveness of various approaches to Africanization. This necessarily involves a discussion of corporate historical constructions of racial identity which is largely neglected in organization studies.

The second sense in which Decker moves in a culturalist direction is that while she invokes theory to provide a richer understanding of a singular event, Africanization in West Africa, the event is not relegated to an illustration of theory or a means to theory development. Decker's central argument is that parallels can be drawn between this event and Affirmative Action in the United States, and more importantly Black Economic Empowerment in South Africa in the 1990s and early 21st century. The aim is not to produce a universal explanation for postcolonial transitions, and such transitions are by definition historically specific, or singular, arising from the historical legacy of racism and colonialism that is rarely mentioned in organization studies (cf. Cooke, 2003). Considering the hitherto overlooked similarities and differences between the history of West Africa and contemporary South Africa provides insights into both contexts, but this is not the same as theory generation predicting replication in other historical contexts.

Both of these studies can be seen as culturalist in that they are clearly concerned with the construction of gender or racial identities. But obviously neither of them displays the kind of disregard for archival evidence that business historians would probably expect from deconstructionist history (Amatori and Jones, 2003). Business historians such as Galambos (2003: 26) also argue that a "focus on class, gender, and race" in history necessarily means a move to the left politically and "away from the subject matter and central concerns of business history." Unfortunately this conflates business history with the conservative, pro-business outlook of business historians who write commissioned histories oriented to explaining the secrets of business success or failure. But as Mills and Decker demonstrate, there is no reason why business archives cannot be used to research culturalist questions of gender or race informed by organization theory, as well as, or instead of business strategies and structures.

NARRATIVE RECONSTRUCTION AND DECONSTRUCTION

The move from constructionist to deconstructionist history is associated with a shift away from a concern over whether history is or should be scientific and towards an interest in the similarities and differences between history and fiction, or a displacement of "the Scientific Attitude" by "the Rhetorical Attitude" (Fay, 1998). One reservation we have with the reconstruction-construction-deconstruction perspective (Munslow, 2003) is that it has obviously been constructed in order to present an epistemological progression towards deconstructionist enlightenment. This sense of progression pervades historians' accounts of history and cultural theory (e.g., Gunn, 2006; Clark, 2004), but it contradicts deconstructionist skepticism towards progress in history. It could be said that deconstructionist historians have yet to find an appropriate deconstructionist style of writing for the recent history of their own discipline (cf. White 1998[1978]).

For constructionists it makes sense to draw a sharp distinction between unscientific narrative history and scientific history that eschews narrative in favor of clearly defined analytical categories. In effect this differentiation separates the relatively small field of academic history that is subject to the fads and fashions of theory from the "great mass" of history that is produced in an unselfconscious narrative form, regardless of whether or not it is fashionable (Stone, 1979: 4). In relation to organizations this mass of narrative history is represented by what we have called the genre of corporate history that expresses the narrative historical identities of organizations (Rowlinson et al., 2010). Nearly all organizations produce written accounts of their past: on their webpages, in their annual reports, as well as in commissioned published histories. The genre generally includes an "origin story," usually focused on the character of the founder, as well as "turning points" such as "averted disasters, changes in direction, and exemplary past triumphs" (Linde, 2009: 79–85).

Jones, and other leading business historians, have consistently distanced their own so-called "critical" or "objective" commissioned histories, from the more readable public relations company histories which allegedly lack "scholarly depth" (Jones and Sluyterman, 2003: 112; Amatori and Jones, 2003: 3; Jones, 2005: v, 323) and can be dismissed as "inferior journalistic hackwork" (Coleman, 1987: 145). But the need to make such a forceful distinction in itself reinforces the impression that they are actually part of the same recognizable genre, which takes as its object the narrative identity of an eponymous corporate entity. In fact the genre is broader than academic business historians allow for. Some of the best corporate histories written by journalists, such as Pendergrast's (2000) *For God, Country and Coca-Cola*, are actually not commissioned but are thoroughly researched. Pendergrast's founder-centered, chronological narrative presents the history of Coca-Cola as a "microcosm of American history." The story is highly dramatized, with drastic action triggered by small events, and success or failure attributed to personal qualities and abilities. Nevertheless, even though Pendergrast's text is not cluttered with numbered notes, he is scrupulous in disclosing all sources.

The second edition of Pendergrast's (2000) book includes a list of Thirty Business Lessons from Coca-Cola. What this illustrates is the convergence between corporate history and some of the best-selling corporate culture gurus, who often not only include a considerable amount of history in their texts (e.g., Peters and Waterman, 1982; Collins and Porras, 1994; Deal and Kennedy, 2000), but also, albeit unknowingly, deploy the narrative techniques of history (Kroeze and Keulen, 2012). From a deconstructionist position, narrative can be considered as a legitimate method of "doing history," as well as the object of analysis as it appears in reconstructionist history. A deconstructionist approach allows for an appreciation of reconstructionist narrative history and how it works, but in order to differentiate itself a deconstructionist narrative would require a meta-commentary—to discuss how it does what it does with narrative (cf. Linde, 2009: 87)—which as far as we are aware is something that has not yet appeared in either business history or organization studies.

As an example of a self-conscious historical analysis of narrative, Durepos has examined the construction of narratives for Pan Am using the archives of the company that ceased operations in 1991. The method is explicitly derived from actor-network theory (ANT), and represents an actor-network deconstruction of corporate history (Durepos, Mills, and Helms Mills, 2008)—for which Durepos (2009) has coined the term ANTi-history. Bruce and Nyland (2011) have recently followed this approach to deconstruct the orthodox view of Human Relations as a response to the inhumanity of Scientific Management. Using Mayo's published work and unpublished correspondence they show how the "truths" of Human Relations were constructed in order to appeal to business leaders. ANTi-history can therefore be characterized as a variant of deconstructionist history. The self-conscious invocation of theory in the construction of a historical narrative can be contrasted with business history, where even culturalists such as Lipartito do not actually articulate their own theoretical position. But neither does Durepos succumb to the constructionist demand for scientistic theory generation, with generalizable propositions for the construction of corporate narratives.

There has been increasing interest in narrative analysis in organization studies (Rhodes and Brown, 2005), often drawing on theorists and philosophers of history such as White (1987) and Carr (1998). Boje's (2008) work in particular has analyzed the construction of narratives over time for companies such as Wal-Mart, Disney, and McDonald's. This raises a question of whether a distinction can be made between history and narrative analysis. For our purposes, considering the extent of a cultural turn in terms of a self-conscious historical orientation, most narrative analysis need not be counted as history because its authors do not present it as such. In one of his best known studies of Disney, for example, Boje (1995) gives a detailed account of the construction of Disney's historical narratives, but he does not present his analysis as historical even though it is highly suggestive for historical research. In other words although Boje has a sophisticated understanding of history, informed by in-depth reading of historical the-orists such as Ricoeur (1985, 1990a, and 1990b), he doesn't see his own research as history, being more concerned with representations of the past in collective memory. As a result Boje is not constrained to follow the con-ventions of history such as citations to sources.

As a business historian Hansen (2007) has studied narratives within the constraints of the core business history journals, which requires detailed cita-tions to sources, combining organizational culture with narrative theory in a detailed historical study of change in Danish Savings Banks. Through an analysis of press reports and published corporate histories, Hansen demon-strates how it is the historical narratives that represent the past in the present, rather than the unmediated past itself, that enables and constrains organiza-tions undergoing change, and furthermore these narrative representations of the past also change over time (see also Suddaby, Foster, and Trank, 2010). An implication of Hansen's work is that business historians need a greater awareness of their own narratives as representations. Whereas constructionist history generally avoids narrative, lest a false narrative is imposed, the implica-tion of deconstructionist history is that the past can only be accessed through narrative, which needs to be analyzed, and that if narrative is to be constructed then it has to be imposed knowingly.

CONCLUSION

The constructionist move to analytic categories reflects the longstanding unease amongst historians about the status of narrative (e.g., Elton, 1967; Evans, 1997). The constructionist view corresponds to the default scientist view of theory and history in organization studies, with history being justi-fied on the basis that it can generate or test theory. A constructionist consen-sus has increasingly won acceptance in business history, with the expectation that corporate history should no longer follow narrative conventions and instead be structured by analytic categories in order to facilitate generalization (Coleman, 1987). A good example of this would be Jones's (2005) commis-sioned history of Unilever, which provides a broad chronological history of the company as the context for an in-depth exploration of various themes such as brands, franchising, human resources, and corporate culture. The landmark *Oxford Handbook of Business History* (Jones and Zeitlin, 2008), is structured around a similar set of analytical themes, such as big business, family business, networks, and cartels, and "functions," including marketing, human resources, and accounting. In other words it provides a valuable checklist for structuring a constructionist corporate history, even though it avoids questions of meth-odology (Kobrak and Schneider, 2011).

Business historians tend to take a pessimistic view that engaging with organization studies requires them to retreat from narrative historical research and writing (Popp, 2009: 833; cf. Kipping and Üsdiken, 2008: 113; Godelier, 2009). But this rests on a false dichotomy between reconstructionist narrative corporate history and constructionist analytical history. Our argument is that the culturalist turn not only opens up new areas of archival research in business history, in relation to the construction of identities, it can also facilitate a return to narrative. However, the deconstructionist view associated with the culturalist turn is that any historical engagement with the past involves concepts, theories, arguments, and ethical beliefs, whether or not these are acknowledged (Munslow, 2003). If the culturalist turn presents an opening for history in organization studies, then historical researchers need to adopt a "reflexive methodology," as advocated by historians such as Jenkins (1991: 69), with an appreciation of why history is or is not narrativized, and why one narrative is presented rather than another. This reflexivity also calls for an awareness that identities are partially constructed through historical narratives. A deconstructionist historical turn in organization studies also requires a critique of the scientistic, or historicist expectations of theory generation and testing from history.

REFERENCES

Abbott, A. (1992). "From Causes to Events: Notes on Narrative Positivism," *Sociological Methods & Research*, 20: 428–55.

Amatori, F., and Jones, G. (2003). "Introduction." In F. Amatori and G. Jones (eds.), *Business History around the World*. Cambridge: Cambridge University Press: 1–7.

Barrett, F., and Srivasta, S. (1991). "History as Mode of Inquiry in Organizational Life: A Role for Human Cosmogeny," *Human Relations*, 44: 231–54.

Boje, D. (1995). "Stories of the Storytelling Organization—A Postmodern Analysis of Disney as Tamara-Land," *Academy of Management Journal*, 38: 997–1035.

Boje, D. (2008). *Storytelling Organizations*. Thousand Oaks: Sage.

Bruce, K., and Nyland, C. (2011). "Elton Mayo and the Deification of Human Relations," *Organization Studies*, 32: 383–405.

Burke, P. (2008). *What Is Cultural History?* 2nd edn. Cambridge: Polity.

Burrell, G. (1997). *Pandemonium: Towards a Retro-Organization Theory*. London: Sage.

Carr, D. (1998). "Narrative and the Real World: An Argument for Continuity." In B. Fay, P. Pomper, and R. T. Vann (eds.), *History and Theory: Contemporary Readings*. Malden: Blackwell, 137–71.

Chandler, A. (1977). *The Visible Hand: The Managerial Revolution in American Business*. Cambridge, MA: Belknap/Harvard University Press.

Clark, E. (2004). *History, Theory, Text: Historians and the Linguistic Turn*. Cambridge, MA: Harvard University Press.

Clark, P., and Rowlinson, M. (2004). "The Treatment of History in Organisation Studies: Towards an 'Historic Turn'?" *Business History*, 46: 331–52.

Coleman, D. (1987). "The Uses and Abuses of Business History," *Business History*, 29: 141–56.

Coleman, D. (1988). "What is Economic History?" In J. Gardiner (ed.), *What is History Today...?* London: Macmillan: 31–2.

Collini, S. (1988). "What is Intellectual History?" In J. Gardiner (ed.), *What is History Today...?* London: Macmillan: 105–9.

Collins, J., and Porras, J. (1994). *Built to Last: Successful Habits of Visionary Companies*, 1st edn. New York: HarperBusiness.

Cooke, B. (2003). "The Denial of Slavery in Management Studies," *Journal of Management Studies*, 40: 1895–918.

Daly, S. (2007). "Spinning Cotton: Domestic and Industrial Novels," *Victorian Studies*, 50: 272–8.

Deal, T., and Kennedy, A. (2000). *The New Corporate Cultures: Revitalizing the Workplace after Downsizing, Mergers, and Reengineering*. London: Texere.

Decker, S. (2010). "Postcolonial Transitions in Africa: Decolonization in West Africa and Present Day South Africa," *Journal of Management Studies*, 47: 791–813.

du Gay, P. (2000). *In Praise of Bureaucracy: Weber—Organization—Ethics*. London: Sage.

Durepos, G. (2009). "ANTi-History: Toward an Historiographical Approach to (Re) assembling Knowledge of the Past," Ph.D. dissertation (Saint Mary's University, Halifax, Nova Scotia).

Durepos, G., Mills, A., and Helms Mills, J. (2008). "Tales in the Manufacture of Knowledge: Writing a Company History of Pan American World Airways," *Management & Organizational History*, 3: 63–80.

Eisenhardt, K. (1989). "Building Theories from Case-study Research," *Academy of Management Review*, 14: 532–50.

Elton, G. (1967). *The Practice of History*. London: Fontana.

Evans, R. (2001 [1997]). *In Defence of History*. London: Granta.

Fay, B. (1998). "The Linguistic Turn and Beyond in Contemporary Theory of History." In B. Fay, P. Pomper, and R. T. Vann (eds.), *History and Theory: Contemporary Readings*. Malden: Blackwell, 1–12.

Ferguson, N. (2011). "Watch this Man," *London Review of Books*, 33(22), 17 November, Letters (accessed July 18, 2013 in <http://www.lrb.co.uk/v33/n21/pankaj-mishra/watch-this-man>).

Finney, P. (2005). "Beyond the Postmodern Moment?" *Journal of Contemporary History*, 40: 149–65.

Friedman, M. (1953). "The Methodology of Positive Economics." In *Essays in Positive Economics*. Chicago: University of Chicago Press.

Galambos, L. (2003). "Identity and the Boundaries of Business History: An Essay on Consensus and Creativity." In F. Amatori and G. Jones (eds.), *Business History around the World*. Cambridge: Cambridge University Press, 11–30.

Galambos, L. (2004). "The Monopoly Enigma, the Reagan Administration's Antitrust Experiment, and the Global Economy." In K. Lipartito and D. Sicilia (eds.), *Constructing Corporate America: History, Politics, Culture*. Oxford: Oxford University Press: 149–67.

Godelier, E. (2009). "History, a Useful 'Science' for Management? From Polemics to Controversies," *Enterprise & Society*, 10: 791–807.

Goodman, R., and Kruger, E. (1988). "Data Dredging or Legitimate Research Method—Historiography and its Potential for Management Research," *Academy of Management Review*, 13: 315–25.

Gunn, S. (2006). *History and Cultural Theory*. Harlow: Pearson Education.

Guthey, E. (2004). "New Economy Romanticism, Narratives of Corporate Personhood, and the Antimanagerial Impulse." In K. Lipartito and D. Sicilia (eds.), *Constructing Corporate America: History, Politics, Culture*. Oxford: Oxford University Press, 321–42.

Hansen, P. (2007). "Organizational Culture and Organizational Change: The Transformation of Savings Banks in Denmark, 1965–1990," *Enterprise & Society*, 8: 920–53.

Harvey, C., Press, J., and Maclean, M. (2011). "William Morris, Cultural Leadership, and the Dynamics of Taste," *Business History Review*, 85: 245–71.

Hassard, J., and Rowlinson, M. (2002). "Researching Foucault's Research: Organization and Control in Joseph Lancaster's Monitorial Schools," *Organization*, 9: 615–39.

Jenkins, K. (1991). *Re-Thinking History*. London: Routledge.

Jeremy, D., and Tweedale, G. (2005). "Editors' Introduction." In D. J. Jeremy and G. Tweedale (eds.), *Business History*, Vol. I. London: Sage: vii–xxxiv.

Jones, G. (2005). *Renewing Unilever: Transformation and Tradition*. Oxford: Oxford University Press.

Jones, G. (2010). *Beauty Imagined: A History of the Global Beauty Industry*. Oxford: Oxford University Press.

Jones, G., and Sluyterman, K. (2003). "British and Dutch Business History." In G. Jones and F. Amatori (eds.), *Business History around the World*. Cambridge: Cambridge University Press: 111–145.

Jones, G., and Zeitlin, J. (2008). *The Oxford Handbook of Business History*. Oxford: Oxford University Press.

Karnani, A. (2007). "Doing Well by Doing Good—Case Study: 'Fair & Lovely' Whitening Cream," *Strategic Management Journal*, 28: 1351–7.

Kieser, A. (1994). "Crossroads—Why Organization Theory Needs Historical Analyses—and How These Should Be Performed," *Organization Science*, 5: 608–20.

Kilduff, M. (1993). "Deconstructing Organizations," *Academy of Management Review*, 18: 13–31.

Kipping, M., and Üsdiken, B. (2008). "Business History and Management Studies." In G. Jones and J. Zeitlin (eds.), *The Oxford Handbook of Business History*. Oxford: Oxford University Press: 96–119.

Kobrak, C., and Schneider, A. (2011). "Varieties of Business History: Subject and Methods for the Twenty-first Century," *Business History*, 53: 401–24.

Kroeze, R., and Keulen, S. (2012). "Understanding Management Gurus and Historical Narratives: The Benefits of a Historic Turn in Management and Organization Studies," *Management & Organizational History*, 7: 171–89.

Lamoreaux, N., Raff, D., and Temin, P. (2004). "Against Whig History," *Enterprise & Society*, 5: 376–87.

Lamoreaux, N., Raff, D., and Temin, P. (2008). "Economic Theory and Business History." In G. Jones and J. Zeitlin (eds.), *The Oxford Handbook of Business History*. Oxford: Oxford University Press: 37–66.

Linde, C. (2009). *Working the Past: Narratives and Institutional Memory.* New York: Oxford University Press.

Lipartito, K. (2004). "The Utopian Corporation." In K. Lipartito and D. Sicilia (eds.), *Constructing Corporate America: History, Politics, Culture.* Oxford: Oxford University Press: 94–119.

Lipartito, K. (2008). "Business Culture." In G. Jones and J. Zeitlin (eds.), *The Oxford Handbook of Business History.* Oxford: Oxford University Press, 603–28.

Lipartito, K., and Sicilia, D. (eds.) (2004a). *Constructing Corporate America: History, Politics, Culture.* Oxford: Oxford University Press.

Lipartito, K., and Sicilia, D. (2004b). "Introduction: Crossing Corporate Boundaries." In K. Lipartito and D. Sicilia (eds.), *Constructing Corporate America: History, Politics, Culture.* Oxford: Oxford University Press: 1–26.

Maltby, J., and Rutterford, J. (2006). "She Possessed Her Own Fortune: Women Investors from the Late Nineteenth Century to the early Twentieth Century," *Business History,* 48: 220–53.

Martin, J. (2002). *Organizational Culture: Mapping the Terrain.* London: Sage.

Martin, J., and Frost, P. (1999). "The Organizational Culture War Games: A Struggle for Intellectual Dominance." In S. Clegg and C. Hardy (eds.), *Studying Organization: Theory & Method.* London: Sage: 345–67.

Martin, J., Frost, P., and O'Neill, O. (2006). "Organizational Culture: Beyond Struggles for Intellectual Dominance." In S. Clegg, C. Hardy, T. Lawrence, and W. Nord (eds.), *The Sage Handbook of Organization Studies,* 2nd edn. London: Sage: 725–53.

Mayhew, A. (2009). *Narrating the Rise of Big Business in the USA.* New York: Routledge.

Mills, A. (2006). *Sex, Strategy and the Stratosphere: Airlines and the Gendering of Organizational Culture.* New York: Palgrave Macmillan.

Mishra, P. (2011). "Watch this Man. Review of Civilisation: The West and the Rest by Niall Ferguson," *London Review of Books,* 33(21) 3 November 2011: 10–12.

Munslow, A. (2003). *The New History.* Harlow: Pearson Education.

O'Sullivan, M., and Graham, M. (2010). "Moving Forward by Looking Backward: Business History and Management Studies," *Journal of Management Studies,* 47: 775–90.

Pendergrast, M. (2000). *For God, Country, and Coca-Cola: The Definitive History of the Great American Soft Drink and the Company that Makes It,* 2nd edn. New York: Basic Books.

Perrow, C. (2008). "Conservative Radicalism," *Organization,* 15: 915–21.

Peters, T., and Waterman, R. (1982). *In Search of Excellence: Lessons from America's Best-Run Companies.* New York: Harper & Row.

Popp, A. (2006). " 'Though it Is but a Promise': Business Probity in Arnold Bennett's Anna of the Five towns," *Business History,* 48: 332–53.

Popp, A. (2009). "History, a Useful "Science" for Management? A Response," *Enterprise & Society,* 10: 831–36.

Popper, K. (2002 [1957]). "The Poverty of Historicism," London: Routledge.

Rappaport, E. (2008). "Imperial Possessions, Cultural Histories, and the Material Turn: Response," *Victorian Studies,* 50: 289–96.

Rhodes, C., and Brown, A. (2005). "Narrative, Organizations and Research," *International Journal of Management Reviews,* 7: 167–88.

Ricoeur, P. (1985). *Time and Narrative: Volume 2*. Chicago: University of Chicago Press.

Ricoeur, P. (1990a). *Time and Narrative: Volume 1*. Chicago: University of Chicago Press.

Ricoeur, P. (1990b). *Time and Narrative: Volume 3*. Chicago: University of Chicago Press.

Rowlinson, M. (1988). "The Early Application of Scientific Management by Cadbury," *Business History*, 30: 377–95.

Rowlinson, M., and Delahaye, A. (2009). "The Cultural Turn in Business History," *Enterprises et Histoire*, 55: 90–110.

Rowlinson, M., and Hassard, J. (1993). "The Invention of Corporate Culture—A History of the Histories of Cadbury," *Human Relations*, 46: 299–326.

Rowlinson, M., and Hassard, J. (2011). "How Come the Critters Came to be Teaching in Business Schools? Contradictions in the Institutionalization of Critical Management Studies," *Organization*, 18: 673–89.

Rowlinson, M., Booth, C., Clark, P., Delahaye, A., and Procter, S. (2010). "Social Remembering and Organizational Memory," *Organization Studies*, 31: 69–87.

Rowlinson, M., Stager Jacques, R., and Booth, C. (2009). "Critical Management and Organizational History." In M. Alvesson, H. Willmott, and T. Bridgman (eds.), *Handbook of Critical Management Studies*. Oxford: Oxford University Press: 286–303.

Scranton, P. (2008). "Beyond Chandler?" *Enterprise & Society*, 9: 426–9.

Stone, L. (1979). "The Revival of Narrative—Reflections on a New Old History," *Past & Present*, 85: 3–24.

Suddaby, R., Foster, W., and Trank, C. (2010). "Rhetorical History as a Source of Competitive Advantage." In J. Baum and J. Lampel (eds.), *Globalization of Strategy Research*, Vol. 27. London: Emerald, 147–73.

Toms, S., and Wilson, J. (2003). "Scale, Scope and Accountability: Towards a New Paradigm of British Business History," *Business History*, 45: 1–23.

Toms, J., and Wilson, J. (2010). "In Defence of Business History: A Reply to Taylor, Cooke, and Bell," *Management & Organizational History*, 5: 109–20.

Tosh, J. (2010). *The Pursuit of History: Aims, Methods, and New Directions in the Study of Modern History*, 5th edn. London: Pearson.

Üsdiken, B., and Kieser, A. (2004). "Introduction: History in Organisation Studies," *Business History*, 46: 321–30.

Voronov, M. (2008). "Toward Engaged Critical Management Studies," *Organization*, 15: 939–45.

Walker, J. (2004). "White Corporate America: The New Arbiter of Race?" In K. Lipartito and D. Sicilia (eds.), *Constructing Corporate America: History, Politics, Culture*. Oxford: Oxford University Press: 246–93.

White, H. (1987). *The Content of the Form: Narrative Discourse and Historical Representation*. Baltimore: Johns Hopkins University Press.

White, H. (1998 [1978]). "The Historical Text as Literary Artifact." In B. Fay, P. Pomper, and R. T. Vann (eds.), *History and Theory: Contemporary Readings*. Malden: Blackwell, 15–33.

Wilson, B. (2010). "'Stuck with Your Own Face.' Review of *Beauty Imagined: A History of the Global Beauty Industry* by Geoffrey Jones," *London Review of Books*, 32: 31–2.

Zald, M. (1991). "Sociology as a Discipline: Quasi-Science and Quasi-Humanities," *American Sociologist*, 22: 165–87.

Zald, M. (1993). "Organization Studies as a Scientific and Humanistic Enterprise—Toward a Reconceptualization of the Foundations of the Field," *Organization Science*, 4: 513–28.

Zald, M. (1996). "More Fragmentation? Unfinished Business in Linking the Social Sciences and the Humanities," *Administrative Science Quarterly*, 41: 251–61.

Part II

Actors and Markets

7

Mining the Past: Historicizing Organizational Learning and Change

Jeffrey Fear

As anyone knows from having watched Internet firms try to create "communities", people commit to each other; they do not commit to AOL, Microsoft, unless these abstractions become part of an identity. The orientation of a knowledge perspective is to understand the origins of advantages in firms as social communities that are resistant to manipulation by social engineering theories of strategic leadership. We are very skeptical that strategic theories of resources will advance in the absence of a more profound investigation of the cognitive and social foundations of knowledge.

(Bruce Kogut and Udo Zander, "A Memoir and Reflection," 2003: 509)

At the beginning of the 1890s, August Thyssen (the German equivalent of Andrew Carnegie) and his chief technical director, Franz Dahl, used to stand in the middle of the steelworks and discuss new investments. Dahl frequently recommended major initiatives, which Thyssen approved or rejected on the spot. Afterwards, in Dahl's words, an "immense" administration was built, which mediated the information received by Thyssen. An incessant business traveler, Thyssen was increasingly away from the factory floor. Dahl urged Thyssen to buy a heavy, expensive crane from one company, but the purchasing office rejected Dahl's recommendation in favor of a lighter, less expensive crane from another company. Thyssen sided with his purchasing executive. Shortly after installation, the crane collapsed, killing the crane operator. This "drastic," "deeply regrettable," and avoidable loss of life ended up costing more than the expensive crane. Thyssen formulated a new policy that gave authority to the directors of technical departments; purchasing offices had to adhere to their guidelines and recommendations (Fear, 2005: 32).

This simple example illustrates a number of themes to be discussed in this chapter. First, the informal, personal form of enterprise gave way to a managerial corporation. But the famous dictum "structure follows strategy" rarely shows "the processes by which historical actors created and linked strategic goals with an effective organizational structure" (Carlson, 1995: 58). Second, the crane incident demonstrates the emergence of a new routine to prevent past mistakes; we hence have a snapshot about organizational learning. The sedimentation of thousands of such hidden choices within the firm created organizational capacity and shaped future decision making. It is precisely here where historians, as miners, might uncover the forgotten events, choices, or rationales that cemented certain procedures, certain choices—and not others—into the firm. Third, *if* Thyssen had not been as distanced from Dahl, he *might* have made another choice—then again maybe not. The "if" and "might" conditions faced by Thyssen highlight choice and ambiguity; both options were "rational choices," but with distinctly different rationales—leaving aside the alternative that the crane operator would not have been killed. Fourth, by analyzing how *historical actors* viewed, interpreted, and solved problems inside the organization, we can better understand the *process* "in-between," rather than a snapshot of before and after. Such historical motivations, perceptions, processes, and contingencies represent a deep longitudinal context or path-dependent moment (Pettigrew, Woodman, and Cameron, 2001).

This chapter explores the "logics of history" (Sewell, 2005) and maps five intersections in which historical thinking can be used by researchers in understanding organizational change inside businesses. If one only examines process at one point in time without a comparative sense of time and space, the danger is that one develops universalizing theories based on the present, or at one period of time in one culture, missing the "time-bound" and "place-bound" dimension of theory. A close, accurate, but imaginative long- to medium-term reconstruction of the internal life of the corporate organization is integral for developing any sort of theory (Weick, 1989). As Kogut and Zander (2003) argue for strategy studies, "firms as social communities" have their own expectations, dynamics, and identity created by their common, shared history. But that history must first be recovered.

MINING FIVE INTERSECTIONS

Missed Opportunities

If (organizational) learning is a process of discovery and adaptation, of working through new information and alternatives to arrive at new conclusions and new actionable knowledge, which are subsequently utilized to execute new strategies, then an accurate rendition of this internal *process* is necessary in order to understand how (organizational) learning takes place (Langley, 1999). Learning is inherently processual because of its rough temporal sequencing: identification of a problem(s); discerning the nature of the problem(s); deciding to solve the problem(s); and enacting the solution(s)—each often overlapping stage of the process subject to conflicts of interpretation and interests among groups of people (March and Olsen, 1976; Argyris and Schön, 1978; Argyris, 1993, 2003).

This single-loop model, however, might evolve into a double-loop learning process whereby the fundamental norms of the organization are called into question and altered. Understanding this process of double-loop learning (Argyris and Schon, 1978) is particularly important as such fundamental change usually becomes an "event" surrounded by conflicts. Controversies arise precisely because actors do not view fundamental problems or solutions in the same way so that the process by which alternatives are sorted through to find a new direction also need recovering as such options represent alternative paths at a given point in time. Such events leave traces, imprinting themselves on the organization—traces that historical research can uncover (Marquis and Huang, 2010).

Not all actions constitute transformative, significant events that alter organizational structures, behaviors, and culture (see Sewell, 2005: 197–270 for a theory of the "event"). As the theory of the firm increasingly rests upon organizational learning (Dierkes, Antal, Child, and Nonaka, 2001), knowledge creation (Nonaka and Takeuchi, 1995), a knowledge-based view of the firm, a learning organization (Senge, 1990), or a "knowing organization" (Choo, 2006), it also becomes important to understand "how does someone in the organization know what one knows." What makes something a learning event rather than merely an action? How is this knowledge disseminated, absorbed, and enacted across an organization? The answers to these questions need to be mapped to organizational processes in time. By targeting those crucial events, identifying controversial internal debates, or tracing the more subtle but important organizational shifts over time, we might mine yet more insight into this double-loop learning process, which cannot be captured as abstracted variables or causes that eliminate human behavior and time (Pettigrew, Woodman, and Cameron, 2001: 700). Organizational theorists and historians could isolate these transformative events in the past to better understand both successful and unsuccessful transitions.

Process is as important to organizational theorists as it is to historians, yet there is not yet much dialogue between the two disciplines. Aside from economic historians, the social scientific testing of historical data is not generally followed by historians who prefer to "get to know" their subjects as human beings or interpersonal communities with shared identities. The classic works of Alfred D. Chandler (1962, 1990), who theorized the development of the multidivisional structure, managed to synthesize history and organizational studies by developing a model of organizational change centered on the managerial architect at the staff level (Chandler, 1962: 283–323). In later works Chandler stressed the importance of organizational learning in theory, but in practice his own work became increasingly structural as he focused more on industry dynamics and country/corporate competitiveness. In order to bring organizational learning processes to light, we need to learn more about the internal organizational life of business corporations, which is still largely *terra incognita* (Cassis, 1997: 157–67). Lamoreaux, Raff and Temin (1995, 1999) offer a series of edited collections on information, coordination, and learning-by-doing inside the business enterprise, but they are largely American-based and economics-oriented. More cross-national analyses in organizational learning or strategic planning under the impact of different regulatory regimes, ownership structures, and cultures are still needed (Whittington, Cailluet, and Yakis-Douglas, 2011).

Few explicit studies of *internal* organizational processes of businesses exist because historians do not tend to concentrate on the internal life of organizations per se except as an illustration of broader social developments. If studied, the organization itself is a site to analyze something else: class relations in labor history; gender attitudes and how they structure business life; political attitudes or the social attitudes of entrepreneurs; or broader dynamics such as the rise of economies of scale and scope or transaction costs. Sociology and history intersect considerably in social history, but less so in organizational history (Fear, 2001). A recent state-of-the-art survey of business history offered no chapter on the relationship of business history and organizational theory, although two chapters on management studies (Kipping and Üsdiken, 2007) and accounting, information, and communication systems (Boyns, 2007) came close. Neither engages with the vast theoretical literature on organizations stemming mostly from sociology.

Yet this lack of attention to organizational matters and the lack of dialogue between business historians and organizational theorists is a profound missed opportunity, especially as both groups study the business firm itself! Often the same meta-thinkers, including Adam Smith, Max Weber, Talcott Parsons, Clifford Geertz, Karl Weick, and Michel Foucault, have heavily influenced both disciplines. In the 1980s, a simultaneous "cognitive turn" in organizational studies and the "cultural turn" in history took place, often relying on the same theorists. Of the modern group, Clifford Geertz provides an anchor for both fields. Business historians trace their common methodology to Alfred D. Chandler (who was in turn strongly influenced by Max Weber, Joseph Schumpeter, and Talcott Parsons) or, alternatively, Oliver Williamson (transaction cost theory, firm as a nexus of contracts.) So, given these shared intellectual traditions and the common focus on the organization, the lack of dialogue between organizational theorists and business historians is just weird. We have a common set of intellectuals, but somehow not a common language or goals.

Finally, almost all organizational theories at some point rely on "stories" to illustrate or make sense of organizations, say the Toyota-General Motors NUMMI example (O'Reilly and Pfeffer, 2000), the *Challenger* and *Columbia* space shuttle accidents (Choo, 2006: 249–82), Matsushita's Home Baker (Nonaka and Takeuchi, 1995: 95–123), or Fiat's Melfi Factory (Patriotta, 2003). All of these authors are actually engaging some form of historical thinking already.

While there are many fruitful points of intersection, this chapter explores five: (1) the use of retrospective knowledge; (2) the examination of process or narrative; (3) the embeddedness of action in time and place (periodization); (4) historical actors' experience, that is, their knowledge and interpretation of their self (self-understanding, memory, narrative as construction of perception and identity), and (5) historical alternatives, that is, choice under conditions of ambiguity and human agency. With each intersection I want to stress the central role that "understanding" (*Verstehen*, Max Weber) plays in the historical profession, which tends to preclude historians from broader theory-building based on ahistorical "variables" and "causes" and leads them to emphasize explanations based on the thoughts and choices of people in a given context under conditions of ambiguity and, quite literally, an unknown future created by those very choices.

Intersection 1: Retrospective Knowledge

Because a historical perspective is necessarily retrospective, the researcher has access to information that contemporaries did not have about the future and can judge outcomes or the long-term consequences of (quiet) choices for their *significance*—a luxury theorists studying organizations in the present cannot have. Retrospective knowledge is based on the premise that the meaning and significance of events hinge on developments that take place after, sometimes *long* after, the original event takes place. For instance, the US Constitution sidestepped the issue of whether the "people" or the states "consented" to the Union and made compromises regarding slavery, but the long-term consequences of these choices contributed to the Civil War. The *meaning* of this founding compromise changed because of a war nearly eighty years later. A similar process occurred with the signing of the Helskinki Accords in 1975, which recognized the formal sovereignty of Soviet rule over Eastern Europe. At the time, it seemed to reinforce Soviet rule, yet by introducing Principles VII and VIII that guaranteed human rights and certain fundamental rights, the Soviet Union inadvertently unleashed a wave of civil society groups across Eastern Europe demanding greater freedoms. In the longer run, Helsinki helped to undermine Soviet rule from within rather than reinforce it (Judt, 2005: 501–3, 569–70).

Applied to organizational studies, a long-term historical perspective that uncovers a deeply hidden past and path-dependent choices offers the opportunity to re-frame the understanding or theory of a decision-making process occurring later in a briefer moment in time (see Intersection 3) (Jones and Khanna, 2006). One might be able to see a recurrent pattern that could not have been identified without a broader array of organizational learning examples from within the organization over time. Past compromises or subtle changes in internal rhetoric potentially set the stage for subsequent action with unintended results.

Organizational theorists can also reconstruct the *experience* (see Intersection 4) of such crucial turning points, events, or subtle shifts in approach, culture, or language using historical methods (see Part III of this volume). Since organizational learning is the interaction among a great many individuals who learn (or do not learn as the case may be), it is by nature a social process inside individual organizations. Well-constructed, historically accurate, reliable stories are a classic way of showing the process of change among historical actors or groups who perhaps disagreed with one another.

"History" should not be understood as "chronology," single "examples," "case studies," or "stories" mined more or less selectively to support or illustrate a given theory; but as *reconstruction* and *representation* of past (decision-making) processes that permitted individuals, organizations, or societies to arrive at their present condition through choice and human agency. Knowing long-term outcomes alters the *meaning* of events or decisions taken in the past, but a long or medium-term perspective must first be reconstructed.

Intersection 2: Process

It is striking that it is in both professions' interests to reconstruct insightfully the microprocessual world of learning inside organizations so as to derive meaningful model- or theory-building (Langley, 1999). A bad reconstruction will lead to bad conclusions and banal theories. "Stories" or "narratives" can be understood as reconstructions of process. Juxtaposing organizational processes at different junctures in time would also provide a sense of how much an organization changed (or did not), or changed in ways that were intended or unintended (see Intersection 1). Contrasting internal decision-making processes across space—for example by comparing how Japanese, American, or Italian businesses reacted to specific crises, say the oil shocks of the 1970s or the financial crisis of 2008–2010—to test existing theories would prove helpful. They would not only enrich the range of experiences, but also more importantly test the limits of established theory. Here joint ventures among organizational theorists and historians might prove useful for isolating the role of periodization (Intersection 3) or by comparing and contrasting discrete processual sequences at critical junctures.

Consider an example of a technology transfer of an innovative welded pipe process, then called the Fretz-Moon process, from the US to the "US Steel of Germany" (Vereinigte Stahlwerke, USW). In 1929 a young engineer discovered a new welded pipe process in Pennsylvania that appeared to revolutionize pipe welding. It took two years of internal debates to decide whether to adopt it because the USW was riddled with internal merger rivalries of the four main former firms. The technology eventually went to a former Thyssen plant in Mülheim (Ruhr) largely due to the initiative of local plant executives. This long forgotten choice had long-term consequences as it kept Mülheim one of the main centers for welded pipe production on the European continent today when it might have been closed (as were other USW pipe plants after its adoption). In microcosm, however, this "story" illuminated almost the entire dysfunctional decision-making process inside the USW, which eventually forced its reorganization into a multidivisional enterprise. Astoundingly, the process of reorganizing confirmed Chandler's (1962) basic transition model found at General Motors and DuPont, but the USW organizational transition owed little to American examples. Through an entirely *different* process of organizational learning, with different motivations, different needs, and a different institutional-legal environment (including financial constraints with American-led bondholders, a different legal theory of the firm, and negotiations with the new Nazi state), German firms too arrived at a multidivisional form a few years after the first American ones did (Fear, 2005: 606–76).

Examining Thomson-Houston (later General Electric), which absorbed Edison General Electric Company in 1892, Carlson (1995) asked why firms exploiting similar technologies organized themselves in different ways. He found that different "interest groups" within the firm possessed different technological "mindsets" so they had conflicting visions about the future "best use" of the new electric lighting technology, which then determined the strategic direction of the firm. (Note that the future technological options remained open and unknown.) Opinions divided along three interest group lines: ones that stressed marketing and finance (customer-led innovation), manufacturing and engineering (reduction of production costs through scale), and invention and design (designing high quality and technically perfect products). The first option raised the cost of production through customer-led customization; the second option reduced production costs, but might preclude crucial customer-oriented innovations or might lock in a less efficient design that might become obsolete in an infant technology; the last option raised the cost of products considerably but kept Thomson-Houston on the cutting edge of innovation. After intense, often angry negotiations, a series of internal compromises settled many of the debates; one innovative solution was the creation of a central laboratory to permit the invention and design team to use their talents for a bevy of different products. For Carlson, personalities and functional expertise underlay the different mindsets, which created different organizational solutions than at rivals Edison or Westinghouse. Retrospectively (Intersection 1), we know Thomson-Houston won by beating Edison General and Westinghouse, but the success was not preordained.

Both examples of technological adoption, the Fretz-Moon process at the USW and the central laboratory at Thomson-Houston, demonstrate how such forgotten choices or compromises created a path-dependent trajectory for that region or firm/industry for decades to come. Many of these processes took years or decades of learning, institutionalization, and readjustment to work through and prove successful or unsuccessful. In short, historical methods can provide a sense of this messy process of organizational learning, overcoming snapshot, before-and-after, and input-output approaches, but *such processes have to be reconstructed*. Fine-grained research rediscovering micro-organizational processes is by definition specific until a number of cases are built upon, then compared under controlled questioning.

Intersection 3: Embeddedness in Time and Place, or Periodization

By utilizing rigorous historical methods, which stress the proper collection and arranging of data, artifacts, and memory shards from the past, individual case studies can be quite robust in their reliability, their internal validity, and their insight into particular events by positioning them in either historiography (previous interpretations) or a particular set of theories, debates, or issues. This is, in principle, no different than articles found in many management journals. Indeed, a single story framed by a clear set of theoretical issues sometimes works in management journals (for example, see Perez-Aleman and Sandiman, 2008). By definition "unique cases," such as good biographies of key business (Steve Jobs) or political figures (Abraham Lincoln), expose a range of "truths" that cannot be captured by social scientific methods alone. But the theoretical issues raised by a case depends on how the researcher temporally embeds the particular figure or subject in a set of broader questions through periodization.

Stories should be considered the friends, not enemies, of theory, as stories are not inherently atheoretical, but sung in a different key, told in a different genre (see the chapter by Yates in this volume). One can hear the guilt in the voice of Pietra Rivoli, a management scholar, when she wrote the book *Travels of a T-Shirt in a Global Economy*, which did not "test" a particular hypothesis about trade. Yet by reconstructing the history of her single T-shirt, by following its value chain, exposing the lives of people who touched it, and delving into the politics of global trade, Rivoli offers a meaningful, insightful portrait of globalization at the beginning of the 21st century (Rivoli, 2009). Note the language of meaningful and insightful versus proof, testing, and theory. Rivoli is an accidental historian.

Historical reasoning establishes causation and significance by relating events, actions, and actors' reasons to past, present, and future developments based on multiple layers of causation. Historians tend to embed their "story" into previous historiography (prior interpretations) in the introduction so as to differentiate their interpretation from those of others in a more or less theoretical fashion (see Lipartito, this volume). Narratives also signal "theory" by where one starts or ends a story (periodization). The "story" (a beginning, middle, and end) *is* an act of interpretation, selection, and analysis—in competition with other alternatives. All good histories are quite clear about the main causes of particular events even if they are told in a highly fluid narrative.

As an example of this multiple layering and periodization, it is standard in business or economic history to frame an individual history of an established large-scale business within a nested set of temporal frames. One of these frames is likely to be the broader picture of the rise of big business in Japan, the US, and Europe during the Second Industrial Revolution (ca. 1860s to 1950s), with its distinct tendency to large-scale, capital-intensive business. Layered over that first frame might be a second one based on the "first wave of globalization" (built on open trade and the gold standard from the 1870s to 1914) that ended abruptly with World War I and shut down global markets. Then, specific industries would have enormously varying temporal dynamics: chemicals are not furniture or restaurants. Next, different countries had different rules regarding big business, such as anti-trust in the US and pro-cartel legislation in Germany. Then, depending on the individual firm, the personality and personal context of the entrepreneur may have to be taken into account. For historians, deciding the most relevant explanatory layers, from the general to the specific, to situate a given set of developments or events is fundamentally an act of sensemaking built on plots, themes, and recurrent patterns. If one magically transported in time the exact same organization from 1932 to 2012, the context of decision-making would be so different that the same rules would probably not apply. At least with a historian's sensibility, organizational learning or change would have to be embedded in a particular time and place.

Having written an in-depth, historical study of corporate organizational change covering sixty years, I established that the main drivers affecting the management system of German steel firms changed dramatically over time. I would have found it difficult to create a single theory to describe sixty years of learning or change even for a single firm. In some time periods industry economics drove organizational change, in others political economic developments such as labor representation or armaments production predominated, in yet other phases financial and merger issues were paramount. In Germany, certain events such as the loss of World War I and subsequent hyperinflation or, later, Hitler's preparation for war, would be unique. Post-World War II reconstruction might be comparable across Western Europe and Japan, but not for the United States, and certainly not for sub-Saharan Africa, the Soviet Union, China, or Brazil. Learning to cope with severe crises, such as the oil shocks of the 1970s, created an entirely different set of organizational dynamics than various financial crises. The second wave of accelerating globalization in the mid-1980s and after the collapse of communism would be told differently had it been a Chinese firm or an American firm that was the subject of study. Also different management ideas, including Taylorism, Fordism, the M-Form conglomeration, and shareholder value, would be layered over these broader changes to account for how executives understood organizational change (Fear, 2005; Jones, 2005).

Periodization offers a framework for understanding certain environmental contexts that must be considered to understand firm strategies and micro-organizational change. These contextual periodizations are not uncontested, let alone inappropriate for certain countries, so that theories of organizational change and learning might be better considered time-or-space-bound, rather than universal. In part for this reason, a great number of business historians have also taken issue with the "one best way" or linear approach for organizing (big) businesses across time and space (Jones, 2008; Scranton, 2004).

Space-bound contexts are also important. Most pertinent to the study of business and organizational life might be the role of families in business. While the role of families in big business has waned in the UK and US, family blockholders are still important features across Europe, and the norm in many emerging markets. Yet "families" are not constructed on the same value system across the world. English families of the 19th-century Victorian era are not the same as the nuclear family today, which impacts succession in family businesses, a fact that demands a different approach to periodization. Since the 1960s, a decline in the desire for multigenerational family businesses in America and Europe can be observed. A recent trend among German family-owned midsize businesses is to turn over company leadership to the daughters in the next generation, a practice that has been theoretically possible for over a century but culturally not possible due to accepted gender roles. How increasing numbers of female managers will affect organizational behavior and decision-making remains to be seen. Such cultural constructions of family and gender also shape a contextual periodization, which would alter how one interprets long-term change.

Most historians would be highly wary of building "universal" theories that are "ahistorical" (without a sense of time) or "a-cultural" (without a sense of place, say a national or regional context) or "presentist" (viewing the past in an instrumental way through the lens of the present as if the past were there just to create the present), three of the most serious crimes a historian can commit.

Historical methods would most likely be most useful in developing mid-range theories in embedded time-bound conceptual frameworks that hold periodization of particular features of business life constant. For instance, internationalizing a business, which usually engenders considerable organizational change, was different in the 1930s because of economic nationalism, strict capital controls, and difficult travel conditions than in the globalized, jet-, and internet-connected world of the 21st century.

Finally, international comparative studies across space are relatively rare so that by default models mostly develop theories based on modern (i.e., since the 1970s), mostly Western corporations with some key contributions from Japan (Pettigrew, Woodman, and Cameron, 2001: 702–4). It is not surprising that Ikujiro Nonaka and Hirotaka Takeuchi's (1995) enriching model of knowledge creation based on the conversion of tacit to explicit knowledge stemmed from many Japanese examples.

Intersection 4: Historical Actors' Experience, that is, Self-understanding, Perception, Narrative, Identity

Considerable overlap in the realm of knowledge, memory, and narrative as the construction of identity exists in both disciplines of history and organizational studies. This is probably the most fruitful area as the cognitive and cultural turn in each discipline has informed a variety of research projects that have successfully integrated "history" itself as a *representation* of an organization's identity or self-understanding that shapes its sensemaking process (Weick, 1995; Hansen, 2012b). Every organization has informal "stories" about how it works or sometimes formal histories (or at least websites) that present the company in some way. The imprint of the past (even incorrect memories or myths) influences the present by shaping an organization's collective identity (or identities) and expectations of the possible in the present for the future: "Courtaulds without fibres would not be Courtaulds" (Owen, 2010: 165). Historians' major contribution to a theory of organizational learning might be locating exactly how the past resides in the present and what present collective memory has conveniently—or inconveniently—forgotten about past events or choices (see Intersection 5 on historical alternatives; Anteby and Molnár, 2012). If an analysis of organizational change is the goal, then contrasting a prior state with a later state—and understanding the processes of learning "in between" (Intersection 2) by which the later state came into being, then one must understand how historical actors perceived their own situation in their terms.

Research on the impact of founders and environmental conditions at the time of founding for the future trajectory and organizational identity of companies form important streams of research in both professions (Marquis and

Huang, 2010; Marquis, 2003; Johnson, 2007; Stinchcombe, 1965; Tedlow, 2006, 2009). It was Stinchcombe who made the famous claim that vested interests (organizational politics), forces of traditionalism (stasis), or an ideological (cultural) position imprints an organization at its inception and constrains its adaptation in the future. For a historian, this is a hypothesis for further "testing"; each of the three reasons implies very different sorts of explanations and methodologies (Fear, 2001). Here collaboration between scholars of both disciplines would enhance each. A longitudinal sensibility tends to be missing in organizational studies (Anteby and Molnár, 2012), while a stronger explicit theoretical framework tends to be missing in historical studies.

Organizational learning and change implies change in ways of thinking and acting over time. In this sense, the inertia of the origins might be less important than analyzing how the organization managed to alter itself at critical moments in time. IBM arguably reinvented itself four times from a mechanical tabulating company, to an electronic one, to a computing mainframe company with the 360, and finally to an IT consulting service company. Based on the history of Courtaulds, Geoffrey Owen (2010) argues that a sense of long-term corporate culture is less important than the ability of a company to reinvent itself in the short term in order to survive over time. Overcoming "inertia" creates longevity rather than drawing down on a company's origins. Often for an organization to change, it must find ways of re-narrating the story it tells about itself (Hansen, 2012b). Cross-national comparisons dealing with a similar financial crisis or a similar set of disruptive technologies might also sensitize researchers to possibilities for learning and change that break the "inertia" of the founding moment. A deep, "thick description" of change in crisis across many different organizations could expose such triggers and processes of learning (Intersection 2). Andy Grove's classic *Only the Paranoid Survive* (1999) related how hard it was for Intel to overcome its image as a memory producer before it concentrated on microprocessors, selling off the "core business" to find a new one. It is important to note that it took five years of reflection and teaching strategy at Stanford for Grove to situate his own experience and explain why it was so hard to change (Intersection 1). In Intel's case, its "memory producer identity" was inertia; Intel's ability to reinvent itself kept it, paradoxically, "Intel." To think through his experience, Grove too wrote an autobiographical "history" of that strategic inflection point.

However, initial imprinting and/or identity may *not* be a source of inertia. For instance, American and German savings banks had deep common roots that initially prevented both from engaging in most standard bank lending practices to consumers or private businesses. A strong collective identity of safe saving for the future and catering to the common man in the local populace was cemented into the mission of savings banks. The "panic of 1907" triggered a fundamental "change event" in Germany—but not in America.

Interpretations of the crisis differed across the Atlantic. German savings bank officials lobbied to change regulations to permit checking/giro accounts and establish clearinghouses to ensure liquidity with the intention to start lending to small business owners. They were successful in changing overall regulatory policy, including small business loans, but *not* their basic mission and identification of catering to their local community, their original imprinting. Although sometimes outsiders attempted to loosen regulatory restrictions, the mentality of American savings bankers blocked change. Both countries' savings banks retained their *original* "imprinted" identity and mission, but bank *strategies* changed. German bankers reinterpreted their core identity so that it included other banking instruments. The long-term results could not be more different as American savings banks declined until deregulation wiped them out. German savings banks, however, have become the single largest banking group in Germany today utilizing a range of universal banking methods, yet they retain their savings bank original "imprinting." Collectively they act as a counterweight to large commercial banks as they have since the 19th century (Fear and Wadhwani, 2013). Original imprinting can explain the core identity, organizational culture, and mission, but not the subsequent trajectory or how the core identity worked as a reservoir of cultural capital to be *mobilized* in different ways. Original imprinting became a source of revitalization in Germany, but not America.

Similarly, the business historian Per Hansen (2007) studied how historical narratives affected organizational choice. Executives of a large commercial bank and a medium-sized savings bank agreed to a merger in 1973, but political protests and *other savings banks*, who insisted that savings banks were a popular, democratic, philanthropic, local alternative to parasitic "big capital" banks, blocked the merger. Although the merger made perfect economic sense, this imaginary border, the *idea*, stopped it. Using Weick's sensemaking framework, Hansen (2012a) analyzed the 1922 failure of Scandinavia's largest bank. At one level, there is nothing particularly different about asset price bubbles, busts, bank failures, than victims searching for villains and explanations. Yet at another level competing narratives helped "make sense" of the crisis. One narrative focused on the overweening power of the CEO so that personal and bank speculative failure negatively affected the rest of a victimized society. Represented by the Bank Inspector's Office, a second narrative focused on corporate governance and internal management failures. The third narrative focused on the general economic crisis defined as a profound failure of monetary and legislative policy not disciplined by the gold standard; "un-Danish" excesses permitted by cheap and "idle money" led to its collapse. All three narratives pointed to different policy "solutions": nationalization, greater bank regulation, or fundamentally different monetary and legislative policy, respectively. The second narrative came to dominate due to the prevailing attitudes of those in political power and, in part, because the narrative "personalized" complex events with a ready-to-hand "villain." Narratives were a means of interpreting situations. From a historian's perspective, such narratives provide insight into historical actors' mindsets and perceptions, regardless of what today we might view as the "causes" of this particular financial crisis.

The bottom line is that initial imprinting might lead to inertia—then again, it might not—meaning that it is contingent upon how actors at the time interpreted their founding mission at a *later* point in time. Actors thus self-reflect upon their own history as they understood it in a reflexive learning process. One of the crucial requirements for a historically informed theory of organizational change is the integration of how historical actors viewed their world, interpreted their place and choices *in their time*, and how they legitimized a set of actions taken (or not). Most historians do not take behavior as a given, but as something to be explored in the terms and language that historical actors used. What are the language, information, knowledge, logic, measures, standards, or methods—and the "narratives" actors themselves use in their time? That is the only frame of reference *they* could use.

Most historians are particularly sensitive to how actors explain their own experience, uncovering their own ways of sensemaking. Karl Weick (1995: 129) argued: "Stories are powerful standalone contents for sensemaking." Narratives about oneself, the organization, or nation are also crucial ways of creating and maintaining identity. From this perspective, narratives or stories are less important as accurate reconstructions (Intersection 1), than as *representations* of the past that help constitute social reality, frame actors' horizons, and shape decision making itself. By creating identifications that frame the horizons of the possible and choice ("Courtaulds without fibres would not be Courtaulds"), they help create an imagined community of insiders and outsiders, the possible and the impossible. While the historian has the right to view the problem differently than historical actors, or question a particular person's judgment in the past, or use other methods to analyze a particular issue in the past, the historian does not have the right to ignore the actor's own sensemaking, reasoning, and viewpoint. Here historians *try* to read their way into the actors' perspective (understanding) and read the past "forward" (Intersection 5) rather than in restrospect (Intersection 1). Historical actors might genuinely think in different ways (burning witches as a way of purging evil), thus leading to different choices.

Indeed, management theories themselves are ways of conceptualization that influence actors, but these too have changed over time and often resemble "fads" that are nonetheless important for understanding how executives analyzed and behaved at given points in time (Brindle and Stearns, 2001). What business schools are teaching now shapes the learning lenses and imaginative possibilities of their students as they move into the business world. Enron used to be taught as a strategy case of reinventing stodgy Second Industrial Revolution companies using financial innovation; now Enron is taught in business ethics courses. Frederick Taylor's *The Principles of Scientific Management* (1911) influenced real-life practices. Teaching a shareholder value goal of the firm turns executive attention to share price considerations first; they, in turn, see the firm differently. Not armed with Michael Porter's "five forces" framework, early 20th-century executives might view strategy through different lenses. Entrepreneurs themselves might *perceive* their industry differently (and thus their choices), especially in emergent industries such as automobiles (see Kirsch et al. in this volume) or smartphones. The shift to a knowledge-based view of the firm of the early 21st century not only reflects the shift to a "post-industrial" society, but also reimagines how to conceive firms. Reimagining, re-viewing the firm means opening individuals to other pathways of learning.

By restoring voice to historical actors, we can again hear the ways in which they made sense of their world that might reshape a theory of learning at different points in time. The sociologist Mitchel Abolafia argued in his study of the Federal Reserve that we need a sharper "theory of action that takes account of the interpretive process that guides action. ... Such an approach brings attention back to the economic actors themselves, focusing on their efforts to construct the market" (Abolafia, 2005: 204, 223 respectively). Understanding interpretive process would be central for a concept of organizational learning. For instance, accounting systems are a profound way of "seeing" the firm and its economic performance as they produce a story over time in figures—an "account" (note the linguistic connection to "story," Fear, 2005), yet those ratios are constructed on certain assumptions and not others. A strategy guided by return on investment is different than one guided by return on equity or share price maximization. It is precisely at this intersection where organizational theorists and historians can work most closely together.

Intersection 5: Historical Alternatives

Recovering past interpretations also means recovering alternative choices and potential paths, that is, contingency and historical agency. Exactly the opposite of retrospective knowledge, historians attempt to read evidence "forward," that is, from the point of view of actors who had no other way to know anything about the future. Indeed their choices *made* the future out of a range of possible futures.

Since learning presumes some sort of knowledge, there is a profound philosophical issue at stake when actors have to decide *without knowing* the future. Frank Knight (1921) famously made the distinction between unmeasurable "uncertainty" versus some form of measurable risk. Uncertainty can be further distinguished between conditions of ambiguity and simple unawareness. Economics and organizational theory work regularly with notions of bounded rationality; that is, actors make decisions with limited information (imperfect knowledge), have cognitive limits, and a finite amount of time to make choices—leaving aside decision making under emotional cross-currents of fear, anxiety, or rage. To take it one step further, actors cannot know the future; "non-knowledge" or "unknowledge" is the *absence*, not *lack* of knowledge, as if the future were somehow knowable (Svetlova and van Elst, 2012; Popp, 2013).

The future does not yet exist until actors' choices, in infinite combinations with other people's choices, create new conditions in the timeline that actors cannot possibly know because they are by definition *new*. The consequences of the internal combustion engine are near infinite and it was not an automatic winner vis-à-vis other alternatives such as the electric car (Kirsch et al. in this volume). Switching on a light bulb requires an electrical engineering grid and has changed human behavior such as enabling a 24/7 consumer culture or three shifts of work. Genuine surprise at events or crises (the Titanic, 9/11, or the 2008/9 financial crisis) illuminates the limits of existing knowledge paradigms and rules, which trigger new learning. Precisely at moments of surprise, disruption, crisis, or controversy, existing rules, power structures, and assumptions are questioned that permit researchers to expose how actors re-learned, re-interpreted, and made adjustments. Crises are bad for those in the midst of them, but excellent vantage points for researchers. (A theory of "surprise," in fact, might be a particularly lucrative research path.)

Particularly in the entrepreneurial or inventive act, knowledge of the future is not just ambiguous, uncertain, or unanticipated, but quite literally unknown. As the historian Walter Friedman (2013) reminds us, the lucrative "science" of economic forecasting was born by the desire to banish uncertainty and divine the future, yet the very act of forecasting (if it convinced a large enough number of people) altered or reshaped the economy or stock market itself in the near future. Despite these shifting sands of alternative futures, people still make more or less informed choices based on past experience, rules of thumb, routines, accepted performance standards, management theories, their education, their "gut," and act in the face of an absent future though under circumstances not of their choosing and not just as they please. Historians term this "human agency."

Ironically, this past "forward" thinking in alternatives, historical approach is implicitly institutionalized in the case method teaching of many business schools, which provide a sort of "real-life" rendition of business problems, that is, a "history" of that decision-making moment even if the case is just a few years old. Class discussion demonstrates that students interpret the same case facts differently, draw upon different case facts, and read the situation differently based upon their experiences and assumptions. If it were the "real world," depending on the classroom's choices, future history would be made. It is often a great teachable moment, if the majority's "good" choice at the time based on available information proves a disaster in the future—the advantage of retrospection (Intersection 1). It is a way of learning vicariously from the experiences of others without ruining a company oneself.

Why is it important to think in such a past "forward" manner (Raff, 2013)? First, we all do it because it is all the information we have: "performance data shown represent past performance, which is not a guarantee of future results" (Vanguard website). Second, it helps to re-situate context from the perspective of historical actors themselves, rather than from present theoretical perspectives or retrospective knowledge of the past. We need to understand different learning processes at different times or in different spaces (national, regional, ethnic, ideological contexts).

Third, juxtaposing those differences in learning with what is expected by the researcher creates *reflexivity* on the researcher's own assumptions or models—the essence of double-loop learning. For example, the accounting scholars, H. Thomas Johnson and Robert S. Kaplan (1991) went back to history to revalorize the efforts of Alexander Hamilton Church, who argued for a forgotten, alternative way of assessing the profitability of the firm by including commercial and administrative costs in manufacturing accounting of individual products so as to move beyond the physical conversion cost accounting methods (cost efficiency) as advocated by Frederick Taylor. Johnson and Kaplan critiqued the overuse of return on investment ratios developed in the early 20th century that dominated the way American business "thought" at the time. This rediscovery of a lost alternative eventually contributed to their conceiving a "balanced scorecard" of measurements.

Fourth, managerial and financial accounting are crucial ways that managers create fundamental information and knowledge about a firm. Accounting knowledge effectively shaped decision-making, learning, and behavior inside the firm as it was the information available to historical actors (Fear, 2005). But accounting measurements and ratios have built in alternative assumptions and have varied over time and place, so that organizational learning and knowledge were different.

The bottom line is that business school professors already have a certain familiarity with agency and contingency if they use the case method. Thinking in alternatives, and taking alternatives seriously, means that one can uncover how (historical) actors think about their world in their time rather than imposing on them the assumptions of the present. That juxtaposition of timeframes in past and present creates reflexivity about the assumptions that "we" (or the specific researcher) hold in the present, that is, "it need not be this way." But it is a particularly important perspective to hold if a theory of organizational learning and knowledge creation is at stake because it raises the elemental question of how actors learn and know about their own organization, what information they access to explain themselves, and how they interpret the knowledge that they do have. Rather than just "testing" present models about organizational learning or change "on" the past (still a possibility!), we can

learn about alternative patterns of organizational learning and uses of knowledge "in time" and "from" the past.

CONCLUSION

One of the key powers of historical perspective is the ability to reflect intel-
ligently on the temporal distance between past and present so as to generate
new learning. Rather than just seeing the past as a mine for quarrying further
examples, like diamonds in the rough, a joint alliance between organizational
scholars and historians might act more like diamond cutting, refining theory further so that its implicit universalism becomes more sensitive to time,
place, context, and longitudinal process. A long-term historical perspective
also might ameliorate the "anatomizing urge" of much organization theory to
"butcher" living organizations on the autopsy table of universalizing theory
(Burrell, 2003: 526). Mid-range theorizing can provide the building blocks
for high-level theory or formalization as expected by more social scientific
methods. Sometimes it takes a collection of mid-range cases in dialogue with
theory to slowly change our existing models, but this requires further disciplinary dialogue between organizational theorists and historians.

Suddaby et al.'s (this volume) plea to historicize institutional and organizational change has parallels in political science, which has sought to explain
why capitalism has evolved differently over time by understanding institutional
change (Wolfgang Streeck, 2009; Mahoney and Thelen, 2010). Development
theorists have recently arrived at a similar conclusion on the need for "dialogue"
between history and development theory so that policymakers can be more
realistic about the way policies can be articulated into the flow of a society's
history, as a country is not a laboratory but a more or less uncontrolled experiment (Bayly, Rao, Szreter, and Woolcock, 2011). Behavioral economics has
made inroads into the neoclassical paradigm. One might reflect on why organizational theory, development economics, and political science are turning to
more situationist, behavioral, and contextual perspectives at this juncture in
history. After all, "organizational learning" existed in firms well before the concept arose in theory (Fruin, 1994; Fear, 2001). Why does the *concept* or *theory*
first appear in the mid-1970s, roughly with Argyris and Schön's *Organizational
Learning: A Theory of Action* (1978) and popularized by Peter Senge's *Fifth
Discipline* (1990), over a century after the advent of the modern corporation?

In management studies, knowledge itself became a strategic "resource."
Not surprisingly, the knowledge-based theory of the firm emerged out of the
"resource-based view" of the firm (Kogut and Zander, 1992, 1993, 2003). The
importance of this shift from "resources" to knowledge is analogous to the
shift from analog to digital because knowledge can be copied many times

over, a multiplier effect generating increasing returns, rather than a "resource" that diminishes, depreciates, or experiences a trade-off with another resource that must be arranged internal to the corporation. Kogut and Zander (2003) stressed the cognitive properties of individuals inside networks and institutionalized contexts, which placed a premium on understanding the distinctive aspects of multinationals as "strategies are made in social communities located in institutional settings. Strategy is a *situated* practice" (Kogut and Zander, 2003: 509–10). However, a knowledge-based theory of the firm requires uncovering and understanding the deep processes, resources, and cultural knowledge extant in the firm and its people, that is, how the firm became that way, its history, how it became situated.

One of the most important ways in which business historians might help organizational theory most is by deconstructing and situating the term "knowledge" itself, which in spite of distinguishing between "tacit" and "explicit," remains abstract and static rather than "processual and evolving, inherently provisional, and situated (socially and technically)" (Håkanson, 2010). Such "knowledge" had to be learned, disseminated, and replicated over time, but chances are it was also negotiated, debated, and contested within the firm as different groups of people fought to determine the future direction of the firm. This is where hagiographic histories of firms do a disservice to both history and organizational theory. Kogut and Zander (2003) made an important point that coordination often fails not because people fail to communicate or that they are acting by guile, but because their identities simply get in the way. Håkanson (2010) notes that the integration and re-combination of knowledge requires the coordination and reconciliation of knowledge across epistemic communities, but it too is "fraught with difficulties" because of a lack of common codes, tools, and theories. These authors implicitly suggest that interdisciplinary research also fails for the same reasons that technology or knowledge transfer or diversification strategies fail within firms. They cannot cross community, epistemic, identity lines.

If standards of social scientific "objectivity" and writing are relaxed, particularly since both business historians and organizational theorists have the modern business corporation as their primary unit of analysis, we might find ways to bridge those lines that intersect so often. Histories are most often simply "told" in a different way than social science methodologies, genres, or journal formats precisely because they are often (not always) designed to show processual time. *Timing*, chance, a key encounter, an opportunity missed, a frown or quick glance, and so on are part of that narrative strategy in a story. Kogut and Zander (2003) reminded their readers that "knowledge is often best understood and remembered via stories." Stories are our friends, quasi-natural ways of learning, disseminating, and retaining knowledge. There is a voracious appetite for good analyses about successful businesses or the recent financial crisis. But "stories" are just a different way of analyzing. Integrating history

Organizations in Time

into organizational theory might mean loosening some of the scientific claims of a universal "management science." After all, historically speaking, the "management of men" used to be spoken of as an "art," a skill, an exercise in rhetoric, even a quality of personal character. This might make organizational theory less universal, but more actionable. It is time that disciplinary boundaries are made more "liquid"; after all, in an age of liquid modernity and border-crossing by firms, should not academic disciplines be more fluid too?

REFERENCES

Abolafia, M. Y. (2005). "Making Sense of Recession: Toward an Interpretive Theory of Economic Action." In V. Nee and R. Swedberg (eds.), *The Economic Sociology of Capitalism*. Princeton: Princeton University Press: 204–26.

Anteby, M., and Molnár, V. (2012). "Collective Memory Meets Organizational Identity: Remembering to Forget in a Firm's Rhetorical History," *Academy of Management Journal*, 55(3): 515–40.

Argyris, C. (1993). *Knowledge for Action*. San Francisco: Jossey-Bass.

Argyris, C. (2003). "Actionable Knowledge." In H. Tsoukas and C. Knudsen (eds.), *The Oxford Handbook of Organizational Theory: Meta-Theoretical Perspectives*. Oxford: Oxford University Press: 423–52.

Argyris, C., and Schön, D. A. (1978). *Organizational Learning: A Theory of Action Perspective*. Reading, MA: Addison-Wesley.

Bayly, C.A., Rao V., Szreter, S., and Woolcock, M. (2011). *History, Historians and Development Policy: A Necessary Dialogue*. Manchester: Manchester University Press.

Boyns, T. (2007). "Accounting, Information, and Communication Systems." In G. Jones and J. Zeitlin, (eds.), *The Oxford Handbook of Business History*. Oxford: Oxford University Press: 447–69.

Brindle, M. C., and Stearns, P. H. (2001). *Facing Up to Management Faddism: A New Look at an Old Force*. Westport, CT: Quorum Books.

Burrell, G. (2003). "The Future of Organization Theory: Prospects and Limitations." In H. Tsoukas and C. Knudsen (eds.), *The Oxford Handbook of Organizational Theory: Meta-Theoretical Perspectives*. Oxford: Oxford University Press: 525–35.

Carlson, W. B. (1995). "The Coordination of Business Organization and Technological Innovation within the Firm: A Case Study of the Thomson-Houston Electric Company in the 1880s." In N. Lamoreaux and D. Raff (eds.), *Coordination and Information: Historical Perspectives on the Organization of Enterprise*. Chicago: Chicago University Press: 55–99.

Cassis, Y. (1997). *Big Business: The European Experience in the Twentieth Century*. Oxford: Oxford University Press.

Chandler, A. D. (1962). *Strategy and Structure: Chapters in the History of the Industrial Enterprise*. Cambridge, MA: MIT Press.

Chandler, A. D. (1990). *Scale and Scope: The Dynamics of Industrial Capitalism*. Cambridge, MA: Belknap Press.

Choo, C. W. (2006). *The Knowing Organization: How Organizations Use Information to Construct Meaning, Create Knowledge, and Make Decisions*. Oxford: Oxford University Press.

Dierkes, M., Antal, A. B., Child, J., and Nonaka, I. (eds.) (2003). *Handbook of Organizational Learning and Knowledge*. New York: Oxford University Press.

Fear, J. (2001). "Thinking Historically about Organizational Learning." In M. Dierkes, B. Antal, J. Child, and I. Nonaka (eds.), *Handbook of Organizational Learning*. Oxford: Oxford University Press: 162–91.

Fear, J. (2005). *Organizing Control: August Thyssen and the Construction of German Corporate Management*. Cambridge, MA: Harvard University Press.

Fear, J., and Wadhwani, R. D. (2013). "Populism and Political Entrepreneurship: The Universalization of German Savings Banks and the Decline of American Savings Banks, 1908–1934." In H. Berghoff, J. Kocka, and D. Ziegler (eds.), *Doing Business in the Age of Extremes*. Cambridge: Cambridge University Press: 94–118.

Friedman, W. (2013). *Fortune Tellers: The Story of America's First Economic Forecasters*. Princeton: Princeton University Press.

Fruin, M. (1994). *The Japanese Enterprise System: Competitive Strategies and Cooperative Structures*. Oxford: Oxford University Press.

Grove, A. (1999). *Only the Paranoid Survive: Only the Paranoid Survive: How to Exploit the Crisis Points that Challenge Every Company*. New York: Crown Business.

Håkanson, L. (2010). "The Firm as an Epistemic Community: The Knowledge Based View Revisited," *Industrial and Corporate Change*, 19(6): 1801–28.

Hansen, P. H. (2007). "Organizational Culture and Organizational Change: The Transformation of Savings Banks in Denmark, 1965–1990," *Enterprise and Society*, 8(4): 920–53.

Hansen, P. H. (2012a). "Making Sense of Financial Crisis and Scandal: A Danish Bank Failure in the First Era of Finance Capitalism," *Enterprise and Society*, 13(3): 672–706.

Hansen, P. H. (2012b). "Business History: A Cultural and Narrative Approach," *Business History Review*, 86(4): 693–717.

Johnson, H. T., and Kaplan, R. S. (1991). *Relevance Lost: The Rise and Fall of Management Accounting*. Boston: Harvard Business School Press.

Johnson, V. (2007). "What Is Organizational Imprinting? Cultural Entrepreneurship in the Founding of the Paris Opera," *American Journal of Sociology*, 113(1): 97–127.

Jones, G. (2005). *Multinationals and Global Capitalism: From the Nineteenth to the Twenty-first Century*. Oxford: Oxford University Press.

Jones, G. (2008). "Alfred Chandler and the Importance of Organization," *Enterprise and Society*, 9(3): 419–21.

Jones, G., and Khanna, T. (2006). "Bringing History back into International Business," *Journal of International Business Studies*, 37: 453–68.

Judt, T. (2005). *PostWar: A History of Europe since 1945*. New York: Penguin.

Kipping, M., and Üsdiken, B. (2007). "Business History and Management Studies." In G. Jones and J. Zeitlin (eds.), *The Oxford Handbook of Business History*. Oxford: Oxford University Press: 96–119.

Knight, F. H. (1921). *Risk, Uncertainty and Profit*. Boston: Houghton Mifflin.

Kogut, B., and Zander, U. (1992). "Knowledge of the Firm, Combinative Capabilities, and the Replication of Technology," *Organization Science* 3(3): 384–97.

Kogut, B., and Zander, U. (1993). "Knowledge of the Firm and the Evolutionary Theory of the Multinational Corporation," *Journal of International Business Studies*, 24(4): 625–45.

Kogut, B., and Zander, U. (2003). "A Memoir and Reflection: Knowledge and an Evolutionary Theory of the Multinational Firm 10 Years Later," *Journal of International Business Studies*, 34: 505–15.

Lamoreaux, N. R., and Raff, D. M. G. (1995) (eds.). *Coordination and Information: Historical Perspectives on the Organization of Enterprise*. Chicago: Chicago University Press.

Lamoreaux, N. R., Raff, D. M. G., and Temin, P. (1999) (eds.). *Learning by Doing in Markets, Firms, and Countries*. Chicago: Chicago University Press.

Langley, A. (1999). "Strategies for Theorizing from Process Data," *Academy of Management Review*, 24(4): 691–710.

Mahoney, J., and Thelen, K. (2010). *Explaining Institutional Change: Ambiguity, Agency, and Power*. Cambridge: Cambridge University Press.

March, J. G., and Olsen, J. P. (1976). *Ambiguity and Choice in Organizations*. Bergen, Norway: Universitetsforlaget.

Marquis, C. (2003). "The Pressure of the Past: Network Imprinting in Intercorporate Communities," *Administrative Science Quarterly*, 48: 655–89.

Marquis, C., and Huang, Z. (2010). "Acquisitions as Exaptation: The Legacy of Founding Institutions in the U.S. Commercial Banking Industry," *Academy of Management Journal*, 53(6): 1441–73.

Nonaka, I., and Takeuchi, H. (1995). *The Knowledge-Creating Company: How Japanese Companies Create the Dynamics of Innovation*. Oxford: Oxford University Press.

O'Reilly, C. A., and Pfeffer, J. (2000). *Hidden Value: How Great Companies Achieve Extraordinary Results with Ordinary People*. Boston: Harvard Business School Press.

Owen, G. (2010). *The Rise and Fall of Great Companies: Courtaulds and the Reshaping of the Man-Made Fibres Industry*. Oxford: Oxford University Press.

Patriotta, G. (2003). *Organizational Knowledge in the Making: How Firms Create, Use, and Institutionalize Knowledge*. Oxford: Oxford University Press.

Perez-Aleman, P., and Sandilands, M. (2008). "Building Value at the Top and Bottom of the Value Chain: MNC-NGO Partnerships," *California Management Review*, 51(1): 24–49.

Pettigrew, A. M. (1992). "The Character and Significance of Strategy Process Research," *Strategic Management Journal*, 13(S2): 5–16.

Pettigrew, A. M., Woodman, R. W., and Cameron, Kim S. (2001). "Studying Organizational Change and Development: Challenges for Future Research," *Academy of Management Journal*, 44(4): 697–713.

Popp, A. (2013). "Making Choices in Time," Enterprise & Society, 14(3): 467–74.

Raff, D.M.G (2013). "How to Do Things with Time," Enterprise & Society, 14(3): 435–66.

Rivoli, P. (2009). *The Travels of a T-Shirt in the Global Economy: An Economist Examines the Markets, Power, and Politics of World Trade*. Hoboken, NJ: John Wiley & Sons.

Scranton, P. (2004). *Endless Novelty: Specialty Production and American Industrialization 1865–1925*. Princeton: Princeton University Press

Senge, P. M. (1990). *The Fifth Discipline: The Art and Practice of the Learning Organization*. New York: Doubleday.

Sewell, W. H. (2005). *Logics of History: Social Theory and Social Transformation*. Chicago: University of Chicago Press.

Stinchcombe, A. L. (1965). "Social Structure and Organization." In J. G. March (ed.), *Handbook of Organizations*. Chicago: RandMcnally: 142–93.

Streeck, W. (2009). *Re-Forming Capitalism: Institutional Change in the German Political Economy*. Oxford: Oxford University Press.

Svetlova, E., and van Elst, H. (2012). "How Is Non-Knowledge Represented in Economic Theory." Available at <http://arxiv.org/abs/1209.2204>.

Tedlow, R. (2006). *Andy Grove: The Life and Times of an American*. London: Portfolio.

Tedlow, R. (2009). *Giants of Enterprise: Seven Business Innovators and the Empires They Built*. New York: HarperCollins.

Temin, P. (ed.) (1991). *Inside the Business Enterprise: Historical Perspectives on the Use of Information*. Chicago: Chicago University Press.

Weick, K. E. (1989). "Theory Construction as Disciplined Imagination," *Academy of Management Review*, 14: 516–31.

Weick, K. E. (1995). *Sensemaking in Organizations*. London: Sage.

Whittington, R., Cailluet, L., and Yakis-Douglas, B. (2011). "Opening Strategy: Evolution of a Precarious Profession," *British Journal of Management*, 22: 531–44.

8

Schumpeter's Plea: Historical Reasoning in Entrepreneurship Theory and Research

R. Daniel Wadhwani and Geoffrey Jones[1]

Joseph Schumpeter began his now-famous article on "Creative Response in Economic History" with this plea: "Economic historians and economic theorists can make an interesting and socially valuable journey together, if they will" (Schumpeter, 1947: 149). Though the article is most often cited for the distinction it developed between "adaptive" and "creative" responses in business, Schumpeter's main purpose was to call for the use of historical methods in the study of entrepreneurship. To Schumpeter, the very nature of entrepreneurship—the empirical difficulty of identifying it *ex ante*, the way it "shapes the whole course of subsequent events and their 'long-run' outcomes," the great extent to which its character differed from place to place and over the course of time—suggested that historical research and reasoning were necessary in understanding how it worked within capitalist economies (Schumpeter, 1947: 50, 1954; McCraw, 2007; Swedberg, 1991).[2]

In recent years, a number of scholars have renewed Schumpeter's plea for the use of historical reasoning in entrepreneurship research (Cassis and Minoglou, 2005; Jones and Wadhwani, 2008; Baumol and Strom, 2008; Landström and Lohrke, 2010). Following Schumpeter, these scholars insist that "history matters" for understanding and studying entrepreneurship. Yet, with few exceptions (Forbes and Kirsch, 2010; Popp and Holt, 2013), the theoretical reasons

[1] Earlier versions of this chapter were presented at the Academy of Management Annual Meeting, the Babson Entrepreneurship Research Conference, and the University of North Carolina, Chapel Hill. We thank Howard Aldrich, Daniel Forbes, Dmitry Khanin, David Kirsch, Hans Landström, and Sanjay Jain for their comments.
[2] While Schumpeter inspired a wave of historically oriented research into entrepreneurship in the years after World War II, this interest in historicism has not persisted in the management-based entrepreneurship scholarship that has developed since the 1980s. See Jones and Wadhwani, 2007; Wadhwani, 2010.

why and *how* history matters in our understanding of entrepreneurship have remained underdeveloped. How specifically does history matter in entrepreneurship theory? What exactly is it about historical reasoning that may offer unique insights about the entrepreneurial process?

In this chapter, we draw on both theories of history and entrepreneurship theory to elaborate on the ways in which historical processes play an integral role in entrepreneurship. Specifically, we build on several lines of historical theory about time, context, and change, and apply them to entrepreneurship theory to show how they illuminate aspects of the entrepreneurial process that more traditional social scientific reasoning about behavior and cognition miss. Our intention is not to suggest that historical reasoning is an alternative to good cognitive and behavioral social science of entrepreneurship. Rather, it is to point out why and how historical reasoning may serve as an essential complement to other approaches to the subject, and to establish a theoretical foundation for a turn toward historicism that, in some ways, has already begun (Casson, 2010; Landes, Mokyr, and Baumol, 2010; Graham, 2010).

We begin by establishing foundational definitions of entrepreneurship and history and explain why entrepreneurship theory lends itself to historical reasoning about time, context, and change. Next we examine three specific modes of historical reasoning about temporality and causation to illustrate how each helps illuminate certain dimensions of entrepreneurial theory and process. In each instance we provide specific examples of research problems or processes that the form of historical temporality helps illuminate and we highlight areas for further research. We conclude by discussing some of the implications of our ideas for future research in entrepreneurship.

HISTORICISM IN ENTREPRENEURSHIP THEORY

Entrepreneurship researchers employ a variety of definitions for the subject they study, making it necessary for us to clarify the foundational concepts on which this paper is built. In particular, we work in the long intellectual tradition that understands entrepreneurship as, at core, relational or functional (Schumpeter, 1934; Shane and Venkataraman, 2000) rather than as a particular behavior (Stevenson and Jarillo, 1990) or type of organization (Gartner, 1985). We do so not only because of the long historical tradition of conceiving entrepreneurship in such terms (Wadhwani, 2010), but also because the great variation in entrepreneurship over historical time makes it problematic to characterize it based on any particular organizational type or behavior (Casson, 2010).

We build from Shane and Venkataraman's (2000: 218) conceptualization of the theoretical domain of entrepreneurship research as encompassing "how, by whom, and with what effects opportunities to create future goods and services are discovered, evaluated, and exploited." Entrepreneurship, in this view, occurs at the nexus of enterprising individuals and potentially lucrative but uncertain entrepreneurial opportunities (Shane and Venkataraman, 2000; Shane, 2003). Such entrepreneurial opportunities may include both so-called "low level" opportunities, such as arbitrage, the exploitation of which moves markets toward equilibrium (Kirzer, 1997) and "high level" opportunities involving innovations that create dis-equalibria and change in markets (Schumpeter, 1934). We leave aside until later the question of whether such opportunities form objective realities that entrepreneurs discover (Shane, 2003) or are somehow constructed or created by entrepreneurs themselves (Sarasvathy et al., 2005).

Uncertainty arises from the fact that unlike opportunities to manage resources within existing means-ends frameworks or according to established decision-making rules, entrepreneurial opportunities involve the identification and successful exploitation of new means, ends, or both (Shane and Eckhardt, 2003; Casson, 1982; Casson, 2010) and that this process requires conjectures about the future conditions of markets that are not reflected in information and prices today (Casson, 2010; Shane and Eckhart, 2003; Knight, 1921). Entrepreneurship thus involves cognitive processes, such as remaining alert to opportunities (Kirzner, 1997) and making judgments (Casson, 1982, 2010) about prospects for the development of future markets and goods, in addition to successfully organizing resources to exploit these potential opportunities.

CONTEXT, TIME, AND CHANGE

Conceived in these terms, entrepreneurship theory inherently (though too often only implicitly and uncritically) employs underlying theoretical constructs of context, time, and change. Indeed, if we understand entrepreneurship theory to encompass the conditions that lead to the existence of entrepreneurial opportunities (Shane, 2003; Shane and Eckhardt, 2003), then context is an essential component of entrepreneurship. Contexts—which may be defined as the sequence of events and conditions that give rise to specific opportunities—define whether the introduction of a particular good, resource, technology, or organizational form constitutes an entrepreneurial opportunity or not. It also largely shapes the payoffs, uncertainties, and information associated with the opportunity. Context determines the existence of some opportunities and not others. It suggests that understanding the origins of opportunity sets in any given context is *as important* as understanding individual and firm-level cognition and behavior in the entrepreneurial process.

The same can be said for the related construct of time. All opportunities exist "in time," and, as a practical matter, no specific act or organization can be defined as entrepreneurial without reference to the time in which it is embedded. (See Wadhwani and Bucheli, this volume.) For an economic actor today rather than a century ago to conceive of mass manufactured and marketed cars produced on assembly lines can in no way be considered an act of entrepreneurship, whereas a century ago the exploitation of this opportunity transformed transportation. Similarly, for an actor to spot an arbitrage opportunity after it has already cleared cannot be considered entrepreneurial. As both a practical and theoretical matter, then, the categorization of behavior or cognition as entrepreneurial cannot exist outside the related construct of time.

Finally, entrepreneurship—particularly Schumpeterian innovative entrepreneurship—explicitly involves the construct of change (Gunther McGrath, 2003). Change, in this sense, cannot and should not be reduced to the more simple assertion that entrepreneurship affects economic growth. Change, as Schumpeter (1947) and others theorized it, involved redirection and restructuring in the makeup and operation of markets. Entrepreneurship "changes social and economic situations for good," Schumpeter (1947: 150) insisted. Change is hence not simply a longitudinal but also a directional construct and is crucial to one of (Schumpeterian) entrepreneurship theory's central claims of being able to explain nonlinear transformations in the states of markets.

Context, time, and change can thus be considered constructs embedded within the very nature of entrepreneurship theory. Despite their seemingly "intuitive" nature, however, such constructs need explication. What is it about contexts, for instance, that makes them relevant to the entrepreneurial process? How is time actually manifested in entrepreneurial processes? What exactly does it mean that entrepreneurship "changes conditions for good?" Elaboration on *the temporality of entrepreneurship,* we contend, can help us understand dimensions of entrepreneurial processes that remain hidden in ahistorical accounts. Yet temporality remains not only under-theorized in entrepreneurship theory, but also largely unexplored in the mainstream empirical work in the field. Entrepreneurship scholarship has largely focused on studying individual and firm-level behavioral and cognitive processes, and is rarely longitudinal (Chandler and Lyon, 2001), let alone historical in the sense of incorporating structural change and retrospective analysis. Context, time, and change are rarely included, and even more rarely considered critically as entrepreneurial constructs requiring research, analysis, and explanation.

HISTORICAL THEORIES OF TEMPORALITY

Historical theory provides a valuable way forward in this regard because it provides well-developed explanations of how time, context, and change relate to behavior, cognition, and causation. Here it is important to distinguish between the popular conception of "history" as a description of a series of events that took place in the past (what the philosopher R. G. Collingwood called "cut and paste" history and Arthur Danto called a "chronicle"), and the distinct intellectual traditions of reasoning, analysis, and interpretation about human history that is the occupation of historians and philosophers of history. The latter can, in fact, be defined as a set of ways of reasoning analytically about time, context, and change and how these relate to human thought and behavior (Collingwood, 1946; Braudel, 1958; Carr, 1986; Hodgson, 2005; Sewell, 2005). Rather than viewing behavior as discrete, replicable, and timeless, it theorizes behavior as fundamentally embedded in and interacting with historical contexts and sequences. As an intellectual tradition, historicism usually calls for context-bound explanations rather than for timeless "general theory" and hence has a relatively well-elaborated set of theories of time and context as they operate in the social and economic world.

In particular, historical theory can be thought of as introducing a set of "temporalities" for understanding the relationship between time and causation (Sewell, 2005). These temporalities embed human behavior and cognition in particular constructs of historical time, in turn establishing specific ways of understanding how time shapes experience and causation, including the entrepreneurial process. It is our contention that understanding these temporal constructs and their relationship to entrepreneurship theory can (1) contribute to a more complete understanding of the entrepreneurial process, (2) illustrate some of the reasons for differences in theories about the existence of entrepreneurial opportunities, and (3) be applied in ways that advance a number of streams of entrepreneurship research.

The rest of the chapter outlines three theories of historical temporality and how they relate to entrepreneurship theory and research. (See Table 8.1 for a summary.) We explain how each provides a theory of historical time as it relates to behavior, cognition, and causation, as well as how each relates to entrepreneurship theory. In each case we also identify examples of entrepreneurial processes that the form of temporality can help illuminate. Lastly, we point out lines of research that may benefit from the types of reasoning we discuss.

HISTORY AS STRUCTURE

Historical Theory

Perhaps the most common construct of historical temporality in the social sciences is what might be termed historical structuralism, the contention that temporally remote developments, stretching back decades or even centuries, can establish rules, routines, mentalities, or other institutions that shape choice and causation in the present. Historical time (or times), in this sense,

Table 8.1 Historical temporalities and their relation to entrepreneurship theory and research

Temporality	Structural	Sequential	Constitutive/Cognitive
Historical Theory	Braudel (1958)	David (1985)	Dilthey (1910)
	Hodgson (2001)	Sewell (2005)	Carr (1986)
			Ricoeur (1983)
Temporal Constructs	Longue durée	Path dependence	Historicity
	Historical institutionalism	Sequencing	Historical narrative
		Events & contingency	
Value to Entrepreneurship Theory	Variations in supply of entrepreneurial talent	Temporal boundaries of opportunities	Entrepreneurial cognition & identity
	Variations in entrepreneurial institutions, opportunities, and allocation of risk	Relationship between entrepreneurship & structural change	Entrepreneurial agency & opportunity "creation"
	Variations in entrepreneurial forms		Alternative paths of structural change
Examples	Baumol (1990)	Schumpeter	Sabel and Zeitlin (1997)
	Kilby (1971)	Jones (2000)	Popp and Holt (2013)
Relevant Research Streams in Entrepreneurship	Effects of institutions on entrepreneurship	Knowledge spillovers	Entrepreneurial cognition & identity
	Variation in entrepreneurial forms	New market emergence	Opportunity creation & effectuation
	Social allocation of entrepreneurial uncertainty	Institutional entrepreneurship	Entrepreneurial bricolage
	Entrepreneurship & economic growth	Entrepreneurial clusters	Alternative paths of development

act as deep institutional structures shaping cognition and behavior, and can only be identified by examining cognition and behavior over long periods of time and by exploring the origins of social and economic phenomena of interest. History, in this sense, constitutes and constructs choices and behaviors (Wadhwani and Bucheli, this volume).

Historical structuralism is predicated on the position that the foundational basis of social and economic behavior can vary over time and place, but does so at such a pace or so infrequently that it may be imperceptible to social scientists working with shorter durations of time (Braudel, 1958). A theoretical generalization about behavior or causation that may be valid today may or may not be applicable to behavior in the past or the future, when laws, culture, and social relations may have been different (Hodgson, 2005). Accordingly, behavior that is entrepreneurial and the source of creative change in the context of early 21st-century American capitalism may simply be destructive or lack any meaningful sense as entrepreneurship in the context of the early 20th-century Japanese economy. The value of history, in this regard, is in uncovering slow or infrequently changing relationships and patterns that often imperceptibly govern social and economic relationships and transactions.

Historians and historical social scientists often deal with such variation over long time spans by delineating "periods" or "eras" when foundational assumptions about behavior and cognition appear to be coherent when applied to the subject under consideration. Differences between eras may exist because the institutions shaping behavior differ over time and place. Institutions, in the historical sense, can include the rules, norms, customs, traditions and assumptions that guide behavior and cognition in particular settings (Hodgson, 2005; North, 1990). Such institutions, of course, include the formal political and legal regimes that define the basis for exchange in capitalist economies. But they also include the cultural norms, assumptions, and mentalities that shape economic behavior and cognition in a variety of ways (Hansen, 2007).

While this view of institutions is somewhat similar to that of the "neo-institutional theory" commonly employed in organizational research, in practice historical structuralism typically differs in examining longer temporal spans and in its interest in the interrelatedness of institutions rather than in identifying specific rule and norm formation at the level of the field or organization. Such an approach to historical time, though most closely associated with the Annales School of history during the 20th century, has in recent decades become common in economic history (North, 1990), historical sociology (Tilly, 1984), and comparative political science (Skocpol, 1979; Pierson and Skocpol, 2002).

The purpose of using a historical structural approach is different from that of using a "general theory" one in that the goal of the research is not to create generalizations about behavior that transcend time and place but rather to create valid generalizations that hold true for meaningful boundaries of period and geography and to identify the underlying historical structures that shape behavior. In this sense, historical structuralism places emphasis on understanding the geographical and temporal boundaries under which certain behavioral patterns hold and identifying the institutions that shape behavior in that context (Braudel, 1958). Social scientists sometimes incorrectly take this context-bound nature of historical generalizations to mean that historical reasoning is atheoretical. Rather, historical structuralism offers a way to account for the wide variations in behavior historians find over time and place by taking into account the higher-level webs of institutions that shape this variation (Hodgson, 2005).

As a result, historical structuralism typically calls for research that examines behavior over long spans of time, with particular attention to the boundaries of time and geography when particular patterns of behavior and exchange hold true. Research that accounts for variation over such temporal spans allows us to understand: (1) how historical structures and institutions affect entrepreneurial behavior, cognition, and opportunities and (2) understand the origins and dynamics of the relevant historical institutions.

Relevance to Entrepreneurship Theory

Historical structuralism is particularly useful to entrepreneurship research and theory in that it helps us better understand how institutions shape the types of entrepreneurial opportunities available in a given context and the range of behaviors entrepreneurs engage in when discovering and pursuing these opportunities. It helps us understand, for instance, how institutions shape the costs, risks, uncertainties, information, cognitive interpretations, and payoffs associated with various types of opportunities, as well as the modes and patterns of discovery and exploitation that come to be accepted and legitimized.

In practice, historical institutionalism provides several benefits to entrepreneurship researchers. First, it diminishes the risks of fallacies created when generalizing about behavior based on evidence from developed countries in the present. Specifically, it helps avoid drawing problematic generalizations about either the timelessness or the fundamental novelty of entrepreneurial behavior today without examining the contextual variations that historical evidence provides. Second, and more importantly from the point of view of theory development, it allows researchers the opportunity to examine the relationship between institutions, opportunities, and entrepreneurial behaviors that is difficult to examine by focusing on familiar contexts in the present alone. That is, scholars need the significant variations in context that historical research provides in order to understand how institutions shape entrepreneurial opportunities and behaviors (Baumol and Strom, 2008; Landes, Mokyr, and Baumol, 2010).

Two examples highlight how understanding historical variations in time and place helps us better understand and develop theory regarding the relationship between institutions, opportunities, and entrepreneurial behaviors. William Baumol's (1990) well-known article on productive, unproductive, and destructive entrepreneurship provides an excellent illustration of how a critical understanding of historical context and variation can help create useful and robust entrepreneurship theory that is nevertheless embedded in historical time. Building on theories of the supply of entrepreneurship, Baumol argues that, in fact, the allocation of entrepreneurship between productive and unproductive ends varies much more widely than the total supply of entrepreneurial skill and hence is more important to long-term innovation and productivity growth of a society. The allocation of entrepreneurial efforts toward productive or unproductive opportunities, in turn, largely reflects the relative payoffs to these types of opportunities based on the legal and cultural institutions of a time and place. The development of this theoretical concept, for Baumol, depends primarily on his use of historical variation in patterns of entrepreneurship over time, since contemporary evidence provides little in the way of sufficient differences to substantiate his claim. "Since the rules of the game change only very slowly," explains Baumol (1990: 895), "a case study approach to the investigation of my hypotheses drives me unavoidably to examples spanning considerable periods of history and encompassing widely different cultures and geographic locations." Baumol shows how the nature of entrepreneurial behavior, the types of opportunities exploited, and the impact of this on productivity and growth has varied significantly based on the institutional foundations of a society.

Kilby (1971) uses a similar research approach to examining contextual variation in order to understand the relationship between political-legal institutions and entrepreneurial behavior. Drawing on his own studies of entrepreneurship in West Africa, he pointed out that neoclassical views of entrepreneurship that emphasized the pursuit of new market opportunities and the assembly of resources as the behavioral foundations of entrepreneurship were too limited to capture the behavioral reality of what African entrepreneurs actually did. Kilby pointed out that, in mature Western economies, stable political-legal processes and a market for good managerial talent could simply be acquired from the environment or market. Western neoclassical thought had hence focused on the opportunity identification and resource-assembly aspects of the creative and unique work of entrepreneurs that could *not* simply be acquired through external market mechanisms. In developing countries, however, entrepreneurs usually needed to create these elements of political-legal process and sound managerial control in order to launch a productive new business; because of their lack of availability in the market or environment, these behaviors were in fact essential elements of the entrepreneurship process (Kilby, 1971). Kilby's work hence uses variations in the institutional context to show how entrepreneurs in settings with unclear property and political rights needed to acquire these rights and protections as an integral part of the entrepreneurial process itself.

Relevance to Entrepreneurship Research

In recent years, neo-institutional research and reasoning has grown more popular among entrepreneurship scholars (Boettke and Coyne, 2009; Hwang and Powell, 2005), but it has only begun to address the range of theoretical issues subject to historical institutional analysis. For instance, research on international entrepreneurship and "born-global" companies may lend itself to productive use of historical institutionalism to build theories about the conditions under which viable opportunities arise for new firms that are internationally oriented from the start. A "born-global" firm is usually defined as a start-up company that "from inception seeks to derive significant competitive advantage from the use of resources and the sale of outputs in multiple countries" (Oviatt and McDougall, 1994: 49, 2005; McDougall and Oviatt, 2000). Though such patterns of international entrepreneurial behavior are sometimes assumed to be relatively new, international ventures based on cross-border opportunities and global networks of relationships have arisen in many different periods and places in the early modern and modern eras. Network relationships, particularly ethnic diaspora networks, were arguably more important to international trade and new business development in the early modern period than multinational firms (Baghdiantz McCabe et al., 2005). While American firms have traditionally expanded abroad incrementally, "born-global" strategies have been an integral part of European and Asian start-ups and new firms in other parts of the world for well over a century. On the eve of World War I, for instance, there existed thousands of British companies that operated exclusively in foreign countries based on existing relationships with other firms and entrepreneurs. Similar "born-international" patterns often existed for companies from small countries with limited domestic markets (Wilkins and Schroter, 1998). Such historical variations in cross-border opportunities and how they are exploited by entrepreneurs lend themselves to research questions that employ an historical institutional approach. In what institutional contexts are international entrepreneurial opportunities exploited by start-up firms or networks of entrepreneurs rather than by established organizations? What institutional and contextual conditions have led to changes in the way in which American entrepreneurs have pursued cross-border opportunities? What are the causes of comparative national or regional differences in the ways in which entrepreneurs pursue these new business opportunities? Extant historical research in international business and entrepreneurship suggests that such questions are addressable using historical methods and evidence.

Historical institutionalism can also be used to further our understanding of how institutions shape the allocation of entrepreneurial risk and uncertainty. Much of the research in this area has focused narrowly on bankruptcy (Lee, Peng, and Barney, 2007), an institution whose development and impact on entrepreneurial opportunities and behaviors certainly lends itself to historical analysis. But bankruptcy laws are only one instance of an institution that over time has shaped the social allocation of the entrepreneurial risk of failure. Historical variation in laws and customs regarding such issues as new product liability, fiduciary responsibility, employment contracting, and intellectual property offer the promise of helping expand our understanding of how a range of other institutions shape the allocation of specific kinds of risks that entrepreneurs may face. Moreover, they offer the opportunity to understand how such institutions develop, what considerations other than optimizing entrepreneurship have shaped their development, and how they relate to one another. In other words, historicism provides an opportunity to develop a deeper and more contextualized understanding of how the institutions shaping the allocation of entrepreneurial risk have developed.

Historical institutionalism can also be used to productively understand variations in the types of organizations entrepreneurs have established or controlled in order to pursue new business opportunities. A growing historical literature illustrates that the variety of firm types available to entrepreneurs differed significantly over time and place and this work opens up the possibility of understanding how laws and institutions shape the organizing process and resources that entrepreneurs use to pursue opportunities, including the ways in which they contract with resource providers to the venture (Lamoreaux, 1998; Casson, 2010; Wadhwani, 2011). Historical institutionalism hence helps us investigate variations in firm founding and organizing practices that are difficult to consider when examining the more limited variation that we see in the present.

Ultimately, then, historical structuralism offers entrepreneurship research a better and more dynamic way to understand the relationship between institutional contexts and entrepreneurship by providing a broader range of variation in institutional arrangements.

HISTORY AS SEQUENCE/PROCESS

Historical Theory

Historical structuralism examines variations in institutional context and their impact on entrepreneurial opportunities and behavior that are difficult to identify by examining entrepreneurship cross-sectionally, or over short periods of time. By itself, however, historical structuralism does not provide an explanation of the role of entrepreneurship in economic change. To better understand change, we have to turn to historical theories of time that involve sequences, processes, and conjunctures of actions and behaviors. Historical sequencing, in this sense, calls on researchers to untangle how past choices and behaviors change the conditions under which present and future ones are made. "It is sometimes not possible to uncover the logic (or illogic) of the world around us except by understanding how it got that way," economic historian Paul David (1985) has explained. The fundamental assumption is that both behavior and structure are path dependent; choices, actions, processes, and events at one moment in time can alter markets and social relationships, in turn changing the conditions and contexts under which subsequent cognitive and behavioral acts take place (Sewell, 2005). Rather than seeking the remote temporal structures that condition behavior in the present, the temporally relevant construct in explaining change is the sequence of events and developments that make a particular behavior or cognitive act possible and relevant.

An important implication of this view of temporality is that behavior and cognition cannot best be understood as discrete, replicable acts subject to uniform sets of causes, but rather need to be understood as parts of sequences of actions and events in order to understand their logic or illogic (Sewell, 2005). The causes and effects of cognitive or behavioral acts are, in this sense, contingent on their particular moment in time and place in relationship to the events and developments that precede, overlap, and follow them. Cause and effect are hence themselves dependent on an act's position in a relevant sequence of events and developments.

Fundamentally, this sequential view of temporality implies that change, and not just time and context, are relevant to understanding behavior and cognition. Similar cognitive and behavioral actions take on different meanings and consequences based on their position and relationship to the events and developments around them. Behavioral and cognitive acts are hence important to understand in part because of their potential consequences, as they change the structure and conditions under which subsequent actions are understood (Sewell, 2005).

Relevance to Entrepreneurship Theory

Path-dependent historical perspectives have, at least in name, been increasingly adopted by social scientists, particularly those studying the "evolution" of organizations and industries (Nelson and Winter, 1982; Aldrich and Ruef, 2006; Murmann, 2003). Their adoption by mainstream entrepreneurship researchers, however, has generally been much slower. This may be attributable, in part, to an assumption that *de novo* start-ups and entrepreneurial behavior more broadly are less subject to path-dependent processes and constraints on behavior than established firms. But we believe that for most of the topics that scholars of entrepreneurship actually study, path-dependent assumptions are far more realistic than the atemporal ones often used. In understanding founder backgrounds and the identification of new opportunities, in specifying how resources flow (or do not flow) to new opportunities, in understanding the success or failure of novel ventures, in conceptualizing incumbent-new venture dynamics, and in understanding spillover and spawning patterns, to name just a few theoretical topics in entrepreneurship research, path-dependent processes can play an important role.

Schumpeter in fact emphasized that path dependence was perhaps the most important reason entrepreneurship needed to be studied historically. "Creative response changes social and economic situations for good," he explained. "This is why creative response is an essential element in the historical process" (Schumpeter, 1947: 150). The implications he drew were two-fold. First, entrepreneurship shaped economy and society by opening up new possibilities that had not existed before *and* by closing off other paths to change that once existed. And second, to fully understand entrepreneurship's impact on the process of economic change one needed to study it not as a discrete behavior or event but as a *sequence* of behaviors and events. Economic historian Arthur Cole (1959, 1968) elaborated on this second theoretical point through his concept of the "entrepreneurial stream," the notion that the pursuit of one entrepreneurial endeavor changed conditions in such a way as to create new opportunities for further entrepreneurial endeavors in a sequence of events that shaped how business systems or orders evolved. Cole argued that the key link was the production of information and knowledge in the entrepreneurial process; new business created new practical knowledge and tangible resources that in turn served as the basis for more new entrepreneurial opportunities.

Situated in the theoretical language used by entrepreneurship researchers today, sequential reasoning suggests that entrepreneurial opportunities and their exploitation are best understood not as distinct conditions and behaviors but rather as sequences of alternating opportunity conditions and exploitation behaviors. Such temporal sequences allow us to understand how the pursuit of one opportunity leads to the opening up of new sets of opportunities while foreclosing or diminishing the attractiveness of opportunities that previously existed. Exploiting one entrepreneurial opportunity changes the opportunity set available and the relative attractiveness of each because the process of entrepreneurial exploitation creates new information, productive knowledge, resource conditions, and productive platforms that fundamentally shift the landscape in which opportunity sets exist.

Understanding longer sequences of opportunity conditions and entrepreneurial actions offers several advantages that examining large sets of discrete entrepreneurial behaviors lack. First, it helps to better account for the factors shaping entrepreneurial choice and behavior. Specifically, it allows us to understand path-dependent factors that constrain and enable entrepreneurial choice. Second, in many cases, it helps us better account for the impact of entrepreneurial behavior in the evolution and changing structure of industries, markets, regions, and whole economies. Such structural changes wrought by entrepreneurial activity are often not apparent by focusing on a single entrepreneurial action or even a single entrepreneur; rather it is only by studying sequences of entrepreneurial opportunities and their exploitation that it is possible to understand significant structural change. In this way, it helps link a set of behaviors at the individual and firm level to structural change at the industry and economy level.

Take, for example, an illustration of this sequential process that influenced Schumpeter's theorization of the process of creative destruction: railroadization in 19th-century America. The introduction of railroad technology and organizational forms by entrepreneurs in the 19th-century US represented an important set of entrepreneurial events in their own right. Railroads constituted some of the largest and most successful new businesses in 19th-century America and by themselves contributed significantly to national wealth. But their impact on the broader set of entrepreneurial opportunities and patterns of exploitation was even greater. The advent of fast, reasonably priced transportation changed relative prices for a whole host of other goods and services and created new sets of opportunities for entrepreneurs in other industries, from finance, to agriculture, to distribution and retailing. The rapid growth in markets available to many of these businesses in turn created opportunities for organizational innovations that had not existed previously. While the success of railroad entrepreneurs created the knowledge, resources, and platform conditions for a broad set of new entrepreneurial opportunities, they also foreclosed the viability and attractiveness of other opportunities, most notably for those entrepreneurs who had identified or were exploring opportunities related to the once-thriving canal business. It was, in fact, by studying such historical processes that Schumpeter sharpened his understanding of the path-dependent nature of entrepreneurial opportunities and his understanding of the process of creative destruction, as Thomas McCraw (2007) has pointed out. The entrepreneurial process that railroadization introduced at once changed the range of opportunities and behaviors considered entrepreneurial and transformed the structure of a host of markets and industries in the US. However, such insights were possible only by examining the historical sequence of opportunities, their exploitation, and their consequences.

Jones (2000) and Jones and Wale (1998) provide another example of how historical sequencing helps us understand the context for entrepreneurial opportunities and the way entrepreneurial processes create large-scale structural changes. They examine *de novo*, "free-standing" British companies in the late 19th century that established their agricultural or infrastructure-building operations in distant lands with no apparent strategic advantages, with the possible exception of access to British capital markets back home. At first, these companies seem—like other *de novo* start-ups—to be fundamentally free from the constraints of past decisions and routines. However, the authors show that such apparently *de novo* companies usually in fact belonged to a cluster or network of large British trading companies doing business abroad. The start-ups were founded as

new spillover opportunities but maintained close ties to the trading companies on which they relied for a host of services. Jones and Wale show
that these start-ups can best be understood as spin-offs resulting from the
path-dependent evolution of the trading companies, designed to exploit
opportunities as time passed. As the bigger trading companies expanded
operations from trading to financial and insurance services and eventually into local construction and production, they often spun off allied small
independent companies that focused on particular opportunities in agriculture, mining, or transportation (Jones and Wale, 1998; Jones 2000). The
production of knowledge resources and infrastructure created by the pursuit of one venture led to the creation of knowledge about other opportunities in a long sequence that led to the creation of novel links across the
early global economy. In summary, these start-ups were formed as part of
broader path-dependent evolution of a group of firms or an industry. They
also forged some paths of development while forgoing others through this
sequence of entrepreneurial actions by shaping the structural linkages of
the emergent global economy.

Fundamentally, then, these examples suggest that a sequential temporality is necessary to understand the structural impact of entrepreneurial processes on industries and economies. Without unraveling sequences of events,
actions, and opportunity sets, we may be able to understand such factors as the
impact of entrepreneurship on economic growth, but we cannot understand
how entrepreneurship affects economic change. Sequential reasoning is hence
a requirement for understanding of entrepreneurship as a dynamic, multilevel
theory.

Application to Entrepreneurship Research

Sequential historical reasoning is particularly important to the development
of streams of entrepreneurship research that aim to address the relationship
between individual and firm action and structural changes in regions, industries, and economies. Despite repeated calls for more multilevel research of
this sort, it remains a small fraction of the scholarship published by entrepreneurship scholars (Chandler and Lyon, 2001).

The promise of research on sequential historical processes can be seen in
its prospective application to a number of streams of scholarship that seek
to tie individual and firm-level choices and actions to structural changes in
markets. One of these is the growing interest of entrepreneurship scholars in
the process of knowledge spillovers from existing firms as a basis for the emergence of new entrepreneurial opportunities (Audretsch and Keilback, 2006;
Agarwal, Audretsch, and Sarkar, 2007). The theoretical work in this area provides an inherently sequential theory for the emergence of new opportunities

and their impact on structural change in industries and markets. The best empirical work conducted to date, however, has tended to focus primarily on the *rates* at which various types of existing firms spin out other firms, in part because such questions allow for the use of consistent datasets and rigorous analytical methods (Agarwal, Echamadi, Franco, and Sarkar, 2004). Valuable as such studies are, one of the promises of research into knowledge spillovers is precisely in helping us understand how they affect subsequent opportunities and the development of new markets, a process that path-dependent historical reasoning allows researchers to explore. While the data and methods needed to explore such sequential processes may not be as "clean" (and hence subject to differing interpretations and criticisms), they address questions that are in fact theoretically more important in our understanding of entrepreneurship and its impact on industries.

Sequential historical reasoning and historical sources are equally promising for research on entrepreneurship in the context of market emergence. As Forbes and Kirsch (2010) have pointed out, historical sources are particularly valuable for examining the origins of new industries. Conventional methods of studying industries as comprised of similar "producer firms" fall short in considering industry emergence because the relevant actors and actions that may lead to existence of new markets often antedate the first recognizable "producers" and the market itself is ambiguous (Santos and Eisenhardt, 2009). Researchers hence typically have to track the origins of the new market opportunity to a broader set of relevant actors, organizations, and modes of interaction in the period before the first recognizable producers have existed. A number of studies that have traced the origins of new industries to the period before the emergence of new producers have used historical sources and methods to identify the actors and sequences of actions that laid the foundations for industry emergence (Christensen, 1993; Garud, Jain, and Kumaraswamy, 2002; McKenna, 2006). A fuller understanding of the origins of new industries may thus require the use of a more eclectic array of historical data and archives and an understanding of the broader context that allow one to identify relevant actors as well as the sequence of developments that lead to the emergence of a particular market (Forbes and Kirsch, 2010).

For similar reasons, historical sequences are integral to understanding processes of institutional entrepreneurship, in which institution formation establishes a platform for change by opening up subsequent opportunities for entrepreneurs to enter a market. Though the methodology is not always explicitly framed in terms of historical sequencing, studies that examine the process of institutional entrepreneurship often do so by documenting sequences of opportunities and their exploitation (Garud et al., 2002; Greenwood and Suddaby, 2006).

Though each of these streams of research is based implicitly on sequential temporal reasoning, none of them explicitly theorize the temporal dimensions of their explanations of entrepreneurship. A better and more explicit accounting of temporal sequencing and its implications for theory and research design in these areas can not only enhance our understanding of the entrepreneurial process but also help researchers better understand the implications of this view of temporality for contingency, agency, and structural change.

HISTORY AS CONSTITUTIVE/COGNITIVE

Historical Theory

Structural and sequential temporalities view history as establishing external conditions that constrain and enable human action. History matters because individual choice and action are limited or enabled by institutional rules or the antecedent sequence of events leading up to the event or action under consideration. A third body of historical theory, in contrast, posits that history plays a constitutive role in how human actors experience and understand their world, and is hence an elemental part of human cognition and action itself (Dilthey, 2002; Carr, 1986; Ricoeur, 2004). The past, in this sense, "appear[s] as an element of our experienced world," as the philosopher of history David Carr (1986: 4) has put it. "The historical world is always there and the individual not only observes it from the outside but is intertwined with it." In their introduction to this volume, Wadhwani and Bucheli refer to this as the cognitive approach to historical reasoning.

In the constitutive/cognitive perspective, historical time is an essential dimension of the sensemaking and sensegiving of human actors. Individuals understand their own sense of being (Heidegger, 1962) in large part through their engagement with time; their perception and understanding of the past and its implications for possible directions for the future are integral to how they experience choice and action in the present. The temporality of experience includes not only an individual's personal experience of time, but also one's awareness of a "social" past that shapes one's relationship to social groups (e.g., family, ethnicity, nation) and to collective identities (Carr, 1986). The "historicity" of experience (Gadamer, 1975) hence constitutes how human actors understand their own identity, what they experience in the present, and how they see the possibilities for action in the future. The only way to understand cognition and behavior, in this view, is to examine a subject's own historical self—that is, the ways in which actors of interest make sense of their own historical context and how they understand its implications for their range of choices and actions for their future.

Unlike the structural and sequential views of temporality, the constitutive view emphasizes that historical time is not only important from the perspective of the critical and reflective observer trying to actively make sense of social and economic behavior, but also from the perspective of the subjects of

research themselves. Understanding the choices and actions of social and economic actors, it suggests, requires unraveling the logics of their own historical experiences and cognitive outlooks (Dilthey, 2002 [1910]; Collingwood,
1946). Only by understanding how actors perceive and interpret the past can
we understand how they make sense of their options for action in their present with some future intent in mind. Thus, the perceived past becomes an
integral part of the agency of actors in the social and economic world.

In recent decades, the constitutive/cognitive view of historical temporality has been most closely associated with scholars focused on how historical
sensemaking operates through the narrative form, with its attendant temporal
structure of perceived beginnings, middles, and possible endings (Carr, 1986;
Hansen, 2012). In this view, the historicity of actors' sensemaking takes the particular form of narrative accounts of their understanding of a past that shapes
how they understand the origins of their situation, the range of choices that
they have in the present, and the implications of these choices for possible endings in the future. The goal of scholarship on historical narrative, in this perspective, is to unpack how subjects' historical narrative shapes their behavior
and cognition.

Relevance to Entrepreneurial Theory

From the perspective of entrepreneurial theory, the constitutive approach to
historical reasoning is valuable for at least two reasons. First, it highlights an
important element in the cognitive dimension of the entrepreneurial process
that is often overlooked by existing research and theory. Almost all functional
and relational theories of entrepreneurship emphasize the entrepreneur's
subjective judgment under conditions of uncertainty about the existence
of an opportunity and whether it can, in fact, be exploited. Casson (2010),
for instance, emphasizes that entrepreneurial judgment is shaped not only
by an entrepreneur's superior access to information but by "memory" and
by an entrepreneur's interpretive theories about the meaning of the limited
and imperfect information he/she has. Kirzner's (1997) concept of "alertness"
serves a similar role if we understand it to mean the identification of familiar
fact patterns that suggest the existence of an opportunity. Such notions beg
the question of where an agent's interpretive theories or their familiarity with
particular fact patterns come from. Constitutive historical approaches provide
one way to locate the origins of an entrepreneur's interpretive schema of what
does and does not constitute an opportunity.

That is, constitutive historicism helps us account for how entrepreneurs'
understanding of their own historical context shapes the nature of the opportunity they pursue (Gerschenkron, 1966; Sabel and Zeitlin, 1997; Popp and Holt,
2013). Two entrepreneurs presented with a similar objective situation may
interpret them in very different ways based on their historical understanding

of the ways events have unfolded and the possible directions they may take in the future. Hence, unraveling an entrepreneur's cognitive processes vis-à-vis a set of opportunities requires analyzing how his/her historical mentality has shaped not only his/her outlook but the very nature of the opportunity itself. In this perspective, it makes sense to consider entrepreneurs as not only "discovering" opportunities but, in a way, "creating" them through the historical interpretation they bring to bear. Thus, unlike the structural or sequential views, the constitutive perspective on historical temporality allows that economic actors may in fact play some role as creators and not simply discoverers of opportunities (Sarasvathy et al., 2005).

Second, the constitutive/cognitive approach helps us take into account historical contingencies that lead to alternative paths of development. Because entrepreneurs may hold differing interpretations of historical context and the way events are unfolding, they may choose to exploit different opportunities or similar opportunities in different ways, leading to fundamentally different outcomes for the development of the organization of markets and industries. The historically shaped interpretive differences between entrepreneurs indicate that such alternative paths of opportunity development and exploitation may not be predictable in advance, but can be understood and explained *ex post* by historical reconstruction of the entrepreneur's thought process, an approach that Schumpeter thought promising.

Historical research on alternative patterns of industrialization highlights both the cognitive dimensions of this approach to entrepreneurship, as well as its implications for the development of markets and industries. For instance, Sabel and Zeitlin (1997) have shown that industrialization proceeded in very different ways in the United States, Western Europe, and Japan based on entrepreneurs' understanding and assessments of their historical moment in narratives of development and change. In particular, while mass production and mass consumption became a common opportunity for American entrepreneurs to exploit during the Industrial Revolution, this pattern differed in other parts of the world where entrepreneurs interpreted significant risk to investing in the fixed costs of mass production systems. Despite keen awareness of the technologies and productions systems based on mass production and consumption and their potential for driving changes in costs and profits, entrepreneurs in industries such as Swiss watch-making, British metalworking, and French weaving chose opportunities associated with more flexible production techniques and specialized markets in order to hedge against what they interpreted as uncertainties that made mass production an inappropriate opportunity for their historical setting. Understanding the assessment process of these entrepreneurs, Sabel and Zeitlin (1997: 11) emphasize, requires investigating how they saw themselves and their organizations within the developing historical narratives of the moment. "The present is connected to the future by the possibility of imagining alternatives," they explain. "The present is connected to the past because of the necessity of imagining the future as a re-elaboration, however fanciful, of what has gone before."

Similar research emphasizing the historical contingency of entrepreneurial decision making now shapes how economic and business historians view the "Americanization" of economies and business models after World War II. Despite preconceived notions of the broad adoption of American management techniques of production and firm organization following World War II, careful historical research shows that entrepreneurs around the world were more critical in evaluating the opportunity to adopt leading American techniques based not so much on difference in information about these opportunities but differences in their interpretation of local historical conditions and the possibilities this implied for the future (Zeitlin and Herrigel, 2000). In this sense, entrepreneurs were selective and strategic in what elements they borrowed from the American model and recombined with existing management, organization, and technologies based on their historical understanding of the possible trajectories in which local markets might evolve.

Application to Entrepreneurship Research

From the point of view of entrepreneurship research, historical approaches that involve reconstructing entrepreneurs' understanding of their historical conditions and their place within historical narratives holds promise in several ways. First, it offers an approach that may deepen our understanding of how entrepreneurs identify and assess opportunities. In recent years, entrepreneurship scholars have begun to examine the importance of personal narrative accounts in understanding the entrepreneurial process, primarily from the perspective of literary and cultural theory or from the perspective of psychology (Krueger, 2003; Gartner, 2007). Yet these tend to hinge on individual differences in traits, personalities, or personal experience, discounting the importance of collective judgments or mentalities that might shape the interpretation of opportunities in particular times and places. Constitutive historical reasoning hence offers an opportunity to further deepen our understanding of entrepreneurial sensemaking about opportunities by understanding how entrepreneurs' understanding of their own historical situation shapes their reasoning about new business opportunities (Popp and Holt, 2013). For similar reasons it can contribute to emerging research on how entrepreneurial identity formation takes place.

The constitutive approach to historical reasoning may be particularly useful to researchers interested in documenting the ways in which entrepreneurs not only discover opportunities but also create and shape them. Historical research can provide access to sources (such as archival records, diaries, letters) that provide insight into how an entrepreneur's mindset and actions actually shaped and reshaped the opportunity they pursued. Historical research hence provides a rich opportunity to ground the "opportunity creation" perspective in more extensive empirical evidence.

Moreover, unlike existing approaches to cognition focused on the individual, the historical approach offers an opportunity to link these sensemaking processes to structural variations in the organization of markets, industries, and economies. By using comparative-historical methods to examine how various entrepreneurial suppositions about opportunities and the future unfold over time, historians' investigation of mentality is able to untangle how actors' assumptions about the past and future play out in their effects on markets. As a result, they allow us both a longitudinal and multilevel approach to understanding the entrepreneurial process and how individual cognition ends up being linked to structural change at the market and industry levels. In doing so, it offers us a way to study important interrelations and interactions over time between individual entrepreneurs, organizations, and industries, to which much of mainstream entrepreneurship has paid little attention.

CONCLUSION

This chapter has contributed to our understanding of the theoretical and methodological relationship between entrepreneurship and historical reasoning. Building on assertions that "history matters" in entrepreneurship research, it has elaborated on why time, context, and change need to be understood as essential constructs within functional and relational theories of the entrepreneur. Moreover, it has articulated a set of ways in which historical theories of temporality allow us to better understand these constructs and how differing views of historical temporality illuminate specific features of the entrepreneurial process, including the origins and distribution of opportunities, the historically embedded nature of the opportunity recognition and assessment process, and the sequences by which individual and firm-level actions lead to structural changes in industries and economies. In each instance, we illustrate these relationships with examples and point to research streams that could benefit from adopting the form of temporal reasoning.

The chapter has several implications for research that seeks to embrace historicism in the study of entrepreneurship. First, it suggests that in order to be successful, historical research on entrepreneurship needs to address its temporal constructs and assumptions explicitly and reflectively. Entrepreneurship theories inherently involve temporal dynamics that historical research and reasoning are uniquely well positioned to reveal. Historical perspective allows researchers to examine the significance of an action in relation to developments before *and after* it, a point of view Schumpeter (1947) argued was essential for understanding entrepreneurship. But, as the chapter has shown, historical perspective can employ different views of temporality and context, each with its own insights about the agency of entrepreneurs and the nature of entrepreneur-ial opportunities. The promise of historical research hence lies not in offering a single method or approach to studying entrepreneurial processes, but rather in offering different temporal and theoretical angles onto a single phenomenon.

The chapter has methodological as well as theoretical implications. The varieties of reasoning discussed here are not easily subject to research using the conventional quantitative and qualitative methods normally used by entrepreneurship researchers. They involve consideration of long spans of time and a historical point of view, making consistent data sources, oral interviews, and ethnographies difficult to find or of limited use. Archives and other historical primary sources are typically essential, but are almost inevi-tably somewhat incomplete. Even when evidence is available, it demands that researchers engage in the inexact process of interpretation and contextualiza-tion given the long spans of time and shifting circumstances involved. (For a fuller explanation, see the chapters on sources and methods in Part III.) The demands of this kind of historical analysis are extraordinarily high, requir-ing that researchers not only analyze behavior and choice but also place their subjects of examination within a remarkably broad and deep set of contexts.

Yet the reward, we would argue, is the development of richer and more robust research and conceptualization of entrepreneurship and its role in the process of historical change. Schumpeter's plea for an active exchange between historical approaches and theories of entrepreneurship is as trenchant to the state of scholarship and understanding in the field today as it was more than half a century ago. The prize is a richer and deeper understanding of entrepre-neurship and how it shapes and reshapes the modern world.

REFERENCES

Agarwal, R., Audretsch, D., and Sarkar, M. B. (2007). "The Process of Creative Construction: Knowledge Spillovers, Entrepreneurship, and Economic Growth," *Strategic Entrepreneurship Journal*, 1(3–4): 263–86.

Agarwal, R., Echambadi, R., Franco, A., and Sarkar, M. B. (2004). "Knowledge Transfer through Inheritance: Spinout Generation, Development, and Survival." *Academy of Management Journal*, 47: 501–22.

Aldrich, H., and Ruef, M. (2006). *Organizations Evolving*. London: Sage.

Audretsch, D., and Keilback, M. (2006). "Entrepreneurship, Growth and Restructuring" In Mark Casson et al. (eds.), *The Oxford Handbook of Entrepreneurship*. New York: Oxford: 281–310.

Baghdiantz McCabe, I., Harlaftis, G., and Pepelasis Minoglou, I. (2005). *Diaspora Entrepreneurial Networks: Four Centuries of History*. New York: Berg.

Baumol, W. J. (1990). "Entrepreneurship: Productive, Unproductive, and Destructive," *Journal of Political Economy*, 98: 895.

Baumol, W. J., and Strom, R. (2008). "Entrepreneurship and Economic Growth," *Strategic Entrepreneurship Journal*, 1: 233–7.

Boettke, P. J., and Coyne, C. J. (2009). "Context Matters: Institutions and Entrepreneurship," *Foundations and Trends in Entrepreneurship*, 5: 135–209.

Braudel, F. (1958). "Histoire et sciences sociales: la longue durée," *Annales*, 13: 725–53.

Carr, D. (1986). *Time, Narrative, and History*. Indianapolis: Indiana University Press.

Cassis, Y., and Pepelasis Minoglou, I. (eds.) (2005). *Entrepreneurship in Theory and History*. New York: Palgrave.

Casson, M. (1982). *The Entrepreneur: An Economic Theory.* Totowa, NJ: M. Robertson.

Casson, M. (2010). *Entrepreneurship: Theory, Networks, History.* Cheltenham: Edward Elgar.

Chandler, G., and Lyon, D. (2001). "Issues of Research Design and Construct Measurement in Entrepreneurship Research: The Past Decade," *Entrepreneurship Theory and Practice*, 25: 101–16.

Christensen, C. (1993). "The Rigid Disk Drive Industry: A History of Commercial and Technological Turbulence," *Business History Review*, 67, 531–88.

Cole, A. H. (1959). *Business Enterprise in Its Social Setting*. Cambridge, MA: Harvard University Press.

Cole, A. H. (1968). "Meso-Economics: A Contribution from Entrepreneurial History," *Explorations in Entrepreneurial History*, 2nd Series, Vol. 6, No. 1.

Collingwood, R. G. (1946). *The Idea of History.* Oxford: Clarendon Press.

David, P. (1985). "Clio and the Economics of QWERTY: The Necessity of History," *American Economic Review*, 75: 332.

Dilthey, W. (2002 trans. [1910]). *The Formation of the Historical World in the Human Sciences.* Princeton: Princeton University Press.

Forbes, D., and Kirsch, D. (2010). "The Study of Emerging Industries: Recognizing and Responding to Some Central Problems," *Journal of Business Venturing* 26: 589–602.

Gadamer, H. G. (1975). *Truth and Method*. New York: Continuum.

Gartner, W. (1985). "A Conceptual Framework for Describing the Phenomenon of New Venture Creation," *Academy of Management Review*, 10: 696–706.

Gartner, W. (2007). "Entrepreneurial Narrative and a Science of the Imagination," *Journal of Business Venturing*, 22: 613–27.

Garud, R., Jain, S., and Kumaraswamy, A. (2002). "Institutional Entrepreneurship in the Sponsorship of Common Technological Standards," *Academy of Management Journal*, 45, 196–214.

Gerschenkron, A. (1966). "The Modernization of Entrepreneurship." In Myron Weiner (ed.), *Modernization: The Dynamics of Growth*. New York: Basic Books: 246–57.

Graham, M. B. W. (2010). "Entrepreneurship in the United States, 1920–2000." In David Landes, Joel Mokyr, and William Baumol, *The Invention of Enterprise: Entrepreneurship from Ancient Mesopotamia to Modern Times*, Princeton: Princeton University Press.

Greenwood, R., and Suddaby, R. (2006). "Institutional Entrepreneurship in Mature Fields: The Big Five Accounting Firms," *Academy of Management Journal*, 49: 27–48.

Gunther McGrath, R. (2003). "Connecting the Study of Entrepreneurship and Theories of Capitalist Progress: An Epilogue." In Z. Acs and D. Audretsch (eds.), *Handbook of Entrepreneurship Research: An Interdisciplinary Survey and Introduction.* Boston: Kluwer Academic Publishers: 515–32.

Hansen, P. (2012), "Business History: A Cultural and Narrative Approach," *Business History Review* 86(4): 693–717.

Hansen, P. H. (2007). "Organizational Culture and Organizational Change: The Transformation of Savings Banks in Denmark, 1965–1990," *Enterprise and Society*, 8(4), 920–53.

Heidegger, M. (1962). *Time and Being.* Trans. by John Macquarrie and Edward Robinson. New York: Harper & Row. From the German original of 1927.

Hodgson, G. (2005). *How Economics Forgot History: The Problem of Historical Specificity in Social Science.* London: Routledge.

Hwang, H., and Powell, W. W. (2005). "Institutions and Entrepreneurship." In *Handbook of Entrepreneurship Research.* New York: Springer US: 201–32.

Jones, G. (2000). *Merchants to Multinationals: British Trading Companies in the Nineteenth and Twentieth Centuries.* Oxford: Oxford University Press.

Jones, G., and Wadhwani, R. D. (2008). "Entrepreneurship," *Oxford Handbook of Business History.* New York: Oxford University Press.

Jones, G., and Wale, J. (1998). "Merchants as Business Groups: British Trading Companies in Asia Before 1945," *Business History Review*, 72: 367–408.

Kilby, P. (ed.) (1971). *Entrepreneurship and Economic Development.* New York: Free Press.

Kirzner, I. M. (1997). "Entrepreneurial Discovery and the Competitive Market Process: An Austrian Approach," *Journal of Economic Literature*, 35: 60–85.

Knight, F. (1921). *Risk, Uncertainty, and Profit.* Boston: Houghton Mifflin Company.

Kreuger, N., Jr. (2003). "The Cognitive Psychology of Entrepreneurship." In Z. Acs and D. Audretsch (eds.), *Handbook of Entrepreneurship Research: An Interdisciplinary Survey and Introduction.* Boston: Kluwer Academic Publishers: 105–40.

Lamoreaux, N. (1998). "Partnerships, Corporations, and the Theory of the Firm," *American Economic Association Papers and Proceedings*, 88: 66–71.

Landes, D., Mokyr, J., and Baumol, W. (eds.) (2010). *The Invention of Enterprise: Entrepreneurship from Ancient Mesopotamia to Modern Times.* Princeton: Princeton University Press.

Landström, H., and Lohrke, F. 2010. *Historical Foundations of Entrepreneurship Research.* Cheltenham: Edward Elgar.

Lee, S.-H., Peng, M., and Barney, J. (2007). "Bankruptcy Law and Entrepreneurship Development: A Real Options Perspective," *Academy of Management Review*, 32: 257–72.

McCraw, T. (2006). "Schumpeter's *Business Cycles* as Business History," *Business History Review*, 80: 231–61.

McCraw, T. (2007). *Prophet of Innovation: Joseph Schumpeter and Creative Destruction.* Cambridge, MA: Belknap Press of Harvard University Press.

McDougall, P., and Oviatt, B. (2000). "International Entrepreneurship: The Intersection of Two Research Paths," *Academy of Management Journal*, 43: 902–8.

McKenna, C. (2006). *The World's Newest Profession: Management Consulting in the Twentieth Century.* New York: Cambridge University Press.

Murmann, J. P. (2003). *Knowledge and Competitive Advantage: The Coevolution of Firms, Technology, and National Institutions.* Cambridge: Cambridge University Press.

Nelson, R. R. and Winter, S. (1982). An Evolutionary Theory of Economic Change. Cambridge, MA: Belknap.

North, D. (1990). *Institutions, Institutional Change, and Economic Performance.* Cambridge: Cambridge University Press.

Oviatt, B., and McDougall, P. (1994). "Toward a Theory of International New Ventures," *Journal of International Business Studies*, 25: 45–64.

Oviatt, B., and McDougall, P. (2005). "Defining International Entrepreneurship and Modeling the Speed of Internationalization," *Entrepreneurship Theory and Practice*, 29: 537–54.

Pierson P. and Skocpol T. (2002). "Historical Institutionalism in Contemporary Political Science." In I. Katznelson, H. V. Milner (eds.) *Political Science: State of the Discipline*. New York: W. W. Norton: 693–721.

Popp, A., and Holt, R. (2013). "The Presence of Entrepreneurial Opportunity," *Business History*, 55(1): 9–28.

Ricoeur, P. (2004). *Memory, History, Forgetting*. Chicago: University of Chicago Press.

Sabel, C., and Zeitlin, J. (1997). *World of Possibilities: Flexibility and Mass Production in Western Industrialization*. New York: Cambridge University Press.

Sarasvathy, S. D., Dew, N., Velamuri, S. R., and Venkataraman, S. (2005). "Three Views of Entrepreneurial Opportunity." In Z. Acs, and D. Audretsch (eds.) *Handbook of Entrepreneurship Research*. New York: Springer.

Schumpeter, J. (1934). *Theory of Economic Development*. Cambridge: Harvard University Press.

Schumpeter, J. (1947). "The Creative Response in Economic History," *The Journal of Economic History*, 7: 149–59.

Schumpeter, J. (1949). "Economic Theory and Entrepreneurial History." In *Change and the Entrepreneur*. Cambridge, MA: Harvard University Press.

Schumpeter, J. (1954). *History of Economic Analysis*. New York: Oxford University Press.

Sewell, W. (2005). *Logics of History: Social Theory and Social Transformation*. Chicago: University of Chicago Press.

Shane, S. (2003). *A General Theory of Entrepreneurship: The Individual-Opportunity Nexus*. Cheltenham: Edward Elgar.

Shane, S., and Eckhardt, J. (2003). "The Individual-Opportunity Nexus." In Z. Acs and D. Audretsch, *Handbook of Entrepreneurship Research: An Interdisciplinary Survey and Introduction*. Boston: Kluwer Academic Publishers: 161–91.

Shane, S., and Venkataraman, S. (2000). "The Promise of Entrepreneurship as a Field of Research," *Academy of Management Review*, 25: 217–26.

Stevenson, H., and Jarillo, J. C. (1990). "A Paradigm of Entrepreneurship: Entrepreneurial Management," *Strategic Management Journal*, 11: 17–27.

Swedberg, R. (1991). *Schumpeter: A Biography*. Princeton: Princeton University Press.

Tilly, C. (1984). *Big Structures, Large Processes, Huge Comparisons*. New York: Russell Sage Foundation.

Wadhwani, R. D. (2010). "Historical Reasoning and the Development of Entrepreneurship Theory." In *Historical Foundations of Entrepreneurship Research*. Cheltenham: Edward Elgar.

Wadhwani, R. D. (2011). "Organizational Form and Industry Emergence: Nonprofits and Mutuals in the Emergence of the Personal Finance Industry," *Business History*. Forthcoming.

Wilkins, M., and Schroter, H. (eds.) (1998). *The Free-Standing Company in the World Economy*. New York: Oxford University Press.

Zeitlin, J., and Herrigel, G. (2000). *Americanization and Its Limits: Reworking U.S. Technology and Management in Postwar Europe and Japan*. New York: Oxford University Press.

9

Historicism and Industry Emergence: Industry Knowledge from Pre-emergence to Stylized Fact

David Kirsch, Mahka Moeen, and R. Daniel Wadhwani[1]

INTRODUCTION

In recent years, organization scholars' interest in accounting for the emergence and evolution of industries has led to a growing engagement with historical settings and sources (Ventresca and Mohr, 2002). A turn toward the past can be found in scholarship across many theoretical schools in macro-organizational research, including neo-institutionalism (Hargadon and Douglas, 2001; Leblebici et al., 1991), organizational ecology (Hannan and Freeman, 1987), evolutionary economics (Gort and Klepper, 1982; Nelson and Winter, 1982), and socio-cognitive perspectives (Henderson and Clark, 1990; Tripsas and Gavetti, 2000). Indeed, this research has often included efforts to draw on historical evidence not only from recent decades, but also from the more distant past (Haveman and Rao, 1997) and to examine industries over long spans of time (Tripsas, 1997).

The increasing use of data and sources from the past raises the broader question of exactly how historical research and reasoning is valuable in the study of industries. The predominant response to this question in mainstream organizational studies might be described as one focused on the identification of "historical mechanisms," a perspective that views history as a context for examining theoretically relevant questions about how time and the sequence of organizational events shape the evolution of markets. The research that draws on historical evidence to examine imprinting (Marquis, 2003), evolutionary change (Murmann, 2006; Aldrich and Ruef, 2006), and path dependence

---

[1] The authors contributed equally.

(Sydow, et al., 2009) in industries can all be categorized as fitting this approach to the past. History, from this perspective, offers organizational scholars a long retrospective lens for identifying and testing theoretical mechanisms and processes by which industries emerge and change. We believe this approach is important to the future of history in studies of industries, and have employed it in our own work.

In this chapter, however, we explore a different and less widely used approach that can be characterized as one based on "historicism." Growing out of the intellectual traditions of source criticism and hermeneutic philosophy (Grondin, 1994), historicism posits that human thought and action cannot be adequately understood without accounting for its antecedents and contexts (Herder, 1968 [1791]). The task of understanding human actions, unlike that of explaining natural phenomena, rests on one's ability to adequately reconstruct the cultural and historical context shaping the subject's knowledge (Dilthey, 2002 [1910]; Collingwood, 1994 [1946]) rather than imposing one's own categories of thought on the subject of inquiry. Time and change present significant challenges in understanding human actors and actions because researchers cannot take for granted that they understand the context for action in the past, and because researchers' own knowledge and conceptual assumptions can inhibit the ability to reconstruct that context (Gadamer, 1975). As such, historicism highlights how time and change shape both the perspectives and choices of the historical actors one studies, *and* how these historical perspectives and choices constrain researchers and others in the present in their efforts to understand and explain the past. Employed in this way, history is valuable because it offers us a well-developed intellectual tradition for grasping and addressing the challenges involved in making sense of how organizational actors understood their industries and made decisions over the course of time.

Such an approach to studying industries, we contend, is especially appropriate at a moment when management scholars have placed increasing emphasis on knowledge formation and cognition as central to the constitution of organizations and markets (Porac et al., 2002; Spender, 1989). Knowledge and cognition-based views of industries inherently raise questions about how organizational actors came to know their industry (and its constituent technologies, applications, business models, competitors, etc.) *and* how scholars reconstruct this knowledge formation process given that the passage of time can create significant obstacles to how we in the present understand the past. In short, it raises questions of how time—in this instance, the time that lapses in industry emergence and evolution—shapes knowledge. These are precisely the kinds of questions historicism has long addressed.

In particular, we show how such an approach can highlight aspects of industry emergence and evolution that are systematically left out or elided both by the passage of time and by our own social scientific models of industry evolution. These processes of elision and exclusion, we argue, are inherent in industry knowledge formation as both contemporary actors and subsequently the social scientists studying them come to focus on certain knowledge as constituting the industry. An awareness of what gets excluded or elided over time is thus crucial for understanding what our explanations systematically leave out and for understanding the process of knowledge formation about an industry. Specifically, we highlight three forms of elision and forgetting that take place in conventional social scientific accounts of industry evolution and show how historical sources and methods hold particular value in helping organizational scholars reconstruct paths and alternatives that are forgotten in the process of emergence. We begin by briefly outlining why and how predominant models of industry evolution tend to leave these elements out and then turn to three case studies that highlight both the processes of exclusion and how historical research might be used to recover omitted industry knowledge and paths of potential development. We conclude by drawing out the implications of the chapter for how we think about alternative explanations, contingency, and choice in the emergence and evolution of industries.

TEMPORAL ASSUMPTIONS AND THE STUDY OF INDUSTRY EVOLUTION

Industries form indispensible units of analysis for organizational researchers. Yet defining and studying industries present particularly difficult problems. More so than other units of analysis—the firm, the entrepreneur, and the state, for instance—the concept of industry immediately presents researchers with the challenge of defining the identity and boundaries of the object of study. Which firms are part of the industry and which are not? Should one include other relevant actors—for example, tastemakers, intermediaries, analysts, regulators (Van de Van and Garud, 1989; Khaire, forthcoming)? How does one account for ideas, relationships, and knowledge in defining the industry (Porac et al., 2002)? And, temporally, when does an industry begin and when does it end (Forbes and Kirsch, 2011)?

The problems in defining the industry and its constituent parts are not just scholarly; they are also practical ones related to knowledge, identity, and boundary formation for organizational actors themselves (Santos and Eisenhardt, 2009). Firms define competitors and design strategy based on their understanding of who comprises the competition (Porac et al., 1995). Entrepreneurs identify opportunities based on their knowledge of the markets and industries in which they will compete. And states must define industries as a necessary step in articulating who and what they are regulating. Questions about what defines an industry are hence central to both how researchers conceptualize industries in theory, as well as how actors think and behave in practice.

The most common scholarly response to this inherent ambiguity has been to rely on functional social scientific definitions of industries and their temporal dynamics in order to establish a foundation for rigorous analysis. Sharp functional definitions that characterize an industry as, for instance, a population of firms that produce substitute goods (Porter, 1980), compete for the same resources, appear in the same industry registry, or identify each other as competitors (White, 1981) have the distinct advantage of focusing research on the development of measurable observations that can be tracked over time and used to test hypotheses. Yet in imposing functional parameters on the often ambiguous and changing definition of an industry, such approaches may also systematically leave out processes at work in industry formation that are already somewhat obscured by time and change. A historicist perspective—one that recognizes industry knowledge as contextually embedded—highlights the temporal assumptions of such functional models and the simultaneous processes of knowledge formation and elision surrounding industries that such models are likely to leave out.

To illustrate this, we use as our example the classical model of industry evolution based on populations of producer firms, as represented by the shaded arrows in Figure 9.1. The model marks the inception of an industry as the moment when a commercial product is first introduced (Gort and Klepper, 1982; Klepper and Graddy, 1990), and characterizes subsequent stages of the industry life cycle based on patterns of producer firm entry and exit. Although a dictionary definition of emergence[2] may refer to any

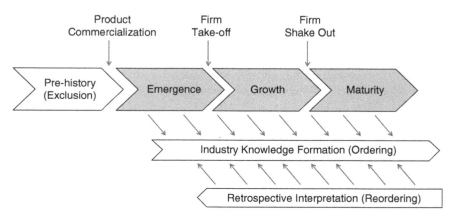

Figure 9.1 Historicism and the industry life cycle model

---

[2] The Merriam-Webster dictionary defines emergence as the act of coming into being through evolution.

act of emerging, in the life cycle model the time period immediately after product commercialization is known as the emergence stage (Agarwal and Tripsas, 2008) and is characterized by the entry of a small number of firms, high levels of uncertainty, and experimentation. The emergence stage is followed by the rapid entry of firms during the subsequent period, such that the industry experiences a sharp takeoff in the number of firms (Agarwal and Gort, 1996; Golder and Tellis, 1997). Consolidation and decline in the number of producer firms mark the beginning of a period of industry maturity, which is typically accompanied by the establishment of a dominant design (Abernathy and Utterback, 1978; Tushman and Anderson, 1986; Utterback and Suarez, 1993). These industry life cycle patterns have been documented across a variety of contexts, and have come to form the foundation for a number of theoretical schools, including organization ecology (Hannan and Freeman, 1977), technology management (Abernathy and Utterback, 1978; Tushman and Anderson, 1982), and evolutionary economics (Gort and Klepper, 1982; Klepper and Graddy, 1990).[3]

Yet, while the life cycle model has provided a powerful foundation for identifying empirical regularities that fall within its parameters, it also illustrates how the temporal framing and assumptions of such functional models of historical change and evolution may obscure other important processes at work in industry formation. The unshaded arrows in Figure 9.1 highlight the three forms of elision—that is, the processes of exclusion, ordering, and reordering of industry knowledge. Though typically elided by functional models of organizational change like the industry life cycle, historicism can render these processes visible. One such process pertains to the *exclusion* of phenomena that fall outside the temporal boundaries of the model. For instance, developments that predate the moment of product commercialization in Figure 9.1 are typically left unexamined in the standard life cycle model, even when this pre-history of the industry includes decisions about technologies, applications, and business models that are crucial to the subsequent evolution of the product and its market.

Second, the model assumes that historical information on industry and firm behavior (such as entries, exits) represent real-time observations rather than a process of retrospective sensemaking and industry knowledge formation that organizational actors were themselves experiencing in time. Yet, as the cognitive view of industries (Porac et al., 2002) suggests, participants themselves go through their own processes of defining and selecting which firms and products constitute the industry (Porac et al., 1995) and how they are to be categorized and valued (Khaire and Wadhwani, 2010). The historical sources and information available to organizational research reflects this process of

---

[3] For a thorough review of this literature, please see Agarwal and Tripsas (2008).

exclusion and inclusion in the creation of industry knowledge rather than direct observations of organizational actions. Indeed, rarely is industry data actually collected at the moment of the first firm's entry, and most archival sources often represent the subsequent efforts of organizational actors or regulators to make sense of the industry. As Lipartito's chapter points out, archival evidence is never neutral, and good historical reasoning requires a critical stance on questions of why certain information was even recorded and preserved as significant "knowledge" of the industry (Ricoeur, 2004). After all, any process of choosing, recording, and preserving information involves excluding some things to focus on others to establish *order* in one's under-standing of an industry. Like other functional models, the life cycle framework elides the fact that the information and observations that are tracked and pre-served for organization scholars to analyze do not offer unfiltered observations of behavior, but rather reflect participants' own changing understandings of the industry and their beliefs of what ought to be recorded.

Lastly, scholars' perceptions of industry formation are shaped by expecta-tions established by their own position in historical time, as they look back from the present into the past. This retrospective view *reorders* what we observe about industries and their emergence in light of both subsequent developments and the conceptual biases we hold, emphasizing what we under-stand to be of *post hoc* importance while marginalizing other developments in the industry emergence process. For example, researchers seeking to explain industry emergence reflect back on the events that had occurred during that timeframe once the industry has already moved past the emergence stage. In doing so, they reorder observations in light of what they know about the ensu-ing events and in ways that elide the uncertainty faced by the subjects of their studies.[4] Such retrospective reordering of our observations and interpretations is reinforced by the theoretical and conceptual assumptions we hold.

In the sections that follow, we look at these patterns of exclusion, ordering, and reordering in closer detail using three case studies, and we consider how historical methods can help us recover what has been overlooked and why that is valuable. Table 9.1 provides an overview of the three case studies that fol-low and the arguments they illustrate. The first case examines the importance of pre-emergence, what happens before a product is commercialized and what aspects of this pre-emergence process tend to be lost in organizational accounts. Using the case of plant biotechnology, we discuss the possible alternative com-mercialization paths that tend to be excluded as one particular application becomes dominant, and we consider the value of history in studying the reasons

---

[4] One example of this is identification of the first instance of product commercialization at the moment of an industry's beginning. For the industry actors it may not be clear whether a particular design or business model constitutes the product that embodies industry. However, when researchers view the emergence stage *ex post*, it may seem obvious what exactly the product is, and when exactly the first product was introduced.

Table 9.1 Summary of cases

Temporal Issue	Exclusion and Pre-history	Reordering and Theoretical Myopia	Ordering and Reordering of Industry Knowledge
Case	Plant biotechnology	Savings banking	Automobile
Relevant Organizational Constructs	Industry emergence Technological embeddedness	Boundaries Organizational Forms	Industry knowledge
Prospects for Historical Research	Non-emergence of industries Ecology of innovation Application/value formation Alternative paths & choices	Contingency and uncertainty of industry pathways Social-political identities of industries	Process of industry knowledge construction Historical narratives and counter-narratives of industries Alternative paths & choices

potential industries fail to emerge. The second section examines how theoretical and conceptual myopia associated with retrospective reordering blinds us to alternative explanations and organizational pathways after emergence. Using the case of savings banking in the 19th century, we highlight how historical methods can recover alternative contexts and explanations of industry development. Finally, using the case of the automobile industry, we show how ordering and reordering of information is itself part of the process by which coherent industries come to be identified and re-defined over time. When even basic data are interpreted in contexts that vary from those in which they were created, misunderstandings are possible and historical analysis is needed to recapture the initial industry knowledge that has long since been forgotten.

NON-EMERGENCE OF "MIGHT-HAVE-BEEN" INDUSTRIES: PLANT BIOTECHNOLOGY

A common type of omission in research on the evolution of industries pertains to the events that occur prior to the first instance of product commercialization. Despite its ramifications for the subsequent evolution of an industry, the pre-commercialization time period has been largely overlooked by industry evolution studies. This temporal elision of the pre-commercialization period may stem from the approach of classic industry evolution models in characterizing industries as a group of producer firms and/or in defining industry inception by the first instance of product commercialization. As a result, research has tended to ignore the antecedents of industries and to miss the alternative and failed commercialization paths undertaken by organizational actors. Although a handful of studies have focused on documenting the existence of the pre-commercialization stage (Agarwal and Bayus, 2002; Golder, Shacham, and Mitra, 2009), these studies tend to focus on developments that led to the eventual introduction of a commercial product and the emergence of an industry. The omission of events from the pre-commercialization time period has more significant implications in cases in which a new technology or product was not subsequently commercialized. If a might-have-been-industry never gets to the stage of product commercialization, not only is it typically excluded from examination in the classic industry evolution literature, it is also likely that retrieving its economic traces becomes difficult (Forbes and Kirsch, 2011).

A better understanding of the factors leading to emergence (and non-emergence) of an industry is of great interest to organizational actors and policymakers who seek to commit resources to a new-to-the-world technology and/or product. Analysis of industries that have not emerged and the alternative paths taken during the pre-commercialization period, though understudied, is crucial for navigating the strategic actions needed during the emergence of an industry. As a thorough examination of non-emergence may provide a more complete picture of developments in the pre-commercialization period, it is imperative to consider various research approaches that shed light on this critical phenomenon. We suggest that historical analysis and contextualization of the events related to industry emergence are essential in such endeavors. In particular, historical research can help retrieve what is forgotten about promising technologies and products that were never commercialized and delineate the differences in the patterns of industry emergence and non-emergence.

The case of plant biotechnology serves as an example of how historical methods may be used to better understand some of the underlying processes and factors related to non-emergence of might-have-been industries. The science of plant biotechnology builds on advancements in modern biotechnology techniques and extends them to genetic modification of plants so that their genetic structure can be modified in ways that express valuable traits. In 1977, plant scientists at the University of Ghent in Belgium discovered a gene transfer mechanism in plants (Schell and Van Montagu, 1977) that laid the foundation for plant biotechnology.[5] Later, in 1983, the first transgenic plants—antibiotic resistant tobacco and petunia—were introduced by three independent research groups from the Washington University in St. Louis (Bevan et al., 1983), University of Ghent (Herrera-Strella et al., 1983), and Monsanto (Fraley

---

[5] Schell and Van Montagu (1977) found that Agrobacterium can transfer DNA between itself and plants and can thus be used as a delivery system for genetic modification of plants.

et al., 1983). These technological advancements in plant biotechnology have opened up various opportunities based on which researchers in universities and firms have extended the scientific knowledge of plant biotechnology and have explored alternative ways through which these technological advancements could be transformed into commercially valuable products. One of the best known applications of plant biotechnology is to enhance agricultural productivity of crops such as corn, soybean, and cotton through pest resistance[6] and herbicide tolerance[7] traits. Transgenic crops with enhanced agricultural productivity traits were introduced to the market in 1995 and have experienced an average adoption rate of 90 percent for principal crops by 2011 (James, 2011).

Although accounts of product commercialization based on plant biotechnology suggest enhanced agricultural productivity as the dominant path undertaken by firms, applications of plant biotechnology science were not limited to enhanced agricultural productivity. Since 1977, the possibilities of using plant biotechnology to introduce products related to biofuel, food, environmental remediation, and pharmaceuticals have also been explored. For instance, researchers have invested in development of a genetically modified corn that expresses the enzyme required for ethanol production directly in the corn kernel. In addition, there have been experiments in genetically modifying the chemical composition and enzyme production process of switchgrass and camelina for biofuel applications. These efforts may result in efficiencies in biofuel production by reducing the need for additional enzymes and increasing yield of fuel per ton of crops. Even though these technological investments have been pursued since the early days of plant biotechnology, the first transgenic corn for application in ethanol production was only commercialized in 2012. Another potential application of plant biotechnology is in bioremediation. Bioremediation refers to the use of plants, trees, and grasses to remove hazardous materials such as arsenic, lead, and mercury from the environment. These transgenic plants are modified to be able to tolerate high levels of hazardous materials, extract them from the soil, and transform them to less toxic elements. Researchers have experimented with genetic modification of poplars, tobacco, and arabidopsis to perform bioremediation. Despite extensive university-based research, there has been no instance of product commercialization. A handful of firms have made investments in this area which have not led to any commercial output thus far. Plant biotechnology may also be used to achieve improved nutritional characteristics, appearance, or flavor in the food industry. A few examples of applications of plant biotechnology in the food industry are non-browning apples, vitamin A-enhanced rice, delayed-ripening tomatoes, and high-oleic

---

[6] Pest resistance protects crops against pests before they can damage the crops.
[7] Herbicide tolerance enables crops to withstand the application of some types of herbicides.

soybeans. Despite the technological viability of these applications, none of them has been commercialized on a large scale. Tomatoes with the delayed ripening trait were commercialized in 1994; however, the product was not well received by consumers and was soon removed from supermarket shelves. Despite firms' and universities' technological investments across all of these domains, only the use of plant biotechnology to increase agricultural productivity has emerged as a nascent industry. Other applications have been limited to research experiments or field trials, and yet no instance of product commercialization has occurred in large scale.

Addressing the question of why some of these might-have-been industries did *not* emerge may lead to valuable contributions with regard to understanding why promising technologies or products sometimes fail to serve as the basis for new industries. There are at least three ways in which drawing on historical methods may be crucial in this regard. First, a theoretical understanding of the underlying factors related to non-emergence requires a pluralistic approach that spans multiple literature streams and considers various context-specific explanations. Although the predominant theoretical lens in the study of industry evolution attributes non-emergence of these commercial applications to technological trajectories or firms' investment patterns, preliminary evidence in the context of plant biotechnology highlights additional critical factors. In particular, examination of historical evidence indicates the role of various stakeholders in the broader socio-economic environment (Van de Van and Garud, 1989), the structure of markets, and the availability of innovation ecosystems (Adner, 2006; Hargadon and Douglas, 2001). For instance, product commercialization related to the biofuel industry was impacted by the lack of availability of innovation ecosystems and the lack of effective mechanisms for value capture. While firms have identified the technological and commercial opportunities related to the biofuel industry, commercial viability of any product was dependent on the growth of biofuel producers. Moreover, market imperfections for securing a price premium from farmers required adoption of new transactional models. Unless such an ecosystem was in place, weak prospects of value capture inhibited industry emergence. Alternatively, the history of the application of plant biotechnology in the food industry indicates that supply-side factors such as technology availability and firm-specific resource commitments favored the emergence of the potential industry. However, demand-side factors such as consumer approval of products became a major reason for non-emergence. The explanations for non-emergence of each of these markets indicate the complexity of studying such a multi-dimensional phenomenon, and therefore underscore that conventional methods of hypothesis testing may be inadequate for studying non-emergence. Importantly, heterogeneity in the nature of determinant factors in each application begs for a case-by-case analysis of different settings, rather than a deductive, theory-testing approach that assumes homogeneity across multiple settings. By allowing for careful contextual analysis of the phenomenon, historical methods provide this alternative approach. This theory-informed contextualization may then feed back into theory building that could form the foundation for later connections across seemingly unrelated contexts.

Second, studying non-emergence requires drawing fully on the breadth and depth of industry records available in historical archives. The case of plant biotechnology is a unique context in that firms' technological investments left traces in the form of government records. According to the coordinated framework for regulation of biotechnology, all experiments with a genetically modified organism in an open field are required to be disclosed to the USDA. Thus, the alternative technological paths that were pursued by firms and universities could be reconstructed from these filings. Similar systematic secondary data sources may not be available in the case of other might-have-been industries and therefore call for the use of archival sources of data and possible triangulation across multiple types of historical evidence.

Finally, historical methods enable us to focus on the temporality of events and reconstruct the specific social and economic context that the organizational actors faced during the window of potential industry emergence. Organizational actors are involved in multiple uncertainties during the pre-emergence period. In the case of plant biotechnology, organizational actors had to face technological uncertainty as it related to whether certain technological milestones could be achieved, commercial uncertainty as it related to whether a viable business model could be designed around a given technological invention, demand uncertainty as it related to whether the general public and the target customers would adopt the new products, and regulatory uncertainty as it related to how regulatory institutions would evaluate the new inchoate industries. As time passes, resolution of some of these uncertainties may make researchers insensitive to the extent to which organizational actors needed to experiment with alternative modes of transforming technological opportunities to commercial products. Accordingly, development of functional models may be impacted by the sensemaking of researchers that study the phenomenon *ex post*, and perhaps lead to an incomplete or biased account of the initial phenomenon. Historical methods are, however, sensitive to the meaning of events in their environmental and temporal contexts and thus account for these temporal considerations.

THEORETICAL MYOPIA AND THE RECONSTRUCTION OF ALTERNATIVE EXPLANATIONS AND PATHS: SAVINGS BANKS

Historical reasoning can help make us aware of not only what our models of industrial time and change leave out, but also of how our extant theories color and shape our understanding of the phenomena we are trying to explain. In this second sense, "forgetting" is not a product of temporal spans that fall outside the parameters of the model, but rather the result of a certain retrospective myopia that comes from imposing an extant social scientific explanation on evidence from an industry's past. Historical methods, in this sense, serve not only to highlight the limits of theory-imposed explanations, but also offer contextualized accounts that point to alternative explanations of industry emergence and identify important choices and conjunctures in industry development.

Research that uses transaction cost reasoning to explain the emergence of a market for "savings accounts" in 19th-century America provides a useful illustration of how theory can lead to a myopic reading of historical evidence. Hansmann (1989) and Rasmusen (1988) have argued that ordinary savers in the antebellum US distrusted commercial banks and the general public lacked the ability or information to monitor such institutions. A market for savings accounts appeared only once nonprofit savings banks were established. The nonprofit form served as a kind of organizational innovation that overcame "problems of asymmetric information facing consumers" (Hansmann, 1989: 66) because it imposed constraints on opportunistic behavior by the managers of such institutions. Hence nonprofit savings banks served as the dominant organizational form for deposit banking in the emerging market for savings accounts until the eventual development of state regulation in the late 19th and early 20th century addressed the information asymmetries and monitoring problems that the general public associated with commercial banks. In his influential book, *The Ownership of Enterprise* (2000), Hansmann relies on a series of such historical illustrations to explain his theory of nonprofit and cooperative firms and the allocation of ownership and governance rights in overcoming coordination and monitoring problems in markets.

Hansmann's explanations are plausible, theoretically elegant, and fit observable quantitative evidence from secondary sources. But neither Hansmann nor Rasmusen engages primary historical sources nor tries to contextualize the decision to organize a particular form using sources that reflect the reasoning and worldviews of contemporary decision makers. We learn little about how historical actors actually thought about such decisions and the industries considered are used as illustrations abstracted from the broader economic, social, and political contexts of their time. Did the choices of actors actually reflect transaction cost reasoning, or some alternative way of looking at the world? What other contextual factors shaped the choice of organizational form? Did these nonprofit and mutual forms simply represent instances of individual organizational choice, or fundamentally alternative paths of historical development that are lost to scholars drawing conclusions based on evidence and general theory derived from the present? The implications of these questions are significant for how one approaches historical evidence and what it reveals about the dynamics of markets.

In the case of 19th-century nonprofit savings banks, a closer look and deeper contextualization of the primary source historical evidence shows that while transaction costs and fears of opportunism *were* a consideration, the more important factors were political ones and represented alternative understandings of the relationship between states and organizations in the emerging field of personal finance. Patterns of savings bank founding and the choice of organizational form as nonprofit or joint-stock companies closely followed state boundaries and evolved according to the political dynamics of competition between state and federal regulators, as well as changing constitutional considerations about the relationships between firms and the state. The dynamics of market evolution and organizational choice reflected competing understandings of the relationship between states and organizations, as did the eventual predominance of joint-stock intermediaries in the United States. The importance of these political processes is particularly clear when the US is compared to other countries, where organizational forms and markets for savings accounts developed very differently due to differences in state-organizational field relationships. In short, industry emergence in savings banking was shaped by the actions and interests of states in ensuring economic order and security, and in financing their own administrative capabilities. Historical contextualization can thus help highlight alternative explanations of industry emergence that theory often obscures, in this case because industry and organization theories tend to assume a limited state.

The case discussed in no way suggests that an approach to historical evidence based on "theory testing" or "theory elaboration" is wrong; indeed, we believe there is real value to using historical evidence to test and elaborate existing theory. However, it does suggest how such approaches to history are by themselves very limited because they typically reproduce assumptions and hypotheses that organizational scholars already hold, rather than opening the researcher to explanations and alternative contextualizations that may in fact be more important in explaining the historical phenomenon under consideration. Theoretical myopia, in such instances, blinds us to alternative understandings by shaping what we gather as relevant evidence on industries, limiting the contexts in which we understand what constitutes the industry, and discounting alternatives and contingent choices made by organizational actors. In short, it *reorders* knowledge of industry emergence based on the assumptions and categories of extant social scientific theory.

An alternative way of engaging historical evidence involves an approach that takes more seriously the need to interpret and understand industries and choices from the point of view of organizational actors. This deeper, contextual approach reads historical evidence from the past "forward" in ways that do not foreclose alternative organizational paths and dynamics in markets as inevitably doomed to failure. This view is not deaf to theory, but is open to contextual dynamics and alternative routes to industrial and market change that existing theoretical lenses tend to marginalize. To be certain, no such effort at interpreting an industry's past on its own terms is likely to be entirely successful. As professional historians and philosophers of history often point out, some element of retrospective bias is inherent in historical reasoning; our very choice of topics and contexts, after all, is inherently shaped by questions and problems that arise in our present (Danto, 1965; Gadamer, 1975). However, an awareness of how retrospective bias and theoretical myopia can shape our explanations of the historical dynamics of industries can be a useful corrective as we gather and interpret historical evidence in ways that are sensitive to the interpretive problems at hand. In particular, a number of principles commonly employed by historians and historical social scientists can be useful here.

One such approach involves greater attention to the broader historical contexts in which organizational choices and industry dynamics take place. Such contextualization helps researchers understand decisions and interpret the dynamics of an industry within the broader economic, social, political, and cultural world in which they took place, rather than seeing industry histories and dynamics as separable. Consider, for instance, how Schneiberg and colleagues (2002, 2007, 2008) approach the historical evidence on cooperatives and mutuals in the early 20th-century US with both attention to their broader context and an awareness of the limits of existing theories in understanding these variations in organizational form. Schneiberg does not ignore theory, and himself draws on institutional theory (2002) in particular. Using both historical evidence and secondary sources from the late 19th and early 20th centuries, he argues that cooperatives and mutual firms often represented an alternative vision of the emergence of corporate forms of organization in the United States, and that these alternative forms—even when they failed—constituted part of the institutional environment that later entrants used to "create new paths" that didn't fit existing institutional choices. Schneiberg's theoretical insights come from an approach that is based on contextualizing the evolution of industries and organizational populations more broadly, taking into account the social and political movements around them. His work hence demonstrates both how historical evidence on markets and organizations, when contextualized using both historiography and contemporary historical evidence, can lead to both new theoretical claims (2008) and an understanding of alternative paths of development in markets and economies that existing theories tend to make invisible. Historical contextualization allows scholars to account for developments shaping industries and firms that lie outside the immediate domain of organizational competition and survival. Studies of industry dynamics and evolution have understandably tried to isolate factors specific to firms and the industry. However, the problem with such approaches is that concepts of industries and firms are themselves embedded in historical time. Historical contextualization hence is crucial for understanding industry dynamics as themselves embedded in broader developments.

The use of contemporary accounts and sources that reveal the "voices" of contemporary actors can also help researchers avoid the myopia imposed by existing explanations. Hansen (2007), for instance, examines the decline of nonprofit savings banks in late 20th-century Denmark using sources that help explain how contemporary Danes understood the narrative identities of commercial banks and savings banks. He traces the rise in the 19th century and persistence in the 20th of the "premise that savings banks offered a democratic and popular alternative to commercial banks, founded on a different set of values and different understanding of financial services" (Hansen, 2007: 928). Not until the late 20th century does the strength of this basic identity segmenting the industry deteriorate, eventually replaced by the distinction between "local" and "big" banks. It is important to note that Hansen does not shy away from theory, and in fact embraces a narrative theoretical perspective on industry dynamics. But his use and careful reading of sources that reveal the voices of contemporary actors allows him to distinguish between the way in which actors "ordered" their understanding of their industry and the secondary interpretive operation by which he uses current theory to "reorder" their experience. Maintaining this distinction in turn allows him to take into account both uncertainty and choice in the evolution of the industry.

SUBMERGENCE AS FORGETTING: THE NON-EMERGENCE OF AN ELECTRIC VEHICLE-BASED TRANSPORT SERVICE

Our third vignette looks at how the uncertainty of industry emergence is "forgotten." In the case of the automobile industry, industry knowledge and uncertainty associated with the pre-emergence phase was "submerged" not just by the arrival of a dominant design, but also by the emergence of a dominant narrative that naturalized the superiority of internal combustion and marginalized the electric vehicle as one of several paths-not-taken. Our counter-narrative examines the fate of one early industry-level datum, shows how careful historical analysis can help recover the story of the industry that did not emerge, and suggests ways that the prevailing dominant narrative may have suffered for its lack of historical awareness.

In 1899, the United States automobile industry was still in its infancy. Numerous "firsts" had been recorded; the first vehicles had been built, sold, raced, and crashed. *Horseless Age*, the first industry trade journal, had been founded. And the motor vehicle had begun to appear in broader cultural fora such as general newspapers. Perceiving the potential import of this nascent sector, that year the Bureau of the Census collected data on the production of automobiles in the United States by mode of propulsion, reporting that 1,681 steam, 1,575 electric, and 936 gasoline automobiles were manufactured.

The Census report suggests that, prima facie, steam- and electric-powered automobiles dominated the initial motor vehicle market, with gasoline (internal combustion) in a lagging position.[8] For decades, observers have trotted out these data to make a range of points about the early history of the American auto industry. From prominent historians (Flink, 1990) to journalists (Motavalli, 2001) and filmmakers (Paine, 2006), secondary accounts of the emergence of the automobile industry have stressed that steam- and electric-powered vehicles *lost* the technological competition to internal combustion in spite of their initial market advantage. Researchers interested in path-dependent technological change have been particularly interested in the observed pattern of early adoption decisions: Arthur's theory of lock-in (Arthur, 1989) suggested, for example, that random sequences of adoption may result in a threshold event leading to the selection of an ultimately "inferior" technological solution. Conversely, believers in the rationality of markets for technological choice have used the Census report to defend the rationality of the rise to dominance of internal combustion. Internal combustion, according to this argument, overcame its slow start due to its superior technological attributes. We take no position on these underlying arguments. We note only that in the century or more since it was first produced, this particular datum has been invoked time and again to support a range of claims and counter-claims about the emergence of the early market for automobiles in the United States.

In many respects, the Census report and other data about the earliest stages of the industry have been very valuable for scholars and have had lasting impacts upon historical interpretation. But what if the Bureau of the Census datum failed to capture an important distinction that characterized the emergent automobile market? What if this fundamental nugget of information about the emergent automobile market—the seemingly incontrovertible observation that production of internal combustion-powered vehicles initially *trailed* production of steam- and electric-powered ones—was incomplete?

In prior work, one of the authors has looked at the early history of the market for electric vehicles and found that the adoption of internal combustion as the technological standard for the emerging motor vehicle market occurred over time, in fits and starts, as different business concepts (Sloan, 1990 [1963]) were tested in the marketplace. The competing technologies were not competing against each other on some hypothetical consumer's mental blackboard, but were instead embedded in technological systems that built upon incommensurable and fragmentary mental schemas, unevenly developed infrastructures

---

[8] Setting aside the handful of truly unique vehicle designs (i.e. those powered by compressed air or a coal-fired boiler), these three modes of propulsion did accurately capture technological variation in the production of motor vehicles in the United States.

and, most important for present purposes, firm-level differences in business models.

Indeed, the most important distinction between early competitors in the emergent automobile industry may well have been the split between companies that sought to make and *sell vehicles* and those that sought to *sell transportation service* (Kirsch and Mom, 2002). The Census reported production by mode of propulsion, but in so doing failed to report on the critical business model competition that was in fact wracking the industry and would go on to define the industry structure that would emerge in the years immediately following. The largest vehicle manufacturer in the United States in 1899 was the Electric Vehicle Company (EVC), and it relied upon a fee-for-transport service business model. Competing against horse-drawn livery companies for well-heeled urban customers accustomed to traveling by hansom cab, the EVC built, owned, and operated its own electric vehicles and generated revenue by selling transportation service.

Can we update our interpretation of these early events to take account of this critical industry knowledge? What would a business-model adjusted Census report have found in 1899? Though specific production numbers are hard to pin down, the EVC and its related companies manufactured approximately 900 of the 1,575 electric vehicles counted in the famed Census report. These vehicles were never sold to individuals and were never intended to be operated by individuals. By contrast, the vast majority of both steam- and internal combustion-powered vehicles enumerated by the Census were produced for sale to individual consumers (though some were subsequently used for commercial purposes). Taking business model into account approximately 5/6 of vehicles produced in the United States in 1899 were intended for sale to end consumers. Internal combustion, in this view, can never be said to have "trailed" electric vehicles. Consumers didn't choose a technology as much as they chose a mode of using motor vehicles. For the thin slice of wealthy American consumers who could afford to either buy an automobile or buy transportation service from a transportation service company, most preferred to own and operate their own vehicle(s). Transportation service never represented more than a small share of the emerging vehicle market.

A book chapter is hardly the place to take on decades of historiography on the automobile industry. Thus, this discussion of the US Census' 1899 report on automobile manufacturing is explicitly not intended to relitigate the history of the emergence of the American motor vehicle industry. Rather, we extrapolate from this brief account of how a specific piece of information has been understood—and perhaps misunderstood—by those who have sought to make sense of an economically and socially important instance of industry emergence to better understand the challenge of getting emergence right.

First, neither the paths-not-taken nor their implications are always self-evident. For most of the history of the automobile industry, the failed emergence of the electric vehicle was either invisible or, where seen, was understood as the result of a deterministic process of technological selection that was briefly led astray by the misguided efforts of a handful of self-dealing New York and Philadelphia-based Robber Barons (Rae, 1955). The US Census report from 1899 could be and was interpreted to support that account. The story of the emergence of an alternative transportation system built upon a different, service-based business model was submerged by accounts of the emergence of the dominant, sales-based business model that also happened to be associated with internal combustion. Recovering the alternate account from the margins of the mainstream narrative invites scholars to ask new questions about the general process of industry emergence. By being mindful of the possible paths-not-taken, scholars may be able to better understand the evolutionary dynamics that operate in the "long now" when flexibility gives way to structure.

Second, time—or more properly, temporality—matters for our understanding of any narrative of emergence. Scholars need to understand and be sensitive to the full sweep of the process of emergence, from the exploration and experimentation that characterizes the pre-history of an industry to the full range of *ex post* attempts to construct or order the events in ways that support both cognitive sensemaking of recent and distant events and the range of narrative accounts in which interests are vested. Therefore, temporality cannot be taken as a given. Rather, narratives and schema themselves emerge in tandem with underlying economic and social stabilization processes. Early participants in the emergence of the automobile industry *ordered* events according to their own biases and assumptions about how the future of the industry would unfold. Based on prevailing industry knowledge, few foresaw the complete dominance of internal combustion and how that dominance would reconfigure everything from popular music to urban geography. Instead, at the time the Census study was conducted, expert observers believed in "separate spheres"—the idea that each technology would eventually find its own unique set of applications. In the intervening century, scholars have reinterpreted and *reordered* early events for their own purposes, highlighting attributes that prior observers would have interpreted through their own temporal lenses. In this instance, even well after the fact, the interpretation of market emergence requires sensitivity to the ways that previous observers have ordered and reordered accounts of the past in dialogue with the ever-changing present.

CONCLUSION

In this chapter, we have highlighted how historicism can raise management researchers' awareness of the ways in which time and change shape how both organizational actors and the social scientists studying them perceive industries and their dynamics. Our goal in highlighting patterns of forgetting and elision in studies of industry emergence has not been to suggest the replacement of conventional social scientific accounts with historical ones; good functional models can provide useful insights into general patterns of industry emergence and development. Rather, our intention is to highlight why and how the historical reasoning and methods outlined in this book provide a useful *complement* to standard social scientific accounts precisely because the use of overlooked archival evidence and careful historical reasoning can help organizational researchers reconstruct what other disciplinary approaches and the process of time erase. In this sense, we argue that the kinds of historical sources and methods outlined in the last section of this book ought to be employed by organizational researchers precisely because they offer insights into issues and questions that extant theory does not effectively address. By way of conclusion, therefore, we highlight several ways in which historical research and reasoning can make unique contributions to the study of industry formation.

Stylized Facts, Historical Narrative, and Alternative Theories

One such area of promise is in the use of archival sources, which have been largely ignored by organizational researchers, in order to create new analytical narratives of industry formation. Mainstream social science research on industry emergence has produced accounts that reflect consensus judgments and capture so-called "stylized facts" about the sources and antecedents of new industries (Helfat, 2007). The very term, stylized fact, conveys the necessary narrative pruning of many foreclosed, and possibly, forgotten developments. There are many benefits of stylized facts: often emergence needs to be studied comparatively, across time and space, and stylized facts help draw out commonalities as they relate to the underlying phenomenon of interest. The traditional model of industry evolution, with its established periodization of the phases of emergence, would not be possible without some degree of "stylization" of the phenomenon across industries, regions, and time. The parsimony of such accounts is necessary for analytic tractability. However, deeper inquiry through the application of heterodox, historical methods—while complex, more time-consuming, and less parsimonious—can produce narratives that capture unique features of the process of emergence that have been excluded or submerged by time and theory. Where the stylization of facts would naturally elide these features, new historical narratives can reconstruct them and point the way to alternative explanations of emergence. As Ricoeur (1984) points out new narratives create "semantic innovation" in our understanding of the subject under consideration by "grasping together" actors, actions, causes, and time in novel comprehensive explanations. An embrace of the reflective and analytical use of historical narratives of industry emergence, in this sense, can provide a powerful approach to identifying alternative theoretical explanations precisely because they uncover evidence, meaning, relationships, and causes that existing models cover up.

Choice and Agency

In reconstructing alternative paths and patterns of development, historical methods also provide insights into the nature of choice and agency in the development of industries. Indeed, historical methods and reasoning allows the reconstruction of at least three aspects of agency and choice in industry evolution: uncertainty, reflection, and the identification of alternative paths. In providing *ex post* explanations for organizational choices, most models of industry evolution necessarily discount the nature of the uncertainty faced by organizational actors. The result is a very limited understanding of how actors actually make choices under conditions of uncertainty, and often include strong assumptions about limitations on reflective action. Indeed, linear social scientific models of development inherently suggest that organizational actors are unable to learn from and respond to previous patterns of development (Gerschenkron, 1966; Sabel and Zeitlin, 1985). Historical accounts, in contrast, allow researchers to reconstruct both how actors experienced the uncertainties surrounding particular choices, and their "creative responses" (Schumpeter, 1947) to the conditions they faced, including their ability to reflect on choices they face in light of previous developments (Gerschenkron, 1966). Such a perspective also allows scholars to understand possible alternative paths of industry development and change, including ones that have failed. Given the deep uncertainties that characterize industry emergence, the ability to understanding decisions and choices in context is crucial, and historical sources and methods provide a useful way forward.

Industry Knowledge Construction

Finally, historical research has value in helping organizational researchers understand the very processes by which elision and forgetting take place. As organizational researchers gain a greater appreciation of the role of knowledge and cognition in industry formation, the empirical questions of what gets forgotten and why in the process of industry knowledge formation will necessarily become of increasing importance in understanding emergence. Industry knowledge, after all, is constituted not just of product knowledge, but also of a wider set of cognitive issues about what actors know and assume to be product, the nature of the value being exchanged, the questions of who comprises the competition, and so on (Porac et al., 2002). Answers to such cognitive questions inherently raise related inquiries into what is excluded from understandings of the industry, as well as what becomes assumed in the creation of "recipe knowledge" (Spender, 1989). In this way, understanding the processes of exclusion and elision are as important as questions of how actors develop social knowledge of what constitutes the industry. Studying this process of forgetting necessarily requires an approach that is able to reconstruct actors' own understandings of an industry in the past. It is, of course, precisely in dealing with these opportunities and challenges for reconstructing the past that history provides a long intellectual tradition from which organizational researchers could benefit.

REFERENCES

Abernathy, W. J., and Utterback, J. M. (1978) "Patterns of Industrial Innovation," *Technology Review*, 80(7): 40–7.
Adner, R. (2006). "Match your Innovation Strategy to your Innovation Ecosystem," *Harvard Business Review*, 84(4): 98–107.
Agarwal, R., and Bayus, B. (2002). "The Market Evolution and Sales Takeoff of Product Innovations," *Management Science*, 48(8): 1024–41.
Agarwal, R., and Gort, M. (1996). "The Evolution of Markets and Entry, Exit and Survival of Firms," *The Review of Economics and Statistics*, 78(3): 489–98.
Agarwal, R., and Tripsas, M. (2008). "Technology and Industry Evolution." In Scott, S. (ed.), *Handbook of Technology and Innovation Management*. Chichester: John Wiley and Sons: 3–56.
Aldrich, H., and Ruef, M. (2006). *Organizations Evolving*. London: Sage.
Arthur, W. B. (1989). "Competing Technologies, Increasing Returns, and Lock-in by Historical Events," *The Economic Journal*, 99(394): 116–31.
Bevan, M. W., Flavell, R. B., and Chilton, M. D. (1983). "A Chimaeric Antibiotic Resistance Gene as a Selectable Marker for Plant Cell Transformation," *Nature*, 304: 184–7.
Collingwood, R. G. (1994). *Idea of History*. New York: Oxford University Press.
Danto, A. C. (1965). *Analytical Philosophy of History*. Cambridge: Cambridge University Press.
Dilthey, Wilhelm. (2002 [1910]). *The Formation of the Historical World in the Human Sciences*. Princeton: Princeton University Press.
Fear, J. R. (2003). "Thinking Historically About Organizational Learning." In M. Dierkes, A. Berthoin Antal, J. Child, and I. Nonaka (eds.), *Handbook of Organizational Learning & Knowledge*. Oxford: Oxford University Press: 162–91.
Flink, J. (1990). *The Automobile Age*. Cambridge, MA: MIT Press.
Forbes, D. P., and Kirsch, D. A. (2011). "The Study of Emerging Industries: Recognizing and Responding to Some Central Problems," *Journal of Business Venturing*, 26(5): 589–602.
Fraley, R. T., Rogers, R. B., Horsch, P. R., Sanders, J. S., Flick, S. P., Adams, M. L., Bittner, L. A., Brand, C. L., Fink, J. S., Fry., G. R., Gallupi, S. B., Goldberg, N. L.,

Hoffman, N. L., and Woo, S. C. (1983). "Expression of Bacterial Gene in Plant Cells," *Proceedings of the National Academy of Science*, 80: 4803–7.

Gadamer, H. G. (1975). *Truth and Method*. New York: Continuum.

Gerschenkron, A. (1966). "The Modernization of Entrepreneurship." In Weiner, M. (ed.), *Modernization: The Dynamics of Growth*. New York: Basic Books: 246–57.

Golder, P. N., and Tellis, G. J. (1997). "Will it ever fly? Modeling the Takeoff of Really New Consumer Durables," *Marketing Science*, 16(3): 256–70.

Golder, P. N., Shacham, R., and Mitra, D. (2009). "Innovations' Origins: When, by Whom, and How are Radical Innovations Developed?" *Marketing Science*, 28(1): 166–79.

Gort, M., and Klepper, S. (1982). "Time Paths in the Diffusion of Product Innovations," *The Economic Journal*, 92(367): 630–53.

Grondin, J. (1994). *Introduction to Philosophical Hermeneutics*. New Haven: Yale.

Hannan, M. T., and Freeman, J. (1977). "The Population Ecology of Organizations," *American Journal of Sociology*, 82(5): 929–64.

Hannan, M. T., and Freeman, J. (1987). "The Ecology of Organizational Founding: American Labor Unions, 1836–1985," *American Journal of Sociology*, 92(4): 910–43.

Hansen, P. (2007). "Organizational Culture and Organizational Change: The Transformation of Savings Banks in Denmark, 1965-1990," *Enterprise and Society*, 8: 920–53.

Hansmann, H. (1989). "The Economic Role of Commercial Nonprofits: The Evolution of the Savings Bank Industry." In H. Anheier and W. Seibel (eds.), *The Third Sector: Comparative Studies of Nonprofit Organizations*. Berlin: de Gruyter: 65–76.

Hansmann, H. (2000). *The Ownership of Enterprise*. Cambridge, MA: Harvard University Press.

Hargadon, A. B., and Douglas, Y. (2001). "When Innovations Meet Institutions: Edison and the Design of the Electric Light," *Administrative Science Quarterly*, 46(3): 476–501.

Haveman, H. A., and Rao, H. (1997). "Structuring a Theory of Moral Sentiments: Institutional and Organizational Coevolution in the Early Thrift Industry," *American Journal of Sociology*, 102(6): 1606–51.

Helfat, C. E. (2007). "Stylized Facts, Empirical Research and Theory Development in Management," *Strategic Organization*, 5(2): 185–92.

Henderson, R. M., and Clark, K. B. (1990). "Architectural Innovation: The Reconfiguration of Existing Product Technologies and the Failure of Established Firms," *Administrative Science Quarterly*, 35(1): 9–30.

Herder, J. G. (1968 [1791]). "Reflections on the Philosophy of the History of Mankind." In F. E. Manuel (ed.), *Classic European Historians*. Chicago: University of Chicago Press: 79-118.

Herrera-Stellara, L. A., Depicker, M., Van Montagu, M., and Schell, J. (1983). "Expression of Chimaeric Genes Transferred into Plant Cells Using a Ti-Plasmid Derived Vector," *Nature*, 303: 209–13.

James, C. (2011). Global Status of Commercialized Biotech/GM Crops: 2011. International Service for the Acquisition of Agri-biotech Applications. *ISAAA Briefs*.

Khaire, M. (Forthcoming). "Fashioning an Industry: Socio-Cognitive Processes in the Construction of Worth of a New Industry." *Organization Studies*.

Khaire, M., and Wadhwani, R. D. (2010). "Changing Landscapes: The Construction of Meaning and Value in a New Market Category: Modern Indian Art," *Academy of Management Journal*, 53(6): 1281–304.

Kirsch, D. A., and Mom, G. P. A. (2002). "Visions of Transportation: The EVC and the Transition from Service- to Product-Based Mobility," *Business History Review*, 76(1): 75–110.

Klepper, S., and Graddy, E. (1990). "The Evolution of New Industries and the Determinants of Market Structure," *The Rand Journal of Economics*, 21(1): 27–44.

Leblebici, H., Salancik, G. R., Copay, A., and King, T. (1991). "Institutional Change and the Transformation of Interorganizational Fields: An Organizational History of the US Radio Broadcasting Industry," *Administrative Science Quarterly*, 36: 333–63.

Marquis, C. (2003). "The Pressure of the Past: Network Imprinting in Intercorporate Communities," *Administrative Science Quarterly*, 48(4): 655–89.

Motavalli, J. (2001). *Forward Drive: The Race to Build the Clean Car of the Future*. London: Earthscan.

Murmann, J. P. (2003). *Knowledge and Competitive Advantage: The Coevolution of Firms, Technology, and National Institutions*. Cambridge: Cambridge University Press.

Nelson, R. R., and Winter, S. G. (1982). *An Evolutionary Theory of Economic Change*. Cambridge, MA: Harvard University Press.

Paine, C. (2006). Who Killed The Electric Car [Documentary]. Culver City, CA: Papercut Films.

Porac, J. F., Thomas, H., Wilson, F., Paton, D., and Kanfer, A. (1995). "Rivalry and the Industry Model of Scottish Knitwear Producers," *Administrative Science Quarterly*, 40: 203–27.

Porac, J. F., Ventresca, M. J., and Mishina, Y. (2002). "Interorganizational Cognition and Interpretation." In J. Baum (ed.), *Blackwell Companion to Organizations*. New York: Blackwell: 579–98.

Porter, M. (1980). *Competitive Strategy*. New York: Free Press.

Rae, J. B. (1955). "The Electric Vehicle Company: A Monopoly that Missed," *Business History Review*, 29(4): 298–311.

Rasmusen, E. (1988). "Mutual Banks and Stock Banks," *Journal of Law and Economics*, 31: 395.

Ricoeur, P. (1984). *Time and Narrative*. Vol. 1. Chicago: University of Chicago Press.

Ricoeur, P. (2004). *Memory, History, Forgetting*. Chicago: University of Chicago Press.

Sabel, C., and Zeitlin, J. (1985). "Historical Alternatives to Mass Production: Politics, Markets and Technology in Nineteenth-Century Industrialization," *Past and Present*, 108(1): 133–76.

Santos, F. M., and Eisenhardt, K. M. (2009). "Constructing Markets and Shaping Boundaries: Entrepreneurial Power in Nascent Fields," *Academy of Management Journal*, 52(4): 643–71.

Schell, J., and Van Montagu, M. (1977). "The Ti-plasmid of Agrobacterium tumefaciens, a Natural Vector for the Introduction of nif Genes in Plants?" *Basic Life Science*, 9: 159–79.

Schneiberg, M. (2002). "Organizational Heterogeneity and the Production of New Forms: Politics, Social Movements and Mutual Companies in American Fire Insurance, 1900–1930," *Research in the Sociology of Organizations*, 1: 39–89.

Schneiberg, M. (2007). "What's on the Path? Path Dependence, Organizational Diversity and the Problem of Institutional Change in the US Economy 1900–1950," *SocioEconomic Review*, 5: 47–80.

Schneiberg, M., King, M., and Smith, T. (2008). "Social Movements and Organizational Form: Cooperative Alternatives to Corporations in the American Insurance, Dairy, and Grain Industries," *American Sociological Review*, 73(4): 635–67.

Schumpeter, J. (1947). "The Creative Response in Economic History," *The Journal of Economic History*, 7: 149–59.

Scranton, P. (2000). *Endless Novelty: Specialty Production and American Industrialization, 1865–1925*. Princeton: Princeton University Press.

Sloan, A. (1990 [1963]). *My Years with General Motors*. New York: Doubleday/Currency.

Spender, J. C. (1989). *Industry Recipes: An Enquiry into the Nature and Sources of Managerial Judgement*. New York: Blackwell.

Sydow, J., Schreyogg, G., & Koch, J. (2009). "Organizational Path Dependence: Opening the Black Box," *Academy of Management Review* 34(4): 689–709.

Tripsas, M. (1997). "Unraveling the Process of Creative Destruction: Complementary Assets and Incumbent Survival in the Typesetter Industry," *Strategic Management Journal*, 18(1): 119–42.

Tripsas, M., and Gavetti, G. (2000). "Capabilities, Cognition, and Interia: Evidence from Digital Imaging," *Strategic Management Journal*, 21: 1147–61.

Tushman, M. L., and Anderson, P. (1986). "Technological Discontinuities and Organizational Environments," *Administrative Science Quarterly*, 31(3): 439–65.

Utterback, J. M., and Suárez, F. F. (1993). "Innovation, Competition, and Industry Structure," *Research Policy*, 22(1): 1–21.

Van de Van, A., and Garud, R. (1989). "A Framework for Understanding the Emergence of New Industries," *Research on Technological Innovation Management and Policy*, 4: 195–225.

Ventresca, M. J., and Mohr, J. W. (2002). "Archival Research Methods." In Baum, J. (ed.), *Blackwell Companion to Organizations*. New York: Wiley: 805–28.

White, H. (1981). "Where Do Markets Come From?" *American Journal of Sociology*, 87: 517–47.

10

The State as a Historical Construct in Organization Studies

Marcelo Bucheli and Jin Uk Kim[1]

INTRODUCTION: POLITICAL HISTORY AND BUSINESS SCHOLARSHIP

An important component in business scholarship is its focus on the relationship between state and firms. Some notable indicators include the founding of a specialized journal, *Business and Politics*, and the rise of influential sub-disciplines such as corporate political activity (Hillman and Hitt, 1999; Hillman et al., 2004). Other more general evidence of the discipline's deep interest in state–firm relationship is reflected in the rich literature subsumed under the umbrellas of resource dependence theory (Pfeffer and Salancik, 2003), neo-institutional theory (DiMaggio and Powell, 1991), and bargaining power perspective (Fagre and Wells, 1982; Kobrin, 1984; Vernon, 1971a, b; Wells, 1977), which analyze how external pressures from the various sources in the environment, often the state, influence firm behavior. These works have consistently shown that firms do not operate in a vacuum and that politics and political actors exert significant influence on corporate behavior. They further show that how firms manage the political environment may have critical implications for organizational success. Indeed, few contemporary business scholars would deny that incorporating the political dimension into the discipline has enhanced its academic rigor and practical relevance. However, prior works have typically been "firm-centric" in that most focus on how businesses are influenced by the top-down political pressure coming from the central state based on the assumption that the state is a unitary, stable, and pre-formed entity that can be incorporated into the analysis as a fixed variable

[1] The authors wish to thank Kenneth Lipartito, Luis Felipe Sáenz, John Hassard, R. Daniel Wadhwani, and JoAnne Yates for input on earlier versions of this chapter.

(e.g., Oliver, 1991; Pfeffer, 1972; Salancik, 1979). These works, while insightful, neglect the fact that the state itself has a history and that this history is an important determinant of its relationship with non-state organizations as well as the wider institutional environment. In the words of North, Wallis, and Weingast, "by overlooking the reality that all states are [also] organizations, this approach misses how the internal dynamics of relationships among elites within the dominant coalition affect how states interact with the larger society" (2009: 17). Considering the fact that history was, for a long time, almost by definition political history, this omission is particularly crucial.

The general argument of the current chapter then is that the state and the institutions it implements can be usefully understood as the outcome of the antecedent conflicts among heterogeneous societal groups with different economic interests, values, and norms over the distribution of economic rent and rationalizations upon which to base actions and decisions. The state is thus conceptualized as a coalition of heterogeneous groups and interests competing in a quasi-market wherein "influence and control are negotiated and allocated" (Pfeffer and Salancik, 2003: 36). Consequently, the winning coalition of the competition shapes the institutional environment to the advantage of the triumphant in order to increase its share of the economic rent and implement its norms and values. Firms, in turn, respond to these shifts in various ways to either mitigate the negative effects or take advantage of the changes. In essence, by highlighting the internal dynamics of the state, the shift parameters, and how these parameters influence business firms, we explicate the link between the political process and business through the lens of political history.

We hope to achieve two interrelated goals through the current chapter: first is to demonstrate that incorporating the state as a contested variable can provide new insights for scholars working on state–firm relationship and organizational studies in general. Understanding the processual details of the antecedent conflicts (e.g., the attributes of the competing groups, how the conflict unfolds) and the outcome (e.g., winners/losers) of the political process opens up avenues for organizational research based on a dyadic understanding of state–firm relationship. The second objective is to provide a toolkit for scholars to overcome a barrier that has inhibited the integration of political history and business scholarship. A common trouble that business scholars encounter when incorporating political history into their analysis is that historians do not have a widely accepted methodology. As Lipartito and Yates discuss in this volume, historians are generally reluctant to define a particular methodological approach in their works, fearing that the methodology itself may constrain the ability to flesh out the subtleties and complexities of the historical process. The current chapter hopes to mitigate some of these troubles by demonstrating how the approaches developed by economic and political historians inspired by the works of Acemoglu and Robinson (2006, 2007),

North (1990, 1991), and North, Wallis, and Weingast (2009) among others can be usefully employed for this task.

In the next section, we begin with a brief explanation behind what we mean by political process and its relationship to the wider social order. We also introduce the concepts of institutional environment, institutional arrangements, and organizations to position the relevant actors, state and business firms, within the conceptual framework. The third section analyzes the sources of change or the shift parameters in the political process and how the change process unfolds through the conflicts among different societal groups in an iterative process. The fourth section provides a more detailed look into the mechanisms underlying how changes in the state and the resulting institutions influence the legitimacy of firms. The penultimate section discusses how firms respond to these changes and presents historical examples of how different strategies lead to various outcomes. Concluding remarks follow.

INSTITUTIONAL ENVIRONMENT, INSTITUTIONAL ARRANGEMENT, AND SOCIAL ORDERS

Institutional environment refers to the "set of fundamental political, social and legal ground rules that establishes the basis for production, exchange, and distribution" (Davis and North, 1971: 6), while institutional arrangements are those "between economic units that govern the ways under which these units cooperate and compete" (Davis and North, 1971: 7). These arrangements include the relationships that organizations establish with other organizations, including the state, and societal actors. All actors, state and organizations, play according to the "rules of the games" of the institutional environment to pursue their respective objectives (Leftwich, 2006). Economic historians studying the institutional environment are typically interested in what conditions led some countries or regions to have the "right" set of institutions that enabled continued economic growth. They commonly point to rule of law, constraints on organized violence through systems of checks and balances, respect for private property rights, and judicious third-party enforcement of contracts as key determinants of prosperity (Campbell and Lindberg, 1990; Scott, 2008; Weingast, 1995, 2003). Scholars who are primarily concerned with issues arising at the level of institutional arrangements focus on the various modes of governance organizations, especially business firms, adopt in a given institutional environment. Williamson (1971, 1979, 1981), for example, argues that organizations adopt particular forms of structure and governance in order to reduce transaction costs generated by problems of opportunism, uncertainty, and bounded rationality in an imperfect market. Economic sociologists, on the other hand, point more to inter-organizational relationships or

networks rather than governance structures as key to understanding the institutional arrangement (Granovetter, 1985), an approach that can be especially
useful in understanding inter-organizational as well as state-firm relationship
in emerging economies (e.g., Boisot and Child, 1996). In international business, Buckley and Casson (1976)[2] applied transaction costs logic to explain the
existence of vertically integrated multinational corporations as transnational
institutional arrangements that business firms adopt in order to economize on
transaction costs arising from cross-border corporate activities.

The constellation of these elements, the players (organizations, including the
state), the interactions among them (institutional arrangement), and the rules
of the game (institutional environment), comes together and shapes the general patterns of social organization which North et al. (2009) call *social orders*.
Social orders can be broadly categorized under two ideal types: (i) limited access
orders; (ii) open access orders; according to the attributes of the "(institutional
environment) that support the existence of specific forms of human organization, the way societies limit or open access to those organizations... (and) how
societies limit and control violence (2009: 1)" in the political competition for
economic rent. In limited access orders, select groups form dominant coalitions in order to control or limit the access to economic rent by other actors
in the institutional environment. Each group holds the capabilities to resort to
collective action, which often involve organized violence, to alter the arrangement when the opportunity for more economic rent arises or when its share
of the rent is threatened by other groups. Politics in limited access orders are
thus akin to a temporary truce, held together by each group's common interest
in limiting the access to economic rent by other groups. Albeit fragile, organized violence is limited and social order is maintained as the interest of each
dominant group is aligned and the "rules of the games" governing the political
competition for economic rent is dictated by these dominant groups.

In contrast, open access orders are Weberian states wherein the legitimate use
of violence is subservient to the political system rather than to any particular
group. The rights of constituents are defined by impersonal, formal constitutions
which stipulate and guarantee the right of citizens to form and join depersonal-
ized, special-purpose organizations. The opportunity to compete for economic
rent thus becomes not a privilege of select groups but that of all citizens who meet
the minimum criteria of citizenship. Therefore, in open access orders, competition over economic rent follows the process of creative destruction in the market
wherein rent generating capabilities held by any societal group can be quickly

---

[2] We are fully aware that Buckley and Casson's internalization theory of multinational enterprises and Williamson's transaction cost economics developed independently from one another.
Yet we categorize both Williamson and Buckley and Casson under the single category of "transaction cost logic" as their analytical framework regarding the existence of the firms and the
parameters determining firm behavior are largely identical.

eroded by others who develop more innovative capabilities that can yield more economic rent for them in the market, a point first made by Schumpeter (1942).

The distinction between open and limited access social orders shows why contemporary business scholarship and organizational studies in general have neglected political history in their works. Most organizational scholars have conducted studies based on the assumptions derived from open access orders where economic organizations have limited relationship with the political competition as they primarily compete and interact in the market and only marginally in politics. In contrast, economic organizations in limited access orders are inherently political since success in the competition for economic rent depends more on political connections and less on innovative capabilities in the market, making state-firm relationships significantly more crucial for both practitioners and scholars. Of course, this is not to suggest that businesses in open access orders are completely apolitical but simply to emphasize that the effects of the political process on the businesses are more direct and conspicuous in limited access orders. More specifically, the distinction between open and limited access orders provides a partial explanation why scholars studying businesses operating outside the developed economies (typically open access orders) have been more acutely aware of the dynamics between state and firms. For example, those who study the relationship between regime type and businesses have found that shifts in regime type between dictatorship to democracy have significant ramifications for the general security of business investment, especially in terms of the sanctity of private property rights (Feng, 2001; Henisz, 2000; Henisz and Zelner, 2001; Jensen, 2008). This is especially important for business firms operating in industries that require location-specific investment that cannot be easily shifted from one place to another (Fagre and Wells, 1982; Vernon, 1971a, b; Wells, 1977). Multinationals operating in these types of industries face decreasing bargaining power vis-à-vis the domestic government as long as they increase their investments since increased investment decreases the credibility of the corporations' threats to leave the country in response to arbitrary changes in the institutional environment, a process known as "obsolescing bargaining power" (Vernon, 1971a, b). Many central states of the countries in which a multinational firm invests have the power to change the institutional environment by altering the rules related to the foreign investors' property rights (Kobrin, 2009).

In sum, this section has defined the key elements of our conceptual framework: institutional environment, institutional arrangement, and social orders. We have also demonstrated some preliminary examples of how regime types and changes in the political process may influence the state-firm relationship, especially with regards to the sanctity of private property rights. In the next section, we take a more detailed look into the shift parameters within the political process and how they shape and re-shape the institutional environment.

POLITICAL PROCESS AND SHIFTS IN THE
INSTITUTIONAL ENVIRONMENT LEVEL

Among the corpus of political science literature analyzing the source of political transitions, the conceptual framework developed by Acemoglu and Robinson (2006, 2007) can be usefully employed to open up the black box of the state and relate the political process with changes in the institutional environment. Similar to North et al. (2009), Acemoglu and Robinson assume that the political status quo or equilibrium in a society is a function of the conflicts over economic rents between different groups or social classes. Each party in the conflict has an ideal set of political institutions from which they can obtain the maximum economic benefit; those who garner more political power eventually triumph in this internal struggle for control and define the final institutional outcome (Leftwich, 2006).[3] Even when written political arrangements express a wide and equalitarian distribution of economic and political power (*de jure* power), the group with greater political power will possess the *de facto* power to access economic rent. For those groups who do not benefit from the existing institutional environment, the only option is to change the status quo through a direct challenge against the system with an eventual change of the institutions rather than organizing themselves under the pre-existing rules of the game.

Consider the case of Argentina, as described in Acemoglu and Robinson (2006: 6–7). The first supposedly democratic election in the country's history was held in 1862 and gave *de jure* power for the people to participate in the political process after nearly half a century of violent internal strife. However, the elections were frequently rigged and the *de jure* right for citizens to participate in the political process was more a ritualistic practice. The established power represented through the National Autonomist Party (Partido Autonomista Nacional—PAN), backed by commercial elite groups such as exporters of agricultural goods, maintained its *de facto* monopoly over the political process until 1916. The rising social discontent, however, led to a power shift from the PAN to the Radical Civic Union (Unión Cívica Radical—UCR) led by Hipólito Yrigoyen. This power shift led to more political power towards the new coalition and, therefore, opportunities to access economic rent by previously disenfranchised groups such as laborers and small-scale farmers. Put

---

[3] Following Parsons (1963: 237), we define political power as the "generalized capacity to secure the performance of binding obligations by units in a system of collective organization when the obligations are legitimized with reference to their bearing on collective goals and where in the case of recalcitrance there is a presumption of enforcement by negative situational sanctions - whatever the actual agency for that enforcement." This definition moves political power away from its capacity to enforce unilateral coercion and focuses on its ability to garner consensus among constituents and, put crudely, "get things done" by mobilizing the societal constituents towards the desirable—as defined by the winning coalition—collective goal.

into our current framework, the traditional elite's *de facto* monopoly over the access to economic rent became undermined by the power transition from PAN to UCR. In response, the conservatives, composed of fascist sections of the military, the agricultural exporters, as well as other business interests (e.g., the US oil multinational Standard Oil Company of New Jersey), overthrew the Yrigoyen government through a military coup in 1930 and re-established conservative domination and the institutional environment was restructured in favor of this winning coalition. This conservative coalition or "Concordancia" lasted for slightly more than a decade until another military coup led by Juan Domingo Perón dislodged the previous coalition from their monopoly position. Perón's coalition reconfigured the rules of the games more favorably towards a radical, pro-labor path which led to dramatic increases in wages and social security benefits to centrally redistribute the wealth from the rural to the urban sector. Perón was then again deposed through another military coup in 1955 only to return to power in 1973. Subsequent distributional conflict surrounding pro-Perón and anti-Perón struggle led to successive collapses of dictatorial regimes as well as democratically elected ones and each transition saw drastic changes in the institutional environment that opened/limited access to economic rent for each winning/losing coalition of societal groups.

A similar interpretation of history can be read from Marx (1992 [1876]) who argued that the Western political and economic system emerged from a long struggle between the bourgeoisie and the feudal order in Europe that culminated in the former's triumph in the French Revolution. The shift in social order started in the European medieval cities surviving the fall of the Roman Empire, places where the merchant class created a legal system that is beneficial to its commercial interest but that conflicted with the feudal order (Berman, 1977; Laski, 1917; Pirenne, 1937, 1954, 1969). This movement continued until the bourgeoisie finally destroyed the feudal order and appropriated all the means of production (e.g., communal lands remaining from the Middle Ages) available to the lower classes (Marx, 1992 [1867]). This built the platform for the bourgeoisie to continue their expansion around the world with Britain and Holland leading the way to implement the first capitalist world empires (Hill, 1984, 1990; Cameron and Neal, 2002; Adams, 2007; Hobsbawm, 1996). As Marx (1988 [1852]) described in the *Eighteenth Brumaire of Louis Bonaparte*, the consolidation of this shift came when, after surviving serious challenges from the lower classes in the European-wide 1848 revolutions, the bourgeoisie created a political system that set the foundations of liberal democracy.[4] This system ensured the bourgeoisie's perpetuation of its economic power by making private property rights sacred. At the same time, the social order implemented by the bourgeoisie gave *de jure* political rights to other social groups

---

[4] As Moore (1966: 418) famously summarized "no bourgeois, no democracy."

(Marx, 1988 [1852]). The consolidation of liberal democracy and capitalism in certain Western countries after the 1848 revolutions did not, however, mean that the system remained unchallenged. Liberal democracy and capitalism faced the rising threat of communism and fascism beginning in the 1930s and throughout World War II, and an even stronger communist threat during the Cold War. Subsequent reforms such as the New Deal, the anti-trust legislation, social welfare, and anti-racial and gender discrimination legislations à la civil rights movements, among others, ensured the stability of the existing institutions and mitigated the internal disruption that threatened liberal democracy and capitalism (Dudziak, 1988; Eichengreen, 1996).

Extending Marx's reasoning, Bowman (1996), Handlin and Handlin (1945), Kaufman (2008), and Maier (1993) argue that in the case of the United States, the commercial legislation, originally adapted from Britain, and its adaptation after independence responds to the interest of the commercial elite, part of the winning coalition in the war of independence. Similarly, Beard (1912, 1913), in his classic studies, argued that the US constitution itself was designed to create an institutional framework that protected the economic privileges of the commercial class. In Acemoglu and Robinson's (2006) terms, the triumphant groups in this political process ensured their *de facto* power over their access to economic rent while giving other groups only *de jure* ones.

To sum up, this section has explicated how changes in the political process—that is, the internal dynamics of the state—can be understood as a competition among different societal groups over economic resources. The key point is that the "rules of the game" governing the environment are never neutral and are designed to distribute advantage to some and disadvantage to others. Furthermore, these "rules of the game" that the state implements shift as a function of the outcome of the antecedent conflict among societal groups who battle over access to economic rent. More explicitly, the shift parameter in the institutional environment is the changing balance of political power among different coalitions of groups; the groups which emerge triumphant in each struggle reconfigure the institutional environment in their favor in order to maximize their access to economic resources while limiting it to others. Next, we turn to how these shifts affect the legitimacy of economic organizations and the institutional arrangement between business firms and states.

CHANGES AT THE INSTITUTIONAL ENVIRONMENT LEVEL AND ORGANIZATIONAL LEGITIMACY

Legitimacy is the "congruence between the social values associated with or implied by their activities and the norms of acceptable behavior in the larger social system" in which the disparity between the value associated by organizational activities and the societal norm leads to "legal, economic and other social sanctions" (Dowling and Pfeffer, 1975: 122). In this view, legitimacy is an "operational resource that organizations extract...from their environments [and] employ in pursuit of their goals" (Suchman, 1995: 576) as the relevant audiences will be more willing to supply resources to legitimate organizations and confer persistence and stability. Furthermore, organizations, both states and firms, control the legitimation process through instrumental and purposive acts which generally leads to frequent opposition with other societal entities which hold different social values and norms of acceptable behavior.[5]

While the two previous sections focused exclusively on the issue of economic rent, the political process of the state can also be understood as a search or competition for "rationalizations upon which to base actions and decisions" (Pfeffer and Salancik, 2003: 192). That is, societal groups compete not just for economic rent but also for the dominant norms and values guiding what is legitimate or not in a society. Historical studies show ample evidence behind how conflicts among different societal groups lead to state-level changes that lead to shifts in norms and values behind what is considered legitimate for business firms. In their study of rate regulation in American fire insurance from 1906 to 1930, Schneiberg and Bartley (2001) show that regulations regarding big businesses became solidified through pressures from a coalition of disenfranchised social groups—farmers and small businesses—who opposed the growing power of big businesses. The movement was instigated by a legitimacy crisis of powerful businesses that were violating principles and came under increasing public scrutiny. The driving force in this mobilization of the anti-business coalition, as the authors show, was to exploit the legitimacy crisis of big businesses as an opportunity to affect the political process to institute the new rules of the regulatory game pertaining to organizational legitimacy. Over time, opposition groups were able to garner enough political power to challenge the status quo and were able to move the state to implement appropriate mechanisms to constrain the big businesses.

More dramatic examples of such shifts in organizational legitimacy can be seen in cases where the government running the state itself is replaced by another one, as happened with the creation of Israel in 1948 in the territory previously known as Palestine. Kalev et al. (2008) studied the evolution of

---

[5] We acknowledge that our conceptualization of legitimacy is simplistic and does not incorporate the insights of the "institutional camp" (e.g., DiMaggio and Powell, 1991) who sees legitimacy not as operational resources but constitutive beliefs that do not evolve simply because of political changes. How the deeper, taken-for-granted, cognitive dimension of society and legitimacy evolve in response to the political process is an important topic (see Henisz and Zelner, 2005 for example) but is beyond the scope of the current chapter.

management principles in the so-called joint productivity councils (JPCs) and how the creation of the state of Israel influenced the legitimacy of the councils. These JPCs sought to introduce scientific management to the Palestinian industrial sector during the British mandate (1923–1948) but this arrangement contradicted the official British plans for Palestine. The official plan of the British government did not endorse the industrialization and modernization of the various industrial sectors in Palestine and, as a result, the British authorities never established any rule, regulation, or other platform to legitimize the goals of the JPCs. After the creation of the state of Israel in 1948, however, the JPCs fate changed dramatically as the newly installed Israeli government devoted enormous material and non-material support to the JPCs. The Israeli government promoted the JPCs as a conduit to establish scientifically guided industrial sectors which were seen as an integral part of the state's economic projects for building a new nation state as well as gaining legitimacy as a "normal" state in the eyes of the international community. Eventually the JPCs, previously neglected and peripheral organizations, gained significant legitimacy, power, and resources to lead Israel's economic policy with the active political endorsement of the state.

On the flip side, dramatic changes in the state may delegitimize previously legitimate organizations. For instance, the radical changes brought about by the French Revolution were accompanied by the new regime's systematic effort to punish those business firms that had benefited from the *Ancien Régime*, even when these firms were far from being remnants of the feudal order and had actually played in important role in facilitating the expansion of French commerce around the world (implicitly congruent with the larger agenda of the bourgeoisie class (Bouton, 2012). Similarly, Rood's (1976) study on the expropriation of assets of foreign businesses in African countries that were decolonized in the 1960s provides us with another good example. Many newly installed governments in Africa seized property and assets owned by non-Africans in their territories. Foreign corporations protested the government seizure of their property as illegitimate and as one that breached in the sanctity of contracts and property rights. African rulers as well as the majority of their supporters, on the other hand, considered their actions to be completely legitimate since they did not see any reason to follow the rules of the games regarding private property, originally mandated and implemented by their former colonial masters, when their own nations did not even exist and, therefore, had no say in the process of designing the rules of the game governing the institutional environment. Contrary to Western countries, where the norms and values underpinning liberal democracy and market economy have long been established and became taken for granted via a long historical process of political conflicts including the French Revolution (1789), the English Civil War (1640), the English Glorious Revolution (1689), the Dutch Revolt (1567–1647), and the American Revolution (1775–1783), rulers of the new

African countries and their constituents believed that the existing system had been unjustly imposed on them by foreign powers. When some multinationals responded that their contracts were protected by the international law, the African leaders countered that the said international law had been written by those who had colonized Africa for centuries and unjustly expropriated the continent. Thus, the African leaders saw the international organizations and multilateral institutions backing these international laws to be illegitimate and that they were under no obligation to follow laws that were created when their nations did not even exist.

Analyzing the shifts in organizational legitimacy as a consequence of regime changes also challenges the prevalent idea that more democratic ones secure private investors' property rights better than authoritarian ones because of the constraints democratic regimes have to act arbitrarily (Feng, 2001; Henisz, 2000; Henisz and Zelner, 2001; Jensen, 2008). In a pioneering political theoretical study, Bueno de Mesquita, Root, Silverson, and Morrow (2005) define two main political actors in every political system: the first one is the selectorate, which is the group of people endowed to choose a government and, the second one is the winning coalition, which is a subset of the selectorate and has political power over the rest of the selectorate and those disfranchised members of the society. Based on this framework, the authors argue that democratic pluralistic societies tend to have large winning coalitions while dictatorships tend to have small winning coalitions and predict that a ruler will try to stay in power by distributing the economic rent among those of his/her winning coalition as either public or private goods. If the ruler is supported by a small winning coalition, he/she will distribute the national income as private goods among that small group whereas if he/she is supported by a large winning coalition, he/she might distribute this income as public goods among his/her supporters. An authoritarian regime can, therefore, create a friendly institutional environment towards the private sector (or at least some members of it) in a way that benefits the economic elites in power. The groups not benefiting from the existing arrangement may not have any other option than scheming to overthrow it and replace the rulers and the rules in detriment to those previously benefiting from it. If the regime shifts from a dictatorship to a democracy, the previously existing system would be delegitimized as well as the organizations benefiting from it and the democratic regime would actually delegitimize and challenge the property rights of the economic organizations that benefited from the previous regime.

We illustrate these dynamics with some historical examples. Between 1917 and 1938, Mexico witnessed increasing tensions between foreign oil companies and the government. Foreign oil corporations enjoyed a generous open door policy under the long dictatorship of Porfirio Díaz (1876–1911), a general who ruled with an iron fist and invited all kinds of foreign corporations in order to modernize his country. The Mexican economy grew at spectacular rates during the Díaz administration, but an increasingly large segment of the population, including some members of the elite, resented the fact that the fruits of the economic growth were distributed among Díaz's inner circle. In 1910, members of the elite rebelled, ousting the dictator and sparking a revolutionary process throughout the country. Mexico fell into a chaotic situation with several revolutionary groups fighting against each other but gradually stabilized by the end of the 1910s. In 1917, the new ruling group wrote a new constitution declaring the subsoil of the country property of the state. The multinationals protested, arguing that this action was confiscatory and went against the sanctity of contracts but the government did not change the new law, using the illegitimate nature of the Díaz's regime to justify its actions (Womack, 1991). These examples of firms having their property rights challenged after a political transition from a totalitarian regime to a pluralistic one show how careful we need to be when assuming that democracies guarantee property rights better than dictatorships. The existence of the business friendly regime of totalitarian People's Republic of China should be a gentle and very contemporary reminder of the need to explore different interpretations.

In sum, this section has outlined how changes in the institutional environment, instigated by changes in the dominant coalition or ruling body of the state, may affect the legitimacy of the organizational actors. In all of the examples, the legitimacy of business firms either came under scrutiny or became empowered depending on the outcome of the political process in which societal groups with different norms, values, and interests came to control the state and reshaped the institutional environment. Firms, however, are not passive recipients of the changes and may actively respond and even shape the emerging institutional environment through various measures. The consequences of these actions depend greatly, again, on the outcome of the shift in the internal dynamics of the state, as we will see in the next section.

LEGITIMIZATION STRATEGIES AND INSTITUTIONAL CHANGE

While legitimacy is clearly a necessary element for firms to survive and prosper in a given institutional environment, not all members of the society need to consent unanimously to their legitimacy. More specifically, legitimacy is "a conferred status and... [is] always controlled by those outside the organization... [but] it need not be conferred by a large segment of society for the organization to prosper" (Pfeffer and Salancik, 2003: 194). Since society is composed of various groups, each with different norms and values, organizations are often faced with conflicting demands from the environment and legitimacy may be secured once its activities are aligned with the interests, values, and norms of certain societal groups who hold more power within the institutional environment. For example, firms can neutralize real or potential changes in the institutional environment by having their boards composed of individuals connected to legitimizing institutions (Etzion and Davis, 2008). Evans (1979) and O'Donnell (1982) add that in the case of multinationals, they can try to legitimize their activities by allying themselves with the domestic elite and sharing a common political and economic agenda. Boddewyn and Brewer (1994) and Kostova and Zaheer (1999) add that a company can reduce legitimacy challenges by integrating elements and politically influential individuals of the host country within its corporate structure.

However, aligning the organization's interest with one set of groups may restrict its ability to adapt to other conflicting demands stemming from changes in the state (Pfeffer and Salancik, 2003) and may undermine its legitimacy in the long run. The Chilean operation of International Telegraph and Telephone (ITT) in the 20th century is an illustrative case. In the 1920s, the US telecommunication giant appointed influential Chilean elites as board members, most of them from the right-wing Conservative and Liberal parties who represented Catholic and secular elites respectively, in order to secure the company's legitimacy within the country. At the time, Chile was largely an agrarian society with most of its population barred from political participation. In the following decades, however, the country industrialized and urbanized and the political landscape shifted dramatically. Two new parties emerged, representing the rising middle class (Christian Democratic Party) and the working class (Socialist Party) respectively and came to dominate the political scene by the 1960s, relegating the Conservative and Liberal parties to the periphery. ITT, however, retained the old oligarchs of the Conservative and Liberal parties on the company board, and this came to undermine their legitimacy over time. Specifically, ITT's monopoly became extremely unpopular among the middle and working class due to the company's expensive and unreliable service. The Christian Democrats and the Socialists moved towards expropriation of the multinational and both used ITT's board composition as a way to delegitimize the firm as a relic of an oligarchic past. The situation deteriorated even further when a cable leak to the media exposed that ITT was actively collaborating with forces that were planning to overthrow the left-wing government of president Salvador Allende. This effectively sealed ITT's fate and the government expropriated the firm with little political opposition and much fanfare from the public (Bucheli and Salvaj, 2013).

Another strategy that scholars promote is for firms (especially multinationals) to approach the government, especially in corporatist or highly interventionist states, with specific projects that fit with the government agenda for national industrial development (Lenway and Murha, 1994; Murtha and Lenway, 1994). Again, historical examples show that this strategy may backfire due to shifting political dynamics and changes in the institutional environment. South Africa's transition from Apartheid regime to the African National Congress (ANC) represents a case in point. After the ANC came to power, some members of the party argued that government contract works granted to businesses during the Apartheid regime should be annulled as they are remnants of the country's shameful racist past. While the threat never materialized, businesses that had major contracts with the past regimes experienced a serious threat to their legitimacy and, consequently, their chances of survival in the new institutional environment as their previous strategy ultimately backfired under the new regime (Bond and Sharife, 2009).

Other historical examples can be used to bolster claims made by organizational scholars. Oliver (1991), for example, proposes that when the institutional environment shifts, organizations might choose compromise as a legitimization strategy. Firms may follow a strategy by which they try to balance the expectations of multiple constituencies and accommodate to the existing institutional environment. In her studies of British firms in de-colonized Africa, Decker (2007, 2008) shows how some multinationals followed a strategy of "Africanization" of their image and embraced the new African countries' economic development projects. Another example would be that of Moreno (2003) who shows how, after the expropriation of Mexican oil in 1938, many American firms decided to embrace Mexican nationalism and even celebrate the expropriation and protectionist economic model.

Another good example is the case of United Fruit Company in Central America. During the first half of the 20th century, Guatemala, Honduras, and Panama specialized almost exclusively in banana exports, most of them controlled by a single multinational, the US-based United Fruit Company. United Fruit also controlled or built a substantial portion of these countries' infrastructure and had influential members of domestic elites on the company's payroll. These elites worked as government officials and also collaborated to topple governments that tried to limit the firm's power (Bucheli, 2008; Dosal, 1993; Taracena, 1993). Things changed in 1952 when, after decades of military dictatorship, Guatemala became a democratic country and its newly elected president, Jacobo Arbenz, planned an agrarian reform to distribute some of United Fruit's lands to the peasants. Arbenz and his followers justified this action arguing that the dictatorial governments the firm had under its control had awarded the generous concessions the multinational enjoyed. A military coup eventually overthrew Arbenz in 1954 and the new government stopped the challenges against United Fruit (Bucheli, 2008; Schlesinger and Kinzer, 1990). During the following years, however, after a series of institutional changes in Central America that gave more power to social groups that had felt excluded from the benefits of the banana industry, United Fruit saw its legitimacy and operations challenged all over those countries (Bucheli and Kim, 2012). Even though many of these countries continued to be ruled by right-wing military dictators who were supportive of United Fruit's dominance, these generals could not continue to ignore the increasing discontent and were forced to approve some social reforms. As a consequence, during the 1960s, the company gradually rid itself of its production assets (mainly plantations and transportation infrastructure) and shifted its focus more towards the international marketing of the fruit (Bucheli, 2005). This process intensified after 1974 when the oil crisis triggered widespread economic crisis in these already poor oil-importing countries. Scared that the economic crisis would turn into political turmoil, the Central American dictators increased taxation on the operations of United Fruit. The company opposed this measure but the dictators surprisingly turned to their old enemies such as labor unions and other dissident forces against United Fruit (Bucheli, 2008). In short, changes in the institutional environment, ruling coalitions, and governments' legitimization strategies eventually affected United Fruit's legitimacy before the Central American societies, forcing the company to change its tactics and eventually acquiesce to the demands of the new winning coalition.

The last example is that of Venezuelan dictator, Juan Vicente Gómez, who ruled Venezuela from 1908 until his death in 1935. He used oil wealth generated by multinationals to reinforce the power of his small winning coalition of military men and landowners. Oil multinationals provided easy and ever growing rent to this small loyal circle and the close relationship between multinational corporations and dictatorships led to endemic corruption and general disregard for the welfare of the larger population. The height of this close relationship was when Gómez allowed the oil companies themselves to write the oil legislation stipulating the terms of dividing the economic rent generated from oil production (McBeth, 1983). But once the post-1952 democratically elected leaders came to power, the state began demanding more concessions from the foreign oil companies so that it could distribute the revenue to a wider segment of the population who voted them into power. Under severe pressure and threat of losing their legitimacy, the multinationals ceded some of their operations to the government and increased their investment in social welfare such as health, education, and housing (Bucheli and Aguilera, 2010; Tinker-Salas, 2009).

Insights from these historical works and the framework of this chapter can also be used to give a different interpretation regarding the existence of business groups. Kaplan and Harrison (1993) claim that firms can organize themselves against potential threats coming from changes at the institutional environment level by collectively organizing themselves through political organizations to influence lawmakers. This can be true for highly stable open access orders like the United States or Western Europe where the sanctity of private property rights is enshrined in the rule of law and this principle is judicially enforced systematically. But in limited access orders where existing institutional arrangements benefit only select groups within a society, the ruler can be tempted to shift alliances and create a new winning coalition by approaching those who have not benefited from the existing institutional environment. In this case, the organizations whose legitimacy can potentially come under question can group together and defend their interests collectively. One form of collective response that is highly prevalent in emerging economies is what the literature has called the "business groups." These are conglomerates "[in which] participants are linked by relations of interpersonal trust, on the basis of similar personal, ethnic, commercial, background" (Leff, 1978: 663). Business groups usually have investments in a wide range of industries, are composed of firms in which some particular (and influential) individuals belong to the boards of several of these firms, and, because of their influence, usually have a strong say in economic policy through extensive political connections (Granovetter, 2005) and have dominated the economies of countries such as South Korea, Mexico, Brazil, Argentina, Chile, Colombia, India, and Japan (Guillén, 2000; Khanna and Palepu, 1999, 2000; Khanna and Rivkin, 2000). In general, most business groups around the world emerged not only during periods of protectionist industrialization policies when the business elites needed the help of governmental protection such as high tariffs and subsidies but also (particularly in Latin America) in times when the working class was increasingly demanding better working conditions after electing governments sympathetic to their cause at the expense of business interests (Bucheli, 2010; Guillén, 2000; Schneider, 2004; Silva, 1997). As already mentioned, economic organizations in limited access orders are inherently political because the sanctity of private property rights is not guaranteed under the political system and can be violated arbitrarily in response to changing political dynamics. Business groups, therefore, can be interpreted as a defense mechanism that firms adopt to protect themselves from such arbitrary swings in institutional environment.

To sum up, in this section, we have highlighted how firms choose different legitimization strategies in response to the political process and how these choices interact with changes in the institutional environment over time. Through historical examples, we highlighted how fluctuations in the internal dynamics of the firm, especially in limited access orders, require firms to adopt a variety of legitimization strategies ranging from acquiescence to manipulation (Oliver, 1991). We also showed how adoption of a certain strategy under one institutional environment configured to the interest of particular winning coalitions may backfire in the future when the composition of the winning coalition changes over time as an outcome of the political process.

CONCLUSION

In this chapter, we propose the integration of political history and studies of organization legitimacy, and maintain that such integration can provide new insights for scholars interested in how the political process influences organizational behavior. We conceptualize the state as an organization or quasi-market resulting from heterogeneous groups competing for economic resources, norms, and values, and the legitimacy of organizations depends on the outcome of this political process. To reiterate, we emphasize that the state has a history of its own and this history determines its own legitimacy as well as that of the organizations operating in the institutional environment. When the state undergoes change as an outcome of the political process, the legitimacy and the legitimization strategies of organizations operating in the institutional environment will be affected in various ways.

The incorporation of political history in organization studies should start by determining which were (or are) the actors struggling for power in a particular society and which social groups benefit from the institutional outcome of the political struggle. The less the institutions are perceived to come from within and as being imposed from outside, the more likely the rules these institutions establish will be regarded as illegal and, hence, vulnerable to change. If the institutions are of relatively recent establishment, how powerful are those not benefiting from them? In this case, we can be talking about economically and/or militarily powerful actors who feel left out or we could be discussing large masses of people, who do not identify with the system or, worse, feel exploited by it. What are their means to contest the institutions? These means can be legal or illegal. The more that those opposing the established rules address their interests and legislations based on the existing institutional infrastructure, the less risk will the established institutional framework be under. However, if those who are discontent feel that rules do not matter because the whole institutional system was created to disfavor them, they will use strategies to dismantle the whole institutional system. Depending on a constellation of the many factors involved in the political process that we have outlined in this chapter, businesses can choose to accommodate compromise or acquiesce in response to the changes. These choices will be reflected not only in their relationship with the government or other companies but also in their internal organizations and governance structure.

Furthermore, an analysis of how the rulers of a particular society took power, who supported them during and after the power grab (a large or small winning coalition), and how they took power (clean elections, fraudulent elections, or a military coup) will help us determine the elements of economic policy related to the ruler's political survival. As some of the examples used in this chapter show, the political struggles that determine the legitimacy of the state consequently determine the ensuing institutional environment, arrangements, and legitimacy of businesses. A political order or regime, therefore, cannot be taken as a given or fixed variable, but as one that is constantly changing and that not only affects the firm, but can also be affected by the firm. Incorporating this point into organizational studies through the lens of history, we believe, will open up new avenues of research and fresh insights into old problems.

REFERENCES

Acemoglu, D., and Robinson, J. (2006). *Economic Origins of Dictatorship and Democracy*. Cambridge: Cambridge University Press.

Acemoglu, D., and Robinson, J. (2007). "On the Economic Origins of Democracy," *Daedalus*, 136(1): 160–2.

Adams, J. (2007). *A Familial State: Ruling Families and Merchant Capitalism in Early Modern Europe*. Ithaca: Cornell University Press.

Beard, C. (1912). *The Supreme Court and the Constitution*. New York: Macmillan.

Beard, C. (1913). *An Economic Interpretation of the Constitution of the United States*. New York: Macmillan.

Berman, H. (1977). "The Origins of Western Legal Science," *Harvard Law Review*, 90(5): 894–943.

Boddewyn, J. J., and Brewer, T. L. (1994). "International Business Political Behavior: New Theoretical Directions," *Academy of Management Review*, 19: 119–43.

Boisot, M., and Child, J. (1996). "From Fiefs to Clans and Network Capitalism: Explaining China's Emerging Economic Order," *Administrative Science Quarterly*, 41(4): 600–28.

Bond, P., and Sharife, K. (2009). "Apartheid Reparations and the Contestation of Corporate Power in Africa," *Review of African Political Economy*, 36(119): 115–37.

Bouton, C. (2012). *Trading in the Age of Revolution: Victor DuPont & Cie. and the Leclerc Expedition to Subdue Saint-Domingue, 1802*. Paper presented at the European Business History Association Meeting, Paris (France).

Bowman, S. (1996). *The Modern Corporation and American Political Thought: Law, Power, and Ideology*. University Park: Pennsylvania State University Press.

Bucheli, M. (2005). *Bananas and Business: The United Fruit Company in Colombia, 1899–2000*. New York: New York University Press.

Bucheli, M. (2008). "Multinational Corporations, Totalitarian Regimes, and Economic Nationalism: United Fruit Company in Central America, 1899-1975," *Business History*, 50(4): 433–54.

Bucheli, M. (2010). "Multinational Corporations, Business Groups, and Economic Nationalism: Standard Oil (New Jersey), Royal Dutch-Shell, and Energy Politics in Chile, 1913-2005," *Enterprise and Society*, 11(2): 350–99.

Bucheli, M., and Aguilera, R. (2010). "Political Survival, Energy Policies, and Multinational Corporations: A Historical Study for Standard Oil of New Jersey in Colombia, Mexico, and Venezuela in the Twentieth Century," *Management International Review*, 50(3): 347–78.

Bucheli, M., and Kim, M.-Y. (2012). "Political Institutional Change, Obsolescing Legitimacy, and Multinational Corporations: The Case of the Central American Banana Industry," *Management International Review*, 52(6): 847–77.

Bucheli, M., and Salvaj, E. (2013). "Multinational Corporations' Obsolescing Political Legitimacy: ITT in Chile, 1920–1972," *Business History Review*, forthcoming.

Buckley, P. J., and Casson, M. C. (1976). *The Future of the Multinational Enterprise*, Homes & Meier: London.

Bueno de Mesquita, B., Smith, A., Silverson, R., and Morrow, J. (2005). *The Logic of Political Survival*. Boston: MIT Press.

Cameron, R., and Neal, L. (2002). *A Concise Economic History of the World*. New York: Oxford University Press.

Campbell, J., and Lindberg, L. (1990). "Property Rights and the Organization of Economic Activity by the State," *American Sociological Review*, 55: 634–47.

Davis, L. E., and North, D. C. (1971). *Institutional Change and American Economic Growth*. Cambridge: Cambridge University Press.

Decker, S. (2007). "Advertising and Corporate Legitimacy: British Multinationals and the Rhetoric of Development from the 1950s to the 1970s," *Business History Review* 81: 59–86.

Decker, S. (2008). "Building Up Goodwill: British Business, Development, and Economic Nationalism in Ghana and Nigeria, 1945–1977," *Enterprise and Society*, 9(4): 602–13.

DiMaggio, P., and Powell, W. (1991). "Introduction." In W. Powell and P. DiMaggio (eds.), *The New Institutionalism in Organizational Analysis*. Chicago: University of Chicago Press: 1–38.

Dosal, P. (1993). *Doing Business with the Dictators: A Political History of United Fruit in Guatemala, 1899–1944*. Wilmington, DE: Scholarly Resources.

Dowling, J., and Pfeffer, J. (1975). "Organisational Legitimacy: Social Values and Organisational Behavior," *Pacific Sociological Review*, 18(1): 122–36.

Dudziak, M. (1988). "Desegregation as a Cold War Imperative," *Stanford Law Review*, 41(1): 61–120.

Eichengreen, B. (1996). "Institutions and Economic Growth: Europe After World War II," In N. Crafts and G. Toniolo (eds.), *Economic Growth in Europe Since 1945*. New York: Cambridge University Press: 38–72.

Etzion, D., and Davis, G. (2008). "Revolving Doors? A Network Analysis of Corporate Officers and U.S. Government Officials," *Journal of Management Inquiry*, 17(3): 157–61.

Evans, P. (1979). *Dependent Development: The Alliance of Multinational, State, and Local Capital*. Princeton: Princeton University Press.

Fagre, N., and Wells, L. (1982). "Bargaining Power of Multinationals and Host Governments," *Journal of International Business Studies*, 13(2): 9–23.

Feng, Y. (2001). "Political Freedom, Political Instability, and Policy Uncertainty: A Study of Political Institutions and Private Investment in Developing Countries," *International Studies Quarterly*, 45(2): 271–94.

Granovetter, M. (1985). "Economic Action and Social Structure: The Problem of Embeddedness," *American Journal of Sociology*, 91(3): 481–510.

Granovetter, M. (2005). "Business Groups and Social Organization." In N. Smelser and R. Swedberg (eds.), *The Handbook of Economic Sociology*. Princeton: Princeton University Press: 429–50.

Guillén, M. (2000). "Business Groups in Emerging Economies: A Resource-based View," *Academy of Management Journal*, 43: 362–80.

Handlin, O., and Handlin, M. (1945). "Origins of the American Business Corporation," *Journal of Economic History*, 5(1): 1–23.

Henisz, W. (2000). "The Institutional Environment for Economic Growth," *Economics and Politics*, 12(1): 1–31.

Henisz, W., and Zelner, B. (2001). "The Institutional Environment for Telecommunications Investment," *Journal of Economics and Management Strategy*, 10(1): 123–47.

Henisz, W., and Zelner, B. (2004). "Explicating Political Hazards and Safeguards: A Transaction Cost Politics Approach," *Industrial and Corporate Change*, 13(6): 901–15.

Henisz, W., and Zelner, B. (2005). "Legitimacy, Interest Group Pressures, and Change in Emergent Institutions: The Case of Foreign Investors and Host Country Government," *Academy of Management Review*, 30(2): 361–82.

Hill, C. (1984). *The World Turned Upside Down: Radical Ideas During the English Revolution*. London: Penguin.

Hill, C. (1990). *God's Englishman: Oliver Cromwell and the English Revolution*. London: Penguin.

Hillman, A., and Hitt, M. (1999). "Corporate Political Strategy Formulation: A Model of Approach, Participation, and Strategy Decisions," *Academy of Management Review*, 24(4): 825–42.

Hillman, A., Keim, G. D., and Schuler, D. (2004). "Corporate Political Activity: A Review and Research Agenda," *Journal of Management*, 30(6): 837–57.

Hobsbawm, E. (1996). *The Age of the Revolutions. 1789–1848*. New York: Vintage.

Jensen, N. (2008). "Political Risk, Democratic Institutions, and Foreign Direct Investment," *Journal of Politics*, 70: 1040–52.

Kalev, A., Shenhav, Y., and DeVries, D. (2008). "The State, the Labor Process, and the Diffusion of Managerial Models," *Administrative Science Quarterly*, 53: 1–28.

Kaplan, M., and Harrison, R. (1993). "Defusing the Director Liability Crisis: The Strategic Management of Legal Threats," *Organization Science*, 4: 412–32.

Kaufman, J. (2008). "Corporate Law and the Sovereignty of States," *American Sociological Review*, 73(3): 402–25.

Khanna, T., and Ghemawat, P. (1998). "The Nature of Diversified Business Groups: A Research Design and Two Case Studies," *Journal of Industrial Economics*, 46: 35–61.

Khanna, T., and Palepu, K. (1999). "Policy Shocks, Market Intermediaries, and Policy Strategy: Evidence from Chile and India," *Journal of Economics and Management Strategy*, 8: 271–310.

Khanna, T., and Palepu, K. (2000). "The Future of Business Groups in Emerging Markets: Long-Run Evidence from Chile," *Academy of Management Journal*, 43: 268–85.

Khanna, T., and Rivkin, J. (2000). "Estimating the Performance Effects of Business Groups in Emerging Markets," *Strategic Management Journal*, 2: 45–74.

Kobrin, S. (1984). "Foreign Enterprise and Forced Divestment in the LDCs," *International Organization*, 34(1): 65–88.

Kobrin, S. (2009). "Sovereignty at Bay: Globalization, Multinational Enterprise, and the International Political System." In A. Rugman (ed.), *The Oxford Handbook of International Business*. New York: Oxford University Press: 183–204.

Kostova, T., and Zaheer, S. (1999). "Organizational Legitimacy Under Conditions of Complexity: The Case of the Multinational Enterprise," *Academy of Management Review*, 24(1): 64–81.

Laski, H. (1917). "The Early History of the Corporation in England," *Harvard Law Review*, 30(6): 561–88.

Leff, N. (1978). "Industrial Organization and Entrepreneurship in the Developing Countries: The Economic Groups," *Economic Development and Cultural Change*, 26(4): 661–75.

Leftwich, A. (2006). *What Are Institutions? IPPG Briefing Paper # 1.* London: Department of International Development.

Lenway, S., and Murtha, T. (1994). "The State as a Strategist in International Business Research," *Journal of International Business Studies*, 25(3): 513–35.

Maier, P. (1993). "The Revolutionary Origins of the American Corporation," *The William and Mary Quarterly*, 50(1): 51–84.

Marx, K. (1988 [1852]). *The Eighteenth Brumaire of Louis Bonaparte.* New York: International Publishers.

Marx, K. (1992 [1867]). *Capital.* London: Penguin Classics.

McBeth, B. S. (1983). *Juan Vicente Gómez and the Oil Companies in Venezuela, 1908–1935.* Cambridge: Cambridge University Press.

Moore B. (1966). *Social Origins of Dictatorship and Democracy.* Boston, MA: Beacon.

Moreno, J. (2003). *Yankee Don't Go Home: Mexican Nationalism, American Business Culture, and the Shaping of Modern Mexico, 1920–1950.* Chapel Hill: University of North Carolina Press.

Murtha, T., and Lenway, S. A. (1994). "Country Capabilities and the Strategic State: How National Political Institutions Affect Multinational Corporations Strategy," *Strategic Management Journal*, 15(Summer): 113–29.

North, D. C. (1990). *Institutions, Institutional Change, and Economic Performance.* Cambridge: Cambridge University Press.

North, D. C. (1991). "Institutions," *Journal of Economic Perspectives*, 5(1): 97–112.

North, D. C., Wallis, J. J., and Weingast, B. R. (2009). *Violence and Social Orders: A Conceptual Framework for Interpreting Recorded Human History.* Cambridge: Cambridge University Press.

O'Donnell, G. (1982). *El Estado Burocrático Autoritario: 1966–1973.* Buenos Aires: Belgrano.

Oliver, C. (1991). "Strategic Responses to Institutional Processes," *Academy of Management Review*, 16(1): 145–79.

Parsons, T. (1963). "On the Concept of Political Power," *Proceedings of the American Philosophical Society*, 107(3): 232–62.

Pirenne, H. (1937). *Economic and Social History of Medieval Europe.* New York: Harcourt, Brace.

Pirenne, H. (1954). *Mohamed and Charlemagne.* London: Allen and Unwin.

Pirenne, H. (1967). *Medieval Cities: Their Origins and the Revival of Trade.* Princeton: Princeton University Press.

Pfeffer, J. (1972). "Interorganizational Influence and Managerial Attitudes," *Academy of Management Journal*, 15: 317–30.

Pfeffer, J., and Salancik, G. (2003). *The External Control of Organizations: A Resource Dependence Perspective*. Stanford, CA: Stanford Business Books.

Rood, L. (1976). "Nationalisation and Indigenisation in Africa," *Journal of Modern African Studies*, 14(3): 427–47.

Salancik, G. R. (1979). "Interorganizational Dependence and Responsiveness to Affirmative Action: The Case of Women and Defense Contractors," *Academy of Management Journal*, 22(2): 375–94.

Schlesinger, S., and Kinzer, S. (1990). *Bitter Fruit: The Untold Story of the American Coup in Guatemala*. New York: Anchor.

Schneiberg, M., and Bartley, T. (2001). "Regulating American Industries: Markets, Politics, and the Institutional Determinants of Fire Insurance Regulation," *American Journal of Sociology*, 107(1): 101–46.

Schneider, B. R. (2004). *Business, Politics, and the State in Twentieth-Century Latin America*. Cambridge: Cambridge University Press.

Schumpeter, J. A. (1942). *Capitalism, Socialism, and Democracy*. New York: Harper Colophon.

Scott, W. R. (2008). *Institutions and Organizations*. London: Sage.

Silva, E. (1997). "Business Elites, the State, and Economic Change in Chile." In S. Maxfield and B. R. Schneider (eds.), *Business and the State in Developing Countries*. Ithaca: Cornell University Press: 152–188.

Suchman, M. C. (1995). "Managing Legitimacy: Strategic and Institutional Approaches," *Academy of Management Review*, 20(3): 571–610.

Taracena, A. (1993). "Liberalismo y Poder Político en Centroamérica (1870–1929)." In V. Acuña (ed.), *Historia General de Centroamérica: Vol. 4*. Madrid: FLACSO: 167–253.

Tinker-Salas, M. (2009). *The Enduring Legacy: Oil, Culture, and Society in Venezuela*. Durham: Duke University Press.

Vernon, R. (1971a). *Sovereignty at Bay*. New York: Basic Books.

Vernon, R. (1971b). "The Multinational Enterprise: Power versus Sovereignty," *Foreign Affairs*, 49 (July): 736–75.

Weingast, B. (1995). "Economic Role of Political Institutions: Market-Preserving Federalism and Economic Development," *Journal of Law, Economics and Organizations*, 11(1): 1–31.

Weingast, B. (2003). "Rational Choice Institutionalism." In I. Katznelson and H. V. Milner (eds.), *Political Science: The State of the Discipline*. New York: W. W. Norton: 660–692.

Wells, L. T. (1977). "Negotiating with Third-World Governments," *Harvard Business Review*, 55(1): 72–80.

Williamson, J. (2011). *Trade and Poverty: When the Third World Fell Behind*. Boston: MIT Press.

Williamson, O. E. (1971). "The Vertical Integration of Production: Market Failure Considerations," *American Economic Review*, 61(2): 112–23.

Williamson, O. E. (1979). "Transaction-Cost Economics: The Governance of Contractual Relations," *Journal of Law and Economics*, 22(2): 233–61.

Williamson, O. E. (1981). "The Modern Corporation: Origins, Evolution, Attributes," *Journal of Economic Literature*, 19(4): 1537–68.

Womack, J. (1991). "The Mexican Revolution, 1910–1920." In L. Bethell (ed.), *Mexico Since Independence*. Cambridge: Cambridge University Press: 125–200.

Part III

Sources and Methods

11

Understanding Historical Methods in Organization Studies

JoAnne Yates

Because historical methods offer benefits to and are beginning to appear in research on organizations in the business and management literature, it is important for scholars in organization studies to understand historical methodologies. Providing such guidance is particularly necessary since in articles published in historical journals, historians typically do not explicitly articulate their historical methods, favoring a more narrative approach. The lack of explicit articulation, however, does not indicate an absence of methods, but rather different norms for writing research articles and books in the different fields. Indeed, historical scholars of organizations also need to understand the methods and genres of qualitative organizational research, in order to adapt their own as needed to continue to gain visibility in the organizational literature.

This chapter begins the job of describing historical methods by comparing them to methods familiar to scholars of organization studies. Methodologies for doing contemporary organizational research are often classified very roughly into qualitative and quantitative. Each type, of course, includes subtypes (e.g., experimental and field-based quantitative approaches and ethnographic and discourse analytic qualitative approaches). When we introduce the historical approach into the mix, surface resemblances make it tempting to classify it into the qualitative category, with the exception of economic history, which falls more into the quantitative category. But we need to be careful not to conflate the methods of business history with those of qualitative research. While they share some characteristics, they differ in others. Using the resemblances as a starting point, this chapter compares historical and qualitative methods to more common quantitative methods, to highlight both similarities and differences among the three. Understanding historical methods as simply a variety of qualitative methods is not as straightforward or useful as it may initially appear either to historians or to scholars of organizations. Scholars in both fields can learn from the differences between qualitative and historical methods, as well as from the similarities. And both can usefully be viewed in contrast to quantitative research.

This chapter initially focuses on describing and comparing historical methods as seen primarily in historical journals and books with qualitative and, as a baseline, quantitative methods as seen in the organizational literature. By the end, my emphasis shifts to recommendations for how historical scholars may want to modify their approaches to the genres of historical writing to increase their chances of acceptance in mainstream management publications. In the more prescriptive final section of the chapter, I will suggest that such modifications include valuing articles more highly as the unit of publication, and giving explicit attention to theory and methods in articles. Such changes will make it easier to publish good historically grounded scholarship in organization and management outlets, and will increasingly expose scholars of organizations to the value of a historical perspective in organizations.

THE QUALITATIVE–QUANTITATIVE SPLIT IN MANAGERIAL AND HISTORICAL RESEARCH ON ORGANIZATIONS

To ground subsequent discussion, we must start by briefly exploring the distinction between qualitative and quantitative methods, a split which exists in both organizational studies and in historical research on organizations. The two terms suggest a clear distinction—one uses numbers and the other does not—but this most obvious characterization oversimplifies. Quantitative research certainly uses numbers as the primary data; moreover, it typically analyzes the carefully chosen numerical data using elaborate statistical methods to test hypotheses generated from theory. This research can statistically analyze data obtained from a lab experiment designed for those purposes (e.g., in areas that draw on the field of psychology), or by analyzing empirical data gathered from the field (e.g., in areas that draw on economics or sociology). But just the presence of numbers doesn't guarantee that a piece of research is using quantitative methods. Quantitative methods refer to methods designed specifically to use quantitative data to test theory-based hypotheses. Such hypothesis testing requires that the numbers be a carefully chosen sample that fits statistical requirements, and that the analysis must follow approved statistical methods. Quantitative methods are best used to measure effects and outcomes and to test hypotheses.

We tend to think of qualitative studies as using words (or images or thoughts) as data, rather than numbers. Typically, qualitative studies systematically organize and interpret the words to derive meaning in relation to existing theories, as well as to suggest new theories. Nevertheless, studies using qualitative methods (e.g., ethnographic, interview-based, or discourse analytic studies) may include numbers, as well—for example, counts of incidents or coding of data. Importantly, however, these numbers are used to describe, interpret, and triangulate findings (e.g., Barley, 1986; Orlikowski and Yates, 1994) rather than to test theory-based hypotheses statistically. Although qualitative data may be coded and counted, and coding may involve computing inter-rater reliabilities, for example, the data is ultimately used to explore, triangulate, interpret, and generate new theory, rather than to test hypotheses based on existing theories. Qualitative research demonstrates its value in exploring phenomena, illuminating processes and meanings, and studying change.

This distinction between the two uses of numerical data also resonates with those familiar with both business history and economic history. Economic historians differ from business and many other types of historians in that they are much more likely to start with theory-based hypotheses, to develop a numerical data set from historical sources, and then to perform statistical analysis of the data to test the hypotheses (e.g., Lamoreaux, Sokoloff, and Sutthiphisal, 2009). In this sense, economic history shares similarities with quantitative organizational research. Business history, on the other hand, typically uses numbers to describe and triangulate findings and interpretations (e.g., Chandler, 1977; John, 1995; Yates, 2005), more like qualitative organizational research. Both historical methods (with the exception of economic history[1]) and qualitative organizational methods are oriented towards *theory building* rather than *hypothesis testing*. Historical methods offer great value in exploring historical phenomena, illuminating processes and meanings within a historical context, and studying change over more extended periods of time and within specific historical contexts.

In the next several sections, I will argue that historical methods (other than those used in economic history) share many similarities with qualitative methods, but also display some differences that make it difficult simply to classify historical research on organizations as a type of qualitative organizational research.

---

[1] In what follows, when I refer to historical methods, I exclude the methods of economic historians unless otherwise specified.

SAMPLING AND ACCESS

Both historical and qualitative methods for studying business and organization are typically used to study a specific case (or a very small number of cases), not the whole population or a large random sample of the population, as is common in quantitative research. The term "sample" is more often associated with quantitative methods than with qualitative methods, so in many cases, qualitative management researchers do not refer to samples at all (e.g., Kellogg, 2011; Vaast and Levina, 2006). When they do, they may claim to use *theoretical* rather than *statistical* sampling (e.g., Graebner and Eisenhardt, 2004). Theoretical sampling is intended to assure that the cases provide all the categories relevant to the theory being built (Eisenhardt, 1989; Glaser and Strauss, 1967; Miles and Huberman, 1994). Of course, all the relevant categories might not be clear to the researcher before beginning the study, but studying multiple organizations comparatively can help provide an adequate theoretical sample. Still, Eisenhardt and Graebner (2007: 27) note that single cases may be theoretical samples, too: "Theoretical sampling of single cases is straightforward. They are chosen because they are unusually revelatory, extreme exemplars, or opportunities for unusual research access."

With the exception of economic history, most historical treatments of organizations, in line with qualitative organizational studies, eschew statistical sampling. They rarely explicitly address any alternative notion of sampling, however. Indeed, historians (like some qualitative organizational researchers) typically start with the phenomenon, rather than with theory. That is, they may choose a historically significant phenomenon to study, rather than a sample designed to illuminate theory. For example, Graham and Shuldiner (2001) studied the phenomenon of R&D and innovation in Corning, and Carlson (1991) studied the role of Elihu Thomson in building the electrical system and the firm General Electric. When Chandler (1977) set out to study the emergence of the multidivisional form in big business, he was somewhat more explicit about his choices, but still with no reference to sampling or theory. He chose to study a set of firms that grew and took on the new form early—DuPont, General Motors, Standard Oil, and Sears, Roebuck—fixing on the firms he felt, based on preliminary research, to be the most innovative (Chandler, 1977: 1–3). In each of these works, the argument could be made that the case(s) studied made up a theoretical sample, but that claim was not made; instead, to the extent that a claim was made, it was based on the historical significance of the case study.

The case study approach is thus shared by the two types of research, but talked about in different ways. Historical treatments of organizations share another concern related to use of case studies: both historical and qualitative organizational studies typically depend on the ability to get *access* to appropriate data on the case. The nature of access and the issues that surround it differ, however.

Qualitative organizational researchers study organizations to which they can gain adequate access and permission to publish.[2] Since they typically want access not just to a predefined set of data (e.g., to a specified set of archival data or the results of a survey, as is often the case in quantitative research), but to people to be interviewed and work practices to be observed, that access can easily expose proprietary information. Thus organizations, and especially their lawyers, make it particularly difficult to gain such access on terms to which academics can agree. Corporate lawyers often insist on reading anything researchers desire to publish before it is submitted to a journal or presented at a conference, a requirement which is resisted by academic researchers and lawyers. At this point the challenge for the scholar is two-fold: (1) to assure in advance that representatives of the corporation have access to the resulting articles and presentations only to confirm that the researcher has disguised the organization and any of its proprietary information, not to censor the scholar's interpretations of what he/she has studied or conclusions based on them; and (2) that the firm has a specified amount of time (e.g., one or two months) within which they must read any outputs of the study for this purpose, so they can't indefinitely delay release of a manuscript, thus effectively suppressing publication. Given these difficulties, qualitative organizational research is very much dependent on gaining access, a process that can depend as much on serendipity as on deliberate choice. In the articles that result from the research, however, such scholars often explicitly address why the organization(s) studied is appropriate given the theory being studied (e.g., Yates, Orlikowski, and Okamura, 1999).

Similarly, those using historical methods typically study organizations for which they can gain access. In this case, however, gaining access means locating contemporaneous documentation (often in company or independent archives) and occasionally (for more recent historical studies) individuals who will agree to oral history interviews. Locating documentary sources on an organization is difficult and subject to survivor bias—that is, organizational records are more likely to be available if the organization still survives or if it has been absorbed by another healthy organization (Forbes and Kirsch, 2010; Kirsch, 2009). Organizations that simply die rarely leave accessible records. Moreover, access to archival documents does not guarantee the right to cite or reproduce them. Archives may be the repository for some items that have a specific time window before they can be consulted and cited, for example. Thus it is common for archives to require that historians submit a detailed list of all items to be cited or reproduced, for approval before publication.[3] Historians do not disguise firms or individuals, making it harder to negotiate

---

[2] This description of access problems faced by organizational researchers comes from conversations with colleagues at my own institution and others who have struggled with this issue.

[3] Among the several archives in which I conducted archival research for Yates (2005), only the MetLife Archive did not require such a sign-off.

favorable terms of access to a firm's records in its own corporate archives. As a condition of access, the firm may require final approval of any publication based on the records. Occasionally, publication may be delayed or prevented by corporate lawyers worried about legal or reputational risk.

Sometime archival data on business organizations that would otherwise be almost impossible to access becomes public, through legal or governmental action. This happens in anti-trust cases such as the many cases around the early computer industry (e.g., the Hagley Museum and Library has "a large body of materials generated by the Sperry-Honeywell lawsuit that revolved around the question about who invented the first electronic-digital computer" (<http://digital.hagley.org/cdm4/document.php?CISOROOT=/p268001coll1&CISOPTR=954&REC=1>), as well as a large collection of IBM Anti-Trust Suit records (<http://digital.hagley.org/cdm4/document.php?CISOROOT=/p268001coll1&CISOPTR=1295&REC=2>). In some cases, government expropriation has also resulted in public availability of records, as with the archives of British and American oil companies in Mexico, which were expropriated in 1938 (see the Mexican government oil archive website <http://petroleo.colmex.mx/index.php/archivos/47>). Then access only requires traveling to a repository or gaining online access to it, with no restrictions on citation.

With respect to the importance of access in choosing a case, then, historical research seemingly resembles qualitative research—both depend on access, which involves a significant component of serendipity. The exact access issues, on the other hand, vary. In the qualitative research case, they involve access to individuals and spaces within the organization. Once the researcher has obtained access, he/she creates data by observations, interviews, and so on. In business history, access issues typically involve access to unpublished documents, which often are found either in corporate archives of the organization itself or in independent archives that maintain archival collections from many organizations. For any historical study beyond the reach of human memory, the data is limited by what has survived—the researcher cannot create additional data but only discover and interpret what exists. The incompleteness of historical sources makes it necessary for historians to have procedures and conventions for their analysis, as is discussed in subsequent chapters. Nevertheless, a creative approach to discovering data beyond corporate records (e.g., consulting personal diaries, trade publications) can broaden what is discovered.

Historical research on organizations shares another characteristic with qualitative organizational research. Because their samples are small (one or more case studies) and limited by access, both types of research have sometimes been accused by quantitative researchers of lacking representativeness or of using a non-scientific approach. The two types of research deal with this potential vulnerability to criticism in somewhat different ways, shaped in part by the differing genres of scholarly writing they draw use.

GENRE DIFFERENCES IN EXPLICITNESS OF
METHODS

Qualitative organizational researchers are part of a broader social science community that has institutionalized genre norms for writing scholarly articles, in turn based on the genre norms for writing articles in the hard sciences (Bazerman 1981).[4] They have had to deal with the criticism of being non-scientific or non-representative more frequently than historians of organizations have had to, and thus they have developed a more conventionalized way of dealing with the issue, in the context of the scientific and social scientific article genre. In the methods section of an article,[5] the author announces explicitly that this is an *inductive, theory-building,* or *exploratory* field study (not a deductive, hypothesis-testing, or confirmatory study). Often he/she then cites a handful of canonical citations (e.g., Eisenhardt, 1989; Glaser and Strauss, 1967; Miles and Huberman, 1994; Strauss and Corbin, 1998) to explain and justify in social scientific terms the choice of site/sample and methods. As already noted, he/she sometimes talks about theoretical (rather than statistical) sampling to justify the choice of site or case study. The analytical methods are typically described as using successive rounds of coding and systematic interpretive analysis to draw (inductive) findings from the qualitative data. After presenting the findings and grounded theorizing based on them, the author then discusses the study's limitations, including referring to the small and unrepresentative sample. Finally, such articles typically close with suggestions for future research such as testing hypotheses based on the newly developed grounded theory in other settings and with broader samples. Indeed, although the researchers who do grounded theory rarely test theory-based hypotheses themselves, the articles almost always refer to the need to further test the theory induced from the case (e.g., Kellogg, Orlikowski, and Yates, 2006). This recommendation for testing suggests a cycle of building theory using qualitative methods, then testing it (or, more accurately, testing hypotheses based on it) using quantitative methods, thus justifying the role of qualitative research in the scientific process.

In contrast, business and organizational history draws on the genre of historical writing, which is not based on norms for the scientific article and rarely has an explicit section dealing with research methods. When a piece of business history is about a single noteworthy example, typically business historians do not feel the need to mention its lack of representativeness, as the audience would not assume that it is representative (e.g., the extensive

---

[4] I have found attention to genres of communication valuable both in my historical studies of communication and information systems (Yates, 1989) and in studies of recent, computer-mediated communication in organizations (e.g., Orlikowski & Yates, 1994).

[5] Books are relatively rare in this field, but they deal with this issue in much the same way.

historical literature on Du Pont or IBM). Often, however, historians note the extent to which firms are atypical (e.g., in the lead in developing new management methods, as Chandler (1962) indicated in the cases of Du Pont, General Motors, Standard Oil, and Sears) or typical (Scovill in Yates, 1989) in their historical period. Whether a case or subject is typical or atypical, a historian writing about it will usually place it historiographically by explaining competing lines of historical interpretation. If the historian deals with several examples and wants to assert a more general pattern, he/she weaves in references to contemporaneous published sources in addition to archival ones to demonstrate that the pattern exists more broadly, or that the chosen organizations are typical of what is in the broader literature of the time (e.g., Chandler, 1977). Alternatively, the historian may trace a pattern in published materials of the era, and then show how that pattern is manifested in particular historical firms or industries (e.g., Yates, 1989). Any discussion of such methods more often appears in footnotes than in the text of the book or article. Thus historical research on organizations does not usually attempt to inoculate itself from criticism of being non-scientific or non-representative by explicitly addressing sample and methods, differentiating it from most recent qualitative organizational research.

Although the genres used by historical and qualitative researchers in studying organizations differ in these obvious ways, they share one underlying similarity to each other and contrast to quantitative research, though the genre differences affect how it is revealed. Because both methods are inductive and theory building, rather than hypothesis testing, both research approaches allow for the possibility that new ideas will emerge in the research process. Researchers in qualitative organization studies typically begin a piece of research with an open-ended question or general focus that gets revised and refined in light of the data, allowing unexpected insights to emerge from the empirical data. For example, the study that resulted in Orlikowski and Yates (1994) did not start out looking at genre repertoires, but just at the evolution of specific genres in email around a specific project. The concept of the genre repertoire and its uses as an analytical tool emerged from the research and iterative analysis. Similarly, historical research on organizations can reveal new, emergent insights based on the data. In researching *Control through Communication* (Yates, 1989), for example, I started with a question about how 20th-century business genres evolved from 19th-century communication practices in business. Although I had several ideas about what factors played a role in the evolution, including technology for producing and reproducing communication (e.g., the typewriter and carbon paper), I did not anticipate the important role of document storage technology (filing), which emerged from my analysis of the published and unpublished sources.

In their finished work, however, both types of researchers tend to foreground the thesis that emerged inductively, rather than beginning with the question posed and taking the reader through the journey leading to the thesis. This foregrounding is done in different ways in the genres used by the two types of researchers. The social science article genre typically has a section, placed immediately after the introduction, that surveys the relevant theory leading to the current research. Quantitative researchers can usually write this section before they have any results, as their hypotheses to be deductively tested are derived from theory before the research is carried out. Qualitative researchers, on the other hand, could not write this section in advance as researchers are not sure what existing theory will be relevant until they have completed their analysis of the data. Nevertheless, once they complete the analysis, they typically follow the genre norms and put much of the theory that they will draw on in building their new theory in this theoretical literature section. As in the case of the stylized presentation of methods, they follow this order to be consistent with the presentation of research more clearly seen as "scientific"—that is, the testing of theoretically derived hypotheses—thus obscuring the more inductive way in which they arrived at the relevant theory to discuss.

Historians are not so explicit in this strategy, but they typically write their books and articles around the thesis that emerged from their research, not around the inductive process that took them to it (e.g., Yates, 1989). Moreover, they typically begin a book or article by laying out the historiography of the phenomenon—the history of its interpretation by other historians. Although the genre norms that lead them to this order are not based on the norms of the social scientific article as are those of the qualitative organizational researchers, they both end up emphasizing the grounded theory or interpretation that has emerged and de-emphasizing its emergent quality.

In summary, business history shares an empirical, emergent orientation with qualitative research on organizations—both allow the data to drive any theory building, rather than using the data to test a pre-determined theory-based hypothesis. The differing genre norms around sample, theory, and methods, however, may make the similarity less evident. Both, however, foreground what has emerged rather than organizing around its emergence.

TEMPORALITY IN ORGANIZATIONAL AND HISTORICAL RESEARCH

An important dimension of organizational research, both qualitative and quantitative, is whether it is longitudinal or cross-sectional—across time or at a particular point in time. Longitudinal research looks for change over time and the factors that cause or shape that change. Qualitative research on organizations can take either orientation. Thus the category of qualitative research does not require a longitudinal orientation. In comparison, all historical methods are, by definition, longitudinal. Indeed, change over time is at the heart of the historical enterprise, although the length of time covered can be measured in years, decades, or centuries. Thus historical research on organizations has most in common with the more restricted category of qualitative *and* longitudinal research.

Temporality enters into historical work in another way that distinguishes it from qualitative longitudinal organizational research. Because the time period being studied is in the past, the focal events have a future as well as a past. That is, historians are likely to make sense of a particular event or period of time in terms of what came before it and what came after it. Historical accounts often include flashbacks to earlier periods to help the audience understand the origins or influences on the focal events. Such flashbacks also may appear in qualitative organizational research, often in the form of a summary of what is known about the organization before the time of the study. Unlike contemporary studies, which are assumed to be current except in cases where a significant event has occurred since data gathering, historical studies may also look forward in time. That is, the significance of the focal events is often made clear by later events. Thus the interpretive task of the historian involves an additional temporal dimension—making sense of the focal events in terms of subsequent history, as well as previous history.

There is another temporal similarity between longitudinal qualitative research and historical research: long time to publication. For all its acknowledged value in organizational research, longitudinal research comes with a temporal cost: it typically takes much more time to conduct. Qualitative longitudinal research requires the researcher to spend a considerable amount of time "in the field," observing or interviewing over an extended period of time (months or years, typically). After this field time, the researcher must spend even more time analyzing the voluminous interview and field notes, coding and recoding them, and seeking patterns in an iterative process (see Pettigrew, 1990, for a useful overview of one researcher's method). Thus such studies take more time to prepare for submission to journals, making them less common than quantitative studies or than cross-sectional qualitative studies.

Historical research is also very time-consuming. Of course, a researcher's time in the archives is not identical to the time covered by the study, as is the case with the organizational field researcher. But it is still a considerable amount of time—often longer than the field researcher's time in the field—followed by a similarly long period of analysis and writing, extending the time to reach publication. And while historical researchers analyze their historical data collected from the archives differently than do qualitative organizational researchers, since historians have no tradition of explicitly coding historical data in the way suggested for qualitative data in the canonical sources cited earlier, historians do, of course, implicitly "code" their data, sifting through it and re-coding it as new themes emerge. Either way, it is a time-consuming process.

Historical methods and qualitative longitudinal methods of studying organizations both take a great deal of time to complete. Cross-sectional qualitative work may also take considerable time, but typically not as much as a longitudinal qualitative study. These varying time scales for different types of work, added to the greater difficulty of getting access to organizations for any kind of qualitative work, suggest one reason why qualitative longitudinal research is relatively rare among tenure-track faculty in business schools (but see, for example, Kellogg, 2011). It is considered by most a riskier route to tenure. Historical methods share the problem of long time to publication, as well as the focus on empirical data from a period of time (though the historian's period is likely to be longer) that can show change over time. But they also differ from longitudinal qualitative studies of organizations in illuminating another dimension of time: the historical researcher may—indeed must—interpret the temporal period being studied from a later point in time, and thus must take into account subsequent events in the interpretation.

VARIETIES OF AND PREFERENCES FOR DATA

One area in which historical researchers on organizations differ from qualitative organizational researchers is in their preferred type of data. Qualitative organizational research often involves serious ethnographic as well as quasi-ethnographic methods, using close observation and/or oral interviews as primary data-gathering methods; in contrast, historical methods depend more on analysis of documents, though interviews (typically thought of as oral histories) are valued by some for more recent research. Indeed, qualitative organizational methods strongly privilege observational and interview data over written documents, typically distrusting the latter. Ethnography-oriented qualitative researchers often assume that documentation is created for the record and as such is distorted to create the record the writer wants to create—not the "truth." Subjects are assumed to reveal something closer to the truth orally rather than in writing, even if it is colored by the passage of time, the shaping of memory, and the personal filters of the researcher (Van Maanen, 2011).

Historical methods, on the other hand, privilege data from the time studied, which is typically either recorded in writing or embodied in an artifact, over retrospective data, such as memoirs written much later or oral history interviews about something that happened in the past. Although oral history interviews have gained some ground among historians for use in more recent history, historians often assume that such retrospective accounts are distorted to create the version of the past that subjects would like to project. They assume that such distortion is even more problematic in memoirs, where follow-up questions cannot prod for more detail. Thus in terms of preferred data types, historical research on organizations differs from qualitative organizational research as understood by most organizational researchers.

That said, this area seems to be one in which qualitative researchers could learn from historical researchers, just as historians could learn from qualitative organizational researchers. Each tends to oversimplify its less favored data-collection method. Historians, for example, do not necessarily take statements in written contemporaneous records at face value, as organizational researchers may assume. They look at written records in the context of the era, of the document series, of the technology of document creation and reproduction, of other documents from other sources, and so on. In Yates (1989), I drew considerable evidence about the technology of document production and reproduction from the physical documents I located in various archives (e.g., press copies vs. carbon copies, typewritten vs. handwritten documents). Published books from that same period allowed me to triangulate with the archival documents. Qualitative organizational researchers would benefit from broadening their acceptable sources of data to better triangulate the oral testimony they gather with contemporaneous written records. Indeed, using documents from the era to ground oral interviews (e.g., by explicitly referring to them in framing questions, or by implicitly taking them into account in interpreting statements made in oral interviews) may improve the data gained from them. Similarly, historians may distrust oral retrospective accounts too much, and thus lose another source of data for studying more recent history, data that can be triangulated with and seen in the context of contemporaneous written data. Organizational researchers are not uncritical of the statements informants make, and historians can learn from them in this regard.

Ideally, both types of researchers could benefit from both types of data, triangulating to improve the trustworthiness of both. At this point, however, data preference differentiates historical research from qualitative research.

PUBLICATION GENRES

Although I have addressed some specific aspects of the social science article genre earlier, the preferred publication genres of qualitative and historical scholars represent a central difference between the two types of research. Qualitative management research, like quantitative management research, is almost always aimed at journal publication. Indeed, business schools, within which most organizational researchers are employed, value articles much more highly than they value books, since most books written by faculty at these schools are not scholarly works, but either textbooks or books aimed at translating scholarly work for a popular business audience. Most management scholars do not typically consider books refereed (despite the fact that university presses always have outside reviewers assess manuscripts before acceptance and many are turned down), in part because the peer reviewing is not double blind as article reviewing is intended to be. Although this preference for articles is widely held in organizational studies, longitudinal ethnographic studies occasionally lead to publication of scholarly books, as well (e.g., Kellogg, 2011; Weeks, 2004). Researchers are often discouraged from writing such books before tenure, however, since they don't fit the normal profile of business school publications and may not be given much weight in the tenure decision. If an organizational scholar decides to write a book in spite of these barriers, he/she often writes articles on the way to the book, to satisfy requirements to show progress and publications.

The unit of publication in history, including business history, is most often the book. Although historical journals have proliferated and articles are more common now in historical fields, the key metric for historians of organizations within the field of business history is the book. Books are viewed by historians as providing a more detailed and better supported argument concerning change over time, while articles are typically seen as isolating one piece of a more involved argument (and thus not seeing it in its broader context) or, alternatively, giving an overview of the more involved argument without adequate evidence to support it. Books are also viewed as peer reviewed by historians, reflecting the scholarly (and blind but not double blind) review process university presses use in deciding whether to accept a manuscript for publication and what changes need to be made in the manuscript before publication. The norm of weighting books more heavily leads to a much more punctuated pattern of production among historians.

This preference for books and the resulting temporal pattern of production do not fit well with the demands of promotion and tenure at the management schools that employ most organizational scholars, quantitative and qualitative.

CONCLUSIONS AND RECOMMENDATIONS

This chapter has provided an overview of how historical research on organizations compares to more typical quantitative and especially qualitative approaches to organizations seen in the management literature. Table 11.1 provides a summary of the comparisons across the three categories of research. As the table illustrates, there are many more similarities between qualitative and historical methods for studying organizations than either has with quantitative methods. Yet historical methods diverge from quantitative methods in significant ways, as well. The similarities and differences have implications for how management researchers will view and accept historical research on organizations, and how historians of organization may need to adapt to gain access to the management world. To the extent that historians of organizations wish to gain acceptance in this world, historians may need to modify some of their genre norms and preferences to make them more similar to those of organizational scholars. At the same time, historians of organizations also need to more explicitly differentiate their work from various types of qualitative organizational research, just as ethnographers differentiate their work from case studies based on interviews alone.

The many similarities noted in this chapter suggest that the qualitative wing of organization studies might be open to embracing historical treatments of organizations. Historical methods, like qualitative methods, allow organizational scholars to interpret phenomena and processes, and to build new theory. Both eschew statistical sampling for theoretical or historical sampling, and both depend on access that is likely to be more difficult to attain (though access in historical research includes survival of records, adding another dimension to the concept). Both historical and qualitative studies of organizations are empirically oriented and emergent, opening the researcher to novel and unexpected findings and theories that cannot emerge using the traditional, deductive, hypothesis-testing methods of quantitative research. Historical research is, by definition, longitudinal, like some but by no means all qualitative research. And both are best used to explore new phenomena, illuminate processes, interpret meanings, and understand change.

Historical methods may be differentiated along some dimensions, as well. Qualitative organizational researchers generally prefer observation and oral interviews to documents, while historical researchers preferred contemporaneous documents, images, and artifacts to interviews. As discussed earlier, this is surely a difference that could be turned into an advantage for both, since understanding and using all types of data to triangulate findings will benefit both qualitative and historical research. Because historical research is, by definition, in the past, it always has a future (up to the historian's present), which creates an additional temporal dimension. That difference, also, creates value that organizational researchers are likely to appreciate.

The differences that seem most likely to put off organizational researchers, and to make historical work seem quite different from (rather than potentially a close relative of) qualitative research on organizations are genre differences. Qualitative researchers model their research output on the articles of quantitative social science, which are in turn modeled on those of natural scientists (Bazerman, 1981); historical researchers model their research output on the books written by academic historians from the humanities. The differences that organizational researchers (both qualitative and quantitative) are likely to see in the genres of organizational historians include the strong preference

Table 11.1 Historical methods in organizational research: A comparison

	Quantitative methods	Qualitative methods	Historical methods
Primary research purpose	Hypothesis testing	Interpretation and theory building	Interpretation and theory building in historical context
Strongest applications	Measuring effects, outcomes	Exploring phenomena; illuminating processes, meanings, change	Exploring phenomena; illuminating processes, meanings, change set in historical context
Sampling	Random, suitable for statistical analysis	Theoretical	On historically significant phenomena (implicitly theoretical)
Access	Close-ended, focused on specified data (e.g., via survey)	Open-ended access critical in choice of case study	Survival of and access to documents critical to choice of case
Evidence (preferred)	Pre-defined data sets, typically numerical	Interviews, observation, images, numbers, documents	Documents, numbers, images, artifacts, interviews when possible
Explication of methods	Explicit, modeled on hard sciences	Explicit, with canonical references to support scientific nature	Traditionally implicit
Research orientation	Empirical, deductive, testing theory-based hypotheses	Empirical, emergent, may discover unexpected findings	Empirical, emergent, may uncover unexpected findings
Temporality	Often cross-sectional, but may be longitudinal	Cross-sectional or longitudinal	Longitudinal and historical, having a future as well as a past
Primary scholarly publication genres	Journal articles	Journal articles	Traditionally books

for books over articles and an overwhelming tendency not to address samples, methods, or theory explicitly.

Based on this comparative overview, I'd like to suggest some recommendations for historical scholars of organization who would like to make their research more visible to organizational scholars, and to the world of management research in general. Historians may increase the attractiveness of their work to this audience by taking advantage of the similarities with qualitative longitudinal research, by leveraging areas where both might benefit, and finally by modifying their genre norms where doing so might make their research more accessible.

Evidence and Data Sources

I have noted earlier that both historians and qualitative researchers would benefit from using a variety of data sources in a careful and critical way. Rather than arguing for the absolute superiority of contemporaneous documents as data, historians could use oral interviews and retrospective accounts to supplement and triangulate with their documents, adopting critical perspectives on these sources from ethnographers and other qualitative researchers while maintaining their own critical perspectives on the documentary record. In collaborations and elsewhere, they could also contribute to the work of organizational researchers by helping them appreciate and critically use documentary sources.

Temporality

In the area of temporality, historians have access to a dimension or perspective lacking to most organizational scholars—the view from the future. To the extent that qualitative researchers have such a view, it comes from the gap between the time of their research and the time of their reporting of that research, typically measured in months or no more than a handful of years. Historical researchers can make this difference an asset by explicitly pointing to the longer gap and to the valuable interpretive perspective it gives them.

Choice of Articles vs. Books

This genre preference issue is a serious one for historians of organizations. Organizational scholars clearly favor articles over books, generally devaluing books in a way that makes the standard historical approach of depending primarily on books highly problematic as a path to tenure in organization studies in most management schools. On this difference, I recommend that historians both shift more emphasis to article writing *and* work to convince this audience of the value of books. If article-length treatments are more readily accepted into the management and organizational world, then those conducting historical studies of organizations need to adopt that unit of research publication as an important one (whether by itself or on the way to a book).

At the same time, however, historical researchers need to make the case that the book is also a major unit of research output with its own advantages in interpreting complex phenomena over time and in context. In this, they would share a cause with ethnographers, who also argue, with varying success, that books are not just a stapling together of articles, but an entirely different and more complex and valuable undertaking. Historians may also find allies on this subject among those who were trained in other disciplinary fields that value books (e.g., political science, sociology) but who now teach in management schools. Such a strategy may play out within individual schools and departments, but also needs to play out in the organizational journals by supporting the practice of including book reviews of scholarly books in these journals.

Adapting the Article Genre

Depending more on articles and trying to place them in organizational journals (e.g., *Administrative Science Quarterly, Organization Science, Academy of Management Journal*), rather than just in business history journals or even the top general history journals, also involves adapting the historical article genre to make it more similar to the qualitative organizational article. For example, sources and methods need to be spelled out explicitly and in detail, in a separate section, for articles aimed at organizational journals. In describing the methods, historians would benefit from being able to cite canonical sources justifying historical methods to social scientists and spelling out the methods in ways that are understandable to social scientists (just as qualitative researchers cite the canonical sources on qualitative analysis methods). Perhaps some of the chapters of this book will become such citations in the future. In addition, the same concepts used in some of the existing canonical citations for qualitative research (e.g., theoretical sampling, Eisenhardt, 1989; Glaser and Strauss, 1967; Miles and Huberman, 1994) may be relevant to historical cases.

Canonical citations alone are not enough; more explanation will be required. For example, it will be particularly important for historical scholars to explain how they have dealt with the potential problems of archival data, with or without oral data to supplement it. Explaining all the sources of data used and how they were triangulated and critically analyzed will improve what organizational researchers would call "external validity" (correspondence to the "real world"). If the article deals with events recent enough to allow for interviewing, supplementing the archival data with such interviews will make it more powerful to the organizational audience.

The role and treatment of theory is another area of genre adaptation. To make historical accounts appropriate to general management journals, historical scholars will need to provide a section on theory after the article's introduction and before the section on data and methods. Then they will need to tie it to the findings of the historical analysis—to show their theory building. There are at least two approaches to the theory section, depending on how the paper is framed, though in each case the theory grew out of the historical research itself. In one, the author presents the emergent theory up front, developing it as an extension of existing theory, then uses the historical case as an example of that extension (e.g., Yates and Orlikowski, 1992). Such an approach frames the article as a whole as a theoretical, rather than empirical, paper and presents the historical case study as an illustration of the theory. Alternatively, the author can frame the article as an empirical article. In that case, the theory section up front can discuss existing theory—whether from organizational literature, historical literature, or both—in areas relevant to what will be developed in the article. Then the historical data and interpretation may be used as the basis for developing grounded theory within the presentation of the findings. The author would then write a section preceding the conclusion, often but not always called "Discussion," that shows how the findings of the case study extend and contribute to the theory discussed in the theory section.

Such adaptations of the historical article genre with regard to theory, methods, and framing would make the genre bear more obvious similarities to qualitative organizational studies and thus be more likely to be published in general management outlets.

IN CLOSING

This chapter provides an initial overview of historical methods for studying organizations by comparing these methods to quantitative and qualitative methods used to study organizations. The similarities between historical research and qualitative longitudinal research on organizations provide a useful starting place in legitimizing historical work on organizations in the world of management research. Subsequent chapters will dig deeper into all aspects of historical methods.

REFERENCES

Barley, S. (1986). "Technology as an Occasion for Structuring: Evidence from Observations of CT Scanners and the Social Order of Radiology Departments," *Administrative Science Quarterly*, 31(1): 78–108.

Bazerman, C. (1981). "What Written Knowledge Does: Three Examples of Academic Discourse," *Philosophy of the Social Sciences*, 11: 361–82.

Carlson, B. (1991). *Innovation as a Social Process: Elihu Thomson and the Rise of General Electric, 1870–1900*. New York: Cambridge University Press.

Chandler, A. (1962). *Strategy and Structure: Chapters in the History of the American Industrial Enterprise*. Cambridge, MA: MIT Press.

Chandler, A. (1977). *The Visible Hand: The Managerial Revolution in America Business*. Cambridge, MA: The Belknap Press of Harvard University Press.

Eisenhardt, K. (1989). "Building Theories from Case Study Research," *Academy of Management Review*, 14: 532–50.

Eisenhardt, K., and Graebner, M. (2007). "Theory Building from Cases: Opportunities and Challenges," *Academy of Management Journal*, 50(1): 25–32.

Forbes, D., and Kirsch, D. (2010). "The Study of Emerging Industries: Recognizing and Responding to Some Central Problems," *Journal of Business Venturing*, 26: 589–602.

Glaser, B., and Strauss, A. (1967). *The Discovery of Grounded Theory: Strategies for Qualitative Research*. Piscataway, NJ: Aldine Transaction.

Graebner, M. E. and Eisenhardt, K. M. (2004). "The Seller's Side of the Story: Acquisition as Courtship and Governance as Syndicate in Entrepreneurial Firms," *Administrative Science Quarterly*, 49(3): 366–403.

Graham, M., and Shuldiner, A. (2001). *Corning and the Craft of Innovation*. New York: Oxford University Press.

John, R. (1995). *Spreading the News: The American Postal System from Franklin to Morse*. Cambridge, MA: Harvard University Press.

Kellogg, K. (2011). *Challenging Operations: Medical Reform and Resistance in Surgery*. Chicago: University of Chicago Press.

Kellogg, K., Orlikowski, W., and Yates, J. (2006). "Life in the Trading Zone: Structuring Coordination Across Boundaries in Post-Bureaucratic Organizations," *Organization Science*, 17: 22–44.

Kirsch, D. (2009). "The Record of Business and the Future of Business History: Establishing a Public Interest in Private Business Records," *Library Trends*, 57: 352–70.

Lamoreaux, N., Sokoloff, K., and Sutthiphisal, D. (2009). "The Reorganization of Inventive Activity in the United States During the Early Twentieth Century," *NBER Working Paper Series*, 15: 440. Available at SSRN: <http://ssrn.com/abstract=1498942>.

Miles, M., and Huberman, M. (1994). *Qualitative Data Analysis: A Sourcebook of New Methods*. Thousand Oaks, CA: Sage.

Orlikowski, W., and Yates, J. (1994). "Genre Repertoire: Examining the Structuring of Communicative Practices in Organizations," *Administrative Science Quarterly*, 39: 541–74.

Pettigrew, A. (1990). "Longitudinal Field Research on Change: Theory and Practice," *Organization Science*, 1: 267–92.

Strauss, A., and Corbin, J. (1998). *Basics of Qualitative Research: Techniques and Procedures for Developing Grounded Theory*, 2nd edn. Thousand Oaks, CA: Sage.

Vaast, E., and Levina, N. (2006). "Multiple Faces of Codification: Organizational Redesign in an IT Organization," *Organization Science*, 17: 190–201.

Van Maanen, J. (2011). *Tales of the Field: On Writing Ethnography*, 2nd edn. Chicago: University of Chicago Press.

Weeks, J. (2004). *Unpopular Culture: The Ritual of Complaint in a British Bank*. Chicago: University of Chicago Press.

Yates, J. (1989). *Control Through Communication: The Rise of System in American Management*. Baltimore: Johns Hopkins University Press.

Yates, J. (2005). *Structuring The Information Age: Life Insurance and Information Technology in the 20th Century*. Baltimore: Johns Hopkins University Press.

Yates, J., and Orlikowski, W. (1992). "Genres of Organizational Communication: A Structurational Approach to Studying Communication and Media," *Academy of Management Review*, 17: 299–326.

Yates, J., Orlikowski, W., and Okamura, K. (1999). "Explicit and Implicit Structuring of Genres: Electronic Communication in a Japanese R&D Organization," *Organization Science*, 10: 83–103.

12

Historical Sources and Data

Kenneth Lipartito

Historical research relies on the use and analysis of "sources." These consist of documents, texts, objects, images, moving pictures, sound recordings, and other residues and remembrances from the past. Primary sources are those texts and objects that come to us from the time period of interest, ideally from actors involved in the events and incidents under study. Secondary sources are commentaries and writings on the past from a later date.

Although primary sources may seem the equivalent of "data," and secondary sources the theory or literature of a field, these analogies are not exact.[1] Primary sources are not objective and detached from the historian-user of them, and they generally are not employed to prove or disprove hypotheses developed from pre-existing theory.[2] One reason for the difference is that history is as much about using sources to uncover the codes by which people understand, represent, and shape their world as it is about finding data that can be said to represent that world (Scott, 1999: 113–38). Representation through historical sources is hence never a neutral act. Sources are best understood as fragments of evidence through which a researcher seeks to engage the past in ways that transcend the categories and habits of thought that shape the present. In this sense, sources cannot be defined as a priori data, but are rather defined through the dialogical research process of engaging a historical subject.

In this chapter we will see how historians engage in research to uncover and organize their sources, how they use those sources to construct historical arguments, and how they establish the credibility of their claims and represent

---

[1] Commonly archives are thought of as simply the house of the documents, but as we will see, more recent critical archives studies have suggested that the archive itself shapes the sources and hence cannot be simply treated as a container for historical documents.

[2] It is certainly possible to use sources to test a hypothesis in the way done in more positivist social science, and sometimes historians will do so, but primary sources and their uses raise other issues that call this mode of analysis into question, as we shall see.

their research. We will also consider the practical as well as intellectual challenges involved in identifying and accessing sources, including some discussion of archives useful for conducting research involving business firms.

SOURCES AND THE HISTORICAL RESEARCH PROCESS

The historical research process typically starts by engaging historically interesting questions about the time period or the phenomena under study. This process may include the use of theory to raise such questions, but generally it does not begin with a purely theoretically framed question. Historically significant questions are designed to reveal the nature of the past and to discover processes that shape people and societies over time. For example, historians may want to know the cause of a war, or explain the impact of major economic change—the emergence of the modern corporation, the Great Depression of the 1930s. By focusing on the specific, historians seek to illuminate the general. In this sense, historical research is not antithetical to theory and generalization as some critics claim (see, Burke, 2005).[3] In fact, modern theories of entrepreneurship (Schumpeter), the firm (Chandler), and institutions (North) owe much to historical approaches to these subjects (Schumpeter, 1942; Chandler, 1962; North, 2005; Suddaby, 2006).

There are several reasons good historical research often begins with "historically significant" rather than theoretically driven questions. The first and perhaps most commonly given is that historians are obligated to the past as it really happened. This means not just a statement of facts (though factual accuracy is crucial), but fidelity to the "pastness" of the past. Historians seek to learn things that cannot be found by turning over the thin topsoil of present day human experience as reflected in current theory. People in the past may well have acted, thought, and organized themselves in radically different ways than they do in the present. A historian failing to respect the integrity of the past by trying to "fit" his/her sources into categories derived from contemporary theory would be akin to an anthropologist going to a foreign land with the assumption that the people there must think and feel, act and desire just like he/she does. Put in more theoretical terms, historians believe that structures emerge and change through time. Scholars of the past rightly fear the danger of "exalting to the level of the eternal observations necessarily borrowed from our own brief movement of time" (Bloch, 1953: 80).

---

[3] For a discussion on how a researcher's reading of archival and primary sources can be shaped by his/her social, ethnic, or cultural background as well as for his/her pre-existing theoretical paradigms, see Appleby et al. (1994) and the collection of essays in Burton (2005).

To a degree pastness is akin to what other social scientists have tried to describe with concepts like path dependency or institutional inertia, or more generally eventful temporality (Sewell, 2005: 81–123). On the one hand historical sequences can alter structures, of both meaning (semiotic codes) and material life. On the other hand, the preservation of structures or institutions also occurs by the ways that agents behave in relation to events and occurrences in time. Thus historians do not mine the past for raw materials to buttress timeless theoretical constructions. Instead they show how the movement of events through time may alter what appear to be solid structures and universal theories.

The fluidity of time also makes it difficult to strictly separate dependent and independent variables in the manner of a causal model. Over time, all variables will interact with each other.[4] Historical work is a quest to find and reveal as many interconnections as it can. Whereas many theories recognize that there are unintended consequences in life, historians see their role as explaining how those seemingly unanticipated or unpredictable consequences come about, to bring to light the hidden processes at work beneath the surface of seemingly stable structures and to follow the ramifications of seemingly small and ordinary events over time.

These tasks require two types of research—synchronic and diachronic. Synchronic research is an attempt to get a complete picture of an event or era, to reveal the features of a period in terms that reflect how actors of the time understood their world. It is the historian's task, in the synchronic mode, to reveal the pastness of the past, including how it contrasts with presumptions and presumably settled and universal matters that we take for granted today. The biggest mistake an unskilled practitioner of history can make is to be anachronistic, or to apply explanations from another era (often the researcher's own), to phenomena and practices of a different time and place.

Explaining movement through time also requires a diachronic approach. Here a clear and precise, even minutely detailed chronology is helpful, to reveal the sequence of events that mount up to change. Events are occurrences in the past that alter seemingly fixed and determined structures. They may be sudden sharp breaks with the past—a new technology. Or they may be more like "drift," a gradual buildup of ideas or material resources (or both) that changes how people think or behave. The danger that the unskilled historian can fall into here is to employ an explanation of change from outside of history—that is, teleology. Teleologies are a form of explanation that rely on some imminent feature seen as emerging from history, or some global process that, in the end,

---

[4] For purposes of analysis some variables can be treated as provisionally independent—one does not need to explain the big bang or the process of geomorphism to understand how Columbus sailed to the New World. Those variables that can be treated independently, however, are often of little explanatory interest.

operates as the final cause of historical developments. Nineteenth-century philosophers of history, including Hegel and Marx, devised teleologies that they believed revealed and explained history: the spirit of rationality emerging from the chaos of events for Hegel; the dialectic of class conflict driving new modes of production for Marx. Modern historians generally avoid teleology in favor of contingent explanations. They see no necessary sequences of events following in history, only possible and probable outcomes and interconnections that have knock on effects from one event to the next.

Historical explanation is not, on the other hand, about observing sufficient variation or making formal comparisons to isolate causal variables. Such work might be a preliminary task of historical explanation.[5] But the historian is not satisfied with reductive models of causation. Such models only work if the statistical methods can be said to eliminate "random" variation to get at underlying structures. Events, by this methodology, become either random perturbations that do not affect underlying structures, or effects dictated by the structural parameters. For the historian, who will watch the interplay between structures and events, the notion of an underlying fixed structure misses the point. It is the temporality of society that matters, the playing out of event upon structure, upon further events that gradually reshape a period or era of interest. This requires a different research strategy than that employed in social research that seeks mechanistic cause and effect relationships.[6]

Historical investigation involves interplay between induction and deduction. Historians formulate questions of historical significance, determine the proper chronology, and perhaps devise some provisional hypotheses. They go to the primary sources, step back to draw preliminary conclusions and revise their initial inquiry, then return to the sources again, often repeating this sequence several times. In this regard historians use methods similar to those of "grounded theory." They engage in a back and forth tacking between their sources and analysis, attempting to construct explanations of the problem under study (Glaser and Strauss, 1967: 6, 28, 45).

---

[5] Scholars dedicated to a rigorous social science model of history may bring questions to the past derived from current theory. They may find that what they can do with their theory is quite limited, however. Sources often do not present themselves in ways amenable to present day theory, which was built with a different world of data. Available sources may both confirm and disconfirm theories, without there being sufficient information to ever resolve the issue. Creative scholars can find ways of filling the gaps, but in doing so they may be forced to narrow their research and questions to those few things that can be researched in ways that comport with contemporary theory. Thus theoretical rigor risks missing what is most interesting and valuable about the study of the past.

[6] The cause of change may come from the articulation of new meanings, even new types of language, which change how people think of and what people believe about the world. Or they may come from changes in technology or economic processes or even environmental shifts that change the distribution of resources among actors.

Given this open-ended, interactive process, the data on which analysis can be performed are unstable. At the beginning the sources themselves may be unknown or poorly understood and are likely to remain incomplete, gradually coming into focus through the back-and-forth process of posing questions, investigating sources, reframing questions, discovering new sources. Rather than being bedrock reality against which researchers can test their theories and hypotheses, historical sources are more like tectonic plates, seemingly stable at first, but actually continually sliding and taking new shape as historians plumb their depths. One cannot separate out the analysis and writing of history from the process of research in the fashion implied in positivist social science. There is no "view from nowhere" on the past. Asking questions of the past and conducting research is a hermeneutical process, in that one's reading of a source will change as one's knowledge of text and context grows (Megill, 2007: 86–7).

THE SOURCES AND THEIR USE

Historians have evolved rules and practices of research, verification, and validation to allow them to make legitimate claims about the past. They verify sources by assessing their authenticity. They ask questions of documents—who created them, for what purpose, and why were they preserved? They derive the significance of a source by placing it in context—that is, comparing it with other similar sources or different sources produced at the same time period, much as an archeologist judges an artifact by where it lies in the sediment.

PRIMARY SOURCES

For the historian, primary sources are primary. It is the use of documentary records that distinguishes professional historical research from amateur work. Scholars are expected to literally and figuratively breathe the dust of the past, much in the same way anthropologists are expected to do field research in uncomfortable locations or archeologists are expected to dig their fingers into the dirt of the past.

The preference for conducting one's own research on primary sources is not purely romantic. As in any scientific enterprise, validity comes in part from multiple researchers replicating the same results—or more accurately for history, multiple eyes examining the same sources—in their original context. The issue is not just one of assessing the accuracy of earlier work on a topic but seeing new things or questioning conclusions drawn by previous scholars.

The repetition or error or bias until it becomes common wisdom is as much a problem in history as in any field. Going to the sources oneself lends credibility to one's research claims. But in using primary sources historians must also ask what makes for a valid and credible source.

Validity

The first question when engaging in primary research is to ask "what are my sources." This is a deceptively complicated issue. Primary sources will vary by the questions asked. A newspaper, for example, is an excellent primary source for exploring the history of media and communication, but as a narrative reflection on happenings in politics and society, it is one step removed from the actors and events. In the case of business, internal firm records would be the first choice for reconstructing the life of a company, its operations, strategy, and structure. But if one were interested in the firm's public life, then internal records would be far less useful than public statements, advertisements, images, and representations of the business as they appeared in mass media and other public venues.

In the quest for validity, historians engage in source criticism. When going deep into the past, such criticism may mean validating the authenticity of a document—is it real or a fake? But authenticity alone does not end the quest. Even for documents whose genuineness can be readily established, criticism takes the general form of "why was this document or artifact produced, by whom and for what purpose?" These why, who, what queries investigate the situated perspective of the document and its creator. Indeed, a forged document may be as enlightening as a true one, telling the reader something about what people thought was important enough to fake, revealing the conventions of thought, argument, and representation of the time that allowed the inauthentic to imitate the authentic.

The fundamental rule of source validity is that those texts, objects, artifacts, and images that were produced during the time under study are the best primary sources. Within this broad statement are several important nuances. Scholars place special value on sources produced by actors of the time who were involved in the events. Productions and representations lose value the further separated they are from actors and events. In studying pre-Columbian civilizations, the writings and art works produced by the Mayans are "more primary" than are reflections or reconstructions made decades later by Jesuit friars. Likewise, when studying a corporation, one might want records from the firm, or its competitors, regulators, workers, and executives, not studies of the firm or industry conducted by third parties at a later date. When studying the public life of a firm, one would seek materials that were available to others—self-representations by the firm, images and portraits that appeared in the popular press. When the artifacts of a people or event of interest do not exist, then one may have no choice but to be satisfied with observations made by others, or even later in time representations. Historians operate on a scale, with the ideal being an artifact directly from an actor at the time of the event— the thoughts and observations of a battlefield soldier at Waterloo, recorded as the battle unfolded! Needless to say, such examples are rare. The ideal, however, provides one measure by which to assess one's sources.

Credibility

The second dimension of source validity is credibility. All actors are situated. The field officer's perspective on the battle is different than the commanding general's, which is different than the front-line soldier's. Historians try to triangulate among different perspectives to gain a more complete picture of the battle. This is not to say that there exists one single reliable source and others should be discarded. It is the historian's task to seek multiple perspectives before drawing conclusions. Alternatively a researcher may deliberately select one perspective to see how events or processes were reflected through the eyes of that actor or group. To learn about innovation in a large corporation, one might focus only on the engineers and technologists, not because they are correct or more truthful, but because their perspective may reveal the problems of translating technical knowledge into commercial products within a large corporate bureaucracy.

Credible historical research thus can take two forms: that which seeks an objective (outside the mind of the actor) perspective on the past, and that which deliberately engages with actor subjectivity. In one sense, no document produced by a human being, even tools and physical artifacts, can be removed from the human mind. Objectivity in the historian's sense means a source that was not produced with a self-conscious purpose, or one that can be read in a way that effectively ignores the creator's purpose. Historians seeking objective knowledge look at tracks or traces of the past—witnesses in spite of themselves. Material never intended for public disclosure or documents that were not created to make a statement, take a position, or advance a theory might in this case take precedence over that which was written to be read and seen (Rowlinson, 2004).

Historians value these leavings and traces of the past as removing some of the potential for deception, propaganda, and guile. This does not mean, however, that the most important documents are private or internal. Even private and internal documents must be critiqued, as they can simply reveal one actor's perspective, or one part of a larger whole. They can be dead ends, ideas that never saw the light of day, programs started then stopped before they got very far. This issue is especially pertinent when looking at the records of complex organizations like corporations. There are likely to be many internal documents that reflect points of view or projects of some part of the organization,

but which did not have much effect on the actions or strategy of the organization overall. It would be a mistake to give more credence or weight to such
documents simply because they were internal, or because they had not been
seen before. Indeed, just as revealing and "objective" in the historian's sense
can be what librarians call ephemera—materials that were public and aimed at
an audience, but were never intended to be saved. The transient nature of such
materials makes them reliable reflections of day-to-day matters not normally
given much thought, good indicators of how people of the time would have
understood their world.

Traces of the past discussed earlier in the chapter fall into the category of
non-narrative primary sources. They do not construct an argument or story.
People in the past create narratives too, and thus leave behind narrative primary
sources as well. These sources require the scholar to take on the subjectivity of
the actor in explicit fashion. For example, the former CEO who chooses to "tell
all" about his years with his company is producing a narrative primary source.
By one dimension, closeness to the time and events, such a confession would
be of high value. But by the standard of credibility, one would have to look with
skepticism on the veracity of the information. It might be that such a narrative
has all the discrete facts right, but the reliability issue arises from the narrative
itself, as told by an interested party. On the other hand, such narrative sources
allow us to understand how business leaders seek to position themselves in the
flow of history, or how they gain credibility and power through their ability to
construct a narrative, or how they understood the world, and hence why they
acted as they did. By reading against the grain, or purpose of the source, historians can tease out more information than the author intended.

Internal business sources are not necessarily the best sources for all occa-
sions. They do not, for example, help to understand how organizations represent themselves to the public as well as the publicly produced materials of an
organization. Much of the life of any organization is lived publicly—from how
they seek to have themselves portrayed through advertising and public relations material, to how they are seen through media and personal observation.
Public sources can in fact be a better way of understanding representation than
internal documents, which only may reveal what the actors of a firm thought
their message was or how they thought they would be seen. The reception of
the message or image requires looking at the images and messages as viewed
by the receiver, and not as intended by the creator.

SECONDARY SOURCES

Historians engage in a back-and-forth tracking between primary documents
and arguments with fellow scholars in what historians term the secondary

sources.[7] Writings of other scholars provide a guide to primary sources, both in the shallow sense of pointing the researcher to locations where potentially useful sources may be held, but also in a deeper sense. Because the primary sources may be, to modern eyes, unfamiliar, obscure, or even impenetrable, primary research requires help from those who went before.

For example, discovering a set of merchant account books from centuries ago could be the start of a fascinating journey into the past, but even a modern accountant might have trouble deciphering the accounting methods used in the past. Ignorant of the particulars of the task, the researcher might mistakenly read present-day notions into very different practices, falsely assuming that words meant the same thing then as now. As the great scholar Marc Bloch observed, "to the great despair of historians men fail to change their vocabulary every time they change their customs" (Bloch 1953: 34). Secondary works can provide the researcher with insight into how to read these sources, and perhaps more importantly, what sort of use they can be put to and what questions they might address (questions the researcher might not have thought of at the onset).

Thus rather than simply providing a research question that can be then tested in the archives, the secondary literature may allow a scholar to work inductively through a set of sources back to an important question. In this way, the primary sources are refreshed again and again, even when no new documents have been discovered. Rethinking categories of analysis calls into question the existing structure of primary documents, or brings to the surface artifacts once thought useless or uninteresting. For example, when feminist scholars questioned assumptions that women had played little part in history, they rethought traditional, narrow definitions of public life. The result was to expand and open the documentary record, allowing scholars to exploit material on the history of the family in ways that reshaped their understanding of small business and female occupations in the economy, and brought to the surface the importance of voluntary societies, charitable organizations, and women's clubs in politics.

The secondary literature thus provides a way to ask historically relevant questions and offers methodological clues and theoretical insights that can reconceptualize the primary sources. Historians of business, for example, might find that seemingly routine records of an organization can be rethought as texts that reveal submerged patterns. Personnel files of companies might show how ideas about gender, race, or ethnicity were encoded in job categories and worker evaluations, both reflecting the cultural presumptions of the time and

---

[7] For those of a more radical postmodern bent, legitimate representation of the past may also require self-conscious discussions of one's own cultural assumptions going into the archive and a more self-reflective narrative. But in either case, history proceeds by argumentation that brings together competing interpretations.

also building those presumptions into work and the economy. Such seemingly routine files would not on the surface appear to be of great significance, but when thought about with the insights of different theories, the possibilities of different sorts of research emerge. Likewise accounting files and information would seem to be nothing more than a standardized way to represent the financial position of a firm. But when considered historically, such evidence can also reveal how practices of representation have changed over time, what sorts of legal or regulatory mandates firms were responding to, even how business institutions took on different conceptualizations of the purpose and strategies of firms (Johnson and Kaplan, 1991; Fligstein, 1990).

ARCHIVES

Although entirely new and unknown sources arise from time to time, for the most part the process of discovery goes on within archives, which are collections of documents and texts. In its original meaning, an archive was simply a place where documents were stored, literally the house of the magistrate, or *arkheion*, in ancient Greece. The actual location of documents is not important to their validity, which is established through source criticism. But location and institution do affect how historians approach and make use of primary sources. An important part of the historian's task is both mastering the institutional matrix in which documents are embedded, and also finding ways of going around or exceeding any limitations that the matrix imposes.

Archives as Institutions

Archives are institutions. They have purposes and histories themselves. They structure the very records that will serve as historians' sources. For example, government archives reflect the concerns of power and state administration. From the types of records that state actors value and choose to save, to the way in which they arrange categories of information government archives may highlight certain features of the nation's history while marginalizing other groups or identities.[8] Likewise, business archives will reflect the strategies, products, and cultural traditions of the firm. Records surviving from very large firms have often made it easier to understand the growth of the corporation than to track the history of small and medium-sized firms, leading to an overemphasis on the part played

---

[8] For interesting discussions on how archives might be used not only to preserve memory, but also to construct, distort, and even to *bury* pasts that some actors or institutions want to be forgotten, see Hamilton et al. (2002) and Steedman (2002).

by large corporations in the economy. Business records might be saved because they are legally mandated or are useful to certain ongoing functions, or even because they reflect the outlook of the leadership, or the whims of those who do the actual collecting. Other business records may not be archived or may even be "de-accessioned" because they are considered unimportant to firm strategy or identity, or perhaps even harmful to firm interests (Schwarzkopf, 2012). For these reasons, historical researchers must be attentive to possible "silences" as well as the voices given expression in business archives (Decker, 2013).

The inflections archives impose on documents are present even when there is no specific institutional goal or purpose at work. Some archives choose to specialize, taking advantage of existing collections to build strength in a particular area, topic, or part of history. In other cases, archives reflect the interest and idiosyncrasies of donors and givers, who have for various reasons chosen to collect and then turn over their papers, objects, art, and images to an archive. Indeed, those who retain information about themselves, their lives, or their institutions are by definition atypical of the majority of people in a given time, who typically do not do these things. Thus what gets into an archive is in no sense a complete population of documents of some past, nor even a random subset.

The Structure of Archival Records

Once material enters an archive, it has to be processed, sorted, organized, catalogued, and made available to users. How well a collection has been sorted and maintained bears on how easily it can be, quite literally, handled. Rare documents or materials in poor physical condition may only be available at certain times to certain users. Materials may be unavailable for duplication, even non-flash photography. They may be heavy and cumbersome, as with deteriorating, leather-bound accounting ledgers from the 19th century. Handling such materials often requires special treatment, significantly slowing the rate of research. In cases when material is valuable only when used in large quantities, the rate of research can be a significant barrier to completing the desired work. Although public libraries and university archives generally do not charge for their services, this may not be the case with private archives or archives put together by organizations for internal purposes.[9]

Archives house materials, organize them, and develop tools for retrieving them. Documents are generally grouped by collection—reflecting the materials of a particular person or organization—or else constitute a more diverse set of documents assembled by someone else and then given to

---

[9] All of the issues of time are multiplied when material is stored off site and must be recalled in advance, often with a restriction on how much per day. In underfunded archives, insufficient staff may be available to do the physical retrieval.

the archive. Retrieval technology may be simply a hand list—a typewritten description of each object or container (file box). More sophisticated finding aids will include both an overall description of the contents of the collection and its subdivisions, and ideally, a brief description of each item, down to the individual letter or document. But many finding aids go no further than a description of what is in a box containing many folders, each folder containing many papers.[10]

The Problem of Access

Public libraries and university archives are generally accessible to researchers. Time seals, however, may prevent use of collections before twenty-five, fifty, or 100 years have elapsed. Laws protecting privacy—which are unclear and in evolution—may prohibit using material that identifies individuals. Birth, death, and other vital statistics are usually exempt from such laws, but not necessarily records bearing on adoptions, juvenile crime, or social services. The National Archives of the United States are meant to be a public treasury of information on the nation's past, but departments and bureaus of the federal government can classify and restrict access to sensitive material. And all government departments—local, state, and federal—can simply fail to turn over documents, either because they want to retain them for working purposes or because the records' retention policies are in conflict with archival needs. Business firms frequently retain records for legal reasons—tax records, financial disclosure records—but dispose of potentially valuable documents because they are not mandated by law to keep them.

Interpreting the Archives

The self-aware historian looks critically at the cultural mindset represented by the structure and practice of an archive. But he or she then faces a choice of either following the lines of information already laid out or finding ways to creatively manipulate those lines by examining and sorting the documents in a different order. In either case the historian has to understand the collection strategy and purpose that built the archive. A historian can begin by asking,

---

[10] Since collections arrive in archives at various times reflecting various states of the art, the finding aids of archives are often like palimpsests—one layer of information on top of another. Few archives can provide a complete item level description for all their collections, but increasingly digitalization of finding aids allows researchers to conduct off site key word and Boolean searches on at least some collections or parts of collections. Almost invariably, the researcher will spend time consulting with the archivist, or in a large archive the archivist who specializes in the topic or collections of interest.

"What values and accepted practices of archiving guided the collection of documents I am now using?" historicizing the very process of archiving material.

In one sense the task faced by a historian in an archive is similar to that of a contemporary social scientist designing and deploying a research instrument—though it is rather different than an economist using already standardized data from the census or Federal Reserve. In contrast to a survey, however, one cannot "design" an instrument to answer a question. Rather one must assemble what is there and find creative ways to employ it.[11] Historical research therefore often involves breaking open the existing structure of data of the archive. On the one hand, the way material is organized is absolutely invaluable for getting started—imagine the difficulty one would confront with material that is totally unorganized. Some works of history have been written from unorganized material, but the problems of piecing together the data desired can be immense. Nonetheless, scholars can rarely simply follow the structure of documents already in place, particularly when they want to ask new questions or read documents against the grain. Original historical research involves creating out of an existing archive a new, virtual archive organized for the question under study.

PRIMARY SOURCES OUTSIDE OF ARCHIVES

Not all materials that provide primary documentation are found in archives. Many organizations, including businesses, keep various records that they never formally archive. Family and personal papers likewise may provide tremendous insight into the past, but may continue to reside in the possession of individuals (with all the possible problems of gaining access that this brings). When the great business historian Alfred Chandler went searching for a dissertation topic, he found his sources in the house of a family member, a descendent of Henry Varnum Poor, the founder of Standard and Poor's (McCraw, 1991).

Another non-archival category of sources, particularly for the modern era, is so-called gray literature. On many topics, particularly those related to technical matters of finance, accounting, law, and technology, professionals and practitioners from the past produced literature intended for an audience of their peers, as they do today. Such literature falls between primary and secondary sources. On the one hand, it may reveal how fairly abstruse practices from the past actually worked, and open up a whole new world for the scholar, who otherwise would have difficulty grasping what he or she is reading in

---

[11] This is not to say that documents in archives cannot be coded and organized in a more quantitative fashion.

documentary sources. On the other hand, it must be treated with some caution, since the authors of professional literature are themselves interpreters of events and practices going on in their time.

As is true of materials in archives, so with materials outside of archives: the validity of the source does not rest on location but on source criticism that reveals its production history, its perspective, its point of view, its proximity to the event, and its value in addressing the question asked.

BUSINESS SOURCES

The history of business can be written from the same sort of documents used in other types of history. Some of these are external to the firm. These include the papers and records collected by governments in the course of going about their economic functions: the records of central banks; records from the branches of the legal system concerned with commercial transactions, bankruptcy, and contracts; wills, diaries, visual and literary representations, even archeological materials. But the study of business in history also makes use of a unique source of records—those internal to firms themselves, especially large corporations.[12]

Internal records can be used to reconstruct the life of a firm or go into depth on some function of a firm, such as finance, accounting, human relations, R&D, or into some process or practice, such as the forms and methods of internal communication. Records at the firm level may also be used collectively to reconstruct an industry's history and evolution, or discuss competition and information exchange among actors in a sector. Business records have been used to study innovation and failure, strategy, entrepreneurship, the evolution of managerial structures, business-government and business-labor relations, the growth of multinational firms, and corporate responsibility, among other issues (Jones and Zeitlin, 2007; Amatori and Jones, 2003). In addition, the firm's papers may also contain "external" records that bear on the history of government agencies, universities, non-profit entities, standard setting bodies, and other institutions. These records may narrate a relationship with such entities from the firm's point of view, but may also contain more general information as well.

Internal records may be stored in an archive or may remain with a firm. External records will likely be housed in a public or private archive. A number of archives accessible to researchers are notable for their strong collections of business records. Among the most prominent in the United States are the

---

[12] On business archives see O'Toole, *The Records of American Business*. On the distinction between internal and external records, see Forbes and Kirsch, "The Study of Emerging Industries."

Hagley Museum and Library, the Baker Library at Harvard Business School, and the University of Minnesota Library and Archives. Archives kept by business firms themselves vary quite a bit, depending on the state and condition of the firm and the policies of the leadership at a given time.[13]

Accessing and Using Business Records

Records of business firms present special issues to the researcher. The first is access. Though many companies deposit their records with public or university archives, sometimes these records remain restricted or closed, particular on matters that bear on the more recent past. In other cases, firms may retain a right to read anything that uses or quotes from their documents before publication. This arrangement can be a touchy one, and most archivists strive to minimize the degree of outside control. Seeing beforehand a paper that a scholar may publish is one thing; vetting and approving scholarship is another.

Company records that make it into a public archive may reflect specific factors that make the collection unrepresentative of an industry or region. Firms that fail may leave behind no records for future historians (though such records may be traceable through bankruptcy courts). Successful, ongoing enterprises have the resources to maintain good records, but their very investment in their own history may mean they are less willing to let their documents go, and are more wary of how they are represented in scholarly publications. Industries with many small firms will be harder to research, generally speaking, than those dominated by a few large, long-lasting companies. Industries with many firms scattered across the nation or globe will present a still more formidable logistical challenge to the diligent researcher. Often therefore, scholars will have to consider alternative research strategies—for example, focusing on one place or region, or case studies of a few firms.

Many business records are still residing inside of firms. Here the scholar faces a truly unknown situation, often resolved by asking simply "do you have any historical records?" Some firms do have true archives, and the company archivist may be authorized to allow access by scholars. Others have a well-organized records retention department, which is mainly for internal purposes. Still others have only current and legally mandated records. In the last case, this does not mean there are no older historical documents, only that the firm has little interest in them. They may well still exist, moldering in some off-site storage facility. Often simply by asking to see them the scholar will bring their existence to the attention of current management. Firms that have

---

[13] A starting point for locating business records includes Snyder (ed.), *Business History in the United States.* See also the content provided by Virtual Library of Economic and Business History, at the website, <http://www.neha.nl/w3vl/index.html>.

not been interested in their own history may well be quite forthcoming with access, figuring that there is nothing in the past that can harm them. Others will take the opposite track, deciding that the past should stay safely buried. When legal departments get involved, caution often wins out over access, though public relations executives who like the idea that the firm's story will be told can be the historian's ally.

When it comes to gaining access to internal firm records, polite persistence pays. If a company does not have an archivist, an initial letter to the head of public relations, external relations, or the company secretary is a good way to start. An initial rejection by a lower level officer can best be followed by moving up the chain of command. Usually the scholar will not be met with rejection as much as "we don't have anything," or "state specifically what you want to see," or most commonly, no response at all. The first two replies can usually be surmounted. Lower-level workers in a corporate hierarchy generally regard inquiries by historians as a bother that can only get them into trouble. So not answering or answering with a "we don't have anything" requires moving up the chain of command. It frequently turns out that the claim that no records exist is false, and in fact there are often informal historians and cultivators of the corporate memory inside the bureaucracy who would love to discuss the firm's past, and know where the sources are. Demands that one list specifically what one wants to see—impossible when it is not even clear that there are records and what those records are—can be met with a long discussion of the sort of research one is attempting. Explaining that the research is scholarly and not journalistic, that one is not seeking to make an exposé but to do serious research helps to assuage doubts.

The Nature of Firm Sources

Although getting access to firm records is a task itself, the researcher will still be faced with the same problems of source interpretation and source criticism as with any other documents. The further back in time one goes, the less will the sources look like the business records of today. Before the 20th century, there were fewer national institutions that governed private business. For the most part companies did not have the extensive and standardized accounting and financial reporting requirements typical of the 20th century. Internally as well the administrative structures of firms have changed over time, with the development of formal departments for financial, legal, personnel, and technology related matters appearing in the late 19th century, and even then in a small number of very large firms. The growth in size and scale of business has meant more internally generated information, but even in smaller firms the spread of formal managerial science (from the growing professionalization of management in business schools and through consulting firms) has led over time to more information and information in more standardized forms. Conversely, however, scholars delving back into the 18th or early 19th century will quickly see that standardization of information familiar today was absent. Or more precisely, the medium of communication and the organization of information reflected a much different historical context in the past. The first tasks of research is to uncover that context to understand what records matter and why.

One of the main sources for the history of business before the mid-20th century, for example, is likely to be letters. Correspondence by everyone from the CEO down was the typical way that communications were undertaken in 19th-century firms, and indeed by merchants, bankers, and others engaged in trade, commerce, and finance going back centuries. Business correspondence fits well with the framework for historical validity because it was undertaken by an actor of the time, usually at the time of action, but was not intended for public consumption when it was set down. Go too far back in time, when markets were smaller and more local and much economic activity was carried on in person, and one will find less written correspondence. Move forward in time and business correspondence tends to decrease, in part because of the use of formal methods of communication—standardized accounts and forms—and in part because of the rise of the telephone. Somewhat unexpectedly, however, the use of the internet and email and other text-based modes of communication have revived written correspondence in business operations.

Likewise, the nature and variety of accessible business records will vary in different parts of the world. As Decker (2013: 3, 5) points out, business archives "in Africa and other less developed countries...suffer from autocratic suppression of information, complete lack of transparency and accessibility—basically the absence of a functioning bureaucratic system." The result is a host of systematic omissions that create a "breadth and diversity of silences within the material" which researchers need to address in their analytical and interpretive approaches.

The Challenge of Self-Promotion

As firms became more aware of how their image was being read by the public, they also became more interested in controlling their message, sharpening the distinction between communication that was for public consumption from that which was not. To the scholar interested in image, the rise of public relations means a wealth of material to study from the perspective of representation. For the scholar interested in strategy and policy, cutting through the massive amount of information a modern corporation produces and determining which plan, study, memo, or report mattered requires gaining an intimate familiarity with how the firm operated, what the lines of reporting were, and some sense of the internal power distribution among executives. One way of taking advantage of this proliferation of sources is to read them critically and against the intended purpose. Even dead-end information often reflects important matters of the day and can be read as a text both for what it does and does not say and how it says it.

REPRESENTING THE RESEARCH

The authority of a historical study rests on demonstrating extensive research in primary documents. Historians strive to show that the sources they used were not only valid in the sense of trustworthy, but also relevant to the task undertaken, and that their conclusions are original. Originality in this context does not necessarily mean the sources were new or had not been worked before, but rather that the research significantly changes our understanding of a period, process, or institution. A good part of peer review for historical work consists of checking to see that sources cited actually match the claims being made. The logic of historical argument is that if assertions or claims can be backed by a primary source or sources, then the conclusions drawn will be valid as well.

Credibility in history, as in other sciences, rests on repeatability. Although it is unlikely that two researchers would come to the same precise conclusions after using the same documents, the presumption of citation practice is that any other researcher could follow the citations back to the same documents. Citations thus must be of sufficient detail to lead another scholar to the same archive or repository, locate the same document, and find easily the information being cited.[14]

Proclaiming originality is a somewhat more complex process. In both the citations and the text, historians engage in historiographical discourse—a debate or dialogue with others who have worked on the same or related topics over the proper interpretation of the case. With regard to the use of new sources (or familiar sources in an unfamiliar way), this discourse may involve building a new or substantially modified interpretation that could not be established with previous sources. Or it may involve the revealing of a counter or disconfirming example against a well-established paradigm. Or finally it may consist of extending a well-established line of thought in a new direction not previously considered part of the interpretation. In each case, the citation of sources validates the interpretive move.

---

[14] This is the same sort of replicability that is expected in other scientific disciplines. It may be the case, however, that sources used are not easily available to other scholars, or over time are lost or destroyed. Though unfortunate, such events do not necessarily invalidate the historian's research.

Establishing that work is backed by useful, appropriate, and valid research is done in history in ways similar to other disciplines. The historian makes a case that the records support the causal and descriptive claims of the text. Sometimes this requires a direct quotation from the document, but often the claim is backed by an accumulation of multiple documents, no one of which provides a particularly revealing or argument-clinching statement. The clear and precise citing of documentary evidence is presumptive proof that the claim is supported.

Citations in history are usually done through footnotes. Footnotes are used not just to clarify points or to cite relevant literature, but to identify specific documents that support statements made in the text. Each major claim should have backing from one or more primary source, which can be tracked through the footnotes. When evidence is in the form of numbers, images, or information that can be conveyed in tabular form, historians will often embed citations in the text. Quantitative historical work often involves creating new sets of data by drawing out figures from primary documents. Each document used to make the dataset must be cited and ideally linked to particular data in the set.

A second function of the footnote is to engage in a dialogue with other writers on the same subject. Footnotes cite important secondary works that either support the claims made in the paper, or argue that other scholars' work has been now superseded—or at least does not contradict the assertions being made. In this way footnotes are part of the infrastructure of a historical work, carrying on a second level discourse between the author, his or her sources, and other writers. They are thus as much a device of critical thought as of evidence citing (Grafton, 1997: 22–3, 231–4).

History can accommodate other methods of citation as well, though footnotes have advantages in connecting claims with specific documents, when many documents from many archives may have been consulted to build the case. Alternative citation forms may also be able to represent the research as valid. They too, however, must allow other scholars to follow the research back to the archives, connect statements made from the text to documents, and allow for some interpretative interaction between the author and his or her interlocutors. Such tasks can be difficult to accomplish in social science citation methods. For example, placing documents in a single bibliography will fail to distinguish properly between primary and secondary sources. Placing document citations in parentheses in the text may lead to elaborate and overly long citations that disrupt the flow of writing. Abbreviated in-text citations, on the other hand, may be insufficient to lead others back to the specific documents supporting the claims of the text.

Historians usually build some of their claims for validity and appropriateness into their argument. They may do so in direct ways, for example explaining why the sources they used were particularly illuminating for the question, hypothesis, or interpretation of their paper. Often, however, this case will be made more implicitly, as part of the historiographical debate in the text and notes with other authors, for example, who used different sources.

Accommodating the different expectations of other disciplines may require features of representation not commonly included in historical publications. As noted, historical research is "grounded" in that the scholar begins with a historically significant question, delves into the archives, steps back from the initial research to place what he or she has found in context. This hermeneutical process of "tuning" both the questions and research in light of initial discovery might be best discussed in a section of the paper describing the research process.[15] Historians have traditionally "hidden" the messiness of the research process in their final paper, not to deceive but in the same manner that a good craftsperson hides their pencil marks and rough cuts in the final product. Greater transparency of process, however, has recently become an issue in history through the postmodern questioning of the idea of an objective author writing from the standpoint of nowhere. Positioning the author and the author's work in the text explicitly is now within the realm of acceptable practices in history. Such practice could also add a level of transparency in the research process expected in other disciplines.

REFERENCES

Amatori, F., and Jones, G. (2003). *Business History Around the World*. Cambridge: Cambridge University Press.

Appleby, J., Hunt, L., and Jacob, M. (1994). *Telling the Truth about History*. New York: Norton.

Bloch, M. (1953). *The Historian's Craft*. New York: Alfred Knopf.

Burke, P. (2005). *History and Social Theory*. Ithaca: Cornell University Press.

Burton, A. (ed.), (2005). *Archive Stories: Fact, Fictions and the Writing of History*. Durham: Duke University Press.

Chandler, A. D. Jr. (1962). *Strategy and Structure: Chapters in the History of The American Industrial Enterprise*. Cambridge, MA: MIT Press.

Decker, S. (2013). "The Silence of the Archives: Business History, Post-colonialism and Archival Enthnography," *Management & Organizational History*, 8: 1–19.

Fligstein, N. (1990). *The Transformation of Corporate Control*. Cambridge, MA: Harvard University Press.

Forbes, D. P., and Kirsch, D. A. (2010). "The Study of Emerging Industries: Recognizing and Responding to Some Central Problems," *Journal of Business Venturing*, 26: 589–602.

Gaddis, J. L. (2002). *The Landscape of History: How Historians Map the Past*. New York: Oxford University Press.

---

[15] See for example, Khaire and Wadhwani, "Changing Landscapes."

Glaser, B., and Strauss, A. (1967). *The Discovery of Grounded Theory: Strategies for Qualitative Research.* Chicago: Aldine Publishing.

Grafton, A. (1997). *The Footnote: A Curious History.* Cambridge, MA: Harvard University Press.

Hamilton, C., Harris, V. et al. (2002). *Refiguring the Archive.* Dordrecht: Kluwer.

Johnson, H. T., and Kaplan, R. (1991). *Relevance Lost: The Rise and Fall of Managerial Accounting.* Cambridge, MA: Harvard Business Review Press.

Jones, G., and Zeitlin, J. (eds.) (2007). *The Oxford Handbook of Business History.* New York: Oxford University Press.

Khaire, M., and Wadhwani, R. D. (2010). "Changing Landscape: The Construction of Meaning and Value in a New Market Category—Modern Indian Art," *Academy of Management Journal,* 56: 1281–304.

McCraw, T. (ed.) (1991). *The Essential Alfred Chandler: Essays Toward a Historical Theory of Big Business.* Boston: Harvard Business School Press.

Megill, A. (with Steven Shepard and Phillip Honenberger) (2007). *Historical Knowledge, Historical Error: A Contemporary Guide to Practice.* Chicago: University of Chicago Press.

North, D. (2005). *Understanding the Process of Economic Change.* Princeton: Princeton University Press.

O'Toole, J. M. (ed.) (1997). *The Records of American Business.* Chicago: Society of American Archivists.

Rowlinson, M. (2004). "Historical Analysis of Company Documents." In C. Cassell and G. Symon, *Essential Guide to Qualitative Methods in Organizational Research.* London: Sage: 303–11.

Schumpeter, J. (1942). *Capitalism, Socialism and Democracy.* New York: Harper Brothers.

Schwarzkopf, S. (2012). "What Is an Archive—and Where is it? Why Business Historians Need a Constructive Theory of the Archive," *Business Archives,* 105: 1–9.

Scott, J. (1999). *Gender and the Politics of History.* New York: Columbia University Press.

Sewell, W. (2005). *Logics of History: Social Theory and Social Transformation.* Chicago: University of Chicago Press.

Snyder, T. (ed.) (2010). *Business History in the United States: A Guide to Archival Collections.* Washington, DC: German Historical Institute.

Steedman, C. (2002). *Dust: The Archive and Cultural History.* New Brunswick: Rutgers University Press.

Suddaby, R. (2006). "From the Editors: What Grounded Theory is Not," *Academy of Management Journal,* 49: 633–42.

13

Analyzing and Interpreting Historical Sources: A Basic Methodology

Matthias Kipping, R. Daniel Wadhwani, and Marcelo Bucheli

This chapter proposes a basic methodology for studying organizations and organizational fields using historical sources. It is intended primarily for scholars interested in publishing historical research in management and organization journals. However, we also hope to provide those publishing in business and management history journals with tools and language to explicitly describe their underlying methodology.

There has been a surge of interest in historical research in organization studies, which, as Leblebici (in this volume) shows, has translated into a growing number of articles in leading organizational journals that engage historical or longitudinal evidence (see also Kieser and Üsdiken, 2004). Among the broad range of issues of theoretical relevance that have prompted management and organization scholars to engage with historical time and context—and to use historical evidence—one can find, for instance, the study of organizational processes (Langley, 1999; Pettigrew et al., 2001), evolutionary dynamics (Lippmann and Aldrich, this volume), institutional fields and mechanisms (Davis and Marquis, 2005), as well as meanings (Suddaby, 2010). Articles based on historical studies of companies or industries have also occasionally been published in the *Strategic Management Journal* (e.g., Tripsas, 1997; Rosenbloom, 2000; Danneels, 2011; see also Kahl et al., 2012). At the same time, business historians have increasingly used their research to engage with debates in organization and management theory (see Kipping and Üsdiken, 2007; Wadhwani and Bucheli, this volume).

Despite the growing interest in incorporating historical research in organization studies, little attention has been devoted to *how* this research should be conducted. Although there is a long-established tradition of qualitative social research (Yates, this volume), there is wide variation in what organization and management articles consider historical research (see Appendix 3.2 in Leblebici, this volume). At the same time, historians tend to confine their discussions of sources and prior research to footnotes and tend to not explicitly discuss their methods for others to follow. The lack of such explicit discussion of methodology within historical research, in turn, tends to limit the publishability of history in management and organizational journals, where explanation of data and methods are standard practice (Decker, 2013). Thus, as Berg and Lune (2012: 306) note, historical methodology had until very recently been "omitted" by most research methods manuals, or, even worse, "mentioned only in terms of its possible threat to internal validity . . . or its effect on construct validity." This stands in clear contrast to other qualitative approaches such as "ethnography" and "action research," which have been able to explain their methodologies and become accepted as legitimate approaches to organizational research.

One of the main methodological challenges in employing historical approaches to studying organizations lies in the nature of historical sources. As Lipartito (in this volume) points out, historical sources are fragments or traces of evidence from the past rather than a set of systematic observations made by the researcher. Even when sources do seem to present systematic information, questions arise about why that particular evidence was initially collected, how it compares to other sources of information on the same phenomena, and why it has been preserved. Even in the impossible scenario where a "perfect" record of the past did exist, researchers would face the challenge of understanding the motives and meanings of actors and actions in the past in ways that avoid imposing assumptions and categories from the present (see also Berg and Lune, 2012: 307–8). To address these issues this chapter proposes a basic methodology for studying organizations and organizational fields based on such historical sources. We draw on *both* the extant practice in the social science literature and the methodological apparatus of historical research in explaining this methodology.

The remainder of the chapter consists of two main sections. The first section reviews how organizational scholars (mainly in some prominent methods handbooks) and historians have addressed the challenges involved in using historical sources. We try to show that both of these have made certain contributions but that neither has gone far enough in developing a methodological process for interpreting historical sources when studying organizations and organizational fields. The second section outlines such a methodology, which combines source criticism, triangulation, and hermeneutic interpretation. We discuss each of these elements in some detail and provide illustrative examples of how each has been applied in extant studies to address research questions in management and organizational studies. A brief conclusion summarizes the contributions and limitations of the chapter and calls for further discussion of historical methods in organization studies and business history.

HISTORICAL METHODOLOGY IN
MANAGEMENT AND ORGANIZATION
STUDIES: A REVIEW

Limited Suggestions in the Extant Methods Literature

Trying to gain an overview of how historical methodology is defined in management and organizational studies is not easy. The predominant usage of the word "history" in the main journals in the field is actually as part of "event history analysis," which is a fairly widely used statistical technique to analyze the probability of an "event," defined as a discrete change from one state to another, as the dependent variable (Castilla, 2007: ch. 3)—and hence unrelated to the methodology proposed here. But even when it comes to the growing number of articles using historical sources and archives, many of them, as Leblebici (in this volume) points out, avoid explicitly characterizing their research as "history." And, as has been noted earlier, most books dealing with research methods in the social sciences do not make any reference to historical methodology either. Thus, for instance, *The SAGE Handbook of Social Research Methods* (Alasuutari et al., 2008) does not contain a chapter on historical methods and does not even refer to it in the index. The temporal dimension is covered in a chapter on longitudinal and panel research, which deals, however, largely with quantitative data and includes "event history" as one of the specific methods. The only relevant chapter in *The SAGE Handbook of Organizational Research Methods* (Buchanan and Bryman 2009) is one on "Archival Research in Organizations in a Digital Age," which focuses mainly on the preservation of digital records (Moss, 2009).

There is, however, a discussion of historical methods, covering several pages, in a chapter on researching institutional change by Suddaby and Greenwood (2009: 183–7). The authors highlight that these methods have "three distinctive advantages over multivariate and interpretive approaches": attention to process, that is, the consideration of multiple, often messy causes; path dependency, that is, the recognition that past decisions constrain current choices; and social construction, that is, the ability to more easily strip current institutional arrangements of their taken-for-grantedness by identifying their historical origins. At the same time, they remain relatively silent on how to conduct these studies, pointing to the multiplicity and variety of "historical research techniques" (with a reference to Ventresca and Mohr, 2002) and the care taken by historians in identifying the underlying interests when examining sources (with a reference to Carr, 1961).

A similar lack of detail is notable when it comes to widely cited books providing toolkits for qualitative researchers, whether it is *Qualitative Data Analysis* (Miles and Huberman, 1994) or *Case Study Research* (Yin, 2013). While the former does not make any mention of historical analysis, the latter characterizes "archival analysis," "history," and "case study" (in addition to "survey" and "experiment") as distinct methods. "History" is portrayed as similar to case studies in terms of its research questions (how? and why?), but with a focus on past rather than contemporary events.

A few others do give a more prominent place to history, but—on the whole—also provide limited practical guidance for conducting such studies. Thus, Stinchcombe (2005), long a proponent of a historical perspective in organizational studies (see in particular his earlier work on foundation conditions, Stinchcombe, 1965; Lounsbury and Ventresca, 2002), makes a strong case for historical research as one of "the four main methods of addressing causal questions in social science"—the others being quantitative, ethnographic, and experimental. In particular, he sees it as the most appropriate way "to study sequences of conditions, actions, and effects that have happened in natural settings, in sufficient detail to get signs of sequences that are causally connected" (Stinchcombe, 2005: 5). While this gives history a prominent place, he remains relatively vague about how it should be studied other than pointing to the need for the "penetration of the details of processes and sequences" (referring to Bearman et al.'s (1999) graphic representation of events in narrative life stories as *one* relevant method, albeit without mentioning others) and, more importantly, using a number of examples for the comparative analysis of various contexts (Stinchcombe, 2005: 230–8; see also Eisenhardt, 1989, 1991).

Berg and Lune (2012), who highlight the marginal position of historical research among the acceptable qualitative methods in the social sciences, also give it a more prominent and explicit place in their own textbook. Quite tellingly, they start their discussion of "What is Historical Research?" by stating what it is *not*, that is, "retelling of facts from the past" or "creative nostalgia," before eventually defining it as entailing "a process that examines events or combinations of events in order to uncover accounts of what happened in the past" (p. 306)—a description that even many historians would not agree with (see, e.g., Carr, 1961) and that seems unlikely to endear it to organizational researchers who emphasize social construction (see for instance Suddaby and Greenwood, 2009).

In terms of methodology proper, it is significant and telling that Berg and Lune (2012) pair their chapter on social historical research with "oral traditions," while they confine the analysis of archival records, which have much more importance in historical research than oral history (see Lipartito, in this volume) to a different chapter dealing with "unobtrusive measures," albeit largely limiting their contribution to an overview of the wide variety of archives available. They ultimately note that "researchers should be cautious in the use of archival data" without providing an exact reason for this warning, but suggesting that scholars "use multiple procedures (triangulation) when working with archival data in order to reduce possible sources of error (missing data, etc.)" (Berg and Lune, 2012: 283–96; quotes p. 296;

for a detailed discussion of triangulation see pp. 316–9, this volume). They also provide a typology of the data used by social historians, distinguishing primary sources (produced by eyewitnesses); secondary sources (from those "not immediately present"); and tertiary sources (which involve a distillation or condensation of the former). They then elaborate on what they refer to as "external" and "internal" criticism of these sources in order to determine, respectively, their genuineness and meaning (pp. 309–17; see our discussion of source criticism).

A detailed discussion of archival documentation and analysis can also be found in Ventresca and Mohr (2002). They contrast "historiographic," "eco-logical," and "new archivalist" modes of analyzing archival data and clearly favor the latter, since it combines more rigorous, quantitative approaches with the "key sensibilities of the historiographic approach," in terms of "exploring the nuanced, meaning-laden, action-oriented foundations of organizational processes" (p. 810). However, as Lipartito (in this volume) shows, much of the available archival data does not lend itself to the kind of systematic, quan-titative analysis necessary for the techniques of the "new archivalism" or for population ecology or, similarly, for so-called cliometric history, conducted in particular by the "new" economic historians (for a summary and critique of the latter see in particular Boldizzoni, 2011). Ventresca and Mohr (2002) recog-nize these problems, but the guidance they provide is rather limited: "the care-ful and detailed scrutiny of the archival materials," where "the researcher reads through large amounts of archival information (often from un-standardized sources) in a disciplined fashion as a way to gain insights, make discoveries and generate informed judgments about the character of historical events and processes" (pp. 814–15).

Specific suggestions of how to deal with company archives are made in a short essay by Rowlinson (2004) in another handbook on qualitative organiza-tional research. He first addresses a number of misconceptions about the use of archival documents in organizational studies, including that "archival research is not a proper method of empirical organizational research because instead of being directly generated in the course of organizational research, historical data is merely collected" (p. 302) and then recounts his own experience as a researcher "poring over documents in the Cadbury library" as part of a larger project examining changes in the work organization of the British company (p. 303). He describes in detail how he decided which documents to consult among the large number contained in the archives (i.e., those related to the topic of the research project) and the "procedure" he used to identify them: "to flick through the pages [of various minutes] trying to spot any item of interest" (p. 305). He characterizes the notes or photocopies taken of these documents as his "data," "generated in the craft-like fashion of a historian" (p. 305) and has subsequently used them to address other research questions using a pro-cedure he describes as similar to "coding for interviews" ("to identify themes and connections between the events recorded"), albeit made more difficult by the variety of different sources (pp. 307–8).

Rowlinson (2004: 308–9) also discusses the differences between company documents intended for public consumption and those meant to remain confidential, as well as the bias towards the view from the top ("senior management"). In general, he emphasizes the problem of studying everyday life in the organization, given the absence of documents recording the personal experiences and feelings of its members, be they workers or board members. Finally, he contrasts the way historians interpret the data and construct their narrative with similar endeavors by other qualitative researchers, that is, ethnographers, highlighting that the former stress singularity while the latter insist on typicality. In his view, this explains the extensive use of footnotes in historical writing ("it is in the footnotes that the nature and interpretation of the evidence is laid out") and the use of "stylization" and even "fictionalization" by organizational ethnographers, intent on demonstrating the generalizability of their findings (Rowlinson, 2004: 308–9).

Thus, while—in part—recognizing the value of historical research, the extant social science literature offers a rather limited, piecemeal approach to address the challenges resulting from the nature of historical sources. Consequently, there is little clear guidance on how to analyze and interpret this kind of evidence in order to generate valid and reliable insights for the study of organizations and organizational fields. It should therefore not be surprising that the growing use of historical sources and contexts in organizational research seems to have taken place applying widely varying approaches and techniques for analysis and interpretation. To some extent, such methodological variation is reasonable and healthy. But, it also limits a broader use of incomplete sources from a temporally distant past in organizational research and the publication of its results in management journals.

History as an "Opaque" Craft

Unfortunately, historical scholarship typically provides little explicit explanation or guidance on the methods used (cf. Chandler, 1962). Reflective historians are well aware of this practice. As the philosopher of history, Hayden White (1995: 243), explains, "history is rather a craftlike discipline, which means that it tends to be governed by convention and custom rather than by methodology and theory and to utilize ordinary or natural languages for the description of its objects of study and representation of the historian's thought about those objects" (here quoted from Rowlinson, 2004; see also Evans, 2001: 66 and, for the description of history as a "craft" by the influential American historian Bernard Bailyn, Ekirch, 1994). In his treatise on "how historians map the past," historian John Lewis Gaddis (2002: XI), who would otherwise agree with little of White's view of history, makes a similar observation: "We recoil from the notion that our writing should replicate, say, the design of the Pompidou Center in Paris, which proudly places its escalators, plumbing, wiring and ductwork on the *outside* of the building, so that they're there for all to see." This lack of explicit discussion of methods, however, creates a significant barrier to interdisciplinary discourse between history and organization studies. As Decker (2013: 2) points out, the "issue is that historians are not explaining their methodology, and in fact are missing a language and a format to do so that are compatible with the approach in social sciences."

The conventions of historical writing and presentation mask what is, in fact, a well-established methodological tradition of thought and practice on the nature of historical sources and how to analyze and interpret them. As an academic discipline, history in fact owes its very origins to methodological concerns about the nature of sources and how to use them to make valid and credible claims about the past (Novick, 1988). The 19th-century scholars who moved history into the academy were particularly concerned about establishing a methodology akin to the scientific method, that would make history "objective" by establishing rules and procedures for the treatment and analysis of sources. This effort to develop history as a "human science" included the development of methods for understanding and reconstructing the perspective of historical actors, in addition to procedures for rigorous examination of sources (Dilthey, 2002 [1910]).

Though scholars in the 20th century raised appropriate doubts about the possibility of achieving perfect historical objectivity (Gadamer, 1975), methods for critiquing and using historical sources remained central in defining the differences between sound and unsound scholarship (Bloch, 1954 [1946]; Carr, 1961; Gottschalk, 1950). Indeed, explanations of historical methodology became *more* sensitive to a number of problems involved in the use and interpretation of sources, including issues related to language and discourse (Appleby et al., 1995: 207–23), the role of power in silencing some voices from the past (Said, 1991; Spivak, 1988), and the interpreter's perspective (Gadamer, 1975) in the identification and analysis of sources. These issues are now central to methodological debates and discussions in the discipline (for summaries, see Howell and Prevenier, 2001; Donnelly and Norton, 2011).

More importantly, beyond the philosophical debates and treatises on analyzing sources in the discipline, historians have developed new practices for dealing with sources as they incorporated new types of evidence and interpretive challenges into the historiographical tradition. The evolution of academic history from a discipline focused on the political past to one encompassing economic, social, cultural, and even natural phenomena has led to encounters with new types of sources and new analytical and interpretive techniques (Appleby et al., 1995; Howell and Prevenier, 2001). Hence, behind what appears to be disinterest by historians in explicit discussions of methodology lies what is in fact a vibrant and evolving body of methodological thought and practice focused on the analysis and interpretation of sources.

In the subsequent section of the chapter, we will draw on these practices, together with relevant suggestions in the social sciences literature already outlined, to propose a basic methodology to study organizations and organizational fields using historical sources.

ELEMENTS OF BASIC HISTORICAL METHODOLOGY IN ORGANIZATION STUDIES

The proposed methodology is designed for the analysis of historical texts. We define such texts broadly to include a wide range of written documents, the spoken word, as well as artifacts that constitute traces of the past. In some regards, the methodological issues of source analysis in history are similar to the methodological issues already well examined by text and discourse analysis in organization studies (highlighted for instance by Rowlinson, 2004; see also, for the widely used "discourse analysis," Phillips and Oswick, 2012). However, the nature of historical sources raises a number of specific issues related to their analysis and interpretation. First, sources are not direct observations of action, and certainly do not provide comprehensive or controlled evidence on the subject under consideration. Second, sources are typically fragments or incomplete accounts that were produced by authors with personal or institutional perspectives that may not be readily apparent. And third, sources from the past may have been produced in cultural and social contexts very different from our own that need to be taken into account in their interpretation.

The basic methodology we describe in what follows draws on both the historiographical tradition and qualitative methods in organization studies to propose a set of analytical and interpretive processes for addressing the issues already mentioned. Specifically, the methodology involves a number of elements, viz. (i) the critique of each text to determine its external as well as internal validity; (ii) a triangulation of various sources to reduce bias and increase confidence in the robustness of the research results; and (iii) an iterative process (often referred to as the "hermeneutic circle"), which situates texts within their historical contexts and in relation to other texts. We will describe and illustrate each of these elements in the following. It is important to note here that these elements should not be taken as a set of discrete or sequential steps. The analysis of historical sources is usually characterized by an iterative use of these elements in both inductive and deductive reasoning that fits together evidence and interpretation.

Source Criticism

Both historians and organization scholars turn to historical sources to address research questions or working hypotheses they may have about a phenomenon or theory (see Lipartito, in this volume, for a description of different types of sources). Unlike most of the data used in the social sciences historical sources were not originally created by researchers (through say questionnaires, interviews, or observation) for addressing the research question at hand. Rather, they were created by actors driven by agendas determined by a context that differs from the one of the researcher. Moreover, most of these sources tend to be incomplete or have a biased survival rate. The incompleteness and temporal remoteness of historical sources as well as the fact that they were produced in conditions beyond the control of the researcher creates a methodological concern for understanding the circumstances surrounding their production and has led historians to develop practices for critiquing their use and abuse (Bunzl, 1997; Novick, 1988). Source criticism constitutes one key element of historical methodology and consists of an attempt to establish their validity (through external source criticism) and their credibility (through internal source criticism) (see also Berg and Lune, 2012: 312–17) as well as expectations about source transparency in their relation to the question at hand. We will address each of these in turn, providing illustrations of how they have been addressed in exemplary organizational research.

First, researchers need to establish the *validity* of a source by analyzing the circumstances surrounding its production and preservation. A source's validity establishes its authenticity and pertinence for the research question at hand. This is of crucial importance for historical research on earlier periods, where both the authenticity and authorship of a source is often in doubt (Howell and Prevenier, 2001: 60–8). But even for more recent historical sources it remains important to examine (a) the provenance of a source, including identifying the author of a text or an artifact as well as the time and place it was actually produced; (b) its intended audience and purpose; and (c) the context under which it was written (Donnelly and Norton, 2011).

Incidentally, these concerns help explain the relative preference of historical research for printed rather than oral sources, given that the former allow a researcher to better isolate the circumstances surrounding the production of a source (Donnelly and Norton, 2011). By contrast, historians tend to shy away from the latter—except for purposes of triangulation (see pp. 316–9, this volume)—since the poor memory and cognitive biases of respondents often result in retrospective biases (Golden, 1992; Kirby, 2008). It should be noted here, however, that there is a long tradition of oral history, which has attempted to give voice to those whose position is not reflected in written records (Thompson, 2000).

Analyzing the validity of a source requires attention not only to the *individual* motives surrounding its production, but also to the *institutional* setting in which it was produced. This is particularly important in the context of corporate or organizational records, which are presumed to reflect not only the interests and views of the individual producing them, but of the organizational structure and culture of which they were part. Many organizational sources—such as memoranda, minutes, newsletters, or even contracts—are not solitary documents but part of a communication genre and understanding their validity requires situating them as part of their institutional, organizational, or communicative category (Yates, 1989; Yates and Orlikowski, 1992; Orlikowski and Yates, 1994).

A good example for an extensive discussion of the validity of a source can be found in the study by Arndt and Bigelow (2005) of the shift in hospital administration from female dominated in the late 19th and early 20th century to male dominated by the 1950s. This study sheds light on how gender occupational boundaries were created and changed over time and argues that professional associations played an important role in defining these boundaries. The researchers focus their attention on the American Hospital Association (AHA) and particularly its trade journal *Modern Hospital* as their main source. In order to establish the validity of *Modern Hospital* as a source to use to answer their research question, Arndt and Bigelow discuss, at length, who authored the magazine and the purpose of writing it. For instance, they highlight that it was "founded in 1913," "targeted hospital superintendents and trustees," and "represented the voice of the American Hospital Association's leadership." They also stress that "the leaders of the American Hospital Association had control over its content" (Arndt and Bigelow, 2005: 237–8). They even describe the positions the individual members of the editorial board of *Modern Hospital* had at the time and how that could have affected the qualitative and quantitative information provided by the journal. Establishing the source's validity as a voice of the AHA allows them to convincingly argue that the association was behind the application of "scientific" management thought to hospital administration, which led to a change in the perception of hospital administration from a "sentimental" profession that required caring and loving individuals (characteristics in those times associated with women) toward a perception of this profession as "scientific" and therefore requiring cold analytical thinking (which was associated with men).

Secondly, source criticism is used to establish the *credibility* of a source, which involves assessing a source's trustworthiness or reliability in addressing the researcher's question. A basic principle here is that sources that are closer to the event or action being explained can be considered more credible than sources that are further removed or that relay the content from other sources that were "more primary" in their position vis-à-vis the event under consideration. In this sense, the primacy of a source depends on its relationship to what the researcher is trying to explain. This principle highlights, again, that historical research does not allow direct observation of action or behavior in the past and so researchers have to consider how to weigh the credibility of evidence presented in the sources. Eyewitness accounts are hence preferred over secondhand ones.

For similar reasons, source criticism places heavy emphasis on the question of authorial authority and perspective—the extent to which the producer of a source can be thought of as trustworthy and capable of speaking to the issue at hand. Do they have the competency to address the issue or development of concern? Do they have a reason to shape impressions or hide facts? What are likely to be their biases? Do they have a regular pattern of dependably reporting on the events or developments (Donnelly and Norton, 2011; Howell and Prevenier, 2001)?

Historical method typically places emphasis on weighing the intentionality of the author in producing a source as one way of assessing credibility. Sources that unintentionally convey information are typically considered more reliable because the author has not tried to actively shape the information that is being conveyed about the event. For instance, using a firm's public relations material about labor relations to chronicle its dealings with unions is often seen as less credible because the authors' intention suggests an interest in carefully shaping and framing the information conveyed while "silencing" other information and perspectives.

An example of the examination of source credibility can be found in King and Soule's (2007) study of the effects of anti-corporate political activism on firms' stock prices for the 1962–1990 period in the US. The authors use the *New York Times* as their main source for identifying protest movements targeted at companies. The authors explain the *Times*' position vis-à-vis the events they sought to identify, stating that "because the major financial exchanges are in New York City, the *New York Times* is ideally positioned to cover protests of business corporations." Moreover, they explain why the source is less likely to be subject to selection and description biases than other sources by comparing the *Times*' coverage of protests to that of the *Wall Street Journal* and the *Washington Post* for shorter periods of time. They note that the *Times* is not only more comprehensive than these other newspapers in its coverage of protests but is also more prompt, making it a credible source by which to examine how information about protests is conveyed and, in turn, affects stock price (King and Soule, 2005: 422–4).

Finally, as in any scientific endeavor, research based on historical sources needs to be verifiable (Gaddis, 2002). Historical scholarship is thus typically expected to practice *source transparency*, linking claims and evidence back to specific sources and documents. This explains the extensive use of footnotes in historical writing, noted earlier. It is here where authors describe a particular source in detail, providing information on the document itself and also where it is located. For a primary source, for instance, this would include the name of the person or organization writing the document, the date it was written, and those it was intended for, but also the name of the archive, the box in which the file is located, and, if available, the file number.

The expectation of source transparency makes it difficult to preserve confidentiality/anonymity, as might be required for the more contemporary sources and information used in organizational scholarship. A respect for such requirements tends to already be embedded in the rules governing the use of historical archives, to which a researcher normally has to consent before being allowed access. This does not exclude that in exceptional circumstances the name of the organization where the historical research was undertaken (or of certain informants, for instance, those that were interviewed) might be anonymized.

A good example of a study that provides source transparency is the work by Kalev et al. (2008) on the joint productivity councils established in Palestine before 1948 and their changing role after the creation of the state of Israel. Their study relies heavily on archival sources to show how the idea of the role of these councils changed from being considered useless during the British rule of Palestine, to becoming an integral part of Israel's economic policies aimed at modernizing the country's economy. The authors consider particular letters and memos as crucial for showing this transition and therefore cite them in footnotes, while at the same time using the standard social science citation system for the rest of their references. In this way, they manage to exploit a wealth of primary sources, citing them for other researchers to consult, while conforming to the type of citation required in management journals.

Ultimately, then, source criticism is designed to allow researchers to understand not just what a source tells us about a development or topic of interest, but also the *limits* of relying on that particular source. To overcome those limits, scholars using historical sources have to rely on additional analytical and interpretive procedures, which we detail in the following.

Triangulation

This term originally refers to techniques in geometry, surveying, and so on to determine the location of an unknown point from known points or known points and distances. In the social sciences, where there is a long tradition of "triangulation" (see, e.g., Berg and Lune, 2012: 6; Denzin, 2010), it is generally seen as a way to cross check and, ultimately, corroborate and validate results. Today the term is often used synonymously with "mixed methods," which in turn usually implies a combination of quantitative with qualitative methods (e.g., Buchanan and Bryman, 2009a: 9; Jick, 1979; Miles and Huberman, 1994: 40–3), with some debate about the priority or at least order in which they should be employed. There are, however, some who advocate a broader use of this term and the underlying techniques. In particular Denzin (1970, 1978; here as summarized by Berg and Lune, 2012: 6–7; Bryman, 2004) suggests that triangulation can take place along four "lines of action," involving the use of multiple data (from different sources); multiple investigators (with different researchers gathering and analyzing data independently); multiple theories (applying different perspectives to the same object of study); and multiple methods (which includes combining quantitative and qualitative methods and/or different qualitative methods such as participant observation, interviews, document and text analysis).

The type of triangulation normally applied by historians is the use of multiple data: "Typically, historians do not rely on just one source to study an event or a historical process, but on many, and they construct their own interpretations about the past by means of comparison among sources" (Howell and Prevenier, 2001: 69). This can involve a combination of qualitative and quantitative sources, like the ones used by Vikström (2010) in her examination of women's occupations in the 19th century. The author actually highlights the gender bias in one of these sources—population registers—which she uncovered by triangulating it with qualitative evidence. More common is the combination of different qualitative methods, namely the analysis of archival documentation with interviews. However, as noted by Rowlinson (2004: 305–6) and already explained, historians would put more credence into the former whereas social scientists tend to do the opposite. For instance, in a study of the origins of European integration, a respondent insisted that he had favored the creation of competitive markets, even if his internal memoranda from the time clearly showed the intention to create Europe-wide producer cartels (Kipping, 2002). Most often in historical studies, triangulation would involve looking at different sources, for example, an internal memorandum compared with say an external communication.

Thus, whereas social scientific approaches to the past often search out and value data sources that provide consistent observations about a phenomenon of interest in order to identify and test hypotheses, historical triangulation actually values sources that are different/heterogenous because of the interpretive procedure involved and the aim of avoiding the bias of any one authoritative source, however consistent it may be. There are several reasons for this. First, multiplicity and variety of sources are often a necessity, especially with research examining long-term developments. Here a trade-off has to be made between the time period covered, which increases the chances of identifying continuity and change, and the consistency of the available sources, which tends to decrease, because organizations change the kind of documentation they generate and retain. In these cases, it is crucial to consult various types of overlapping sources that can both complement and corroborate each other.

Second and more importantly, it is actually crucial for historical researchers to use various types of texts to overcome the limits that source criticism identifies about any one source. Sources produced by different authors with different motives and perspectives on the development of interest hence constitute a critical part of historical research procedures for overcoming the limitations identified for a particular source. For instance, to understand the extent to which management education became "Americanized" after World War II requires recourse to sources examining the various actors involved both from the United States and the recipient countries—otherwise one might easily adopt a sender-only perspective, which as various studies have shown would be overly simplistic and mistaken (for a summary Kipping and Üsdiken, 2009).

The reliance of historical interpretation on multiple sources and triangulation procedures is also reflected in how primary and secondary sources are integrated in the process of interpretation and analysis. Whereas both quantitative and qualitative organization studies research tends to limit the use of secondary literature in the interpretation process to the theoretical setup for a study or the post-analysis interpretation of a study's findings, historical interpretation often integrates secondary sources into the analysis and interpretation process itself (Lipartito, this volume). While recognizing the particular weaknesses of secondary sources in their historical "distance" from the development or phenomenon under consideration, the historical procedure of using heterogeneous sources in order to triangulate means that secondary literature can often serve as a "data point" in the interpretation and analysis process—albeit one that requires a particularly critical and careful interpretation (Donnelly and Norton, 2011; see also Berg and Lune, 2012: 316–17). Given the incompleteness of historical sources, the use of secondary sources in this process can be seen as a matter of convenience as well as a matter of methodological adherence to source heterogeneity.

Finally, it is important to understand that triangulation of historical sources is not only used to corroborate evidence; it is often most useful in instances where sources contradict each other. For instance, as Vikström (2010: 212) notes with respect to the "dissonant data" she found in her study on the occupations of 19th-century women such contradictions can be "beneficial in the questioning that it engenders for the gaining, viewing and analysis of knowledge." Confronted with such research results, organizational scholars might take another page from the playbook of historical methodology and be somewhat more assertive—albeit always justifying their choices explicitly: "Sometimes the information they have from various sources is contradictory, sometimes mutually confirming, but the historian's job in any case is to decide which accounts he or she will use, and why" (Howell and Prevenier, 2001: 69).

Following are selected examples for the application of triangulation to reduce bias and corroborate results among the historical studies of organizations and organizational fields. Thus, in her work on the effects of corporate identity in generating resistance to technological change Tripsas (2009: 444–6) explicitly applies triangulation to address potential bias, also generated by the fact that she had formerly been a board member of the company in question, Linco, which made flash memory cards for digital cameras. She actually uses different methods: semi-structured interviews, participant observation, and an analysis of written documentation. The latter consist of three types of sources: (i) the confidential, internal archives of the company, providing insights into how a variety of insiders viewed the organization; (ii) documents addressed towards the outside, such as business plans or SEC filings, showing the kind of identity it tried to project; and (iii) documents generated by observers such as reports by analysts or the media, revealing how outsiders viewed the company. Triangulation of methods and sources thus allows her to compare different perspectives and increase the overall validity of her findings.

An even wider range of sources, combining qualitative and quantitative data, internal archives, published company documents, and external reports, as well as interviews, can be found in a study examining the role of cognition and path dependence on shifts in competitive advantage among the four dominant Finnish retailers between 1945 and 1995 (Lamberg and Tikkanen, 2006). The wide variety of sources not only allows corroboration of the results, but also helps the authors examine the complex interplay between developments in society, technology, and the firms' strategic decisions. Nevertheless, the authors highlight the particular importance of the confidential company records, which should not come as a surprise, given that one of them was trained as a historian: "This archival material lacks the retrospective bias of interview data and was central in the reconstruction of the decision-making criteria underpinning strategic behavior" (pp. 821–2; see also Rowlinson, 2004: 306).

Using almost the whole array of triangulation as laid out by Denzin is the study of changing organizational forms among management consulting firms in the UK by Kipping and Kirkpatrick (2013). While relying on the confidential archives of the industry's main trade association as the main source, which contains statistical data, internal minutes, and a variety of other documentation, they supplement this with material from select consulting firms, published reports by industry observers, secondary sources, both contemporaneous and contemporary, as well as a number of interviews (which can be considered methods of triangulation). They also use investigator triangulation (examining some of the potentially more biased documentation independently) and, one might argue, theoretical triangulation considering alternative readings of the evidence (mainly from the sociology of professions and neo-institutionalism). This combination allows them to cover a significantly longer time period (more than half a century) than comparable studies of other professional service firms and to advance an alternative account of what drives the changes in the modes of organizing among these firms.

Hermeneutic Interpretation

The challenge of analyzing fragmented and incomplete historical sources is further complicated by the problem of interpreting them in the social, cultural, and historical contexts in which they were produced. While there are some traditions of historical scholarship that assume actors in the past thought and acted in essentially economically or socially functional ways, the predominant stance in academic historical research is that the use of historical perspective requires efforts to understand historical actors and sources in their own context—with interests, identities, mentality, and actions shaped by their place in historical time (Dilthey, 2002 [1910]; Collingwood, 1946).

To use the language of organization studies, historical research usually requires researchers to understand historical actors' own ways of sensemaking and sensegiving in order to analyze the sources they produced. To fail to interpret the meaning of sources from the actor's point of view and in their contexts risks imposing categories and methods of thought from the present onto the past that distort our understanding of the event or action. Reconstructing the meaning of historical sources thus requires the procedure of historically contextualizing the source and reading it empathetically. The body of theory that most closely describes the procedure of historical interpretation through contextualization is hermeneutics (Grondin, 1994), a philosophical tradition associated with historicism that deals with the interpretation of the meaning of texts.

At its most basic level, hermeneutics is a theory of textual interpretation that posits that the meaning of language and texts arises through their relationship to the contexts in which they are interpreted. Specific texts, or parts of texts, therefore need to be understood in relationship to contexts and vice versa. The meaning of a text, therefore, can only be derived by moving back and forth between a text and the contexts in which they are understood. This back and forth between text and context forms what is referred to as the "hermeneutic circle" through which interpretations arise (Grondin, 1994; McAuley, 2004; Alvesson and Skoldberg, 2009). Hermeneutics is one of the bodies of theory and methods that organizational scholars have used to interpret organizational texts within their cultural settings and to critically analyze the intent of authors (McAuley, 2004).

Phillips and Brown (1993: 1547), for instance, used a critical hermeneutic approach to study corporate advertising campaigns to show how companies sought to "create and disseminate cultural forms that support preferred patterns of power and dominance." Similarly, Prasad and Mir (2002: 92) used a critical hermeneutic approach to analyze the texts of letters from oil industry executives to shareholders and "juxtaposed them against the 'context' of key historical events" during the turbulent 1970s and 1980s to show how they sought to deflect the crisis of legitimacy they faced from OPEC. Heracleous and Barrett (2001) draw on hermeneutic theory along with rhetorical theory to explore the role of discourse in shaping organizational change. Thus, within organization studies, attention to hermeneutic theory and methods of interpretation is associated most closely with approaches to discourse analysis (Phillips and Oswick, 2012) that are attentive to the context within which texts are interpreted.

In historical research, hermeneutic theory has been influential in explaining and accounting for the researcher's task of understanding and interpreting sources in the historical contexts in which they were produced (Howell and Prevenier, 2001; Ricoeur, 2004). In practice, this is done by interpreting a primary source in relationship to other sources that establish the context for its interpretation, and by using this context to try to understand the author's intention or point of view in producing the source. Historians sometimes refer to this as reconstructing the "voice" of the source (Decker, 2013; Evans, 2000). Secondary sources, in this regard, play an important role in guiding a researcher in identifying the historical contexts within which to interpret a historical source. Understanding the minutes of a corporate broad, for instance, may be facilitated by contextualizing them within what other scholars have explained about the forces shaping the industry at the time the minutes were produced. But, original historical research typically also involves establishing context by understanding a particular source's relationship to other primary sources through an iterative process of moving back and forth between the focal source and other primary sources that situate the source in different, often progressively broader, ways. In this regard, hermeneutic interpretation is related to triangulation (as well as to the discourse analytic notion of intertextuality) because the latter's emphasis on the use of multiple, heterogeneous sources in research helps establish a broader context for the analysis of any one particular primary source.

Khaire and Wadhwani's (2010) study of the emergence of modern Indian art as a market category provides an illustration of the use of hermeneutic processes in the interpretation of sources. The authors study how Indian art emerged from an indistinct form of provincial art to a distinct category in the international art market in the late 20th century, and the implications of this categorization for how the art was valued. They use a series of auction market catalogues covering the period of change as their focal primary sources, but interpret these sources within a series of broader contexts represented by other bodies of sources. These other contexts (which include the market for Indian art, the literature on Indian art history and criticism, and the development of "modern art" over the course of the 20th century) were established by moving outward from the primary source to a set of progressively broader contexts to which the previous sources referred. By placing art market catalogues within these broader contexts, the authors are able to show that the primary source reflected changing understandings of modernism in the late 20th century.

Challenges to the identity of modernism's uniquely Western identity by art historians and critics laid the foundations for the way in which Indian art was understood and appreciated. Over time, auction catalogues, they show, drew on and reflected these changes in how they described the art and how they explained its aesthetic and economic value.

Khaire and Wadhwani's article also shows that hermeneutic interpretation of sources is attentive not only to the cultural and social context in which a source is produced but also to its temporal embeddedness—that is, to the contexts of what came before and after a source was produced as relevant to its interpretation. Hence, they analyze changes in art market catalogues in the late 20th century in the context of the development of "modern art" much earlier in the century as well as from the point of view of the naturalization and institutionalization of the category in the years that followed.

In recent decades, both hermeneutic theory and historical practice have devoted increasing attention to the historical consciousness and the situated perspective of researchers themselves, and the constraints these place on one's ability to reconstruct the past in a way that is not mediated by one's own time and experience (Gadamer, 1975). While such issues are less problematic in the investigation of more recent histories, such as the one presented by Khaire and Wadhwani, they come into sharper focus when researchers attempt to reconstruct meaning from sources in more temporally and contextually distant settings. In such contexts, research that attempts to "understand" sources is shaped not only by the context in which the source was created but also by subsequent developments, including the historical researcher's own historical embeddedness in the present. In this sense, modern hermeneutic theory takes into account the notion that historical perspective on a given subject is not entirely fixed and objective, but rather inherently shaped by a researcher's view of the past from his/her position in the present. Such temporal distance, however, has its benefits as well as its constraints in achieving understanding of a subject that more recent histories and contemporary perspectives cannot achieve. In particular, a critical awareness of how one's position in time shapes understanding offers a way to understand and contextualize seemingly settled ideas in the present and to "deconstruct" accepted stories from the past.

The recent body of historical research on the Hawthorne Studies by organization scholars, particularly Hassard's (2012) account, illustrates how awareness of one's historical perspective is taken into account in the process of hermeneutic interpretation of primary sources. The Hawthorne Studies were conducted in the 1920s and quickly came to be understood as a turning point in labor-management relations by establishing scientific evidence in favor of a "human relations" perspective, which challenged and eventually overturned the principles of F. W. Taylor's system of scientific management. Contributing to recent critical re-evaluations of the motives and impact of the Hawthorne Studies (Gillespie, 1991; O'Connor, 1999; Bruce and Nyland, 2011), Hassard

(2012) questions the accepted view by contextualizing the sources in two new ways: the corporate context of Western Electric, as the site of the studies, and the cultural context "through an examination of its social organization and communal experience." Though he does not use the term, Hassard employs an essentially hermeneutic approach in explaining that his methods were focused on developing a sense of " 'prior context,' or considering the 'parts that imme- diately precede' an event or era and which serve to 'clarify its meaning.' "

These contexts show that the Hawthorne Studies did not represent a major shift in perspective on labor-management relations, but rather reconfirmed a shift toward welfare capitalism that firms like Western Electric had already embraced in response to the social and ethnic background of their labor force and as part of corporate strategy and reputation. "Contrary to the orthodox narrative of management and organization studies, which suggests a theoreti- cal and practical paradigm-shift in the wake of behavioural experimentation," Hassard explains, "the impression from this research is that Mayo and his team *did not so much turn the sociological tide at Hawthorne as swim briskly with it*" (p. 1447). Hassard hence uses temporal distance from the events of study and explicit explanation of how he was contextualizing sources to both decon- struct the accepted understanding of the past as well as to critique assump- tions widely held in our own time about the relationship between scientific studies and organizational practices. In this way, the deconstruction of exist- ing historical narratives through deeper contextualization is used to examine and critique prejudgments held in the present (Gadamer, 1975).

In addition to becoming increasingly aware of how historical perspective in the present shapes interpretation of the past, hermeneutic theory and, to a lesser extent, historical practice has also embraced greater awareness of lan- guage and linguistic forms in contextualizing the interpretation of sources. This has been especially true for the importance of the narrative form (White, 1973; Ricoeur, 1984; Carr, 1986), as both historical writing and many sources from the past conform to elements of narrative style and structure. In this regard, an important theoretical debate addresses the question of whether his- torical research "imposes" narrative interpretations onto the past or whether such narratives in part reflect experiences of historical actors themselves, and hence constitute an important element embedded within primary sources themselves (Carr, 1986). More broadly, this growing attention to language and linguistic forms has opened up a growing area of research at the intersection of historical and communicative theories of organization, such as rhetoric (Suddaby et al., 2010) and discourse (Phillips and Oswick, 2012), particularly to account for processes of organizational change.

For instance, in their study of the "birth of the Kodak moment," Munir and Philips (2005) draw on archival sources to examine "how Kodak man- aged to transform photography from a highly specialized activity to one that became an integral part of everyday life." The "typology of strategies" that the firm used to reshape the institutional field links their primary archival texts to broader discourse. They argue that these texts were "not meaningful individually" but that it is only an examination of the links "to other texts, the way in which they draw on different discourses, how and to whom they are disseminated, the methods of their production and the manner in which they are received and consumed that make them meaningful." Their emphasis on intertextual interpretation of sources is essentially hermeneutic in that it "links texts to discourses and locates both within a particular social and historical context."

Thus, while the hermeneutic tradition remains crucial to historical research, the ways in which it has been practiced have evolved in recent years, and hence vary depending on the researcher's attention to issues of language, power, and perspective. From this point of view, it is more accurate to say that historical interpretation involves a range of practices, all of which emphasize attention to context and the perspective of contemporary actors.

CONCLUSION

While there have been calls for more historical research in the study of organizations and organizational fields, the results, as Leblibici (in this volume) has shown, have been mixed, especially when it comes to the publication of such research in management journals. This stands in stark contrast to other qualitative approaches such as "ethnography" or "action research," which have been legitimized within management and organization studies. The comparatively weak position of the historical approach is, we have suggested, related to the absence of a well-articulated methodological framework—an absence not only detrimental per se, but compounded by the challenges posed by the very nature of historical sources: (i) the records tend to be incomplete, especially if covering long time periods and many actors; (ii) they are not created by the researcher to answer a particular question, but rather represent traces of the past "found" ex post; and (iii) the contexts in which they were originally produced are usually very different from our own.

As we have also shown, efforts in methods handbooks in the social sciences to address these challenges have remained rather limited and piecemeal, leaving organizational researchers interested in an historical approach with little guidance and driving them to develop their own methodologies on an ad hoc basis—with varied success. And while historians have developed an elaborate methodological apparatus since the 19th century and have continued to discuss its philosophical and epistemological underpinnings, most of their publications provide little if any explicit discussion of the challenges posed by the underlying sources and how they were dealt with.

The present chapter provides an attempt to overcome these shortcomings by suggesting a basic methodological framework of how to study organizations and organizational fields using historical sources. It does so by building on the solid foundation of the relevant reflections among historians and the previous efforts by management and organizational scholars. What we have suggested consists of three interrelated elements, which—and this bears repeating—should not be seen as discrete steps or procedures but rather as an iterative processes, where researchers move back and forth between the historical sources and the research question in developing interpretations and findings that best fit the evidence:

Source criticism, which allows the researcher to identify the ways in which any one source is incomplete and biased and hence helps the researcher judge the extent to which it should be trusted in addressing the research question.

Triangulation, which combines insights from different sources and thus complements source criticism in corroborating or identifying contradictions in the claims of any one source, hence strengthening the findings or interpretations of the researcher.

Hermeneutics, which addresses the challenges resulting from the time that has elapsed between the production of a source and the moment of its interpretation by the researcher, by requiring the latter to carefully consider the cultural, social, as well as temporal context in which a given source was produced.

Providing illustrative examples, we show that parts of the proposed methodology have already been applied successfully in the extant management research. We hope that our framework provides more systematic guidance and a methodological language for scholars examining organizations and organizational fields with the use of historical sources—be they social scientists or (business) historians. We consider the framework a starting point for discussion and further elaboration by others interested in the use of historical sources and methods in management and organizational research.

REFERENCES

Alasuutari, P., Bickman, L., and Brannen, J. (2008) (eds.), *The SAGE Handbook of Social Research Methods*. London: Sage.

Alvesson, M., and Sköldberg, K. (2009). *Reflexive Methodology: New Vistas for Qualitative Research*. London: Sage.

Appleby, J., Hunt, L. and Jacobs, M. (1995). *Telling the Truth About History*. New York: Norton.

Arndt, M., and Bigelow. B. (2005). "Professionalizing and Masculinizing a Female Occupation: The Reconceptualization of Hospital Administration in the Early 1900s," *Administrative Science Quarterly*, 50: 233–61.

Bearman, P., Faris, R., and Moody, J. (1999). "Blocking the Future: New Solutions for Old Problems in Historical Social Science," *Social Science History*, 23(4): 501–33.

Berg, B. L., and Lune, H. (2012). *Qualitative Research Methods for the Social Sciences.* Boston, MA: Pearson.

Bloch, M. (1952). *Apologie pour l'Histoire ou Métier d'Historien.* 2nd edn. Paris: Armand Colin.

Bloch, M. (1954 [1946]). *The Historian's Craft.* Manchester: Manchester University Press.

Boldizzoni, F. (2011). *The Poverty of Clio: Resurrecting Economic History.* Princeton: Princeton University Press.

Bruce, K., and Nyland, C. (2011). "Elton Mayo and the Deification of Human Relations," *Organization Studies,* 32: 383–405.

Bryman, A. (2004). "Triangulation." In M. S. Lewis-Beck, A. E. Bryman, and T. F. Liao (eds.), *The SAGE Encyclopedia of Social Science Research Methods,* Vol. 1. London: Sage: 1142–3.

Buchanan, D. A., and Bryman, A. (eds.) (2009a). *The SAGE Handbook of Organizational Research Methods.* London: Sage.

Buchanan, D. A., and Bryman, A. (2009b). "The Organizational Research Context: Properties and Implications." In D. A. Buchanan and A. Bryman (eds.), *The SAGE Handbook of Organizational Research Methods.* London: Sage: 1–18.

Bunzl, M. (1997). *Real History: Reflections on Historical Practice.* London: Routledge.

Carr, D. (1986). *Time, Narrative, and History.* Indianapolis: Indiana University Press.

Carr, E. H. (1961). *What Is History?* Cambridge: Cambridge University Press.

Castilla, E. J. (2007). *Dynamic Analysis in the Social Sciences.* London: Elsevier.

Chandler, A. D. (1962). *Strategy and Structure: Chapters in the History of the Industrial Enterprise.* Cambridge, MA: MIT Press.

Collingwood, R. G. (1946). *The Idea of History.* Oxford: Clarendon Press.

Danneels, E. (2011). "Trying to Become a Different Type of Company: Dynamic Capabilities at Smith Corona," *Strategic Management Journal,* 32(1): 1–31.

Davis, G. F., and Marquis, C. (2005). "Prospects for Organization Theory in the Early Twenty-First Century: Institutional Fields and Mechanisms," *Organization Science,* 16(4): 332–43.

Decker, S. (2013). "The Silence of the Archives: Business History, Post-colonialism, and Archival Ethnography," *Management & Organizational History,* 8(2): 155–73.

Denzin, N. K. (1970). *The Research Act in Sociology.* Chicago: Aldine.

Denzin, N. K. (1978). *Sociological Methods: A Sourcebook.* New York: McGraw-Hill.

Denzin, N. K. (2010). "Moments, Mixed Methods, and Paradigm Dialogs," *Qualitative Inquiry,* 16(6): 419–27.

Dilthey, W. (2002 [1910]). *The Formation of the Historical World in the Human Sciences.* Princeton: Princeton University Press.

Donnelly, M., and Norton, C. (2011). *Doing History.* London: Routledge.

Eisenhardt, K. M. (1989). "Building Theories from Case Study Research," *Academy of Management Review,* 14: 532–50.

Eisenhardt, K. M. (1991). "Better Stories and Better Constructs: The Case for Rigor and Comparative Logic," *Academy of Management Review,* 16(3): 620–7.

Ekirch, R. (1994). "Sometimes an Art, Never a Science, Always a Craft: A Conversation with Bernard Bailyn," *The William and Mary Quarterly,* 51(4): 625–58.

Evans, R. J. (2000). *In Defense of History.* New York: W. W. Norton.

Gadamer, H. C. (1975). *Truth and Method.* New York: Crossroad.

Gaddis, J. L. (2002). *The Landscape of History: How Historians Map the Past.* Oxford: Oxford University Press.

Gillespie R (1991). *Manufacturing Knowledge: A History of the Hawthorne Experiments.* Cambridge: Cambridge University Press

Golden, B. R. (1992). "The Past Is the Present—or Is It? The Use of Retrospective Accounts as Indicators of Past Strategy," *Academy of Management Journal,* 35(4): 848–60.

Gottschalk, L. R. (1950). *Understanding History: A Primer of Historical Method.* New York: Knopf.

Grondin, J. (1994). *Introduction to Philosophical Hermeneutics.* New Haven, CT: Yale University Press.

Hassard, J. (2012). "Rethinking the Hawthorne Studies: The Western Electric Research in Its Social, Political, and Historical Context," *Human Relations,* 65(11): 1431–61.

Heracleous, L. and Barrett, M. (2001). "Organizational Change as Discourse: Communicative Actions and Deep Structures in the Context of Information Technology Implementation," *Academy of Management Journal,* 44(4): 755–78.

Howell, M., and Prevenier, W. (2001). *From Reliable Sources: An Introduction to Historical Methods.* Ithaca, NY: Cornell University Press.

Jick, T. (1979). "Mixing Qualitative and Quantitative Methods: Triangulation in Action," *Administrative Sciences Quarterly,* 24: 602–11.

Jones, G., and Zeitlin, J. (2007) (eds.), *The Oxford Handbook of Business History.* Oxford: Oxford University Press.

Kahl, S. J., Silverman, B. S., and Cusumano, M. A. (eds.) (2012) *History and Strategy, Advances in Strategic Management,* Vol. 29. Bingley: Emerald Group.

Kalev, A., Shenhav, Y., and De Vries, D. (2008). "The State, the Labor Process, and the Diffusion of Managerial Models," *Administrative Science Quarterly,* 53(1): 1–28.

Khaire, M., and Wadhwani, R. D. (2010). "Changing Landscapes: The Construction of Meaning and Value in a New Market Category—Modern Indian Art," *Academy of Management Journal,* 53(6): 1281–304.

Kieser, A., and Üsdiken, B. (2004). "Introduction: History in Organisation Studies," *Business History,* 46(3): 321–30.

King, B. G., and Soule, S. A. (2007). "Social Movements as Extra-institutional Entrepreneurs: The Effect of Protests on Stock Price Returns," *Administrative Science Quarterly,* 52(3): 413–42.

Kipping, M. (2002). *La France et les origines de l'Union européenne, 1944–1952: Intégration économique et compétitivité internationale.* Paris: CHEFF.

Kipping, M., and Kirkpatrick, I. (2013). "Alternative Pathways of Change in Professional Services Firms: The Case of Management Consulting," *Journal of Management Studies,* 50(5): 777–807.

Kipping, M., and Üsdiken, B. (2007). "Business History and Management Studies." In G. Jones and J. Zeitlin (eds.), *The Oxford Handbook of Business History.* Oxford: Oxford University Press: 96–119.

Kipping, M., and Üsdiken, B. (2009). "Beyond Transfer and Translation: The Role of Foreign Models in the Development of Management Education in Germany, Sweden and Turkey." In L. Wedlin, K. Sahlin, and M. Grafström (eds.), *Exploring the Worlds of Mercury and Minerva. Essays for Lars Engwall.* Uppsala: ACTA UNIVERSITATIS UPSALIENSIS, Studia Oeconomiae Negotiorum: 45–68.

Kirby, R. K. (2008). "Phenomenology and the Problems of Oral History," *Oral History Review*, 35(1): 22–38.

Lamberg, J.-A., and Tikkanen, H. (2006). "Changing Sources of Competitive Advantage: Cognition and Path Dependence in the Finnish Retail Industry 1945–1995," *Industrial and Corporate Change*, 15(5): 811–46.

Langley, A. (1999). "Strategies for Theorizing from Process Data," *Academy of Management Review*, 24(4): 691–710.

Lounsbury, M., and Ventresca, M. J. (2002). "Social Structure and Organizations Revisited." In M. Lounsbury and M. J. Ventresca (eds.), *Social Structure and Organizations Revisited*. Bingley: Emerald Group: 3–36.

McAuley, J. (2004). "Hermeneutic Understanding." In C. Cassell and G. Symon (eds.), *Essential Guide to Qualitative Methods in Organizational Research*. London: Sage: 192–202.

Miles, M. B., and Huberman, A. M. (1994). *Qualitative Data Analysis*. London: Sage.

Moss, M. (2009). "Archival Research in Organizations in a Digital Age." In D. A. Buchanan and A. Bryman (eds.), *The SAGE Handbook of Organizational Research Methods*. London: Sage, 395–408.

Munir, K. A., and Phillips, N. (2005). "The Birth of the 'Kodak Moment': Institutional Entrepreneurship and the Adoption of New Technologies," *Organization Studies*, 26(11): 1665–87.

Novick, P. (1988). *That Noble Dream: The 'Objectivity Question' and the American Historical Profession*. Cambridge: Cambridge University Press.

O'Connor, E. (1999). "The Politics of Management Thought: A Case Study of the Harvard Business School and the Human Relations School," *Academy of Management Review*, 24: 117–31.

Orlikowski, W. J., and Yates, J. (1994). "Genre Repertoire: The Structuring of Communicative Practices in Organizations," *Administrative Science Quarterly*, 39(4): 541–74.

Pettigrew, A. M., Woodman, R. M., and Cameron, K. S. (2001). "Studying Organizational Change and Development: Challenges for Future Research," *Academy of Management Journal*, 44(4): 697–713.

Phillips, N., and Brown, J. L. (1993). "Analyzing Communication in and around Organizations: A Critical Hermeneutic Approach," *Academy of Management Journal*, 36(6): 1547–76.

Phillips, N., and Oswick, C. (2012). "Organizational Discourse: Domains, Debates, and Directions," *The Academy of Management Annals*, 6(1): 435–81.

Prasad, A., and Mir, R. (2002). "Digging Deep for Meaning: A Critical Hermeneutic Analysis of CEO Letters to Shareholders in the Oil Industry," *Journal of Business Communication*, 39(1): 92–116.

Ricoeur, P. (1984). *Time and Narrative*, Vol. I. Trans. K. McLaughlin and D. Pellauer. Chicago: University of Chicago Press.

Ricoeur, P. (2004). *Memory, History, Forgetting*. Chicago: University of Chicago Press.

Rosenbloom, R. S. (2000). "Leadership, Capabilities, and Technological Change: The Transformation of NCR in the Electronic Era," *Strategic Management Journal*, 21(10–11): 1083–103.

Rowlinson, M. (2004). "Historical Analysis of Company Documents." In C. Cassell and G. Symon (eds.), *Essential Guide to Qualitative Methods in Organizational Research.* London: Sage: 301–11.

Said, E. W. (1991). *Orientalism: Western Conceptions of the Orient.* London: Penguin.

Sewell, W. (2005). *The Logics of History: Social Theory and Social Transformation.* Chicago: University of Chicago Press.

Spivak, G. C. (1988). "Can the Subaltern Speak?" In C. Nelson and L. Grossberg (eds.), *Marxism and the Interpretation of Culture.* Urbana, IL: University of Illinois Press: 271–313.

Stinchcombe, A. L. (1965). "Social Structure and Organizations." In J. G. March (ed.), *Handbook of Organizations.* Chicago: Rand McNally: 142–93.

Stinchcombe, A. L. (2005). *The Logic of Social Research.* Chicago: University of Chicago Press.

Suddaby, R. (2010). "Challenges for Institutional Theory," *Journal of Management Inquiry,* 19(1): 14–20.

Suddaby, R., Foster, W. M., and Trank, C. Q. (2010). "Rhetorical History as a Source of Competitive Advantage," *Advances in Strategic Management,* 27: 147–173.

Suddaby, R., and Greenwood, R. (2009). "Methodological Issues in Researching Institutional Change." In D. A. Buchanan and A. Bryman (eds.), *The SAGE Handbook of Organizational Research Methods.* London: Sage: 176–95.

Thompson, P. (2000). *The Voice of the Past: Oral History,* 3rd edn. Oxford: Oxford University Press.

Tripsas, M. (1997). "Unraveling the Process of Creative Destruction: Complementary Assets and Incumbent Survival in the Typesetter Industry," *Strategic Management Journal,* 18: 119–42.

Tripsas, M. (2009), "Technology, Identity, and Inertia Through the Lens of 'The Digital Photography Company,'" *Organization Science,* 20(2): 441–60.

Ventresca, M. J., and Mohr, J. W. (2002). "Archival Research Methods." In J. A. C. Baum (ed.), *The Blackwell Companion to Organizations.* Oxford: Blackwell: 805–28.

Vikström, L. (2010). "Identifying Dissonant and Complementary Data on Women through the Triangulation of Historical Sources," *International Journal of Social Research Methodology,* 13(3): 211–21.

White, H. (1973). *Metahistory: The historical imagination in nineteenth-century Europe.* Baltimore, MD: Johns Hopkins University Press.

White, H. (1995). "Response to Arthur Marwick," *Journal of Contemporary History,* 30: 233–46.

Yates, J. (1989). *Control through Communication: The Rise of Systems in American Management.* Baltimore, MD: Johns Hopkins University Press.

Yates, J. and Orlikowski, W. (1992). "Genres of Organizational Communication: A Structurational Approach to Studying Communication and Media," *Academy of Management Review,* 17(2): 299–326.

Yin, R. K. (2013). *Case Study Research: Design and Methods,* 5th edn. Thousand Oaks, CA: Sage.

Index